COSTA RICA
THE COMPLETE GUIDE

Second Edition

©2015 DESTINATION PRESS

ISBN: 978-19407540-0-0

Written & Photographed by James Kaiser

Updated by Suzanna Lourie

This book would not have been possible without the help of many generous people, among them David Boddiger, Steve Mack, Beto Font, Isabella Cota, Alex Leff, Bryan Beasley, Jessica Webb, Stacey Auch, Matt Levin, Clayton Norman, Ben Heneveld, Eli Carmichael, Scott Braman, Adam Preskill, Chip Braman, Barb Braman, Jim Thompson, Adrian Bonilla, Iraci Gaspar, Greg Loehmann, Kevin Castelo, Gibbs Henderson, Jay Tatum, Ryan Johnston, Kelly Born, John Silkey and Jenn Grinels. Special thanks to all of my Spanish teachers, particularly Yami, Pablo and Alejandra. Special thanks to Catherine Zusky and Polly Kaiser for their impressive editing skills, and a very special thanks to Andrea Rincón, a guardian angel without whom this book would not have been possible. As always, special thanks to all of my family and friends, who have always supported me, even when they shouldn't have.

Notice a Change? Although all information in this guide has been exhaustively researched, names, phone numbers and other details do change. If you encounter a change or mistake while using this guide, please send an email to changes@jameskaiser.com. Your input will help make future editions of this guide even better!

Additional Photography & Image Credits
Archivo Nacional: 138, 144, 147, 148, 151, 155, 156, 159, 161
Stock Photography: 40, 57, 76, 77, 84 (chicharron), 87 (maracuya) 112, 113, 119 (leaf-cutter ant), 126 (peccary), 132 (hammerhead shark), 133 (manatee)
Sea Turtle Conservancy (www.conserveturtles.org): 128, 296, 456
Northwind Picture Archives: 139, 140; Bay Island Cruises: 341
Bryan Beasley: 8–9; Avi Klapfer: p.441; INTEL: 163
Darrin O'Brien: 110 (Long-tailed manakin)
Printed in China

COSTA RICA

• THE COMPLETE GUIDE •

Second Edition

1% for Nature

One percent of this book's profits will be donated
to environmental organizations working to preserve
Costa Rica's biodiversity for future generations.

FSC
www.fsc.org

MIX
Paper from
responsible sources
FSC® C005748

JAMES KAISER

BACKGROUND

INTRODUCTION p.11

Welcome to Costa Rica, a tropical paradise filled with stunning scenery, incredible biodiversity and thrilling outdoor adventures. Discover the highlights, find the best of everything and learn how to beat the crowds.

PRACTICAL MATTERS p.14

Visiting Costa Rica is easy—as long as you're prepared. This chapter explains everything you need to know: entry requirements, transportation options, health concerns and the Top 10 Ways to Avoid a Cultural Misunderstanding. From dining etiquette to personal greetings, these simple tips will help you avoid potentially embarrassing situations.

ADVENTURES p.33

Surfing, sportfishing, hiking, river rafting, canopy tours, canyoning, scuba diving—the only question is what not to do in Costa Rica! From the mountains to the sea, experience the country's most popular adventures. Plan ahead and you'll enjoy a vacation that's safe, fun and action-packed.

CULTURE p.47

From ancient rituals to life in the 21st century, discover the cultural roots of the "Happiest Country on Earth." Costa Rica's national character is shaped by coffee farmers in the highlands, cowboys in the dry northwest, Afro-Caribbean residents along the Caribbean coast, and native indigenous tribes.

FOOD & DRINKS p.82

Costa Rica's rustic cuisine is more than just rice and beans, and this section reveals many of the country's lesser known specialties. Venture beyond the basics and you'll find delicious Afro-Caribbean dishes, strange tropical fruits and delicious snacks that go untasted by most tourists.

NATURAL HISTORY p.91

Born of a chain of volcanic islands between North and South America, Costa Rica rose from the sea and connected the continents. Today it serves as a meeting point between multiple ecosystems, attracting a stunning range of plants and animals. Learn about Costa Rica's most amazing feature: its astonishing natural diversity.

WILDLIFE p.106

Simply put, Costa Rica is one of the world's top wildlife destinations. The country's rugged mountains and coastal rainforests are home to dozens of microclimates that shelter tens of thousands of incredible species: monkeys, sloths, parrots, toucans, jaguars, tapirs, nesting sea turtles, poison dart frogs and over 900 bird species!

HUMAN HISTORY p.137

For thousands of years Costa Rica was home to small-scale indigenous societies. Columbus arrived in 1502, but the region was mostly ignored during the Spanish colonial era. After independence, Costa Rica developed an economy based on coffee and bananas. In 1948 Costa Rica abolished its army and invested in its people, becoming one of the most successful countries in Latin America.

DESTINATIONS

SAN JOSÉ & THE CENTRAL VALLEY P.167

Costa Rica's capital and largest city is the political, economic and cultural heart of the country. Though gritty and urban, San José has plenty of good museums and restaurants to keep you occupied.

NORTHERN MOUNTAINS P.191

Famous for volcanoes, cloud forests and outdoor adventures, the Northern Mountains offer a terrific mix of action and natural beauty. Hike to a gorgeous waterfall, soar through the trees on a canopy tour, soak in a natural hot spring or simply relax amid the lush scenery.

SOUTHERN MOUNTAINS P.239

Home to the tallest mountains in Costa Rica, this high altitude region is rugged, remote and well under the tourist radar. But the chilly Southern Mountains are home to some of the country's best hiking, best coffee and most authentic villages.

NICOYA PENINSULA P.271

Stunning beaches, terrific surf and the sunniest weather in Costa Rica. The Nicoya Peninsula is one of Costa Rica's most popular destinations because it offers something for everyone—from big luxury resorts in the northern Nicoya to rustic surf towns in the south. If you're looking for beach time, the Nicoya Peninsula is the place to be.

CENTRAL PACIFIC P.347

The Central Pacific is the transition zone between the tropical dry forests of the north and the humid rainforests of the south. It offers impressive biodiversity and a lush coastline. For many, the combination of great beaches and incredible wildlife is hard to beat.

SOUTH PACIFIC P.399

Wild and remote, the South Pacific is the ultimate eco-destination. Home to the Osa Peninsula, 40% of which is protected as Corcovado National Park, the South Pacific is one of the most biologically intense places on earth. If you're looking for pristine rainforest and stunning wildlife, the Osa Peninsula should be at the top of your list.

THE CARIBBEAN P.443

Long overlooked, the beautiful Caribbean coast is finally getting the attention it deserves. The northern Caribbean is home to Tortuguero National Park, one of the most spectacular sea turtle nesting areas in the Western Hemisphere. The southern Caribbean offers stunning white-sand beaches, lush jungle and a vibrant Afro-Caribbean culture.

CONGRATULATIONS!

If you've purchased this book, you're going to Costa Rica. Perhaps you're already here. If so, you're in one of the most extraordinary places on earth—a tropical paradise overflowing with natural beauty and outdoor adventures. A country that covers less than 0.03% of earth's surface area yet contains 5% of earth's total biodiversity. A country that abolished its army and is one of the most prosperous and developed societies in Latin America.

So who am I, and why should you listen to me? My name is James Kaiser, and I'm the author and photographer of this guide. I first visited Costa Rica in 2006 and immediately fell in love with the gorgeous scenery and friendly people. Having just finished a series of successful guidebooks to U.S. National Parks, I was looking for a new adventure. So after returning home I sold my possessions, packed my bags and hopped a one-way flight to Costa Rica.

This book is the culmination of years of research and exploration. I've logged countless kilometers seeking out Costa Rica's best beaches, best adventures and best national parks. Along the way I learned Spanish, befriended dozens of locals and immersed myself in the culture. In this book I share my experiences—both good and bad—to help you maximize your time to plan the ultimate Costa Rican vacation. I've also included extensive background information about Costa Rica's history, culture and wildlife to help you better understand this remarkable country.

Although physically small, Costa Rica is home to an astonishing variety of landscapes. In a matter of hours, you can drive from a coastal jungle filled with monkeys to a chilly mountain eco-lodge where clouds drift through the trees. There are coffee farms, active volcanoes and incredible waterfalls. There are white sand beaches home to world-class surf breaks and black sand beaches where nesting sea turtles gather by the thousands. And no matter where you go in Costa Rica, the wildlife is off the charts.

You could easily spend a year exploring Costa Rica and not run out of things to do. But if you're like most people, you've only got a week or two. Make that time count! To get the most out of your vacation, you've got to plan your trip wisely. This guidebook puts the best of Costa Rica at your fingertips, helping you maximize your time for an unforgettable vacation.

Now let me show you the best that Costa Rica has to offer!

Puerto Viejo

INTRODUCTION

COSTA RICA IS a tiny country with big attributes: the most peaceful country in Central America, the most democratic country in Latin America and one of the most biodiverse places on earth. The country's name, "Rich Coast," was given by early Spanish explorers who assumed Costa Rica was filled with gold. In reality there was little gold to be found, but the country is home to something even more precious: stunning natural beauty.

Located just north of Panama and just south of Nicaragua, Costa Rica occupies one of nature's most incredible pieces of real estate. Like the rest of Central America, Costa Rica is sandwiched between two continents and two oceans, attracting an amazing diversity of plants and animals from each ecosystem. But even within Central America, Costa Rica's biodiversity is impressive. Its Pacific Coast is the transition zone between the tropical dry forests of the north and the tropical rainforests of the south. Meanwhile a string of mountains runs through the center of the country, sheltering cool cloud forests and freezing *páramos*.

This varied geography supports an astonishing range of flora and fauna. All told, Costa Rica is home to roughly 5% of the world's biodiversity, including nearly 8% of the world's bird species, 10% of the world's butterfly species, 10% of the world's bat species and 20% of the world's hummingbird species. Even more impressive, all this natural wonder is packed into a country just 300 km (186 miles) long by 120 km (75 miles) wide, about half the size of Ohio. No other area of comparable size in the Western Hemisphere contains so much biodiversity.

The people of Costa Rica, who call themselves "Ticos," are the proud stewards of this natural heritage. In contrast to the rest of Central America, which suffered a series of ruthless dictators and bloody civil wars throughout the 20th century, Costa Rica is a stable democracy that abolished its army in 1949 and invested in its people. Today its citizens are among the most educated and prosperous in Latin America. They are also among the most environmentally conscious. Ticos have set aside over 25% of their country as national parks or preserves, and ecotourism is a major part of the economy. As such, Costa Rica has become a powerful role model for other developing countries, demonstrating that environmentalism and economic growth can go hand in hand.

Not surprisingly, Costa Rica's unique combination of peace, stability, natural beauty and environmentalism lures travelers from around the world. Visitors are treated to gorgeous beaches, lush rainforests, active volcanoes and world-class wildlife. And because foreigners have been visiting for decades, Costa Rica is incredibly user-friendly. English is widely spoken, hotels and restaurants are up to international standards and getting around is easy. You don't have to be Tarzan to enjoy Costa Rica's jungles, which is what makes it one of the world's most popular eco-destinations.

BEST OF COSTA RICA

Best Beaches

Nosara (p.328)	Playa Flamingo (p.290)	Santa Teresa (p.325)
Manuel Antonio (p.363)	Tamarindo (p.299)	Cahuita (p.461)
Playa Conchal (p.293)	Punta Uva (p.481)	Uvita (p.391)

Best Uncrowded Beaches

Cahuita (p.461)	Playa Carrillo (p.323)	Playa Matapalo (p.381)
Manzanillo (p.485)	Playa Grande (p.294)	Uvita (p.391)

Best Wildlife Destinations

Carara (p.351)	Gandoca-Manzanillo (p.487)	Sarapiquí (p.188)
Corcovado (p.411)	Monteverde (p.211)	Tortuguero (p.447)

Best Waterfalls

La Fortuna (p.204)	Llanos de Cortés (p.274)	Nauyaca (p.388)
La Paz (p.188)	Montezuma (p.333)	Río Celeste (p.227)

Best Authentic Seaside Villages

Cahuita (p.461)	Manzanillo (p.485)	Puerto Jiménez (p.423)
Drake Bay (p.401)	Montezuma (p.333)	Tortuguero (p.447)

Best Mountain Destinations

Chirripó (p.261)	San Gerardo de Dota (p.257)	Monteverde (p.211)

★The Old Highlights

These are the original destinations that made Costa Rica famous. They are beautiful, fascinating and, these days, often crowded. Though charming and quaint 30 years ago, today they can all be considered "touristy," home to all-inclusive hotels and a steady stream of package tourists. This is not to say they should be avoided. I still enjoy visiting all of these places. I just don't go expecting peace, quiet and bargain prices—especially during peak season.

★Arenal p.193
★Manuel Antonio p.363
★Monteverde p.211
★Tamarindo p.299

★Drake Bay p.401
★Nosara p.311
★Puerto Viejo p.469
★Río Celeste p.227
★Santa Teresa p.325
★Tortuguero p.447
★Uvita p.391

★The New Highlights

Though hardly new, these up and coming destinations remain just a bit off the beaten path, providing the best of "classic" Costa Rica: rustic natural beauty, light development and limited crowds. If you're planning on visiting one or two of the Old Highlights, you should also visit at least one of the New Highlights to round out the flavor of your trip.

PRACTICAL MATTERS

Getting to Costa Rica

BY PLANE

There are two international airports in Costa Rica: Juan Santamaría (SJO) in Alajuela, just outside San José, and Daniel Oduber (LIR) in Liberia, in northwest Costa Rica. Most visitors will want to fly into Juan Santamaría, which is located in the center of the country. If you're planning on spending most of your vacation on the Nicoya Peninsula or in the Northern Mountains, you'll want to fly into Daniel Oduber. Both airports are roughly six hours from Los Angeles, five hours from New York City, four hours from Houston and three hours from Miami.

Note: All visitors leaving Costa Rica must pay a $29 "departure tax." When you arrive at the airport for a departing flight, head straight to the departure tax booth. This tax must be paid before you can check in for your departing flight.

Passport & Visas

All international visitors to Costa Rica must present a valid passport that will not expire within 90 days. At the immigration booth, visitors from North America, Europe and Japan will be granted a visa for up to 90 days. At the end of the 90 day period, you must leave Costa Rica for at least three full days, at which point you can return for another 90 days. In Costa Rica all foreign visitors are required to carry their passport or a photocopy of their passport (including the visa stamp) at all times. This is especially important if you're driving. As soon as you arrive at your hotel, make a photocopy of your passport and leave your actual passport in the hotel safe. If your passport is stolen while you're in Costa Rica, you'll need to contact your country's embassy in San José. The U.S. embassy (Tel: 2519-2000) is located in Pavas, 2 kilometers northwest of Parque Sabana on road 104.

Disease and Vaccinations

Compared to many tropical countries, Costa Rica is remarkably disease-free. You need no vaccinations if you are arriving from North America or Europe. (Yellow fever vaccination cards are required if you're arriving from Bolivia, Brazil, Colombia, Ecuador or Peru). Outbreaks of dengue, which is spread by mosquitoes, occasionally flare up in Limón, Puntarenas and Liberia, but they are not common. Malaria, also spread by mosquitoes, exists only in the most remote areas in the coastal lowlands. The best prevention is strong insect repellent. Far more common is the occasional stomach bug, which is easily treated with antibiotics from a local pharmacy. For the latest Costa Rica health alerts, visit the Center for Disease Control website (www.cdc.gov).

Money & Currency

COSTA RICAN COLONES

Costa Rica's currency is called colón (koh-LONE), which is the Spanish name for Columbus (as in Christopher Columbus). The plural of colón is colones (Koh-LONE-Ehs), and the currency symbol is ₡. As of this writing, the exchange rate is around 550 colones to the dollar, so a ₡10,000 bill is worth about $18. That said, currency rates can fluctuate wildly. Before you depart, check the exchange rate online at www.xe.com and write it down in this book.

Costa Rican coins range from 5 to 500 colones. Costa Rican bills are plastic or paper and come in a rainbow of colors. The artwork is a mix of famous politicians and wildlife. Ticos love nicknames, and they've given nicknames to many of their bills. The red ₡1,000 bill is called *un rojo* ("a red").

DOLLARS

Dollars are widely accepted, especially in tourist areas. In fact, most hotels and many restaurants list their prices in dollars. Whenever dollars and colones are accepted, watch out for the "Exchange Rate Swindle." If something is priced in colónes and you pay in dollars, or vice versa, you will most likely pay an excessive conversion fee. I find it's best to carry a mix of dollars and colónes, or, better yet, pay by credit card.

CREDIT CARDS

Credit cards give you the best exchange rate, which is calculated automatically by the credit card company using daily rates. Credit cards are widely accepted, especially at high end and mid-range establishments. Further down the price chain, you'll encounter more cash-only situations, and in really remote areas cash-only is often the only way to go.

Important note: Many credit card companies charge a 3% "International Transaction Fee" on all foreign purchases. This can add up quickly over the course of a vacation, so check your credit card's terms. I use Capital One, which doesn't charge International Transaction Fees on any of their cards.

ATMS

ATMs are common in all but the most remote villages. They offer the best exchange rate, so they're the best way to take out colónes. ATMs are called *cajeros* ("Kah-HARE-Ohs"), and most dispense dollars as well as colones.

THE AIRPORT CURRENCY EXCHANGE BOOTH

This is a great place to get ripped off. Use the ATM at the baggage claim instead.

TRAVELERS CHECKS

Don't even bother. Nobody accepts them anymore.

Weather & Climate

In Costa Rica there are only two seasons: dry and rainy. In most of the country dry season lasts from December to April and rainy season lasts from May to November. Dry season is called *verano* ("summer") and rainy season is called *invierno* ("winter")—a situation that leads to much confusion among visitors from northern latitudes, where the "summer" and "winter" months are reversed.

Within Costa Rica, however, there is significant variation in the length and intensity of the seasons. In the North Pacific, the driest part of Costa Rica, the dry season can last six months (November to May) and average annual rainfall is 1.7 meters (5.6 feet). In the South Pacific, one of the rainiest places in Costa Rica, the dry season lasts just three months (January to March) and average annual rainfall is 5 meters (16.5 feet). The Caribbean coast, meanwhile, has no clearly defined dry season, and average annual rainfall is 3.5 meters (11.5 feet).

Seasonal weather patterns are due to annual fluctuations in the strength of the trade winds that blow across Costa Rica. During much of the dry season, trade winds (called *alisios*) arrive from the northeast, bringing moist air from the Caribbean that dumps regular rain on Costa Rica's east coast. As this moist air blows up the tall mountains that separate the Caribbean from the rest of the country, it cools and condenses, dumping even more rain on the mountains' Caribbean slope. By the time the air crosses the mountains and descends the Pacific slope, much of the moisture has been wrung out, creating a dry "rain shadow." As dry air blows across Costa Rica's Pacific coast, it blocks moist air that would otherwise arrive from the Pacific. One major exception is the southern Pacific, where the tall Talamanca Mountains create a wind vortex that scoops in some moist air from the Pacific that results in more rain.

During Costa Rican winter, the northeast trade winds diminish and moist air arrives from the Pacific, bringing rain to much of Costa Rica. In the depths of the rainy season—September and October—the rain shadow effect is reversed and the Caribbean coast becomes the sunniest, driest part of Costa Rica.

Not surprisingly, Ticos have many different words for *lluvia* ("rain"). An *aguacero* is a tropical downpour that features intense bursts of heavy rain. *Temporales* are prolonged periods of rain during rainy season. And *pelo de gato* ("cat's hair") refers to fine misty rain often encountered in the mountains.

Because Costa Rica is located just 10 degrees north of the equator, temperatures change very little throughout the year. In most places, temperatures change more throughout the day than they do throughout the year. Within Costa Rica, however, temperatures vary significantly with elevation. Along the coast temperatures average between 25–34°C (77–93°F). At mid-level elevations temperatures average between 17–26°C (63–79°F). And at the highest elevations temperatures average between 5–10°C (41–50°F). Chirripó, Costa Rica's highest peak at 3,819 meters (12,526 feet), experiences freezing temperatures as well as the occasional light snowfall.

When to Visit

DEC–APRIL: The Dry Season
This is the dry season and, not surprisingly, peak tourist season. The busiest weeks are Christmas and Easter when many hotels charge "peak season" prices and reservations must be made far in advance. Dec–Feb is coffee picking season, making it a great time to take a coffee tour (p.69), while Jan–March are the best months to visit the South Pacific, which experiences a longer rainy season (and a rainier dry season) than the rest of the Pacific coast. By contrast, the Nicoya Peninsula, in the northern Pacific, can experience months without a single drop of rain. The downside: the final months of the dry season can be brutally dry on the Nicoya Peninsula, with leafless trees and roads so dusty that motorcycle riders resort to wearing ski goggles and covering their mouths with bandanas. Over on the Caribbean coast, which is rainy year-round, February and March are relatively drier months.

MAY: The Most Underrated Month
The rainy season officially starts in May, and low-season rates kick in for most hotels. But here's a secret: early May really isn't *that* rainy, so you'll most likely enjoy many sunny days with only a handful of afternoon showers. May is also the month between gringos escaping winter and gringos on school break, which means limited crowds just about everywhere. In short, you can enjoy some of Costa Rica's most popular destinations with fewer crowds and lower prices.

JUNE–AUGUST: The Rainy Season
By June the rainy season has officially kicked in everywhere, which means clear, sunny mornings followed by rain showers in the late afternoon. If you're looking for beach time, this is a great time to visit the Nicoya Peninsula, which is drier than the Central Pacific and *much* drier than the South Pacific. That said, you could always get lucky and hit a handful of consecutive sunny days with no rain. *Veranillo* ("little summer") is also a weather phenomenon that usually offers 1-2 weeks of sunshine around mid- to late-July.

SEPT–NOV: The Really Rainy Season (Except for the Caribbean)
September and October are the depths of the rainy season, with October serving up nearly continuous showers. The beginning of November is often still rainy, but by late-November things start to clear up and the transition to the dry season begins. (In the relatively drier Northern Pacific, the dry season often starts in early November.) There is, however, an important exception to these depressingly rainy months: the Caribbean coast, where September and October are the best months to visit. Although the Caribbean is normally the rainiest part of Costa Rica, September and October offer sunny days, calm seas, egg-laying sea turtles and (best of all) low season prices!

Getting Around Costa Rica

BY PLANE

Two local charter services, Nature Air (2299-6000, www.natureair.com) and Sansa (2290-4100, www.flysansa.com), offer regional flights between 13 popular destinations in Costa Rica. Prices generally range from $70 to $150 one-way, depending on the route and the time of year. This is usually the priciest way to get around, but cheap promos are sometimes available. It's always worth checking their websites. That said, most flights within Costa Rica are less than 45 minutes, and for some remote destinations (Tortuguero, Drake Bay, Puerto Jiménez) a flight will spare you an all-day trip on bumpy roads. In addition, the view from the air is spectacular.

BY CAR

Unless you're planning on driving in downtown San José, just about anyone can handle driving in Costa Rica. The roads are filled with potholes and the drivers are often crazy (see right), but having your own car will provide you with complete travel freedom. There are many places where having your own car will let you explore remote beaches, beautiful waterfalls and great restaurants that most tourists miss. There are, however, a few places where having a car is actually more of a hassle, which I mention in the "Getting Around" section of each destination. For a four-wheel drive car rental, which I definitely recommend, prices generally range from $60/day during low season to $120/day during high season. A valid driver's license from your home country is all you need to drive in Costa Rica.

In Costa Rica, the streets have no names, but a private company, NavSat (www.navsatcr.com), has mapped out nearly every road in the country plus restaurants, hotels, etc. If you rent a car in Costa Rica, RENT THE GPS! It's like a gift from the gods that allows you to confidently navigate even the most remote locations. If you don't rent the GPS, you will almost certainly get lost. All car rental companies offer GPS rentals for around $10 per day, and it's worth every penny. If you have your own GPS device, you can also download the map data from the NavSat website. As of this writing, a 10-day version cost $50 and a 30-day version cost $70. Mobile apps like Google Maps and Waze are another option if you purchase a SIM card (p.23), but they are more likely to contain errors.

The government controls the price of gasoline in Costa Rica, so all gas stations, called *bombas* ("pumps"), sell gas at the same price. As of this writing the price of gas was about $1.50 per liter ($5.70 per gallon). In Costa Rica there are three types of gas: regular unleaded, super unleaded and diesel.

Important note: Rental cars are often targets of theft when left unattended. Never leave anything unattended in your car, and make sure you know *exactly* how to lock your car. Some rental cars have an unusual locking procedure that requires holding up the handle as you close the door.

Finally, if you are pulled over by the police while driving, remember that fines are paid at banks, never directly to police officers.

Driving in Costa Rica

Forget every cultural stereotype you've heard about Ticos: polite, laid-back, conflict-averse. When it comes to driving, many Ticos are aggressive, rude and dangerous. Excessive tailgating, passing on blind curves and passing on the shoulder of the road are just some of the moves you can expect to encounter. Much of this has to do with *machismo*—the vast majority of bad drivers are men—but there's also a shocking lack of driver's education. Many Ticos have the attitude that if you can afford a car, you can drive it. Period. A handful of bills is all it really takes to get a driver's license at many government offices. Add in the attitude of most police officers, who view reckless driving as perfectly normal, and things can get *loco*.

What can you do? Sharpen your defensive driving skills. Expect to encounter aggressive drivers and respond accordingly. If someone tries to pass you on a blind curve, slow down and let them pass. If you see someone trying to pass ahead of you, slow down and give them room. Aggressive driving is simply part of the culture. Honking your horn or flashing dirty looks won't accomplish anything—other than confirming your status as an uptight foreigner.

Crazy drivers aside, driving in Costa Rica is a relatively straightforward matter in much of the country, especially the rural areas that most tourists visit. There is, however, one important exception: San José. Costa Rica's capital and biggest city is a mess. The city has grown with virtually no planning, and the driving conditions reflect that. Downtown San José is a confusing maze of unmarked one-way streets, clogged intersections and frequent accidents. To remedy the driving problems in San José, the government has undertaken a series of "solutions" that strike many outsiders as absurd.

To remind drivers to stop at stoplights, stop signs have been placed at many stop light intersections. Thus, when the light is green, you are expected to drive past the stop sign without stopping. Failure to do so risks being rear-ended. At stop signs without a traffic light, however, you are still expected to stop.

To reduce traffic in downtown San José, which suffers from a never-ending series of infrastructure problems, a new law was established: if your license plate ends in 1 or 2, you can't drive on Monday; if your license plate ends in 3 or 4, you can't drive on Tuesday; and so on.

GPS definitely helps out in San José, but in general it's best to avoid driving there altogether. If you're staying within greater San José and thinking of visiting downtown, take a taxi. You'll save both money and peace of mind. And if you must drive through downtown San José, try to do so in the late morning or early afternoon when traffic is lightest.

BY SHUTTLE

A handful of private shuttle companies offer hotel to hotel service between nearly two dozen of Costa Rica's most popular destinations. Prices generally range from $35 to $80 one-way. Shuttles are a terrific way to get around Costa Rica. Although more expensive than buses, they save you the hassle of walking around with your luggage or paying for taxis. Shuttles are also more secure than buses, and some even offer free wifi. Listed below are the most popular shuttles.

Interbus (4100-0888, www.interbusonline.com)

Grayline (2220-2126, www.graylinecostarica.com)

Easyride (4033-6847, www.easyridecr.com)

Montezuma Expeditions (2642-0919, www.montezumaexpeditions.com)

Monkey Ride (2787-0454, www.monkeyridecr.com)

BY BUS

Buses are the cheapest way to get around Costa Rica, offering transportation to just about anywhere for under $20. Downtown San José is the country's major bus hub, though frustratingly there's no central bus terminal. In general buses are modern, clean, prompt and reliable. The only real challenge is that most bus drivers speak no English, and even their Spanish can be impossible to decipher sometimes. In the "Getting To" section of each destination, I list bus schedules and prices. If you're planning on getting around by bus, it's worth visiting the ICT (Costa Rican Tourism Chamber) website (www.visitcostarica.com) for the most up-to-date bus schedule. From the homepage click on "Planning Your Visit" and then select "Bus Itinerary" to download a PDF of the complete bus schedule. Note: Theft can be a problem on buses. If you ride the bus, keep an eye on your luggage and keep your most valuable possessions on your person.

BY TAXI

Taxis are common throughout Costa Rica, but you should only use official taxis, which are red with a yellow triangle on the door. The only exception is official airport taxis, which are orange. It's usually best to have your hotel or restaurant call a local taxi. Whenever possible I've listed taxi phone numbers in the "Getting Around" section of each destination. In Costa Rica it is not customary to tip taxi drivers.

By law, all taxis are required to use a *maría*, an electronic box that automatically calculates the fare. In practice, however, you'll sometimes encounter taxi drivers who refuse to use the maría, especially in remote tourist areas. If your driver refuses to use the maría, agree to a fixed price before you get in the cab. A common scam is for "friendly" taxi drivers to drive trusting tourists to their destination, then demand an exorbitant fare.

In many places unlicensed taxis, called *piratas* ("pirates"), are common. I do not recommend using piratas, but in some small towns there may be no other option. Use your judgement.

The Old Fig Tree

Costa Rican "Addresses"

In Costa Rica, there are no addresses. No street names, no house numbers, *nada*. When giving directions, people say something like "200 meters west of the hospital, 100 meters south, yellow house." Written addresses follow the same format. When I needed something sent to my old apartment, I wrote "100 meters south of Scotiabank." When I asked Scotiabank what their address was, they told me "100 meters east of El Chicote Restaurant."

In Costa Rica, people give directions expressed as distances from known landmarks, where 100 meters corresponds to one block and 50 meters corresponds to half a block. Even when a landmark disappears, it often lives on as an address. Perhaps the most famous is *el antiguo higuerón* ("the old fig tree"), which continued to be used as a landmark long after it fell down.

Not surprisingly, many postmen spend much of their day wandering around in search of the correct address. As a mail worker explained to a reporter: "We once got a letter addressed to 'the guy who is sometimes outside of the post office.'" Even former President Laura Chinchilla admitted she couldn't name the street in front of the President's House.

Although this quirky system worked fine in the oxcart era, it has proven poorly suited to modern times. The Inter-American Development Bank estimates that Costa Rica loses over $700 million a year due to their lack of addresses. (On the plus side, there's not much junk mail.) In the handful of places where people have tried to establish addresses, they have largely been ignored. I know a woman who lives in an expat neighborhood where residents took matters into their own hands and installed their own street signs. She lives on Itabo Street, named for a type of plant found in Central America. One day a Tico visitor arrived an hour late, explaining that he had searched everywhere for the itabo plant, but he couldn't find it. As most Ticos will happily admit, their unusual address system is simply one of their "cultural idiosyncracies."

Hotels

Rather than produce a 1,000-page book filled with hundreds of hotel listings—when all you really need are two or three hotels—I've posted all hotel information free online at www.jameskaiser.com. Along with personal recommendations, I've included links to hotel websites and online review sites.

Hotels in Costa Rica cover the full spectrum, from $10/night hostels to rustic ecolodges to five-star, $1,000/night all-inclusive resorts. In some remote areas, choosing a good hotel will be key to enjoying a great trip. In more popular areas, your hotel may simply serve as a place to sleep while you enjoy activities away from the hotel. Although there are plenty of hotels, the best ones always fill up fast, so I recommend booking your hotel as soon as possible before your trip. This is especially true during peak season (Dec–April) and essential during Christmas, New Years and Easter week.

Restaurants

First things first: Unless you're willing to subsist entirely on typical foods like *gallo pinto* and *casados* (p.82), don't expect meals in Costa Rica to be a bargain. These days prices at most tourist restaurants are comparable to U.S. prices, especially when taxes (13%) and tip (10%) are included, as required by Costa Rican law. Some menus list prices with tax and tip (abbreviated as "i.v.i") included, others do not. When in doubt, ask.

Tipping: A 10% tip is automatically included on your bill, but in upscale restaurants it has become customary to include a bit more for good service.

When you're ready for the bill, ask for *La cuenta, por favor* (La KWEN-Tah, Poor FAH-Voor). *Always* double check the bill. Mistake-ridden bills are disturbingly common in Costa Rica.

As you flip through this guide, you'll notice that I've focused more on tourist restaurants than typical Costa Rican restaurants. This isn't because I don't like typical Costa Rican restaurants. On the contrary, I *love* eating a typical meal at a typical restaurant, and I think every visitor should enjoy that experience. But the truth is that most typical restaurants offer incredibly similar options at incredibly similar levels of quality. There just aren't that many ways to cook rice and beans, which tend to dominate every menu.

Whenever possible, I've included typical Costa Rican restaurants that offer something special (great ambiance, rare specialties, exceptional value), but if you're interested in seeking out typical food just swing by any place that calls itself a *soda*—a word that roughly translates as "diner" in Costa Rica. At just about any soda you will find authentic, reasonably priced food. I love visiting random sodas for a breakfast of gallo pinto—the one dish that every Costa Rican knows how to prepare well. Don't worry too much about finding the "right" soda. Roll the dice. Live a little. It's fun.

Food/Water

In general, it's safe to drink the tap water just about everywhere in Costa Rica, which has made good investments in its water delivery systems. The only place I've ever had problems is on the Caribbean Coast, where the public infrastructure is sometimes lacking. Prepared food is also very safe, especially in tourist areas. I eat everything (including street food) and drink tap water all the time, and I've only had one major stomach issue, which was quickly cleared up after a trip to the local pharmacy. If you have a sensitive stomach, by all means stick to bottled water, which is sold just about everywhere.

What to Pack

No matter where you go, pack sunglasses, a hat, a water bottle and a flashlight. Although sunscreen and bugspray are readily available, it's a good idea to pack your own because the prices in Costa Rica are often double or triple what you'd pay back home. If you're spending time at the beach, shorts, T-shirts and a swimsuit are essential. Unless you're spending all of your time at Nicoya Peninsula beaches between December and March (dry season), you should also pack shoes/boots and a rain jacket due to the country's abundant rain. If you're planning on spending time in San José, pack a pair of long pants (no one in San José wears shorts, and you will stand out as a tourist if you do). If you're thinking about spending time in the mountains, pack at least one sweater. And if you're heading to Costa Rica's highest elevations (Zona de los Santos, Chirripó), pack a winter jacket and warm hat.

Mobile Phone SIM Cards

Costa Rica uses the GSM network, and prepaid SIM cards for mobile phones and tablets are available from telecom providers Kölbi, Claro and Movistar. In general, prices for voice and data are extremely reasonable, and reception is surprisingly good throughout the country with the exception of a few remote areas. If you can't live without mobile internet, it's definitely worth picking up a SIM card when you arrive. Even if you never use it, having access to voice and internet will provide peace of mind. In my experience Kölbi offers the best national coverage. In Juan Santamaría Airport there is a Kölbi counter near gate 6.

The big catch: to use a prepaid SIM card, you need an "unlocked" (aka "unblocked") global phone. In the U.S. and other countries, many mobile service providers "lock" your phone so you can only use it with their service. If you try to use a SIM card from another provider, it won't work. With an unlocked phone, you can use whatever SIM card you like. A quick internet search will reveal multiple options for unlocking your phone. After purchasing your Costa Rican SIM card, pop out your regular SIM, store it in a safe place, and insert the new, local SIM card. When it's time to go home, re-insert your regular SIM.

Emergencies

For all emergencies in Costa Rica dial 911, which connects you to the country's emergency response hotline.

Crime & Security

Crime in Costa Rica is lower than the rest of Latin America but higher than the U.S. or Europe. Petty theft is by far the most common problem. In general, you should never leave anything unattended at the beach or in your car. If you are traveling with valuables, always lock them in the hotel safe or leave them with the front desk of your hotel. Violent crime is rare, especially if you don't mess around with drugs and/or prostitutes.

Car locks: Certain rental cars have a bizarre locking mechanism that requires you to hold up the handle when you close the car door. Failure to hold up the handle will unlock the door when it closes. Rest assured, thieves know exactly which cars suffer from this problem, and they target them. Be sure you know *exactly* how to lock your rental car.

Report any crime to the OIJ, the Costa Rican police (Tel: 800-800-3000). If you're an American citizen, you should also report crimes to the Consular Section of the U.S. Embassy (2519-2000, acssanjose@state.gov).

Health & Medical Care

For a developing country, Costa Rica has a good public health system. In addition, some of its private hospitals offer state-of-the-art facilities and U.S. board-certified physicians. Not surprisingly, medical tourism is booming in Costa Rica due to high quality and low prices.

If you need medical care in Costa Rica, private hospitals are the best option. CIMA (2208-1000, www.hospitalsanjose.net), located in the San José suburb of Escazu, is considered the best private hospital in the country.

In rural areas, pharmacies are your best bet for stomach bugs and minor illnesses, and they are staffed by professionals licensed to prescribe medicine on the spot. If you're feeling ill, the local pharmacy should be your first stop. Note that some rural pharmacies are incredibly fond of injections, even for headaches and mild illness. Feel free to ask for a pill instead.

Medicare does not provide coverage for medical costs outside the U.S., and not all private insurers offer international coverage. It's always best to call your insurer and check. If your insurance provider does offer international coverage, carry your insurance policy identity card at all times. If your insurance provider does not offer international coverage, short-term travel insurance is a good option. The travel section of the U.S. State Department website offers extensive information on international travel insurance (travel.state.gov).

Swimming & Rip Currents

Powerful rip currents (aka riptides) can be a risk at many Costa Rican beaches, especially during strong ocean swells. Because few beaches have lifeguards, it's best to know what to do if you find yourself getting sucked out to sea by a rip current. First and foremost, don't try to swim against the current. Most drownings occur when people try to swim against the current and become exhausted. If you feel yourself getting caught in a rip current, swim parallel to shore until you are free of the powerful current, at which point you can safely swim to shore.

Sunrise/Sunset

Because Costa Rica lies just 10° north of the equator, daylight hours vary little throughout the year. During the winter solstice (the shortest day of the year) the sun rises around 5:50am and sets around 5:20pm. During the summer solstice (the longest day of the year) the sun rises around 5:15am and sets around 6pm.

Beer, Wine & Liquor

If you were immediately drawn to this section, check out page 88. Suffice to say, beer, guaro and rum are readily available throughout the country. Wine is harder to come by in rural areas, and it is often of low quality. If you're planning on buying wine or liquor in Costa Rica, swing by the duty free shops in the airport as soon as you arrive. They offer excellent selection and discounts up to 50%.

Power Outlets

All power outlets in Costa Rica are 110 V with standard US two-prong plugs.

Online Resources

ICT - The Costa Rican Tourism Institute. Their website offers plenty of basic information, plus up-to-date bus schedules (www.visitcostarica.com)

Tico Times - Costa Rica's top English-language newspaper. (www.ticotimes.net)

La Nacion - Costa Rica's top Spanish-language newspaper. If you don't understand Spanish, Google Translate will do the trick. (www.nacion.com)

U.S. State Department - The Costa Rica section of their website offers up-to-date information and travel warnings. (www.state.gov)

Center for Disease Control - One of the top resources for disease and vaccination information. Includes up-to-date info for all countries. (www.cdc.gov)

TOP 10 WAYS TO AVOID A CULTURAL MISUNDERSTANDING

1. Ask for the bill in restaurants

In Costa Rica, as in much of Latin America, it's considered rude for the waiter to bring the bill before the customer asks for it. This has led to more awkward situations between Ticos and gringos than I care to imagine. Consider the following situation: as the Tico waiter patiently waits for the gringo customer to ask for the bill, the gringo customer patiently waits for the Tico waiter to bring the bill. As the minutes drag on, the gringo grows more and more frustrated, especially when he notices that their waiter is *looking right at him*. Finally, the irritated gringo stands up and asks, almost redundantly, for the bill. As the waiter dutifully fetches it, he's left to wonder why so many gringos are so upset when they're on vacation. When you want the bill, simply wave to your waiter, mock scribble onto your palm and ask for *La cuenta, por favor* (La KWEN-Tah, Poor FAH-Voor).

2. Assume it's your responsibility to get the waiter's attention

Although not true everywhere, restaurant service in Costa Rica can be painfully slow and apathetic. For Ticos this is perfectly normal. For gringos, especially those accustomed to service with a smile, it can be incredibly frustrating. If you want something, assume it's *your* responsibility to get the waiter's attention. Don't expect refills or regular check-ins. Trust me, it's better to arrive with low expectations and be pleasantly surprised than to arrive with high expectations and end up frustrated. Whenever you want something, simply flag down the waiter with your hand, say what you'd like and finish it with a polite *por favor*. Example: *Un agua, por favor* ("A water, please"); *Una cerveza, por favor* ("A beer, please").

3. Close car doors *gently*

In Costa Rica, as in much of Latin America, car doors are treated as delicate objects that could shatter at the slightest touch. The way gringos close car doors is considered aggressive, violent slamming. I have absolutely no idea where this cultural difference comes from, but when I mentioned it to my Spanish teacher she told me, in no uncertain terms, that gringos slam car doors because they consider cars to be disposable objects.

Regardless, there's no better way to upset your cab driver than by "slamming" the door when you enter/exit a cab. If the car door closes with anything more than a soft click, don't be surprised if your fare magically rises. The more softly and gingerly you close the door, the better. If it takes two tries to close the door, you're doing great. Rest assured your reflexes will undermine this advice, and the driver of the car will cringe, but at least you'll know why he's upset.

4. Mind your manners

In Costa Rica, as in much of Latin America, manners are *extremely* important and not knowing the basic social protocol is a great way to embarrass yourself. Take the time to learn some basic etiquette and you'll really set yourself apart from the average tourist.

Whenever you greet a female acquaintance, it's customary to lightly touch right cheeks and give a single air kiss. Keep in mind that this is an *air* kiss *near* the cheek, not an *actual* kiss *on* the cheek, which would be considered presumptuous. Male acquaintances, meanwhile, simply shake hands. When it's time to say goodbye, the air kiss/handshake process is repeated.

Whenever you enter or leave a social gathering, you are expected to say hello or goodbye to each person individually. Missing a single person is considered rude, and greeting a roomful of people with a universal "hola" is considered extremely lazy. (Although coming from a gringo, it won't be shocking.)

For both men and women, hugging is considered an intimate gesture normally reserved for family. A hug between non-family is often viewed as too close for comfort.

Finally, it is considered extremely poor manners not to respond to "thank you" with "you're welcome." If someone thanks you by saying *Gracias*, respond with *Con mucho gusto* (Cone MOO-Cho GOO-Sto). In many Latin American countries "you're welcome" is expressed with *De nada*, but in Costa Rica the slightly more formal *Con mucho gusto* ("with much pleasure") is far more common.

5. If you're from the U.S., don't refer to yourself as "American"

From the time they are young children, Latin Americans are taught that "America" stretches from Alaska to Argentina. An "American," therefore, is anyone born in either North, Central or South America. Some Latin Americans, especially those of an "anti-American" persuasion, get upset when U.S. citizens refer to themselves as American. In my experience, most Ticos don't take this too seriously. I can't count how many times I've been asked if I'm *Americano*, and stores throughout Costa Rica sell *Ropa Americana* ("Clothes from the U.S."). But if you'd like to be on your best behavior, describe yourself as *Norteamericano* or "from the U.S."

6. If you're female, be prepared for *piropos*

In Costa Rica, as in much of Latin America, women should expect to receive *piropos* from random men. Translated literally, *piropo* means "compliment," but depending on its context it can also be translated as "flirtatious remark" or "pick-up line." If you're a woman, don't be surprised if some men refer to you as *linda* ("beauty"), *preciosa* ("precious"), *princessa* ("princess"), *reina* ("queen") or even *muñeca* ("doll") or *mamita* ("hot mamma"). It's debatable whether or not this is considered acceptable behavior in Costa Rica. Some Ticas love the compliments; others find them demeaning. The same goes with the whistles and kissing sounds that sometimes greet women as they walk down the street.

7. Do not criticize anything about Costa Rica ... Except the roads

Ticos are incredibly patriotic and incredibly sensitive to any criticism of their country. The one exception is the roads, which every Tico will admit are terrible. Although Ticos love to complain about Costa Rica's problems among themselves, the minute a foreigner (especially a gringo) chimes in with a complaint things can get uncomfortable. Criticizing Costa Rica touches a highly sensitive nerve. Upon meeting a Tico, one of the first things you may be asked is "How do you like Costa Rica?" Correct response: "It's so beautiful and the people are so friendly, but the roads are terrible!"

8. Do not expect politically correct behavior

For better or worse, political correctness is not part of the average Ticos's DNA. Ticos tend to say it like they see it, especially among friends and acquaintances. Elderly people are called *viejo* ("old"), overweight people are called *gordo* ("fat"), short people are called *enanos* ("midgets") and *gringos* are called, well, gringos. No harm is intended, and none is taken. In general, Ticos are very comfortable with their own physical characteristics. As my Tica Spanish teacher once put it, "I'm *gorda* ('fat'), so everyone calls me fat." When I expressed shock, she looked at me as if I was crazy, or perhaps blind. Meanwhile one of my classmates, a black Haitian man living with a Costa Rican host family, was summoned to dinner every night when his host mother called out, *Negrito, la cena!* ("Little black boy, dinner's ready!"). Even if someone isn't *gordo* or *negro*, the names *gordito* ("little fatty") and *negrito* are often used as terms of affection among couples.

Ticos, like many Latin Americans, tend to take a far more relaxed approach towards race than people in other parts of the world. Racial intermarriage is common in Latin America, and racial sensitivity, while present, doesn't touch nearly the same nerve it touches in the U.S. This cultural difference was perfectly illustrated to me one day during a *mascarada* (p.72) where one of the masks used was a black man with big lips and giant white eyes. An African-American girl standing next to me was appalled. The situation escalated when the man in the mask noticed her and asked for a dance.

If you're Asian, expect to be called *chino* ("Chinese") regardless of whether you're Chinese, Japanese, Korean, etc. I once met a Vietnamese-American man, born in Florida, who was living in a small village near Arenal in 2011. One day his neighbors came running up to him in a panic. "We've been looking for you every-where!" they blurted out, "Are you OK? Is your family OK?" "Yes," he responded, "Why?" "The Tsunami!" they exclaimed, referring to the Japanese tsunami that destroyed the Fukushima nuclear plant.

That said, I DO NOT RECOMMEND adopting the "say-it-like-you-see-it" approach on your visit. Sensitivities do exist, and it's a fine line that's often hard for non-Ticos to decipher.

9. When asking directions, don't ask Yes or No questions

One of the strangest quirks of Costa Rican culture is the tendency for some people to give bad directions even when they know the directions are bad. If you ask someone, "Is the ACME Hotel down this street?" they will often say "Yes!" even if they have no idea where the ACME hotel actually is.

There are various theories about this behavior. Some people claim that Ticos are so eager to please that they refuse to *not* give directions. Others claim that, in a country as small as Costa Rica, it's embarrassing to admit that you don't know where something is. Whenever I ask my Tico friends about it, they just laugh. "Yes," they say, "that's *very* Tico" Don't worry, I'm told, it's not because I'm a gringo. "Ticos do that to other Ticos all the time," a Spanish teacher informed me. "When you ask someone for directions," he advised, "look into their eyes. That's the best way to tell if they *really* know where the place is."

Investigative eye-gazing aside, if you need to ask directions, ask open-ended questions. Don't ask, "Is the ACME hotel down this street?" which often results in a "Yes" answer. Ask "Where is the ACME hotel?" There's no guarantee that you'll get the right answer, but at least you'll limit your margin of error.

10. Never approach a problem with irritation or a raised voice

Ticos are *incredibly* sensitive to irritability and raised voices, which are widely regarded as a mortal sin when expressed in response to a problem. In Costa Rica, messing up is generally considered more socially acceptable than being irritable or raising your voice, which is pretty much the exact opposite of how things work in the U.S. In Costa Rica irritation and raised voices are seen as potential stepping stones to confrontation, so avoiding them is a kind of survival mechanism in a small country where everyone knows everyone. It has helped Ticos live peacefully for decades, and it may partially explain why Ticos score so consistently high in happiness surveys.

If something goes wrong during your visit, take a deep breath, relax and explain the problem in as soft and neutral a tone as possible. If you're interested in a prompt solution, do your best not to express any irritation or raise your voice. Trust me, if you approach a problem with irritation and a raised voice, *you* will become the problem and a prompt solution will vanish into thin air.

*Special Bonus Tip
(Not restricted to Costa Rica)

Speaking louder does not equal speaking more clearly

It is one of life's great mysteries why people of all cultures raise their voices when talking to non-native speakers. Speaking louder will seem strange at best, condescending at worst. Raise your clarity, not your volume.

COSTA RICAN SPANISH

The biggest difference between Costa Rican Spanish and general Latin American Spanish is the use of the second person singular *vos* instead of *tu*. Although *tu* is used and understood by everyone, *vos* is preferred among family and friends. Another difference is the common use of *con mucho gusto* ("With much pleasure") in response to *gracias* ("Thank you"). In much of Latin America *de nada* ("You're Welcome") is used in response to *gracias*, but in Costa Rica *con mucho gusto* is far more common.

Ticos are very proud of their accent, which they consider clear and neutral. Unlike some of their neighbors, Ticos clearly pronounce the "s" at the end of words that end in "s." Their neighbors, in turn, complain that Ticos don't properly trill their "r"s, including (most prominently) the "R" in *Costa Rica*.

Words and Phrases

Rather than fill countless pages with basic Spanish words and phrases, I'll simply recommend installing a Spanish dictionary and phrasebook on your smartphone or purchasing a physical phrasebook. Smartphone apps are *perfect* for dictionaries and phrasebooks. They let you to walk around with thousands of quickly searchable words and phrases in your pocket. SpanishDict is a good Spanish dictionary app, and Word Lens visually translates words in real time. My favorite physical dictionary/phrasebook is the *Guide to Costa Rican Spanish* by Christopher Howard.

Ticos use hundreds of words found nowhere outside of Costa Rica. Listed below are some classic Costa Rican phrases and *pachuco* ("slang"). For a complete list, check out the Tico-produced app "Costa Rican Idioms."

Pura Vida [PUR-Ah VEE-Dah]: "Pure Life"
The proud motto of Costa Rica (see page p.54)

Mae [MY]: "Dude"
I like to joke that after I learned *mae*, I understood 50% more Spanish in Costa Rica. *Mae* is derived from *maje*, but what *maje* is derived from is a matter of debate. Some claim it's an old word for "idiot" used in medievel Spain. Regardless, *mae* is used constantly by teenagers and young adults, though it is never used in formal company.

Tuanis [TWAH-Nees]: "Cool"
Tuanis is supposedly derived from the phrase "Too Nice," which is another way of saying "cool" in the English-speaking Caribbean Coast.

Agüevado [Ah-Gway-VAH-Doh]: "Sad/Bored"
This common breakup expression is supposedly derived from *huevos* ("eggs").

Diay [Dee-EYE]: "Well"/"Hey"
There's no direct English translation for *diay* (also written *ydiay* or *idiay*), which is more of an emotional expression/exclamation that an actual word. Ask any Tico for an extended explanation.

Chunche [CHOON-Chay]: "Thingy"
One of Costa Rica's most beloved words, a *chunche* is any old thing—a comb, a hat, a pen—that you can't quite remember the name of. According to politically incorrect Costa Rican lore, the word came about thanks to non-Spanish speaking Chinese immigrants who walked into stores asking for things like "chung" and "chong." This was later shortened to *chunchón*, which ultimately became *chunche*.

¿Cómo Amaneció? [KOH-Moh Ah-Mahn-Ah-See-OH]: "How did you sunrise?"
This fun phrase is a popular way of asking "How are you feeling this morning"

Upe! [OOO-Pay!]: "I'm here!"
Upe! is shouted out as you approach someone's house to notify them of your impending arrival. This is supposedly a shortened version of the traditional religious greeting *"Ave María Purísima Nuestra Señora la Virgen de Guadalupe."*

Fresa [FRAY-Sah]: "Snob"
Fresa literally means "strawberry" in Spanish, but in Costa Rica it's also used to describe someone who's a snob or aspires to be a snob.

Pulpería [Pool-Pear-REE-Ah]: "Corner Store"
Every village in Costa Rica, no matter how small, has a *pulpería*. Some claim the word is derived from *pulpa* ("pulp"), as in fruit pulp sold to make beverages.

Suave un Toque [SWAH-vay Oon TOE-cay]: "Just a minute"
In the land of Tico Time (p.52) this expression comes in handy.

Guachimán [GWAH-chee-man]: "Security Guard"
Pronounced like "watchyman," *guachimán* (or *guachi*, for short) is derived from the English word "watchman," as in night watchman.

Carro [KAR-Oh]: "Car"
In Mexico and Spain the word for car is *coche*, but in Costa Rica they say *carro*.

Birra [BEER-Ah]: "Beer"
Everyone knows cerveza, but *birra* (derived from "beer") is *muy* Tico.

Zarpe [ZAR-pay]: "Final Round"/"Nightcap"
The last drink of the night. If someone offers you a zarpe, it's considered a bit rude not to accept.

Goma [GOH-mah]: "Hangover"
This is what happens after you've had one *zarpe* too many.

CANOPY TOURS

For MANY PEOPLE, visiting Costa Rica without whizzing through the trees on a canopy tour is simply unthinkable. Canopy tours (aka zip-lines) are the country's signature outdoor adventure—a combination of scenery, speed and adrenaline. They're a great way to experience some of Costa Rica's most dramatic landscapes, and they're popular with just about everyone. Even young children and grandparents can enjoy canopy tours. (The minimum age is usually around six, and I've talked to guides who have taken 80-year-olds on canopy tours!)

The typical canopy tour works like this: A long metal cable is suspended between two tall trees, both of which have elevated platforms next to the cable. While standing on a platform, riders hook themselves onto the cable via a harness and pulley system, then zip to the next platform at speeds ranging from 5 to 65 kph (3 to 40 mph). On some tours, the longest cables stretch several kilometers. Most canopy tours offer a dozen or so cables, and trained guides direct riders through each stage of the process.

These days canopy tours are popular throughout the world, but they originated right here in Costa Rica. In the 1980s scientists in Monteverde used a cable and pulley system to study the forest canopy from above. In 1992 an enterprising Canadian named Darren Hreniuk converted the setup into a multi-cable system that focused more on speed than science, and the canopy tour was born. Within a few years canopy tours had spread throughout Costa Rica, and *canopy* (pronounced "CAH-noh-pee") had entered the local lexicon.

Over the past decade, intense competition has forced many canopy tour operators into a kind of adrenaline arms race. No longer content with simply gliding through the trees, tour operators began offering longer/faster cables and new adventures like the "Tarzan Swing," a giant pendulum that involves a brief free fall. The latest craze is the ability to "Fly Like Superman" via a back harness that lets you zoom along the cables belly-down.

In my opinion, the best canopy tours are still found in Monteverde (p.211), where canopy tours began. The rugged mountains offer dramatic terrain and beautiful cloud forest scenery. But rest assured there are great tours—and incredible scenery—throughout Costa Rica. In all but the most remote tourist towns, there will be a good canopy tour nearby.

CANYONING

COSTA RICA'S TROPICAL climate and rugged topography are perfect for canyoning (aka canyoneering), which involves descending steep, water-filled canyons through a combination of hiking, scrambling, swimming and rappelling. Most canyoning tours include dramatic waterfall rappels, and all involve getting dirty and wet. If you're an outdoor junkie looking to get up close and personal with the jungle, you're going to love canyoning.

Although all canyoning tours descend rugged canyons, different operators use different rapelling setups. Some use fixed rapelling platforms near waterfalls (left), while others rappel directly down the face of a waterfall. Depending on the contours of the canyon, you'll need to employ technical footwork and/or down-climbing skills. Unlike canopy tours, where you simply strap in and hold on tight, canyoning involves both physical and mental agility. Trained guides will lead you safely down the canyon, pointing out the best methods and easiest routes.

If you're planning on canyoning in Costa Rica, it's a good idea to bring some basic gear. The most important accessories are closed-toed water shoes (Keen is a great brand), which drain easily and protect your feet. Sandals are useless, and open-toed sport sandals don't offer sufficient protection. Boots and sneakers are adequate, though both tend to get water-logged. Because you'll get wet, it's also a good idea to wear clothes made from synthetic fibers, which dry far more quickly than cotton. Helmets and harnesses are provided by the tour operator.

Costa Rica's most popular canyoning tours are located in Arenal (p.193). Desafío Adventures (2479-0020, www.desafiocostarica.com) leads descents down Lost Canyon, with four waterfalls ranging from 7–70 meters (23–230 feet). Pure Trek Canyoning (2479-1313, www.puretrek.com) leads descents down El Cacao Canyon, which features four waterfalls ranging from 9–49 meters (30–160 feet).

Costa Canyoning (8880-9192, www.costacanyoning.com) offers a terrific canyoning tour in Uvita (p.391) in the Central Pacific, and Psycho Tours (8353-8619, www.psychotours.com) offers a great canyoning tour in Matapalo on the southern Osa Peninsula.

The rainy season, May–November, offers the best canyoning in Costa Rica thanks to swollen waterfalls that add another layer of action and excitement. During the dry season many waterfalls slow to a trickle. But no matter when you go canyoning, expect to be treated to some of Costa Rica's most beautiful (and overlooked) scenery.

HIKING

FROM HIGH-ELEVATION CLOUD forests to coastal rainforests, Costa Rica is home to an incredible range of landscapes, and one of the best ways to experience them is on foot. Spend some time strolling through the forest, and you'll likely encounter fascinating plants and animals that most people miss. Costa Rica's best hiking trails are found in the country's national parks, which are scattered throughout the country.

Costa Rica's most spectacular and challenging hiking destination is Chirripó (p.261), the country's tallest peak. Towering 3,820 meters (12,533 feet) above sea level, Chirripó's rocky summit is reached via a 20-km (12.4-mile) trail that starts in the small town of San Gerardo de Rivas. As the trail heads above tree line, it enters the páramo (p.105), Costa Rica's coldest and most unusual ecosystem. A rugged shelter near the summit offers overnight lodging.

Another hiking highlight is Monteverde (p.211), which is home to Costa Rica's most famous cloud forest. Roughly 13 km (8 miles) of hiking trails criss-cross the misty Monteverde Reserve, and several nearby reserves offer additional hiking. North of Monteverde lies the Río Celeste (p.227) and Rincón de la Vieja (p.236), both of which feature hiking trails to beautiful waterfalls.

The best hiking on the Pacific coast is found in Corcovado National Park (p.411), which covers 40% of the Osa Peninsula. Two trails, one 19.5 km (12.1 miles) long and one 20 km (12.4 miles) long, head to a remote ranger station that offers overnight lodging in the heart of the park. Both trails are long and physically demanding, but they offer some of the best wildlife watching in Costa Rica.

The Central Pacific's most popular hiking destination is Manuel Antonio National Park, where a network of good trails passes through lush rainforest en route to some of Costa Rica's most beautiful beaches. Another good hiking option, especially for birders and wildlife watchers, is Carara National Park (p.351), located 23 km (12.4 miles) north of Jacó.

On the Nicoya Peninsula, the best hiking is found at Cabo Blanco (p.330), near Santa Teresa and Montezuma. Located at the southern tip of the peninsula, this reserve was one of the first protected areas in Costa Rica, offering a mix of jungle, beaches and wildlife.

On the Caribbean coast, Cahuita National Park is home to an easy, 9-km (5.6-mile) trail that wraps around a beautiful peninsula surrounded by beaches. A more challenging hiking trail passes through the rugged Gandoca-Manzanillo Refuge (p.487), located southeast of Puerto Viejo.

RAFTING

COSTA RICA'S RUGGED mountains and abundant rainfall have created a country that's literally overflowing with rivers. By some estimates, only New Zealand has more rivers per square kilometer for a country of comparable size. Unfortunately, most of Costa Rica's rivers are too small to paddle, but a handful are big, beautiful and filled with exciting whitewater. In addition to thrilling rapids perfect for rafting, Costa Rica's rivers are famous for lush, tropical scenery and world-class wildlife. There's nothing like splashing through a series of Class IV rapids, then spotting a toucan or a poison dart frog.

The rafting highlight of Costa Rica is the Río Pacuare, which starts near the town of Turrialba and flows north into the Caribbean. Over the course of 29 km (18 miles) it passes through exciting rapids (Class III–IV) and some of the most beautiful river scenery in Costa Rica (left). Although one-day trips are offered (pick-up and drop-off provided in San José), the best options are 2–3 day trips that include 1–2 nights at a riverside ecolodge. The Pacuare River Lodge (2225-3939, www.pacuarelodge.com) is by far the most luxurious overnight option. Another good choice is the Ríos Tropicales Lodge, run by the folks at Ríos Tropicales (2233-6455, www.riostropicales.com).

The region around Arenal is another great place for river rafting in Costa Rica. Nearby rivers include the Sarapiquí (Class II–III), Balsa (Class II–III) and Toro (Class II–IV). Rafting trips near Arenal are offered by Ríos Tropicales and Wave Expeditions (2479-7262, www.waveexpeditions.com).

About 40 km (25 miles) southeast of Liberia (p.272), rafting trips depart the Rincón Corobicí Restaurant for the Río Corobicí, a calm stretch of river alongside Palo Verde National Park that's great for wildlife watching. For more whitewater, check out the nearby Río Tenorio, which offers thrilling Class III–IV rapids. Rafting trips on both the Tenorio and Corobicí are offered by H2O Adventures (2777-4092, www.h2ocr.com).

The Central Pacific is also home to a handful of fun rivers near Manuel Antonio (p.363). The most thrilling is El Chorro, a narrow canyon that offers Class IV–V rapids even in the dry season. Gentler waves are found on the nearby Río Savegre and Río Naranjo (Class III–IV). Tours are offered by Ríos Tropicales and Quepoa Expeditions (2777-0058, www.quepoaexpeditions.com).

No matter where you end up, the most exciting whitewater is found from June–November, Costa Rica's rainiest months.

SNORKELING & SCUBA DIVING

COSTA RICA IS home to one of the world's most amazing dive sites: Isla Del Coco (p.441), which lies 540 km (335 miles) off the southern Pacific coast. This stunning uninhabited island—the inspiration for Jurassic Park's Isla Nublar—is surrounded by a series of underwater seamounts that attract thousands of schooling hammerhead sharks. Unfortunately, Isla del Coco is only accessible on 8–12 day boat trips that cost $4,500–6,800.

The waters off mainland Costa Rica are far less impressive. Visibility is the main issue—tall mountains and abundant rain create *lots* of runoff—so don't expect crystal clear water close to shore. On the plus side, the nutrient-rich runoff attracts a number of "big game" wildlife, including reef sharks, bull sharks, sea turtles, manta rays and even the occasional whale shark. Although the Pacific coast boasts few coral reefs, if you're a scuba aficionado there's plenty of interesting scenery worth checking out.

The Pacific coast's top dive site is Isla de Caño (p.408), which lies 16 km (10 miles) offshore Drake Bay near the northern tip of the Osa Peninsula. The island's waters are home to some fun seamounts and a modest collection of coral reefs. If you're visiting Drake Bay and fascinated with ocean wildlife, it's also worth contacting Costa Cetacea (p.404), which organizes "Blue Water Safaris" that head 10–20 miles offshore in search of dolphins, whales and other sea creatures.

The Pacific coast's second-best dive sites are located off the northern Nicoya Peninsula, near Playa del Coco (p.281) and Playa Flamingo (p.290). Both towns are home to good dive shops that arrange daily trips to the islands and seamounts lying just offshore.

Costa Rica's most impressive coral reefs are located off the southern Caribbean coast. Cahuita National Park (p.464) protects one of the country's largest coral reefs, which is open only to snorkelers accompanied by a local guide. South of Cahuita, between Puerto Viejo and Manzanillo, there are several additional kilometers of coral reefs lying just offshore. As long as the seas are calm, it's easy to snorkel around these reefs on your own, and two local dive shops offer scuba trips to some of the nearby underwater walls.

SPORTFISHING

THE TROPICAL WATERS offshore Costa Rica are home to world-class sportfishing. The Pacific coast is famous for sailfish and marlin, which are classified as billfish due to the long, stiff bills that protrude from their heads. Sailfish (left) measure up to 3 meters (10 feet) long, weigh up to 100 kgs (220 pounds) and swim up to 110 kph (68 mph)—the fastest recorded speed of any water creature. Marlin come in several varieties, including blue, black and striped. Blue marlin measure up to 4.6 meters (15 feet) long and weigh up to a whopping 900 kg (2,000 pounds)! Both marlin and sailfish are prized by anglers for their long, fierce fight.

The Pacific coast's excellent sportfishing results from pockets of nutrient-rich water that lie 20–30 miles offshore. Peak sailfish season is January–April for the Central and South Pacific, May–August for the Nicoya Peninsula. Peak blue marlin season is November/December and March/April. All billfish sportfishing is catch-and-release in Costa Rica, but popular catch-and-eat species include yellowfin tuna and dorado (mahi mahi).

Because boats consume *lots* of gas heading 20–30 miles offshore in search of sailfish and marlin, offshore sportfishing trips are very expensive. Full-day charters generally cost $1,000 or more. A less expensive option is inshore fishing for species such as roosterfish and snapper.

The Pacific coast's most luxurious sportfishing destination is Los Sueños Marina in Playa Herradura (p.353), which lies just north of Jacó in the Central Pacific. There's also the new Pez Vela Marina (p.377) in Quepos, near Manuel Antonio. In the South Pacific, the top outfitter is Crocodile Bay (p.430) in Puerto Jiménez. There are also a handful of sportfishing boats that operate out of Golfito (p.436), a gorgeous harbor on the eastern shores of the Golfo Dulce. In the north Pacific, the most popular sportfishing destinations are Playa Flamingo (p.290) and Playa del Coco (p.281).

The Caribbean coast is famous for tarpon, which grow up to 2.5 meters (8 feet) long and weigh up to 125 kg (280 pounds). Another Caribbean favorite is snook, which grow up to 1.4 meters (4.5 feet) long and weigh up to 24 kg (53 pounds). Both are fierce fighting fish caught close to shore. The best months for tarpon fishing are September and October. The Caribbean coast's top fishing destination is Barra de Colorado (p.458), a remote village near the Nicaraguan border that's accessible by plane. There's also the small town of Parismina (p.458), located halfway between Tortuguero and Limón.

SURFING

WITH TWO COASTS, 1,200 km (750 miles) of coastline and warm water year-round, Costa Rica is a surfer's paradise. There are nearly a dozen world-class surf breaks, most of which have hotels and restaurants nearby that cater specifically to surfers. Although Costa Rica is Central America's top surf destination, crowds are rarely a problem, and there are still plenty of remote beaches with great waves. There are also a number of terrific surf camps offering lodging, meals and instruction.

A comprehensive surf guide is beyond the scope of this book, but I've done my best to include some basic information about the country's top surf spots. If you're looking for a good surf guide, check out *The Surfer's Guide to Costa Rica* by Mike Parise and Robert Towner. Another good guide is the *Tiquicia Surf Map and Guide*, which is locally produced and available at surf shops in Costa Rica.

The Pacific coast contains the vast majority of Costa Rica's top surf breaks. The northern Pacific, which is dominated by the Nicoya Peninsula, is home to Witch's Rock (p.276) and Ollie's Point, Playa Grande (p.294), Playa Negra (p.307), Nosara (p.311) and Santa Teresa (p.325). Farther south, the Central Pacific's top breaks are Playa Hermosa (p.359) and Dominical (p.383). The south Pacific is famous for Pavones (p.438), the world's second-longest left, and there are also some good waves at Cabo Matapalo (p.427) at the southern tip of the Osa Peninsula. Over on the Caribbean coast, Puerto Viejo (p.469) is home to Salsa Brava, one of the country's most powerful and challenging waves.

If you're new to surfing and looking for good beginner waves, head to Tamarindo (p.299) or Nosara (p.311), both of which are located on the Nicoya Peninsula. In addition to gentle waves and a mellow, beginner-friendly vibe, these beaches are home to some of the top surf camps in Costa Rica. In the Central Pacific, Jacó (p.353) offers good beginner waves, though Dominical (p.383) has better surf schools.

The Pacific's biggest swells arrive from the south from June–October, which corresponds with the rainy season. From Dec-Feb, the northern Pacific is blessed with powerful offshore winds, including the famous Papagayo Winds (p.95). Over on the Caribbean coast, the best waves are found from Dec–April.

For those of a literary bent, Allan Weisbecker has written two popular memoirs about surfing in Costa Rica: *In Search of Captain Zero* and *Can't You Get Along with Anyone?*

CULTURE

THE PEOPLE OF Costa Rica, who call themselves Ticos, are famous for their cheerful outlook, their conflict-averse nature and their laid-back approach to life. These cultural traits, combined with the country's relatively high standard of living, have led some researchers to conclude that Costa Rica is the "Happiest Country on Earth." But beyond the stereotype of the happy, peaceful Tico—which is heavily promoted by politicians, tourist brochures and the Ticos themselves— lies a far more complex reality.

Costa Rica's mythic self-image revolves around *campesinos* ("rural peasants") and *boyeros* ("ox-cart drivers"). These two archetypes, generally portrayed as light-skinned and living in the mountains, occupy an outsized role in Costa Rican culture. Boyeros gather in parades throughout the year, proudly showing off their elaborately painted oxcarts (p.70). At patriotic events, parents often dress their children as campesinos. Boys are dressed in a white shirt, white hat, red bandana, painted on moustache and mini-machete. Girls are dressed in long white dresses with vibrant satin colors and flowers in their hair. Even though three-quarters of Ticos now live in areas classified as urban, the celebration of campesinos and boyeros reflects the rural, self-sufficient mindset that still forms the bedrock of Costa Rican culture—even in the age of highways and shopping malls.

Of course, Costa Rica is more than just light-skinned mountain farmers. Eight indigenous groups are scattered throughout the country, and a vibrant Afro-Caribbean population lives along the Caribbean coast. In Guanacaste, a dry, dusty province in northwest Costa Rica, a typical Tico is a brown-skinned *sabanero* ("cowboy") roaming the plains on horseback. All of these traditional cultural groups, combined with a steady stream of immigrants and expats from Nicaragua, Colombia, the United States and Canada make up the modern social fabric of Costa Rica.

LATIN AMERICAN INFLUENCE

AS PART OF Spanish-speaking Latin America, Costa Rica shares much of its culture with the region as a whole. Like most Latin Americans, Ticos generally take a laid-back, relaxed approach to life. The spirit of *mañana*—putting things off for another day—is a constant theme, and personal warmth is generally given higher priority than personal achievement. Both Catholicism and *machismo* (male chauvinism) form a large part of the culture, though both are less prevalent than they were a generation ago.

Like most Latin Americans, Ticos consider family to be the most crucial aspect of their lives. Nothing—not work, not school, not friends—is more important than family. Many Ticos cannot conceive of the fractured family structures in the U.S., where children happily choose to move away from their hometowns. In Costa Rica, many children live with their parents until they are married, at which point some build a house on their parents' property or purchase a house nearby. If children do move away from home, some talk with their parents on the phone several times a day. Ticos spend the vast majority of their free time with extended family, and family time on Sunday is sacrosanct. The family is the bedrock of Costa Rican society—a steady, reliable source of support in an uncertain world.

The enormous importance of family partly reflects Costa Rica's relatively low level of social trust—the extent to which people trust non-family members. As in much of Latin America, Ticos' intense focus on the family can come at the expense of the community as a whole. This can be seen in the day-to-day functioning of most towns, where public infrastructure is rundown and law enforcement is subpar. Instead of working within the "system" (i.e. the government), which is widely viewed as inherently corrupt, many Ticos simply cover their own houses in metal bars and razor wire. In wealthy neighborhoods families hire private security guards. In both rich and poor neighborhoods homes are neat and tidy on the inside, but public spaces are in disrepair. As a result, home and family offer a refuge from the neglected outside world in a self-reinforcing cycle. Although Costa Rica has low levels of social trust compared to the U.S. and Canada, it enjoys high levels of social trust compared to the rest of Latin America.

Some economists believe that levels of social trust are correlated to income inequality. Latin America famously has the highest level of income inequality in the world, a situation that stems from the colonial era when a small number of Spanish conquistadors ruled over a large number of indigenous workers. In Costa Rica, where settlers tended to work their own land, a more egalitarian ethos evolved. For decades Costa Rica has had one of the lowest levels of income inequality in Latin America, though it remains high by global standards. In fact, on many social indicators (crime, corruption, homicide) Costa Rica scores positively within Latin America but low by global standards.

THE TICOS

LIVING IN A tiny country, Ticos are cultural sponges who eagerly absorb modern influences from the rest of the world. Telenovelas and pop music arrive from Mexico and Colombia, movies and technology descend from the U.S. and European political ideas have long been in vogue. More exotic foreign influences—sushi, yoga—arrive largely in Westernized form.

Yet despite their openness to outside influences, Ticos retain a passionately strong sense of what it means to be Tico. First and foremost, Ticos are cheerful and non-confrontational. Playing nice is a survival mechanism in a small country where everyone seems to know everyone. Although Ticos often complain behind closed doors, anything other than face-to-face niceness is considered rude, and public confrontation is considered disgraceful. When parents were recently polled on "the most important qualities to teach children" the most common response was "good manners." (The least common response was "hard work"). Compared to other Latin Americans, Ticos tend to be less outgoing and more reserved, but they are consistently friendly once engaged in conversation.

Ticos are also incredibly sensitive to stress, which is viewed as a kind of social taboo. There is strong social pressure to avoid anything that might induce stress such as raising one's voice or being irritable. This offers both upsides and downsides. Ticos don't sweat the small stuff, but they often don't sweat the big stuff either. As a result, problems tend to fester and grow worse over time. When problems grow too big to ignore, Ticos often take a fence-sitting approach, shying away from bold solutions that might offend anyone.

In many ways, however, Costa Rican identity is also based on what it isn't. Ticos view themselves as less violent and corrupt than other Latin American countries, less militarized and stressed-out than the U.S. and less uppity and snobby than Europe. In general, Ticos view themselves as a culture apart—a unique people in a strange and tumultuous world.

Ticos' eagerness to view themselves as different has led to many quirks, of which they are quite proud. If you mention their lack of addresses (p.21) or reluctance to admit not knowing where something is (p.29), Ticos will laugh and beam with pride. "Yes," they say, "That's *very* Tico!" They have even given their quirks a name: *idiosincrasia costarricense* ("Costa Rican idiosyncrasies"). Indeed, the stereotype of the bumbling, accident-prone Tico is, for the most part, largely celebrated. One wildly popular Facebook page called *Solo en Costa Rica* ("Only in Costa Rica") is filled with user-submitted photos of bizarre mistakes and accidents encountered in Costa Rica.

Tico pride, even when it comes to their mistakes, is part of an intense patriotism instilled from a young age. Schoolchildren are taught that Costa Rica is an exceptional country that is envied by other countries, and they take that lesson to heart. National pride runs deep, and even mild criticism of Costa Rica by foreigners is considered extremely rude. If it wasn't for their unfailing politeness and their love of laughing at themselves, Ticos would probably come across as a bit smug.

Among some Ticos, there is an unfortunate racial element to their feelings of self-satisfaction. The so-called "White Legend" of Costa Rica is the belief that Costa Ricans are descended primarily from racially "pure" Spanish settlers and European immigrants. Ticos are more light-skinned than their neighbors, and among the upper class blond hair and blue eyes are not uncommon. But genetic testing reveals that the average Tico is 40–60% white, 15–35% indigenous and 10–20% black. Regardless, the White Legend persists. When President Rafael Ángel Calderón Fournier visited Spain in 1992, he was quoted as explaining that Costa Rica had "no Indians" when Columbus arrived.

Ticos & Ticas

The people of Costa Rica proudly call themselves *Ticos*, a nickname derived from a local linguistic quirk. In most Spanish-speaking countries, the diminutive -ito is added to the end of words to indicate a "little bit" of something. Thus, a little *momento* ("moment") is a *momentito*. In Costa Rica, however, people like to add the diminutive -tico, so a little *momento* becomes a *momentico*. Thus, Costa Ricans are affectionately known as Ticos. As Spanish grammar dictates, *Tica* is the feminine version of Tico. Costa Rican men are Ticos, Costa Rican women are Ticas and a mixed group of men and women are Ticos.

La Negrita

The Basílica de los Ángeles in the former capital of Cartago is the holiest church in Costa Rica because it contains the country's holiest object: *La Virgen de los Ángeles*, commonly known as *La Negrita* ("The Little Black Girl"). This six-inch stone statue, which depicts the Virgin Mary holding the baby Jesus, was discovered on August 2, 1635 by a young indigenous girl named Juana Pereira. According to legend, Juana was gathering firewood in the forest when she found the statue on top of a rock. Intrigued, she brought it home and placed it in a box. But when she woke up the next morning, the statue was gone. She returned to the forest and found the statue resting on the same rock. Again she brought it home, again it disappeared, and again she found it on top of the rock. This continued several more times, at which point Juana brought the statue to the local priest, who placed the statue in a secure box. The next morning, however, the statue was gone. Yet again it was found resting on the rock in the forest. Deciding it was a sign from God, the priest built a small shelter around the statue, and today the Basílica de los Ángeles is located where La Negrita was found.

The significance of La Negrita goes far beyond the statue's miraculous disappearance/reappearance. In 1635 Cartago was a racially segregated town, and Juana Pereira lived in a neighborhood known as *La Puebla de los Pardos* ("The Village of Colored People"). Because Spanish religious imagery depicted only white people, the discovery of a dark-colored Virgin struck an emotional chord with the town's indigenous and mixed-race citizens.

In 1824 La Negrita was declared the patron Virgin of Costa Rica, and today she is encased in an elaborate gold fixture in the church. The grotto behind the church is filled with offerings called *exvotos* ("ex-vows"), which represent answered prayers. Most are miniature metal body parts—feet, hands, hearts, eyes—that were miraculously healed. Some exvotos are more unique. There is the crown worn by Miss Costa Rica 1992 and a fishing harpoon used by a shipwrecked gringo who heard about La Negrita on an old radio while adrift at sea and promised to convert to Catholicism if he was saved. In 2012 Warner Rojas, the first Tico to climb Mount Everest, left rocks from the world's highest peak. Although thousands of exvotos are on display, they represent a fraction of the total collection. Since 1635 over two million exvotos have been left at the Basílica, and their numbers continue to grow. Street vendors outside the church sell a wide variety of exvotos to those wishing to pay their respects.

Tico Time

In Costa Rica *Hora Tica* ("Tico Time") is a popular expression used to convey the fact that things rarely start on time. Although Costa Rica is often called the "Switzerland of Central America" due to its rugged mountains and political stability, the thought of comparing the hyper-punctual, watchmaking Swiss to the ultra laid-back, forever *mañana* Ticos has always struck me as hilarious. Showing up 10, 20, even 30 minutes late for an appointment is considered perfectly normal, and punctuality is considered odd. One of the funniest conversations I had about Tico Time was with a Tica who was born in Costa Rica but raised in London. As such, she had a pretty interesting perspective on time. "The thing I don't like about Tico Time," she told me, "is that it only applies to the start of the workday. Closing time is sacred. It's never Tico Time when it's time to close." As more and more gringos have moved to Costa Rica, a new expression has become popular: *Hora Gringa* ("Gringo Time") which, loosely translated, means "Be on time."

COSTA RICAN ART

IT CAN BE argued that Costa Rica's small size, lack of bloody conflicts and strong cultural desire to not criticize or offend have resulted in minimal artistic accomplishments. Compared to the creative vibrancy of much of Latin America, Costa Rica definitely seems a bit uninspired. It doesn't have the famous painters of Mexico, the complex cuisine of Peru or the passion for music and dance found in Cuba, Colombia and Argentina. Costa Rica's most famous artist, the sculptor Francisco Zúñiga, moved to Mexico when he was 24 and has been called "one of the 100 most notable Mexicans of the 20th century." Ouch.

Until recently, most Ticos did not place a high priority on artistic achievements. Ticos are highly utilitarian, and their style reflects this. Architecture is bland, fashion is humble and meals are dominated by rice and beans for breakfast, lunch *and* dinner. Of course, there are exceptions to Tico utilitarianism— the elaborately painted oxcarts (p.70) being the most obvious example. But in general Ticos have been far more focused on relaxing and hanging out than obsessing about artistic greatness. In the early 1970s, newly re-elected president José Figueres decided to change that by establishing the Ministry of Culture. As he famously put it: "Why should we have tractors if we don't have violins?"

Costa Rica's most prominent artistic achievements are mostly literary. Two famous Costa Rican novels are *Mamita Yunai* ("Mommy United"), about struggling banana workers in the 1930s, and *La Isla de los Hombres Solos* ("The Island of Lonely Men"), the memoir of a wrongly convicted Tico who spent decades in a notorious prison on Isla San Lucas (p.341). Costa Rica's most famous writer, Joaquín Gutiérrez, is best known for the popular children's book *Cocorí*, which describes the adventures of a black boy on the Caribbean Coast.

In recent years, a handful of Costa Rican films have made a splash in local theaters, including *Caribe* (2004), *Gestación* (2009), *El Regresso* (2011) and *Italia 90* (2014), a dramatization of Costa Rica's 1990 World Cup run.

Pura Vida

Costa Rica's national motto is *Pura Vida* ("Pure Life"), a multi-purpose expression that represents the best of what it means to be Tico. Pura Vida can be used as a greeting ("How are you?" ... "Pura Vida!"); a way of saying OK ("Want to go to the movies? ... "Pura Vida!"); a way of saying great Great ("How was the movie?" ... "Pura Vida!"); and a way of saying Goodbye ("See you later." ... "Pura Vida!"). The widespread use of Pura Vida is one of the most endearing aspects of Costa Rican Spanish. Ticos are *extremely* proud of their motto, and they *love* it when foreigners give it a try. So say it loud. Pura Vida!

MUSIC

Although not famous for their musical creations, Ticos are voracious consumers of Latin pop music. *Musica tropical*—salsa, merengue, cumbia, bachata—are the rhythms of choice, and no fiesta is complete without musica tropical played at ear-splitting levels. At special events like birthdays and anniversaries, live mariachis are often hired, and marimbas (below) are popular at traditional celebrations. Reggaeton is popular among teens, as are hits from U.S. Latino stars.

Marimbas

Developed in Mexico and popular throughout Central America, the marimba is Costa Rica's most traditional instrument. Marimba music is common at festivals, celebrations and typical dances. Players strike wooden bars with rubber mallets, producing a light chime that's amplified by a hollow tube below each bar. Early marimbas used gourds as amplification tubes—a design that was most likely developed by African slaves based on traditional African instruments.

Calypso Limonense

Costa Rica's Caribbean coast is the birthplace of *Calypso Limonense* ("Calypso of Limón"), a unique style that blends Calyspo and Mento music. Calypso originated in Trinidad and Tabago, where it began as a form of coded news that was sung between slaves who were prohibited from talking with one another. Mento was a similar folk music that originated in Jamaica. When Afro-Caribbean musicians in Limón began mixing Calypso rhythms with a Mento tempo in the early 1900s, Calypso Limonense was born. Originally considered working-class music, it was shunned by local radio stations, so Calypsonians played at bars, beaches and street parties. In the late 1970s, Calypso Limonense arrived in San José and achieved a larger following. Costa Rica's most famous Calypsonian is Cahuita resident Walter Ferguson, who has written over 100 songs. If you want to check out Calypso Limonense, head to Cahuita, which often features live bands on the weekends. Cahuita also hosts an annual International Calypso Festival in early July.

COSTA RICAN POLITICS

WHAT COSTA RICAN culture excels at, above all else, is political stability. Unfortunately, this doesn't quicken the pulse of art majors, foodies or music aficionados, and it makes a lousy souvenir. But it also means that Costa Rica has never embraced anti-U.S. firebrands like Fidel Castro or Hugo Chávez. Compared to the rest of Latin America, Ticos have been rather boring politically—which has served them extremely well. Indeed, Costa Rica's "tropical welfare state," which combines capitalism and private property rights with strong emphasis on education, health care and retirement benefits, is a compelling model for other Latin American countries.

Costa Rica has one main political party: the PLN, *Partido de Liberación Nacional* ("National Liberation Party"), which first came to power following the 1948 Civil War. The PLN is a center-right, Social Democrat party (against both interventionist socialism and laissez-faire capitalism) that supports free trade, the welfare state and conservative social stances (pro-life, anti-gay marriage). Other parties include the center-left PAC, *Partido Acción Ciudadana* ("Citizens Action Party"), the center-left PUSC, *Partido Unidad Social Cristiana* ("United Social Christian Party"), and the Libertarian PML, *Partido Movimiento Liberatrio*, all of which have struggled to gain a dominant foothold.

Elections are treated as important, celebratory occasions, and they are famously clean and transparent. Costa Rica even has a law that no liquor can be sold on election day. But although Ticos are firm believers in democracy, they are distrustful of politicians and authority in general. Many Ticos view government officials as interested in only one thing: *chorizos* ("sausages," Costa Rican slang for "bribes"). In 2010 one unsuccessful presidential candidate, Luis Fishman, tried to harness this popular discontent with the uninspiring slogan *¡El Menos Malo Es El Más Bueno!* ("The Least Worst Is The Most Good!")

In many ways, politics is a family affair in Costa Rica. In the past 30 years, two sons of presidents have been elected as presidents themselves. Although most presidents come from wealthy families, they take great pains to appear humble due to Ticos' strong disdain for snobbery. Presidents often dress casually and travel without bodyguards. In the 1980s, president Luis Alberto Monge even had his wallet stolen by a pickpocket in downtown San José.

In 2010 PLN candidate Laura Chinchilla became Costa Rica's first female president. Halfway through her four-year term, however, her approval rating plummeted to 13%. In 2014 support for the PLN was so low that their presidential nominee, former San José mayor Johnny Araya, dropped out of the race rather than suffer a humiliating defeat. That handed the presidency to Luis Guillermo Solís of the center-left PAC. A former PLN member, Solís denounced the party for corruption and "anti-democratic" practices in 2005. In 2014 Solís campaigned against corruption and promised more inclusive economic growth.

TICOS & NICAS

"In Costa Rica," goes a popular saying, "there are three seasons: the dry season, the rainy season and the season when there are problems with Nicaragua." For centuries Ticos (Costa Ricans) and Nicas (Nicaraguans) have been uneasy neighbors, never missing an opportunity to dislike one another. Unlike Ticos and Panamanians, who get along just fine, Ticos and Nicas exist in a state of permanent agitation.

One could argue the feud really got going in 1824, when Costa Rica annexed the province of Guanacaste, which up to that point belonged to Nicaragua. The annexation was voted on by the citizens of Guanacaste, and it brought Costa Rica stunning beaches, a rich folkloric tradition (p.60) and the eternal ire of Nicaragua. In 1856 the notorious William Walker invaded Costa Rica from Nicaragua, though he was quickly defeated by Costa Rica's army (p.148). In 1955, seven years after Costa Rica abolished its army, Nicaraguan dictator Anastasio Somoza backed a failed rebel attack on Costa Rica and dropped bombs on San José.

Starting in the early 1970s, the Nicaraguan economy entered a period of swift decline following a massive earthquake, the Sandinista overthrow of Somoza and the Contra wars of the 1980s. Today Costa Rica is one of the richest countries in Latin America while Nicaragua is one of the poorest. As a result, tens of thousands of Nicaraguans have flooded across the border in search of work. Today there are officially 400,000 Nicaraguans living in Costa Rica, although the actual number is likely much higher. The vast majority are low-skilled, low-wage workers, employed as janitors, maids or coffee pickers. Many Ticos view Nicaraguans as inherently violent, and they are uncomfortable with the rise of "Costa Nica." Some Ticos complain that Nicas steal jobs and are responsible for much of the country's crime. Nicas respond that they're just doing the work most Ticos refuse to do, and that the majority of crime in Costa Rica is committed by Costa Ricans.

In 2010 tensions flared up again when Nicaraguan troops occupied Isla Calero, a disputed island in the Río San Juan that forms Costa Rica's northeast border. Costa Rica claimed Nicaragua invaded their island. Nicaragua claimed the island was theirs. The standoff lasted for weeks, briefly making international headlines when Nicaragua appeared to justify its actions based on data from Google Maps.

Tensions over Isla Calero ultimately calmed down without violence, but tensions between Costa Rica and Nicaragua remain. There's seemingly no end to all the petty bickering, which even includes an ongoing dispute about the origins of *gallo pinto* (both countries claim to have invented the popular breakfast food). As a Tico once told me, "Costa Rica and Nicaragua are like an old married couple. They constantly argue and fight, but they don't know how to live any other way."

SPORTS & FITNESS

THERE IS ONLY one sport that matters in Costa Rica: *Fútbol* ("football" aka "soccer"). Every town, no matter how small, has a fútbol field where organized games are held nearly every weekend. In fact, a town can't legally qualify as a political district without a fútbol field. The biggest professional teams are *Saprissa* (from San José) and its arch-rival *La Liga* (from Alajuela). Saprissistas and Liguistas are the two most polarized social groups in Costa Rica, though everyone comes together to cheer on the national team, known as *La Sele*, short for *La Selección* ("The Selection"). When La Sele advanced to the World Cup knockout stage in 1990, the president declared a national holiday. When La Sele reached the World Cup quarter finals in 2014, it was considered the greatest moment in Costa Rican sports history.

Although *fútbol* dominates, other sports have become popular in recent years. Surfing is big on the coast, and many public parks offer basketball courts. Tennis and golf are largely the domain of the upper class. Baseball is not at all popular, which is unusual for Central America.

Sadly, physical fitness has declined in recent years thanks to poor eating habits and sedentary lifestyles. Poor Ticos, who spend long days in the field, are generally in good shape, but middle class waistlines have steadily expanded. Today 25% of Ticos are considered obese. Fortunately, physical fitness is now widely regarded as a good thing. This is a big change from the 1970s, when police in a remote village arrested a man for jogging because they determined he must be mad.

MALE & FEMALE RELATIONS

AS IN MOST Latin American countries, *machismo* ("male chauvinism") remains a significant part of the culture. But attitudes regarding women's role in the public sphere have changed dramatically in recent years. Women now make up the majority of university graduates, and Costa Rica has one of the highest percentages of women legislators in the world. Women were granted the right to vote in 1948, and since 1999 political parties have been required by law to include women in at least 40% of electable positions on their party lists. Today Costa Rica ranks as one of the top countries for women's rights in the Western Hemisphere.

On the domestic front, however, many aspects of machismo remain. Many men expect their wives to be submissive at home, and male infidelity is disturbingly common. Having multiple lovers is considered a badge of honor, and men who are faithful to their wives or girlfriends are often teased by their male friends. Many men claim they are simply born *muy caliente* ("very horny") and can't be expected to control their natural urges. Many cheated-on women grudgingly accept this argument, directing their anger more towards the *amante* ("mistress") than their partner. Until 1974 Costa Rican law stated that married women could only divorce adulterous husbands in cases of "open and scandalous concubinage."

Latin machismo does not, however, discourage men from being proudly emotional. Men often extoll their love in passionate declarations, flowery poetry and constant references to *mi amor, mi vida, mi corazón* ("my love, my life, my heart"). Sending mariachis or musicians to serenade a lover is also popular.

Tragically, domestic abuse remains a huge problem, especially in poor, rural areas. Although public violence is disdained by Ticos, it is all too common behind closed doors. According to a 2003 poll, 58% of Ticas reported having been the victim of at least one act of physical or sexual violence, and 24% reported having been the victim of four or more acts of physical or sexual violence. Many women stay with abusive partners because they have no other economic option.

The Happiest Country on Earth

Since 2007 the U.K-based New Economics Foundation has regularly named Costa Rica the "Happiest Country on Earth." The results are determined by multiplying life expectancy by "experienced well-being" (how happy people feel on a scale of 0 to 10), then dividing by "ecological footprint." According to the United Nation's 2013 World Happiness Report, Costa Rica ranked 12th in the world for happiness, second only to Canada (6th) in the Western Hemisphere. The U.N. ranked Denmark first in happiness, while the U.S ranked 17th.

GUANACASTE CULTURE

GUANACASTE IS THE hot, dry province that includes much of northwest Costa Rica and the Nicoya Peninsula. Originally home to the indigenous Chorotega tribe, the province is named for the mushroom-shaped Guanacaste tree, which the Chorotega call *cua-necaztli*, ("ear tree"). The name is a reference to the ear-shaped seed pods that grow on the branches during the dry season.

Although Guanacaste was originally covered by extensive tropical dry forests, large tracts were chopped down during the colonial era to create large cattle *haciendas* ("estates"). As such, the region became famous for *sabaneros* ("horseback riders") who roamed the vast *sabanas* ("savannahs"). Over time, Guanacaste developed a unique culture that incorporated traditions from the Chorotega, colonial settlers and the black slaves who were brought to work the ranches. Horsemanship and the *vaquero* ("cowboy") lifestyle are celebrated, and both *topes* (p.72) and bullfights (p.75) remain extremely popular.

Prior to 1824 Guanacaste belonged to Nicaragua. When Nicaragua erupted in civil war following independence from Spain in 1821, the citizens of Guanacaste voted to be annexed by peaceful Costa Rica. The annexation gave Costa Rica a badly needed dose of folklore, and today the country's most famous traditions come from Guanacaste.

Costa Rica's national dance is the *Punto Guanacasteco*, which features men and women engaged in a fast-paced, passionate courtship frequently interrupted by loud yelps. Men wear colorful clothes and twirl handkerchiefs at the tips of their fingers. Women wear long, flowing dresses with vibrant satin colors. The Punto Guanacasteco, which was supposedly invented by a musician named Leandro Cabalceta while he recovered from a hangover in jail, is traditionally accompanied by marimba music. At certain points during the dance participants stop while a man or woman calls out a *bomba* ("bomb"). This short, four-line rhymed verse generally features witty, sexual or rude themes. Two typical bombas are listed below.

Mi mujer y mi caballo	My woman and my horse
se me murieron a un tiempo	died at the same time
¿Que mujer ni que demonio?	My woman, who cares?
Mi caballo es lo que siento.	My horse is what I miss.
La naranja nació verde	The orange is born green
y el tiempo la maduró;	and ripens over time;
mi corazón nació libre	My heart was born free
y el tuyo lo aprisionó.	and yours imprisoned it.

Punto Guanacasteco

Carnaval, Limón

AFRO-CARIBBEAN CULTURE

AFRO-CARIBBEAN CITIZENS make up roughly 3% of Costa Rica's population, and they are heavily concentrated along the Caribbean coast. Historically neglected by the central government, Afro-Caribbeans forged a unique culture that often shares more in common with Jamaica than Costa Rica.

The first blacks arrived in Costa Rica as slaves with the original Spanish colonists. The slaves worked cattle haciendas in Guanacaste, farms in the Central Valley and cacao plantations along the Caribbean coast. Over time, however, their descendants were largely integrated into the local gene pool.

Starting in the 1820s, Costa Rica's Caribbean coast saw an influx of English-speaking Afro-Caribbeans from Panama and Nicaragua. They hunted sea turtles, planted coconut groves and lived largely self-sufficient lifestyles. At the time the Caribbean coast was almost completely disconnected from the rest of Costa Rica, and Afro-Caribbean settlers traded mostly with local indigenous groups.

In the 1880s a large influx of Jamaican workers helped build the railroad from San José to Limón, and many worked the vast banana plantations that sprang up in its wake. As light-skinned Ticos and black Jamaicans mixed in the plantations, racial tensions flared. Many Ticos viewed themselves racially superior to the Jamaicans, and many Jamaicans viewed the Ticos as lazy, dirty and drunk. When a banana blight destroyed the banana plantations in the 1930s, the United Fruit Company (p.152) offered to transport the black workers to the new plantations on the Pacific Coast. But in 1934 President Ricardo Jiménez signed a decree forbidding the company from transferring "colored" workers so as not to upset Costa Rica's "color balance" and cause "civil commotion." It wasn't until new politicians came to power after the Civil War of 1948 that Afro-Caribbeans born in Costa Rica were granted full citizenship.

Over the past decades tens of thousands of light-skinned Ticos have moved to the Caribbean coast in search of work. Today Afro-Caribbeans comprise just 13% of the region's population. But many Afro-Caribbean influences remain, including delicious Caribbean food (p.86) and Calypso music (p.55). The Caribbean coast is also famous for Creole English (aka *Patois* or *Mek I tel you*), which mixes African speech patterns with English words. "Wh'appen, man?" is a shortened form of "What's happening," "How de morning" is "Good morning" and "How much o'clock?" is "What time is it?"

Although Rastafarianism—or at least the Bob Marley version of it—is incredibly popular, many young Afro-Caribbean citizens now prefer speaking Spanish, much to the dismay of their parents. But youth continue to share their parents' deep suspicion of the Costa Rican government. I once met an Afro-Caribbean woman who proudly displayed a Panamanian flag at her home as a form of protest. As she explained, the Costa Rican government "can just make up whatever rules they want, and it don't matter what the deal was before."

Fiesta de los Diablitos

INDIGENOUS CULTURE

PRIOR TO EUROPEAN contact, Costa Rica was home to an estimated 500,000 indigenous people. Following European contact in 1504, the population was devastated by previously unknown diseases and subjugation by colonial settlers. By 1700 the official Spanish census recorded just 1,300 indigenous people living in 14 villages.

Today roughly 100,000 indigenous people live in Costa Rica—about 2.5% of the total population. They live in 22 indigenous reserves that comprise about 6% of national territory. Until 1991 indigenous people were not even considered full legal citizens of Costa Rica. They were only given *cédulas* (identity cards necessary for voting and access to state services) after staging a protest in which they blocked the roads in downtown San José.

The Bribris are the largest indigenous group in Costa Rica, numbering about 18,000 individuals. Their most famous village is located near Puerto Viejo on the Caribbean coast. The Cabécar are the second-largest indigenous group, numbering roughly 17,000 individuals in the Talamanca Mountains. Because they live in remote, inaccessible areas, the Cabécar retain much more of their culture than other indigenous groups. Both the Cabécar and Bribri share linguistic and cultural roots with South American tribes.

The Boruca, who number roughly 2,000, are famous for the *Fiesta de los Diablitos* ("Festival of the Little Devils"), which is held in the village of Rey Curré, near Palmar Norte on the southern Pacific coast. The festival begins on December 30 with the blowing of a conch shell by the *diablo mayor* ("elder devil"). This is followed by dozens of *diablitos* ("little devils") taunting an improvised toro ("bull") that represents the Spanish conquistadors. The diablitos wear ornate masks, cover their bodies with banana leaves and drink lots of *chicha*, a fermented corn beverage. The multi-day festival culminates on the night of January 2 with the diablitos "killing" the bull and throwing it into a bonfire.

The Guaymí number just 3,000 individuals in southern Costa Rica, but they are part of larger population that numbers over 100,000 in Panama. The women are famous for their colorful dresses, and the Guaymí continue to speak their native language. Both men and women work as migrant coffee pickers in the Southern Mountains, most notably the Zona de los Santos (p.251).

The Chorotegas are the largest indigenous group in northern Costa Rica, with about 11,000 individuals on the Nicoya Peninsula. Descendents of a displaced indigenous group from Mexico, the Chorotega arrived in Costa Rica around 800 AD. They share many cultural traits with the Aztecs, including linguistic roots and a reverence for maize. The Chorotega continue to produce beautiful pottery using traditional methods in the village of Guaitíl (p.344).

Costa Rica's smallest indigenous groups are the Huetar (3,500), who once lived in the Central Valley; the Maleku (1,800), who live in the northern lowlands; and the Térrabas (2,700), who live in southern Costa Rica.

Indigenous Artifacts

Jade Objects

Jade craftsmanship was developed in Mexico around 1500 B.C. and reached Costa Rica around 500 B.C. Exceptionally rare and durable, jade was a symbol of wealth and power coveted by local elites. Imported from Guatemala—the only major source of jade in Central or South America—the green stone was fashioned into pendants, necklaces and earrings.

Decorated Pottery

Simple monochrome pottery was produced as early as 1900 B.C. in Costa Rica. Early pieces reflected South American styles, but around 500 A.D. pottery in northwest Costa Rica acquired styles from the Mesoamerican cultures to the north. Local artisans were soon producing striking multi-color vessels that incorporated human and animal motifs.

Gold Figurines

Gold metallurgy was first developed in the Americas in Peru around 2000 B.C., and gold-working techniques reached Costa Rica by about 500 A.D. Before long gold had replaced jade as the object most valued by local elites. Costa Rica's southern Pacific region produced the greatest number of gold objects thanks to gold deposits on the Osa Peninsula.

Stamp Patterns

Among the most interesting decorative tools were cylindrical stamps covered with repetitive geometric designs. The ceramic stamps were covered in dye, then rolled onto surfaces to create continuous patterns. Although their exact use is unknown, many archaeologists believe the stamps were used to decorate human skin.

Stone Sculptures

Carved stone objects first appeared in Costa Rica around 300 A.D. The most popular early sculptures were three-legged stone *metates*, low-slung tables used to grind seeds and maize into flour. Over time, metate decoration became highly elaborate, often incorporating complex patterns and animal forms. Around 700 A.D. stone sculptures depicting humans appeared. Many of these statues portrayed male warriors holding axes and cradling the decapitated "trophy" heads of their victims. Women were often portrayed holding their breasts, a sign of fertility and sexuality. For all sculptures, durable volcanic rock was the preferred material.

Deformed Skulls

In northwest Costa Rica archaeologists have unearthed human remains with intentionally deformed skulls. This custom, which was also practiced by the Maya and Inca, involved pressing boards against the skulls of infants to permanently reshape the bone structure.

Giant Spheres

Costa Rica's most mysterious artifacts are giant stone spheres from the south Pacific. Measuring up to 2.5 meters (8.2 feet) in diameter and weighing up to 14 tons, they are geometrically precise within centimeters. The spheres, which are made of gabbro, a type of rock formed by cooled magma, are believed to date between 200 BC and 1500 AD. Their purpose, however, is completely unknown.

El Grano de Oro "The Golden Bean"

It's impossible to talk about Costa Rica without talking about coffee. "The golden bean," as Ticos call it, is inseparable from Costa Rica's history and development. The cultivation of coffee in the early 1800s transformed Costa Rica from a poor, remote backwater to an export powerhouse, giving rise to both a stable middle class and a wealthy coffee oligarchy. By the 1850s coffee accounted for over 90% of Costa Rican exports. Its production also kept the majority of Costa Ricans living in the mountains where coffee grows best. Coffee remained a top export through much of the 20th century, and today there are over 93,000 hectares (348 square miles) under cultivation. Because a small country like Costa Rica can't compete on quantity, coffee farmers compete on quality, growing only choice arabica beans. Coffee is cultivated between 600–1,700 meters (2,000–5,600 feet), but the finest coffee is grown at cool, high elevations above 1,200 meters (3,900 feet). Tarrazú, a high-elevation region near the Zona de los Santos (p.251), produces some of the finest coffee in Costa Rica.

Coffee Harvest

In Costa Rica the major coffee harvest lasts from December to March, and during this time plantations are filled with workers hand-picking ripe coffee berries. School vacation, mid-December to early February, is timed to coincide with the harvest so children can help their parents in the field. These days, however, fewer and fewer Ticos pick coffee, preferring higher paying, less-physically demanding jobs. Today about half of coffee pickers are poor migrant workers from Nicaragua and Panama. Pickers start the harvest at low elevation plantations and follow the ripening berries to progressively higher elevations.

Cajuela

The *cajuela* is the traditional woven basket used by coffee pickers in Costa Rica. When filled with ripe coffee berries, a cajuela weighs 12.9 kg (28 pounds). Each year coffee pickers fill roughly 42 million cajuelas in Costa Rica. Each picker earns roughly ₡1,200 ($2.20) per cajuela, and fast pickers can fill 20–30 cajuelas per day.

El Pilón

Essentially a giant mortar and pestle, the *pilón* is carved out of a single piece of heavy wood. It was used in pre-industrial times to separate coffee beans from the outer flesh of the coffee berry. Today automated machines separate the beans from the berry, but pilóns remain a popular decoration in restaurants and homes throughout Costa Rica.

Chorreador

The most popular way to make coffee in Costa Rica remains the *chorreador*. Derived from the verb *chorrear* ("to pour"), a chorreador features a long cloth *bolsita* ("little bag") that holds the coffee grounds. Hot water is poured into the bolsita, and fresh coffee drips into a pot or mug below.

Costa Rica's Best Coffee Tours

Café Britt, Central Valley (p.181)
Diriá Coffee Tour, Nicoya Peninsula (p.345)
Coopedota, Santa María de Dota (p.254)
Don Juan Coffee Tour, Monteverde (p.224)

Boyeros & Painted Oxcarts

In the pre-industrial era, wooden oxcarts were used to transport coffee from Costa Rica's mountain farms to its coastal ports. By the late 1800s, Ticos were decorating those oxcarts with elaborate, colorful designs, and today *carretas pintadas* (painted oxcarts) and *boyeros* (oxcart drivers) are proud symbols of Costa Rica's heritage.

Oxcarts were first used by European colonists to transport crops and supplies. But due to the terrible condition of local roads (some things never change), Costa Rican oxcarts differed significantly from their European counterparts. Instead of using traditional spoked wheels, which clogged easily on bumpy, muddy roads, Costa Ricans constructed solid, durable wheels made out of strong tropical hardwoods.

By the mid-1800s coffee had become Costa Rica's most lucrative export, and each year millions of pounds of coffee were loaded onto oxcarts in the fertile Central Valley and transported to the port of Puntarenas on the Pacific coast. (Although the Caribbean coast was closer to the lucrative European market, it lacked a suitable

transportation route.) By 1848 more than 2,000 oxcarts were transporting coffee along the road to Puntarenas *every day* during peak harvest. Each oxcart carried roughly 700 kg (1,500 pounds) of coffee, and the 100-km (62-mile) trip from San José to Puntarenas took between four and five days.

By the late-1800s boyeros were decorating their oxcarts with colorful designs. Flowers were painted onto the side panels, and a compass rose was added to each wheel. One theory claims these designs were introduced by Italian immigrants from Sicily, where elaborately painted wooden carts are also popular. Indeed, both the Sicilian and the Costa Rican carts feature colorful geometric patterns painted over a reddish base. Another theory is that the oxcart designs were adapted from the flowery baroque style popular in colonial-era churches. Whatever the original inspiration, the designs were added to and embellished over time until a uniquely Costa Rican style emerged.

Although Costa Rican oxcarts are most famous for their colorful designs, they also exhibit musical qualities. Thanks to natural irregularities in the wooden wheels, each oxcart produces a unique melody as it rolls down the road. Many boyeros claim they can identify individual oxcarts based solely on their *canto de carreta* ("song of the oxcart").

Oxcarts are pulled by a team of two *bueyes* ("oxen"), which are attached to the oxcart by a *yugo* ("yoke"). Boyeros guide the oxen with their long, pointed *chuzo* ("pike") and feed them daily rations of *caña* ("sugarcane"). Whenever possible, boyeros select two oxen of nearly identical size and coloration.

Although oxcarts are no longer used to transport coffee, they have become one of the most beautiful and beloved symbols of Costa Rica. Traditional oxcarts are still manufactured by hand in the town of Sarchí (p.181), and boyero parades are held throughout the year. Each year in mid-March, hundreds of boyeros gather in the town of San Antonio de Escazú just outside San José to celebrate the *Dia Nacional de los Boyeros.*

Costa Rica's painted oxcarts are famous for their colorful designs, which mix flowers and flourishes in eleaborate geometric patterns

Topes

One of the most popular traditions in Costa Rica is the *tope* (TOE-pay), a horse parade featuring skilled riders and decorated horses. As riders trot down the street, they often pull over and offer quick rides to children. Spectators dress in traditional *vaquero* ("cowboy") clothes—cowboy hats, cowboy boots, plaid shirts, giant belt buckles—and Mexican ranchero music is often blasted at high volume. Whoops and hollers greet well-decorated horses, acts of showmanship, or particularly busty female riders. Topes are common in small pueblos throughout the country, but the most famous is the December 26th *Tope Nacional*, which features over 3,000 horses in downtown San José.

Cimarronas & Mascaradas

One of the oldest Costa Rican traditions is the *mascarada*, which features a troupe of dancers wearing giant paper-mâche heads depicting devils, animals, celebrities and *La Giganta* ("The Giant Woman"). As dancers twirl around and interact with children, music is played by a *cimarrona*, a band with percussion and brass instruments. *Cimarrona* means "wild," which accurately describes the loud boisterous music. Costa Rica's most famous mascaradas are held in Barva in late March and Cartago on October 31.

Costa Rica's red, white and blue flag was designed in 1848 by Pacifica Fernández Oreamuno, the wife of President José María Castro Madriz. Its colors were inspired by the flag of France and its 1848 revolution (the Third French Revolution), which was much admired in Costa Rica. The official coat of arms, also designed by Pacifica Fernández Oreamuno, shows two merchant ships sailing on two coasts separated by three volcanoes (one for each of the country's three major mountain ranges). The seven stars above the volcanoes represent the seven provinces of Costa Rica.

The Typical Tico House

Although much less common today than in the past, the typical Tico house can still be found throughout the Costa Rican countryside. These small square houses proudly display the three colors of the Costa Rican flag: white walls, a red roof and a blue stripe painted across the bottom. Simple, utilitarian and patriotic, Tico houses are the Costa Rican equivalent of the log cabin in the U.S. Pastoral paintings of the red, white and blue houses are ubiquitous in homes and restaurants, and schoolchildren often make lanterns resembling the houses for the *Desfile de los Faroles* (p.81).

Costa Rican Bullfights

Bullfights, known as *corridas de toros*, are one of Costa Rica's most popular traditions. Unlike the bloody Spanish version, however, Costa Rica's bullfights have a unique Tico twist: instead of people chasing the bull, the bull chases the people. Participants, known as *toreros improvisados* ("improvised bullfighters"), are nonprofessionals who voluntarily enter the *redondel* ("bullring"). Once inside, improvisados taunt the bull by inching closer and closer until the bull charges, at which point they run away or jump over the surrounding barriers to safety. Prizes such as cash and electronics are offered to improvisados who engage in particularly brave acts, such as grabbing a bandana attached to the bull's horns or approaching the bull on both knees. Although common in small towns throughout Costa Rica, the most famous bullfights take place in Zapote (just east of downtown San José) at the end of December.

Costa Rican Legends

La Segua

Costa Rica's most famous legend is the *Segua* (pronounced "SEG-wah"), which is also spelled *Cegua* or *Tzegua*. The legend, which is likely indigenous in origin, is found throughout Central America, but it is particularly popular in Costa Rica. Although there are several different versions, each involves a drunk, womanizing *campesino* ("peasant") who lived in a small village long ago. One night after a hard day in the fields, the campesino headed to a local tavern to drink *guaro* (p.89) with his friends. Well past midnight, the drunk campesino stumbled out of the tavern, then mounted his horse for the long journey home. The night was foggy and dark, and as he headed down a long dirt road he noticed something strange in the distance. Drawing closer, he realized it was beautiful young woman. In the moonlight he could make out her long hair, beautiful face and voluptuous body. Enchanted, the campesino offered the young woman a ride, which she gladly accepted. With an outstretched arm he lifted her onto the back of his horse, and the pair rode off into the night. As they passed coffee fields and cattle ranches, the young woman wrapped her arms tightly around him. He could feel her warm breath on the back of his neck. The campesino, who considered himself quite a lady's man, reached back and gently placed his hand on her leg. The young woman gently stroked his hand with her fingers. The campesino smiled to himself, then turned around to give her a kiss. To his horror, he found himself staring at a disgusting creature with a horse skull for a head and fiery bloodshot eyes. As he let out a scream, the Segua grabbed the reigns of his horse and the pair galloped off into the darkness. Since then, the Segua has tempted many a late night drunkard in Costa Rica. But as everyone knows, you should never give the Segua a ride.

El Cadejos

This large black dog with eyes like burning embers follows people home at night, but El Cadejos is not aggressive or bloodthirsty, and he has never attacked a person. Rather he makes sure that people traveling alone, particularly drunk men, reach their destination without harm. After following someone to their doorstep, el Cadejos vanishes into the night. Long ago, el Cadejos was a rebellious young man who spent his days drinking and arguing, but he was transformed into a supernatural dog obligated to protect others. Although few people have actually seen el Cadejos, many have heard his long claws scraping the ground or the clink of the large chains that dangle from his collar.

La Llorona

During Costa Rica's colonial era, there was a beautiful indigenous girl who fell in love with a handsome Spanish settler. Although the two were deeply in love, they hid their relationship from the girl's father, who disapproved of the Spaniard. Every day the couple met in secret at a remote waterfall where no one could see them together. For months they carried on an illicit romance, but when the girl became pregnant, they could hide their secret no longer. When her father realized what had happened, he was consumed with rage. "You have brought shame upon yourself and upon this family," he screamed at his daughter. He tracked down the Spaniard and killed him in front of his daughter's eyes. When the baby was born several months later, the father ordered his daughter to throw the cursed child into the waterfall where she had disgraced herself. With tears streaming down her face, the girl faithfully obeyed her father's orders. From that day forward, she was condemned to wander the banks of the river in search of the baby she abandoned. Even today, along the banks of many rivers in Costa Rica, you can still hear the soft cries of *La Llorona* ("The Weeping Woman").

Holidays & Festivals

Mid-January - Fiestas Típicas de Santa Cruz
One of the biggest celebration on the Nicoya Peninsula, this "Typical Party" features food, music and dancing in the town of Santa Cruz.

Mid-January - Fiestas de Palmares
The giant, week-long party has the vibe of a country fair and includes concerts featuring big-name Latin American popstars.

Second Sunday in March - El Día Nacional del Boyero
National Boyero day celebrates Costa Rica's famous painted oxcarts and the men (and women) who drive them (p.70). The celebration is held in the town of San Antonio de Escazú near San José.

Late March/Early April - Semana Santa
Easter week is one of Costa Rica's most important holidays. Because it falls near the end of the dry season, it's considered the last big holiday before the "winter" rains set in. During Semana Santa, all liquor sales are suspended on Thursday and Friday throughout the country.

April 11 - Juan Santamaría Day
Costa Rica's national hero, Jaun Santamaría, is honored for his accomplishments in the country's most famous military battle (p.149).

Mid-July - Fiesta de la Virgen del Mar
This nautical festival features a boat parade that pays homage to the patron saint of the sea. Celebrated in Puntarenas (p.349) and Playa del Coco (p.281).

July 25 - Día de Guanacaste
To celebrate Costa Rica's annexation of Guanacaste from Nicaragua in 1824 dances and horse parades are held throughout the province. The largest celebration takes place in Liberia (p.272).

August 2 - La Romería de la Virgen de los Ángeles
The Pilgrimage of the Virgin of the Angels is Costa Rica's most important religious celebration. Over one million *romeros* ("pilgrims") walk to *Basílica de los Ángeles* (p.244) in Cartago to pay homage to *La Negrita* (p.51).

August 15 - El Día de la Madre (Mother's Day)
One of Costa Rica's most important holidays. All workers get the day off, and mothers are treated to presents, serenades and special meals.

September 14 - El Desfile de Faroles

"The Parade of Lanterns," which starts immediately after the country sings the national anthem at 6pm, features schoolchildren carrying red, white and blue lanterns through the streets.

September 15 - Independence Day

The most patriotic day of the year celebrates Costa Rica's independence from Spanish colonial rule (p.81).

Mid-October - Carnaval

The biggest celebration on the Caribbean coast features a large parade in the town of Limón (p.459) with lots of Afro-Caribbean influence. The parade normally falls on the weekend closest to October 12.

Dec 12 - Festival de La Virgen de Guadalupe

Held in the town of Nicoya (p.345), this religious festival combines traditional Chorotega and Catholic beliefs.

Mid-December - Festival de la Luz

The "Festival of Lights" is a nighttime parade held on Paseo Colón in downtown San José. Elaborate floats are decorated with electric lights.

December 25 - Navidad

In Costa Rica, as in much of Latin America, Christmas is celebrated on the 24th of December with a big family dinner and gift giving at midnight. Gifts from *El Niño Dios* ("Baby Jesus") are opened in the morning.

Dec 26 - Tope Nacional

The country's biggest topes (horse parade) (p.72).

Dec 31–Jan 3 - Festival de los Diablitos

The "Festival of the little Devils" is Costa Rica's most famous indigenous celebration. Held in the town of Boruca, near Palmar Norte on the Pacific coast, it features three days of costumed parades and lots of *chicha* (a traditional fermented corn beverage). On the final night of the celebration, masked participants "kill" a burlap bull that represents the Spanish conquistadors.

Dec 31 - Año Nuevo

In Costa Rica, as in all of Latin America, New Years is spent with the family. Popular traditions include: eating 12 grapes as fast as you can at midnight and making a wish after swallowing each grape; walking around the block with a suitcase to bring good travel vibes; wearing yellow underwear to bring money in the New Year.

Independence Day

Independence Day, September 15, is one of Costa Rica's most important holidays. Throughout the country, parades are held featuring children in traditional dress dancing and marching to drums. Independence Day is celebrated throughout Central America, which declared independence from Spain as a whole on September 15, 1821. Each year runners carry a "Freedom Torch" from Guatemala to Costa Rica, arriving in Cartago at 6pm on September 14, at which point Ticos sing the national anthem in unison. The anthem is followed by the *Desfile de los Faroles* ("Lantern Parade"), where children carry red, white and blue lanterns through the streets accompanied by their parents and teachers.

COSTA RICAN FOOD

There's no getting around it—Costa Rica is not known for its food. Compared to the complex flavors of Mexico or the rich cuisine of Peru, Costa Rica doesn't have much to brag about. But while Ticos don't have a sophisticated cuisine, they are experts at simple, home-style cooking. Comfort food. And when prepared with love, preferably *a la leña* ("wood-fired"), it can really be delicious.

That said, most tourists don't taste some of Costa Rica's most delicious foods. Expecting nachos, tacos and burritos, visitors are confronted with chorreadas, patacones and chifrijo. Bewildered, they order a hamburger, which is always the worst thing on the menu. Thus the stereotype of bad food lives on.

The goal of this section is to expose visitors to a wider range of Costa Rican food. Everyone learns about gallo pinto and casados, but seek out some of Costa Rica's lesser known specialties and you may find yourself pleasantly surprised.

Gallo Pinto

No matter where you go in Costa Rica, there is always gallo pinto, a mixture of rice and beans with seasoning provided by onions, celery, red peppers and cilantro. Served for breakfast, it's the national dish of Costa Rica. There's even a popular expression: *Mas Tico que gallo pinto* ("More Costa Rican than gallo pinto"). Translated literally, *Gallo Pinto* means "Painted Rooster"—a reference to the black and white speckling found on some roosters—though it is often called simply "pinto." Gallo pinto is often served with eggs, and salsa Lizano (p.85) is a popular add-on. In my opinion, gallo pinto almost always tastes better in simple, cheap restaurants. Fancy restaurants tend to overprepare gallo pinto, which requires a rustic, homemade touch.

Chorreadas

These sweet corn pancakes are a delicious alternative to gallo pinto for breakfast. Derived from the verb *chorrear* ("to pour"), chorreadas are a combination of corn kernels, flour, milk, eggs and sugar. They are often served with a side of *natilla* (sour cream) and cheese.

Casado

Costa Rica's second-most famous dish mixes beef, chicken or fish with rice, beans, cabbage salad, tortillas and sweet fried plantains. *Casado* literally means "Married Man," a reference to the days when married men working in the fields would bring mixed lunches prepared by their wife and wrapped in a banana leaf. Casados are almost always one of the least expensive and best prepared items at any typical restaurant.

Tamales

Tamales are a mix of corn-based dough, meat, rice and vegetables, wrapped and cooked in a plantain leaf, which imparts a subtle, earthy flavor. In Costa Rica pork tamales are served as the main course for Christmas dinner, and two tamales tied together are called a *piña* ("pineapple"), though nobody seems to know why.

Patacones

Say hello to the most delicious snack you've never heard of. These fried, mashed green plantains are popular throughout Central America and the Caribbean, but they are virtually unknown in Mexico—which is probably why they are largely unknown in the United States. Patacones (pronounced *Pah-tah-coh-nays*) go great with black bean dip or fresh guacamole.

Olla de Carne

Literally "Pot of Beef," *Olla de Carne* is the most popular soup in Costa Rica. Large and filling, it is often served as a main course. Ingredients include yucca, plantains, potatoes, carrots, corn, onion, garlic, cilantro and, of course, a large hunk of beef.

Pejibaye

This starchy, fibrous fruit is one of Costa Rica's most beloved snacks. About the size of a small peach, *pejibaye* (pronounced "peh-hee-BUY-yay") grows on a tall palm tree in bunches of up to 1,000. Native to South America, it has been cultivated in Costa Rica for centuries. The raw fruit is hard and slightly toxic, but when cooked with salt it becomes soft and nutritious. The mild, slightly sweet flavor is similar to chestnuts, and pejibaye is eaten with a dab of mayonnaise or cooked into a rich soup. Costa Rica is the largest pejibaye exporter in the world with roughly 2,000 hectares (5,000 acres) under cultivation. During peak harvest (Aug–Oct), cooked pejibaye is often sold on the side of the road around San José.

Chicharrón

In Costa Rica fried pork is called *chicharrón* (pronounced "chee-char-RONE"), and it is one of the country's most popular bar foods. Salty, greasy and crispy (when cooked right), it's delicious with a squeeze of fresh lime.

Chifrijo

Since it first appeared in the 1990s, *chifrijo* (pronounced "chee-FREE-ho") has taken Costa Rica by storm. Miguel Ángel Cordero Araya, who owns Cordero's 1 Bar in the San José suburb of Tibás, claims to have invented the popular snack, and he has even taken out a patent on chifrijo. The name is a combination of *chicharrón* and *frijoles* ("beans"), which are the two main ingredients. Chifrijo also includes rice and *pico de gallo* (a tomato/onion/cilantro salsa), and popular add-ons include fresh avocado or jalapeños. Although served in a bowl and eaten with a spoon, chifrijo usually comes accompanied with a side of fresh tortillas chips.

Gallos

This simple snack food consists of a heated corn tortilla served with a dollop of beef, chicken or *arracache*, a popular starchy vegetable. *Gallos*, which is literally translated as "roosters," are one of Costa Rica's most popular *bocas* ("appetizers").

Yuca Frita

Yuca, also known as cassava, is a starchy tuber that has been cultivated by indigenous people for centuries. Fried yucca is similar to fried potatoes, but with a slightly sweeter flavor.

Ceviche

Popular in coastal areas from Peru to Mexico, ceviche is prepared by marinating raw fish in citrus juice, which breaks down the proteins and "cooks" the fish. Additional flavoring is often provided by cilantro, onions and chiles.

Tres Leches

This popular Latin American dessert consists of moist sponge cake soaked in *tres leches* ("three milks"): whole milk, evaporated milk and sweetened condensed milk.

Salsa Lizano

Costa Rica's most popular condiment is Salsa Lizano, a sweet, tangy sauce that's added to everything from gallo pinto to tamales. Created in 1920 by the Lizano Company, it's found in homes and restaurant throughout the country. Salsa Lizano's ingredients include water, sugar, salt, onions, carrots, cauliflower, cucumbers, pepper, mustard and turmeric.

CARIBBEAN FOOD

Some of Costa Rica's most delicious food comes from the Caribbean coast, which is home to a large Afro-Caribbean population.

Rice & Beans

The Caribbean coast's most popular dish is rice and beans, but unlike in the rest of Costa Rica, the rice and beans are slow cooked with fresh coconut milk, resulting in a sweet, savory flavor that goes great with *pescado frito* ("whole fried fish") and patacones.

Rondón

Considered the Caribbean coast's finest dish, this savory coconut milk soup features a hearty medley of fish, crab, yucca, plantain, yam, vegetables and spices. The name *rondón* is supposedly derived from the English "run down"—a reference to the days when chefs made the soup with whatever they could literally "run down."

Patty

Also spelled *patí*, this baked empanada is filled with spicy ground meat. The kick comes from habeñero chiles, which are locally known as *chile panameño* (Panamanian chiles).

Pan Bon

This sweet, dark bread is typically made with flour, unrefined sugarcane, butter, mild white cheese, cinnamon, nutmeg, vanilla, raisins and candied fruits. The sweetness of pan bon falls somewhere between regular bread and cake, making it more of a light snack than a true dessert.

FRUIT DRINKS

Dozens of exotic fruits are cultivated in Costa Rica, and delicious fruit drinks are available at just about every restaurant. Known as *frescos*, *jugos* or, when mixed together, *batidos*, they are mixed *con leche* ("with milk") or *con agua* ("with water"). Be aware that many restaurants automatically add sugar to fruit drinks, even sweet ones like pineapple and banana. If you don't want extra sugar, ask for your drink *sin azucar* ("without sugar"). I also recommend ordering drinks that are *natural* (pronounced "NAT-tur-al") over drinks made from *pulpa* ("pulp").

In addition to *papaya*, *mango*, *sandia* ("watermelon"), *piña* ("pineapple"), *fresa* ("strawberry"), *mora* ("blackberry") and *banano* ("banana"), here are a few fruits you may not be familiar with:

Guanábana

It looks strange, sounds strange and tastes delicious. Also known as soursop, *guanábana* (pronounced "Gwah-NAH-Bah-Nah") grows up to 12 inches long and weighs up to 8 pounds. Its thin green skin is covered with sharp points, and its white interior has the gooey consistency of a wet marshmallow. Do not be afraid! Guanábana is one of Costa Rica's most delicious drinks.

Maracuyá

Also known as passion fruit, *maracuyá* (Mah-Rah-Coo-YAH) is filled with crunchy seeds covered with a tart, mucilaginous coating. The seeds and coating are crushed together in a blender, and when sweetened with sugar the intense citrus flavor is divine.

Cas

This sour fruit, which is native to Central America, is about the size of an apple with a somewhat similar texture. The raw fruit is eaten with salt, and when sweetened with sugar its flavor lies somewhere between an apple and a pear.

Agua de Sapo

Popular on the Caribbean coast, *agua de sapo* ("toad water") is a refreshing combination of water, sugarcane, lime and ginger served over ice.

Agua Dulce

This hot, sweet beverage, which is made from boiled water and *tapa de dulce* ("raw cane sugar"), is popular in Costa Rica's chilly mountain towns. After a long day hiking through the cloud forest, a warm mug of *agua dulce* ("sweet water") definitely hits the spot.

Vino de Coyol

This unusual beverage has been produced for centuries by Costa Rica's indigenous Chorotega people. The liquid used to make *vino de coyol* ("coyol wine") is extracted from the coyol tree, a type of palm covered in poisonous spines. According to tradition, coyol trees are chopped down three days after the full moon at low tide, and a sweet, watery sap is then extracted from the trunk. The liquid is left to ferment, and some people claim that if you drink too much vino de coyol, you will get drunk again the next day if you stand in the sun. During the dry season (Dec–April), vino de coyol is often sold on the side of highway in the pueblo of Nambí, 10 km (6.2 miles) north of the town of Nicoya on the Nicoya Peninsula.

Agua de Pipa

The coconut water craze is nothing new in Costa Rica, where *agua de pipa* ("young coconut water")—*pipa* for short—has long been considered one of nature's most refreshing beverages. Suffice to say, the 100% natural version tastes infinitely better than the boxed, chemical-laden stuff they sell outside the tropics. In Costa Rica agua de pipa is sold by *piperos* ("pipa vendors"), who often hang around beaches or set up shop on the side of the road. Piperos chop of the top off the coconut with a machete and provide a straw for easy drinking.

Craft Beer

For decades Pilsen and Imperial were the only locally produced beers in Costa Rica, but recently craft breweries have been flourishing. The most famous and popular is Costa Rica Craft Brewing (p.245), whose signature beers are Libertas, a tropical golden ale, and Segua, a red ale named after Costa Rica's most famous legend. One of the best places to sample a wide variety of Costa Rican craft beers is at the Stiefel Pub (p.178) in San José.

Imperial & Pilsen

These two pale lagers are the oldest and most popular beers in Costa Rica. Pilsen was first brewed in 1888, and Imperial, which is famous for its *aguila* ("eagle") logo, was first sold in 1924. Although many Ticos express a strong preference for one or the other, they are about as different as Coors and Budweiser.

Rum

Made from sugarcane and molasses, and often aged for several years in oak barrels, *ron* ("rum") has long been one of Central America's most famous liquors. Costa Rica's most popular rum in Ron Centenario, though Nicaragua's Flor de Caña is also widely available and considered of slightly higher quality.

Guaro

Costa Rica's cheapest and most popular spirit is *guaro*, which is made from distilled sugarcane. Similar to vodka, though sweeter and with a lower alcohol content (30%), it's often consumed straight or mixed into a guaro sour. To crack down on illegally produced *contrabando* ("moonshine"), the government produces guaro under the Cacique ("Chief") brand.

NATURAL HISTORY

COSTA RICA IS famous for it biodiversity, and with good reason. Though less than half the size of Ohio, it contains roughly 5% of the world's biodiversity. To put that in perspective, the U.S. is 200 times larger, yet it contains just half of the species found in Costa Rica. This incredible biodiversity results from the tiny country's unique geography. Costa Rica is located in the tropics, where nearly two-thirds of earth's species are found. In addition, it is situated between two oceans and two continents, attracting a wide range of plant and animal species from each. Finally, Costa Rica's tall mountains shelter a wide range of species not found in the hot, humid lowlands.

The story of Costa Rica's unique geography began roughly 100 million years ago, when North and South America were completely disconnected. At the time, Central America was nothing more than a channel of water between the continents connecting the Atlantic and Pacific Oceans. As tectonic plates shifted, a chain of volcanic islands formed in the waterway between North and South America. Around 12 million years ago, these islands collided with the northern tip of South America, and by 3 million years ago tectonic action had formed a land bridge connecting North and South America.

Prior to the formation of the Central American land bridge, North and South America had two distinct ecologies. North America was home to raccoons, llamas, horses, bears and saber tooth cats. South America was home to monkeys, armadillos, porcupines, parrots, toucans and giant ground sloths. When the continents connected, thousands of species crossed the land bridge in search of new habitats and new prey. This biological free-for-all permanently shook up the ecologies of both continents. Even today, roughly half the land mammals found in South America arrived via the Central American land bridge. Because Costa Rica was located in the transition zone, it became a mixing point for thousands of species.

But the ecological havoc wrought by the connection of North and South America paled in comparison to the havoc wrecked on Earth's climate. Prior to the rise of the land bridge, a strong ocean current flowed from the Atlantic Ocean directly into the Pacific. Following the closure of North and South America, the Atlantic current was deflected north and a new current, the Gulf Stream, was born. This triggered a chain of events that led to decreased temperatures in the

Arctic, where massive glaciers began to form. In effect, the rise of the Central American land bridge helped trigger the start of the Ice Age roughly 2.6 million years ago. As the global climate cooled, small glaciers formed on Costa Rica's highest peaks. Following the retreat of the glaciers roughly 20,000 years ago, Costa Rica's tall mountains became a refuge for many species of plants and animals adapted to cooler temperatures.

Costa Rica has four mountain ranges. The largest, and most impressive, are the Talamanca Mountains, which extend 150 km (93 miles) from southern Costa Rica into western Panama. The Talamancas are the remnants of the first islands that appeared between North and South America millions of years ago. They are home to Chirripó, the highest peak between Guatemala and Colombia, which rises 3,820 meters (12,533 feet) above sea level. The Talamancas are also home to Costa Rica's largest national park: *La Amistad International Park* ("The International Friendship Park"), 50% of which is located in neighboring Panama. This vast park covers 239 square-kilometers (92 square-miles) and contains an estimated 60% of Costa Rica's biodiversity, though it is largely inaccessible due to its rugged terrain.

Northwest of the Talamanca Mountains are the Central Mountains, Costa Rica's second-highest mountain range. Formed by four volcanoes—Turrialba, Irazú, Barva, Poás—the Central Mountains extend 90 km (56 miles) and form the northern boundary of the Central Valley, where two-thirds of Costa Ricans live. The tallest peak is Irazú, which rises 3,432 meters (11,260 feet) above sea level.

To the west of the Central Mountains lie the Tilarán Mountains, home to Monteverde and nearby Arenal Volcano. To the north are the Guanacaste Mountains, which are formed by a series of volcanoes—Miravalles, Rincón de la Vieja, Orosí—that rise above the hot, dry plains of northwest Costa Rica. The highest peak, Miravalles, rises 2,028 meters (6,654 feet) above sea level. Taken together, the Tilarán and Guanacaste Range stretch 160 km (100 miles).

Costa Rica's two coastlines are remarkably different. The Caribbean Coast is straight, flat and measures just 212 km (132 miles) in total length. Although there are few natural harbors, set back from the coast are the country's only navigable rivers. The Pacific coast, meanwhile, measures 1,016 km (631 miles) long—nearly

Costa Rica is home to an estimated 1.5 million species—roughly 5% of all biodiversity on earth—including over 300,000 insect species, over 900 bird species, over 240 mammal species (nearly half of which are bats), 222 reptile species, 190 amphibian species and 130 species of fresh water fish. There are also 9,000 vascular plant species, 1,200 orchid species and 1,200 hardwood tree species. Perhaps most impressive, each year scientists discover dozens of new plant and animal species, and thousands more likely await discovery.

Costa Rica's National Parks

Today roughly 28% of Costa Rican land is legally protected. Of those 1.4 million hectares (3.5 million acres), 38% are national parks, 18% are forest reserves, 15% are indigenous reserves and 11% are wildlife refuges. All told, there are over 90 protected areas, including 26 national parks. This would be impressive anywhere, but it is particularly notable in a developing country like Costa Rica.

The modern appreciation of Costa Rica's natural resources began in the mid-19th century, when European naturalists arrived on the heels of the newly established coffee trade. They were followed by U.S. naturalists, and by the mid-20th century foreign experts had helped Costa Rica establish its own research institutions dedicated to the study of nature. Before long Costa Rica was producing its own crop of talented scientists.

In 1968 Mario Boza, a Costa Rican forestry student, visited Smoky Mountain National Park in the U.S. Inspired by his experience there, Boza returned determined to create a similar national park system in Costa Rica. Boza teamed up with biology student Alvaro Ugalde, who had spent several months at Grand Canyon, and working together the pair spearheaded the development of a Costa Rican national park system. Poás and Santa Rosa became the first two national parks, followed by Tortuguero and Cahuita on the Caribbean coast. Boza and Ugalde were given critical support from Karen Olson, the wife of president José Figueres (p.156), and subsequent presidents who embraced the concept. By 1978 Costa Rica had established 17 national parks.

Despite the collapse of the Costa Rican economy in the early 1980s, the national park system continued to expand. When La Amistad National Park was created in 1982, it nearly doubled the size of the national park system. By the end of the decade, additional land was protected in "debt-for-nature" swaps initiated by U.S. conservation organizations such as the World Wildlife Fund and Conservation International. In exchange for protecting natural resources, the U.S. government forgave many of Costa Rica's massive foreign debts.

The creation of Costa Rica's national park system, and the subsequent rise of eco-tourism, has helped foster a strong culture of environmentalism in Costa Rica. In 2011, just 8% of Costa Ricans agreed with the statement "Priority should be given to economic development even if it means damaging the environment." With strong public support, the Costa Rican government is pushing forward with bold new initiatives. Blessed with an abundance of hydropower, geothermal and wind energy, Costa Rica has set the impressive goal of becoming the world's first carbon neutral country by 2021.

Land of Volcanoes

Costa Rica is part of the Central American Volcanic Arc, a 1,500-km (932-mile) chain of volcanoes that stretches from Guatemala to Panama. The arc has the greatest density of volcanoes in the world—roughly 1 every 35 km (22 miles)—and it is the most volcanically active region in the Americas. The volcanic arc formed as a result of plate tectonics, specifically the Cocos Plate, which underlies the Pacific Ocean west of Central America, slowly slipping under the Caribbean Plate, which underlies Central America. (The Cocos Plate is moving northeast at a rate of roughly 10 cm per year.) This process, called subduction, is directly responsible for the region's frequent earthquakes and regular volcanic activity. As the Cocos Plate is pushed deep underground, its leading edge melts, sending giant plumes of magma rising towards the surface where they form volcanoes.

Of Costa Rica's four mountain ranges, two—the Central Mountain Range north of San José and the Guanacaste Mountain Range in the northwest—are volcanic in origin. All told, Costa Rica is home to over 200 volcanic features, but just five—Arenal, Rincón de la Vieja, Poás, Turrialba, Irazú—have been active in historic times. The most famous, Arenal, recently went quiet after several decades of regular activity. Conditions permitting, you can drive to the rim of three volcanoes—Poás, Irazú and Turrialba—and hike to the rim of Rincón de la Vieja. It is also possible to hike Cerro Chato, an extinct volcano lying next to Arenal.

five times the length of the Caribbean coast. The Pacific coast is dominated by two major peninsulas, the Nicoya and the Osa, as well as numerous islands and bays. Lying 540 km (335 miles) offshore is Isla Del Coco (p.441), Costa Rica's most remote national park.

Located in the tropics between two oceans, Costa Rica experiences abundant rainfall. The "rainy" season, May–November, is referred to as *invierno* ("winter") while the dry season, Dec–April, is referred to as *verano* ("summer"). But rainfall varies significantly within Costa Rica. The tropical dry forests of the Pacific northwest receive roughly 1.5 meters (5 feet) of rain per year, while the rainforests along the Caribbean coast receive up to 6 meters (20 feet) of rain per year. Temperatures, meanwhile, range from 35°C along the coast to freezing at the country's highest peaks. With so much variation in rainfall, temperature and geography, Costa Rica is home to 12 major "life zones" and dozens of microclimates. This plays a significant role in the country's impressive biodiversity.

Under completely natural conditions, Costa Rica would be almost totally forested. Just 30 square kilometers (12 square miles) of the country lies above treeline. Indigenous groups burned small tracts of forest, but deforestation accelerated with the arrival of European settlers. In 1800 Costa Rica was roughly 90% forested. By 1950 that number had dropped to just 64%, and by 1987 just 21% of Costa Rica was forested. At one point in the 1980s, Costa Rica had one of the highest rates of deforestation in the world. Much of this destruction was to create cattle pasture for beef exports.

Over the past two decades, the situation has improved dramatically. Starting in the 1980s, the government implemented a series of laws that incentivized reforestation efforts. By 1999 roughly 44 percent of Costa Rica was forested, and by 2012 that number had increased to 52 percent.

The Papagayo Winds

Costa Rica's north Pacific coast is famous for the Papagayo Winds, which blow each year from December to March. The winds can blow at speeds of 80 kph (50 mph) for days at a time, with some gusts topping 160 kph (100 mph)—a speed normally found only in major hurricanes. The winds are caused by cold, high pressure systems that descend from North America over the Gulf of Mexico, then flow across Central America towards the Pacific Ocean's low pressure systems. Throughout most of Central America tall mountains slow the wind as it blows west, but in northern Costa Rica and southern Nicaragua a gap in the mountains funnels the wind into a narrow channel. Although the Papagayo Winds are extremely dangerous for boaters, they delight surfers with powerful offshore winds.

Mangroves

Mangroves (*manglares* in Spanish) are found in coastal river areas where freshwater mixes with saltwater. Although most plants can't survive in environments where water and salt levels fluctuate throughout the day, mangroves have developed a series of remarkable adaptations that allow them to thrive. Red mangroves have salt-filtering roots and absorb air through pores in their bark. Black mangroves secrete excess salt through their leaves and send out snorkel-like shoots, called pneumatophores, that help them obtain additional air. Mangroves also provide numerous environmental benefits. They filter water flowing into ocean, buffer coastal areas from storm surges and provide a protective, nutrient-filled nursery for young fish. Pacific coast mangroves are also home to the mangrove hummingbird, a species found only in Costa Rica.

Tropical Dry Forest

Tropical dry forests are found from Mexico to northwest Costa Rica, and they are characterized by deciduous trees that drop their leaves during the long dry season. During this time many leafless trees burst into flower, including "big bang" species that flower en masse, creating extended swaths of pink, yellow or orange trees. Simultaneous flowering attracts swarms of pollinators, and northwest Costa Rica has one of the largest documented bee faunas in the world. Prior to European colonization, tropical dry forests were the most common ecosystem in Central America. As ranching and agriculture spread, however, the forests were cut down, and today they cover less than 2% of their historic range. They are now considered the most threatened ecosystem in the tropics. Fortunately, tropical dry forests are actually *increasing* in Costa Rica thanks to conservation measures in Santa Rosa National Park.

Tropical Rainforest

Tropical rainforests are generally found in regions that experience temperatures above 18° C (64° F) year-round and annual rainfall of at least 2.5 meters (8.3 feet). Although they cover just 6% of land on earth, tropical rainforests contain roughly half of the world's species and two-thirds of its flowering plants. Most of this biodiversity is found in the dense canopy, which typically rises 30–45 meters (98–148 feet) above the forest floor. Despite the dazzling vegetation, however, rainforest soils are relatively nutrient poor. Unlike in northern forests, where layers of fallen vegetation accumulate in the soil each winter, most fallen debris in rainforests is broken down and recycled before it's absorbed by the soil. As a result, most trees have shallow root systems, and large trees rely on above-ground buttressed roots for support. Costa Rica's most impressive rainforest is found on the Osa Peninsula.

Cloud Forest

One of Costa Rica's most fascinating ecosystems is the cloud forest, a lush landscape found only at high elevations in the tropics. Cloud forests—which are named for the clouds that regularly drift through the trees—cover less than 0.4% of the Earth's surface, yet they support nearly 20% of the world's plant diversity. Up to 40% of a cloud forest's total biomass is composed of epiphytes such as mosses, orchids, ferns and bromeliads that grow on trees and absorb moisture and nutrition from passing clouds. Some large trees can support up to 40 kg (88 pounds) of epiphytes. In Costa Rica cloud forests are located between 1,500-2,500 meters (4,920–8,200 feet) and average temperatures are 16–21°C (61–70°F). Costa Rica's most famous cloud forest is Monteverde, but cloud forests are also found in San Gerardo de Dota, San Gerardo de Rivas and Poás Volcano.

Páramo

The páramo is the highest ecological zone in Costa Rica. Found only above treeline in the tropics of South America and Central America, páramos are characterized by small plants such as shrubs, grasses and dwarf bamboo. In Costa Rica páramos are found primarily in the Talamanca Mountains above 3,000 meters (9,842 feet). Although they receive plenty of rain—an average of 1.8 meters (5.9 feet) per year in Costa Rica—vegetation is limited due to freezing temperatures, strong winds and high levels of ultraviolet light. The most extensive páramo in Costa Rica surrounds the country's highest mountain: Chirripó.

BIRDS

Simply put, Csta Rica is one of the world's top birdwatching destinations. This tiny country, sandwiched between two oceans and two continents, attracts migrating birds from both North and South America, and it is home to dozens of species found nowhere else. From lush rainforests along the coast to cool cloud forests in the mountains, Costa Rica's varied habitats support an astonishing variety of birds. All told, over 900 bird species have been identified in Costa Rica. That's more bird species than in the U.S. and Canada combined, and it represents nearly 8% of all bird species on the planet. In addition, roughly 10% of birds in Costa Rica are considered regional endemics (found only in southern Central America).

And here's the best part: in a country as small as Costa Rica, all of these species are incredibly accessible. You can spend the morning watching quetzals in the mountains, drive down to lower elevations to spot toucans and macaws in the afternoon, then finish the day observing shorebirds in mangroves.

Roughly 600 of Costa Rica's bird species are permanent residents, and over 200 species are seasonal migrants, mostly from North America. Many of these "North American" species spend over six months in the tropics, however, so they are better defined as tropical species that go north to breed. Only a few migrants arrive from South America, most likely because South America shares a similar tropical environment. A handful of seabirds migrate from beyond South America, including the South Polar Skua, which migrates from Antarctica, and the Sooty Shearwater and White-faced Storm-Petrel, which migrate all the way from New Zealand.

For birdwatchers, one of Costa Rica's most impressive sights is the biannual raptor migration along the Caribbean coast. Millions of hawks and vultures migrate along Central America's Caribbean coast in the spring and the fall. In Costa Rica they are funneled through a narrow passage between the coast and the Talamanca Mountains. During this time it's possible to view over one million raptors passing through this bottleneck, and a volunteer hawkwatch program is conducted at the Kèköldi Indigenous Reserve (www.kekoldicr.com).

Birders divide Costa Rica into four major zones: the Caribbean slope, the south Pacific slope, the north Pacific slope and the highlands. If you're new to birding, the two most important things you'll need are a pair of good binoculars (at least 7x magnification) and a willingness to get up early. Birds are generally most active in the early morning between 5:30am and 8am.

If you're an experienced birder looking for information on Costa Rica's bird species, the most in-depth book is *A Guide to the Birds of Costa Rica* by the famed naturalist Alexander Skutch. Considered a tropical John James Audubon, Skutch spent six decades studying the birds of Costa Rica. (His house, Finca Los Cusingos, located 130 km south of San José, is open to visitors by appointment: 2738-2070, cusingos@cct.or.cr). Another terrific book is *The Birds of Costa Rica* by Richard Garrigues, which is more visually oriented and contains range maps for each bird.

Macaws

Covered in stunning plumage and growing up to 90 cm (2.9 feet) long, macaws are the largest parrots in the New World tropics. In Costa Rica there are two macaw species: the scarlet macaw (*Ara macao*), which weighs 1 kg (2.2 pounds), and the slightly larger great green macaw (*Ara ambiguus*), which weighs 1.3 kg (2.9 pounds).

Macaws are noisy and conspicuous. Their loud squawk, a guttural *raaak raaak,* is unmistakable and commonly heard in flight. Macaws are often seen flying in pairs or family groups of three or four birds. Although the green macaw's wingspan reaches up to 125 cm (49 inches), macaws aren't built for soaring and must steadily flap their wings to remain airborne.

The macaw's powerful bill, which can generate up to 1,000 pounds of pressure per inch, evolved to crush the hard shells of tropical nuts, which constitute much of its diet. As the famous naturalist Alexander Skutch put it, the macaw's bill combines the destructive powers of an ice pick, a chisel, a file and a vice. A macaw's tongue, meanwhile, is as dexterous as a human thumb. Not only can the tongue rotate hard seeds and nuts into optimal cracking position, it can be used to mimic human speech, which is one of the reasons macaws are considered among the smartest birds on Earth.

Macaws reach sexual maturity at 6–8 years of age and macaw pairs mate for life. Females lay 1–3 eggs, and the firstborn chick receives the majority of the parents' care and attention. Chicks that survive the treacherous first year can live over 60 years in the wild.

The scarlet macaw's historic range extended from southern Mexico to Brazil, and green macaws once flourished from Honduras to Ecuador. Over the past century, however, habitat destruction and theft for the illegal pet trade have eliminated macaws from most of Central America. Today in Costa Rica there are an estimated 1,500 scarlet macaws and just 250 green macaws. The largest populations of scarlet macaws are found in Corcovado National Park and Carara National Park, while a small population of green macaws is found in the northern Caribbean. But not all of the news is bad. Over the past decade, captive release programs organized by nonprofit groups such as the Ara Project (www.thearaproject.org) have released over 100 macaws in Costa Rica. In some locations, macaw populations appear to be increasing.

Resplendant Quetzal
(Pharomachrus mocinno)

Found only in the mountains of Central America, the resplendent quetzal is one of the world's most beautiful birds. The male's iridescent feathers are bright green and blue, its breast is rich crimson and its crown resembles a fuzzy mohawk. Most impressive of all is the male's shimmering tail, which can grow up to 64 cm (2 feet) long. Quetzals were worshipped by both the Maya and Aztec, whose rulers used their tail feathers in ceremonial headdresses. In Guatemala, where the quetzal is both the national bird and the name of the country's currency, legend states that quetzals will die if caged. Though recently disproved, the birds remain a potent symbol of freedom in Central America.

Quetzals are members of the trogon family. Like most trogons the females are less colorful than the males. The majority of their diet consists of wild avocado fruits, and quetzals follow the fruiting cycle up and down mountain slopes. From January to May they spend most of their time in high elevation cloud forests for courtship and mating. In Costa Rica quetzals are commonly spotted in Monteverde and San Gerardo de Dota. Their call is a soft, high-pitched *kyow*.

Barid's Trogon
(Trogon bairdii)

One of 10 trogon species in Costa Rica, Baird's trogon is found in the low-elevation rainforests of southern Costa Rica and Western Panama. The word *trogon* is Greek for "nibbling," a reference to the birds' habit of gnawing holes in trees to make nests. In Costa Rica trogons range from humid coastal rainforest to cool mountain cloud forests. They are famous for their straight tails, upright posture and bold colors, though females are less colorful than males. Baird's trogon is named for Spencer Baird, the first curator of the Smithsonian Institution.

Hummingbirds

Found only in the New World, these tiny, iridescent birds are famous for their ability to hover in place and fly backwards, which, along with their long beaks, helps them consume nectar from flowers. Their impressive range of motion, unique among birds, is made possible by rotation of the entire wing at the shoulder joint. Most hummingbird species can flap their wings dozens of times per second. In flight they have the highest metabolism of any animal other than insects. To conserve energy at night, hummingbirds can enter a state of "torpor," lowering their body temperature and heartbeat in a manner similar to hibernation. Costa Rica has over 50 hummingbird species—more than double the number in the entire U.S.—and they are found in nearly every corner of the country. Costa Rica's largest hummingbird, the violet sabrewing, weighs 11.5 grams (0.4 ounces), while its smallest, the scintillant hummingbird, weighs just 2 grams (0.07 ounces).

Purple-Throated Mountain Gem
(Morpho peleides)

Green-Crowned Brilliant
(Heliodoxa jacula)

Violet Sabrewing
(Campylopterus hemileucurus)

Clay-Colored Thrush
(Turdus grayi)

Given the astonishing variety of colorful birds in Costa Rica, the clay-colored thrush (aka clay-colored robin) seems like a dull choice to be the country's national bird. But despite its bland appearance, *el yigüirro*, as it's locally known, is a highly meaningful choice. Found throughout Costa Rica and mentioned frequently in local folklore, it possesses a series of beautiful calls that change throughout the year. Its most famous song, a series of bouncy whistles, heralds the start of the rainy season. For centuries farmers used the yigüiro's song as a natural reminder to plant their crops. It was also believed (falsely) that the bird sang seven songs— one for each of Costa Rica's seven provinces. The clay-colored thrush is found from Texas to Colombia.

Turquoise-Browed Motmot
(Eumomota superciliosa)

Ranging from Mexico to the north Pacific coast of Costa Rica, the turquoise-browed motmot is one of 9 motmot species in Costa Rica. Motmots, which are found only in the New World tropics, are famous for their tails, which generally include a featherless section and a racket-like tip. The tip of the tail is sometimes swung back and forth like a pendulum, which may be a signal to predators that the motmot is aware of their presence. Motmots eat small prey like insects and lizards. The turquoise-browed motmot is the national bird of Nicaragua.

Long-Tailed Manakin
(Chiroxiphia linearis)

There are 10 species of manakin in Costa Rica, but the long-tailed manakin is by far the most famous. Its bizarre mating ritual is a wonder to behold. Males form long-term partnership duos or trios that sing together to attract females. Calls include a sonorous *To-Lee-do* and a nasal *whaaa, whaaa*. Curious females are treated to an extended "dance" that involves upward leaps and synchronized cartwheels. If the female is impressed, she will mate with the alpha male. Subordinate males must wait until the alpha male dies before they can mate. Females build nests and raise the young with no help from the male. The long-tailed manakin is found in northwest Costa Rica and parts of the central highlands. Males grow up to 12 cm (4.7 inches) long with 15 cm (5.9 inch) tail feathers. Females are olive green with short tail feathers.

Collared Aracari
(Pteroglossus torquatus)

Aracaris are members of the toucan family, and there are two aracari species in Costa Rica. The collared aracari (right), is found in northern Costa Rica and along the Caribbean coast. It is distinguished by its whitish upper bill and a black band over its belly. The fiery-billed aracari, which has a redish-orange upper bill, is found in the Central Pacific and South Pacific. Both species are primarily fruit eaters, but they also eat insects and lizards.

Chestnut-Mandibled Toucan
(Ramphastos swainsonii)

The large bill of the chestnut-mandibled toucan grows up to 20 cm (7.8 inches) long and is used to pluck fruit from trees. Although seemingly thick and heavy, the bill is actually hollow and light. The chestnut-mandibled toucan ranges from Honduras to Ecuador, and in Costa Rica it is found along the Caribbean coast, Central Pacific and South Pacific. Locals claim its high-pitched call sounds like *Dios te dé te dé* ("God shall give you, shall give you").

Keel-Billed Toucan
(Ramphastos sulfuratus)

Famous for its brightly colored bill, which grows up to 15 cm (6 inches) long, the keel-billed toucan ranges from southern Mexico to Colombia. In Costa Rica it is found along the Caribbean coast and in the northern mountains. Keel-billed toucans travel in flocks of up to six birds, seeking out fruits that form the majority of their diet. After slicing a fruit with its bill, the toucan will toss it back and swallow it whole. Its call is a harsh, repetitive croaking sound that has been compared to the winding of an old clock.

Emerald Toucanet
(Aulacorhynchus prasinus)

The emerald toucanet is the smallest member of the toucan family in Costa Rica, measuring 30 cm (11.8 inches) long and weighing just 180 grams (6.3 oz). Although found from Mexico to Bolivia, a blue-throated sub-species is found only in the mountains of Costa Rica and western Panama. The emerald toucanet nests in old woodpecker nests or natural tree cavities. Its call, a loud *rrip rrip rrip*, sounds like a handsaw and is often repeated for several minutes on end.

Roseate Spoonbill
(Platalea ajaja)

This striking pink bird is found in shallow wetland areas on both the Pacific and Caribbean coasts. It uses its large, spoon-shaped bill to sift through the mud in search of crustaceans, insects and small amphibians. Like flamingos, roseate spoonbills derive their brilliant pink coloration from a red pigment in the crustaceans they eat. Without the pigment, they start to lose their brilliant pink coloration. Roseate spoonbills grow up to 80 cm (2.6 feet) long with a 1.3-meter (4-foot) wingspan.

Magnificent Frigatebird
(Fregata magnificens)

Found in coastal areas throughout the New World tropics, these large black birds have a 2-meter (6.5-foot) wingspan. With their wings fully outstretched, they can soar effortlessly for hours on end, riding thermals to heights of 2,500 meters (8,200 feet). Males have a large scarlet throat pouch that is inflated like a balloon during breeding season.

Brown Pelican
(Pelecanus occidentalis)

Brown pelicans are large birds with a wingspan up to 2.5 meters (8.2 feet) across. Their short, stubby legs make them extremely clumsy on land, but they are incredibly graceful in flight. They feed by plunge diving from the air, scooping up fish with their large throat pouch. Large air sacs beneath their skin makes them incredibly buoyant. Brown pelicans are often seen flying in single file V-formation on the Pacific coast, where there are several breeding colonies.

Harpy Eagle
(Harpia harpyja)

This massive eagle, which weighs up to 9 kg (20 pounds) and has a wingspan up to 2.2 meters (7.2 feet) across, is the most powerful raptor in the Western Hemisphere. Using its massive talons, it can snatch monkeys and sloths from trees. Although harpy eagles once thrived from southern Mexico to Argentina, they are now extremely rare in Central America due to habitat loss. In Costa Rica they are found on the Osa Peninsula.

King Vulture
(Sarcoramphus papa)

One of the largest vultures in the Americas, the king vulture's wingspan measures up to 2 meters (6.6 feet) across. Befitting its name, it is generally given feeding priority at a fresh carcass. The king vulture ranges from Mexico to Argentina, and it was frequently depicted in Mayan artwork. It is easily recognized by the fleshy yellow protrusion on its beak, which is called a caruncle.

Jabiru
(Jabiru mycteria)

One of the rarest birds in Costa Rica is the jabiru, a large stork found in wetlands in the Palo Verde and Caño Negro regions. Standing up to 1.5 meters (5 feet) tall, it is the tallest flying bird in Central and South America. Its wingspan, which measures up to 2.8 meters (9.2 feet) across, is the second-largest in the Americas after the Andean Condor. The jabiru is found from Mexico to Argentina, but habitat loss has removed it from much of its former range in Central America.

FROGS

Red-Eyed Leaf Frog
(Agalychnis callidryas)

Considered one of the world's most beautiful frogs, the red-eyed leaf frog is famous for its bright green skin, orange fingers, a blue striped belly and bright red eyes with vertical pupils. Growing up to 7 cm (2.8 inches) long, it is found in low-elevation rainforests from Mexico to Panama. In Costa Rica it is most common on the Caribbean coast. Primarily nocturnal, it spends its days clinging to the underside of broad leaves, scrunching its body into a tight green oval that conceals its colorful markings.

Glass Frogs

These unusual frogs are named for their semi-translucent skin and fully translucent bellies. Viewed from below, their intestines and bones are visible, and in some species it's even possible to see the frog's beating heart. There are 13 species of glass frog in Costa Rica.

Poison Dart Frogs

Strawberry Poison Dart Frog

Found only in the rainforests of Central and South America, these tiny colorful frogs secrete a potent skin toxin that indigenous hunters used to poison their darts. It is believed that poison dart frogs generate toxins by concentrating the stinging alkaloids of ants and insects, which form a large part of their diet. Levels of toxicity vary considerably among species, however, and none of Costa Rica's 8 poison dart frogs are considered deadly. Males of all species are extremely territorial and will wrestle other males away from their chosen space. Costa Rica's largest species, the Green & Black Poison Dart Frog, measures 4 cm (1.5 inches) long, while its smallest species, the Strawberry Poison Dart Frog, measures just 2 cm (3/4 inches) long. The Golfo Dulce Poison Dart Frog, which is found only in Costa Rica, lives in the lush rainforests surrounding Golfo Dulce.

Golfo Dulce Poison Dart Frog

Green & Black Poison Dart Frog

BUTTERFLIES

Costa Rica is home to over 1,500 butterfly species—twice as many as the United States and almost 10% of the world's total. The most famous butterfly is the blue morpho, a stunning iridescent beauty common in both rainforests and cloud forests. Remarkably, the shimmering blue wings of the morpho contain no pigment. Instead, the wings are covered in tiny scales that reflect blue wavelengths of light. Although the top side of the wings are vibrant and unmistakable, the underside is dull brown, which provides quick camouflage.

Blue Morpho
(Morpho peleides)

A morpho's total wingspan can reach 20 cm (8 inches) across. There are over 80 species of morpho in the New World tropics and 7 species in Costa Rica.

Another famous species in Costa Rica is the owl butterfly, named for the large "eyespot" on its wings that mimics the eye of an owl. The eyespot helps scare away predators such as lizards and small birds, while other predators must contend with the upper corner of the owl butterfly's wing, which resembles the head of a snake. Glasswing butterflies employ an even more ingenious method of camouflage: transparent wings.

Costa Rica is also home to an estimated 15,000 moth species. The largest, the white ghost moth, has a wingspan up to 30 cm (one foot) across. Another, the ducktail moth, migrates en masse between the Pacific and Caribbean coasts every few years. Ducktail moth larvae feed on the Omphalea plant, which slowly increases its toxicity to fend off the larvae. When the toxicity becomes too great, the moths venture across the mountains in search of less toxic plants on the opposite coast. The undisturbed Omphalea plants then reduce their toxicity, and every few years the process is repeated.

Owl Butterfly
(Caligo eurilochus)

A popular Costa Rican superstition states that encountering a large, dark moth is a sign that death is near. If the pattern on the moth's wings contains numbers, however, it's considered lucky. After "reading" the numbers on a lucky moth wing, many Ticos will purchase a lottery ticket with the same series of numbers.

Tiger Longwing
(Heliconius hecale)

SNAKES

Costa Rica is home to 137 snake species, the majority of which are nonvenomous. Over 100 snake species belong to the colubrid family, which pose little threat to humans. There are also five species of boa, including the famous boa constrictor, which grows up to 4 meters (13 feet) long.

There are 20 highly venomous snakes in Costa Rica, all of which belong to either the viper or coral families. Vipers include the beautiful yellow eyelash pit viper (right), named for modified scales over its eyes that resemble eyelashes, and the deadly bushmaster, known locally as *matabuey* ("bull killer"). The most famous viper is the much feared *fer-de-lance* (below), which grows up to 2.5 meters (8.2 feet) long and has 2.5-cm (1-inch) long fangs. The fangs inject a powerful anticoagulant that causes massive internal bleeding and a necrotizing agent that rots flesh. Because fer-de-lance are found throughout much of the country, they are responsible for the majority of poisonous snake bites. The name fer-de-lance is French for "spearhead"—a reference to the snake's flat, pointy head. Its Spanish name, *terciopelo* ("velvet"), refers to the snake's velvety sheen.

Eyelash Pit Viper
(Bothriechis schlegelii)

Although rarely seen, coral snakes are the deadliest snakes in Costa Rica. Three of the country's five coral species are easily distinguished by their red, yellow and black banded coloration. Included in the coral family is the yellow-bellied sea snake, which by some estimates is the fourth most poisonous snake in the world. Although common in the waters off the Pacific coast, sea snakes are rarely encountered close to shore, and thus pose little threat to swimmers or surfers.

Fortunately, highly venomous snakes are rarely encountered, and Costa Rica is also the only country in Central America that manufactures snake antivenom. The antivenom is produced by injecting a horse with snake venom, which triggers the natural production of antivenom. The horse blood is then extracted and placed in a centrifuge to extract antivenom.

Fer de Lance
(Bothrops asper)

LIZARDS

Green Iguana
(Iguana iguana)

Costa Rica's 69 lizard species are found throughout the country, from the coastal lowlands to the country's highest peaks. The largest lizard is the Green Iguana (above), which grows up to 1.5 meters (5 feet) long and weighs up to 9 kg (20 pounds). These dinosaur-esque creatures range in color from bright green to dull brown. During mating season the back spines of males turn bright orange. Incredible climbers, they spend nearly all of their lives in trees, and they can survive a 15-meter (50-foot) fall without serious injury. Although green iguanas have sharp teeth, they are primarily herbivores. Iguana meat, which supposedly tastes like chicken, has been enjoyed by local residents for centuries, and in Costa Rica green iguanas are known as *gallina de palo* ("tree chickens"). Although once common from Mexico to Brazil, green iguana populations have declined significantly due to hunting and capture for the pet trade. In Costa Rica they are found on both coasts up to 500 meters (1,600 feet).

The green basilisk lizard (below) is famously known as the "Jesus Christ lizard" for its ability to "walk" on water. Its powerful hind legs and special foot structure propel it across water at speeds topping 1.5 meters (5 feet) per second. When threatened, they can skim across several meters of water—an invaluable defense against predators. Green basilisks are also excellent swimmers, and they can spend long periods of time underwater. They grow up to 1 meter (3 feet) long, and their brilliant green coloration is flecked with small blue and white spots. Males have sail-like crests on their head, back and tail; females have a single crest on their head. They are found in lush rainforests along the Caribbean coast.

Anoles are small lizards that are found throughout Costa Rica. They are famous for their "dewlaps," colorful, fan-shaped throat flaps that males extend to attract females.

Green Basilisk
(Basiliscus plumifrons)

INVERTEBRATES

There are an estimated 370,000 invertebrates in Costa Rica, of which roughly 95% are insects. Although many invertebrates are visible during the day, some are active only at night. In recent years night tours, which seek out Costa Rica's incredible nocturnal insects, have become popular throughout the country.

Jewel Scarab

Beetles that belong to the genus *Chrysina*, known as jewel scarabs, are famous for their iridescent colors, which range from brilliant green to metallic gold and silver. They are often found in cloud forests, and they measure 15–35 mm (0.6–1.4 inches) in length.

Harlequin Beetle
(Acrocinus longimanus)

Harlequin beetles grow up to 7.5 cm (3 inches) long and are named for their colorful back patterns. They are found in low elevation forests throughout the country. The male's unusually large forelegs are longer than its entire body.

Elephant Beetle
(Megasoma elephas)

Measuring up to 12 cm (4.7 inches) long, elephant beetles are part of the Dynastinae sub-family, commonly called rhinoceros beetles. Among the largest beetles in the world, rhinoceros beetles are named for their large "horns," which are used to dig and fight.

Walking Fern
(Trychopeplus laciniatus)

Also known as the moss mimic walkingstick, the walking fern's incredible camouflage helps it blend seemlessly into the mossy cloud forest where it lives.

Tarantula Hawk
(Pepsis sp.)

This giant wasp is a tarantula's worst nightmare. After stinging a tarantula with paralyzing venom, a female tarantula hawk will drag it back to her burrow, lay her eggs on its body and bury the spider alive. When the wasp larvae hatch, they feast on the still-living tarantula.

Red-Legged Tarantula
(Megaphobema mesomelas)

This beautiful tarantula, found in humid forests above 500 meters (1,600 feet), is popular with international collectors thanks to its unique coloration. In Costa Rica it's called *pica caballo* ("horse biter") for the mistaken belief that it bites horses.

Golden Orb Weaver
(Nephila clavipes)

One of the most common spiders in Costa Rica is the golden orb-weaver, which spins a web up to 1 meter (3 feet) across. Its silk is six times stronger than steel, and its web has a golden hue. Golden orb-weavers grow up to 5 cm (2 inches) long.

Leafcutter Ants
(Acromyrmex & Atta sp.)

These industrious ants live in massive colonies that harvest up to 50 kgs (110 pounds) of leaves *each day*. After hauling the leaves underground, the ants chew them and mix them with fecal matter to cultivate a fungus that feeds the colony. Leafcutter ants are found in forests throughout Costa Rica.

MAMMALS

Jaguar
(Panthera onca)

Jaguars are the largest cat species in the New World and the third-largest cat species after tigers and lions. Powerful and athletic, they grow up to 1.9 meters (6.2 feet) long, weigh up to 150 kg (330 pounds) and are renowned for their hunting abilities. Highly sensitive pupils give jaguars extraordinary night vision, and their powerful jaws are strong enough to crush animal skulls and turtle shells. Jaguars prey on peccaries, tapirs, sloths, monkeys, iguanas, birds and smaller cat species. In coastal areas, jaguars stake out beaches during the new moon to feast on nesting sea turtles. After encountering a turtle, a jaguar rips off its head and scoops out the meaty interior with its paws. Jaguars have retractable claws that aid in both hunting and tree climbing. Because they require large areas with adequate prey, a jaguar's range can extend up to 3,800 hectares (15 square-miles). Jaguars generally lead independent, solitary lives, but males and females come together whenever a female is in heat. During this time jaguars mate up to 100 times per day, but despite this impressive statistic, the jaguar penis bone is just 0.8 cm long. Gestation lasts roughly 100 days and females give birth to 1–4 cubs. Roughly 6% of jaguars are born completely black, and they retain this dark coloration throughout their lives. Jaguars can live up to 15 years in the wild. Throughout Latin America they play a prominent role in the mythology of indigenous groups. Costa Rica's Bri Bri believe life on earth was created after Sibú, the supreme god, planted seeds in baby jaguar blood. Biologists believe jaguars are descended from leopards whose Asian relatives crossed the Bering land bridge during the Ice Age. Although once common from the southwest U.S. to Argentina, jaguar populations are now in decline. Human hunting and habitat loss have devastated wild populations. Today jaguars, like all Costa Rican cat species, are found mostly in protected areas.

Margay
(Leopardus wiedii)

Weighing roughly 3.5 kg (7.7 pounds), the margay is the second-smallest cat species in Costa Rica (after oncillas). Margays spend the vast majority of their lives in trees, and they are highly adapted to that environment. Strong claws and unusually flexible ankles make them one of just two cat species that can descend trees head-first (the other is the clouded leopard of Southeast Asia). The margay's long tail aids in balance, and its vertical leap is 2.5 meters (8.2 feet). Although found from Mexico to Argentina, margays are rarely seen due to their nocturnal nature.

Agouti
(Dasyprocta punctata)

These small ground rodents weigh about 3 kg (6.6 pounds) and are found at all but the highest elevations in Costa Rica. Agoutis feed on fruits and seeds, and they sometimes follow monkey troops in search of dropped fruit. Males attract females by showering them with urine, which sends receptive females into a frenzied dance. Females give birth to a litter of 1–4 babies, and newborns are placed in tiny, individual dens inaccessible to large predators. Mothers visit the dens to feed the newborns and eat their excrement, which helps conceal their scent.

White-Nosed Coati
(Nasua narica)

Coatis are one of Costa Rica's most commonly spotted mammals. Known locally as pizotes, they are highly adaptable and habituate easily to people. Coatis range from Texas to Ecuador, and in Costa Rica they are found at all but the highest elevations. Adult males are generally solitary, while females and young travel in packs of up to 25. Males may be excluded from packs because they have a habit of eating young coatis. Adult coatis weigh up to 5 kg (11 pounds).

Baird's Tapir
(Tapirus bairdii)

Tapirs are the largest land-dwelling mammals in Central America and South America, growing up to 2 meters (6.5 feet) long and weighing up to 400 kg (882 pounds). Their most distinctive feature is a long, flexible snout used to gather vegetation. Leaves and stems form the majority of their diet, and tapirs eat up to 15 kg (33 pounds) of food each day. Although large, they are surprisingly athletic. They can climb nearly vertical hills, swim across rivers and run through dense forest at high speeds. Their unusually thick hide—up to 3 inches thick in places—guards against scratches from sticks and helps protect them from jaguars and crocodiles. Called *danta* in Spanish, tapirs are genetically related to rhinos. There are four tapir species worldwide, including three in the New World and one in Southeast Asia. Baird's tapir is the largest tapir species in the New World. They have short dark hair, cream-colored markings on their throats and a small dark spot on each cheek. Their front feet have four toes and their back feet have three toes. Young tapirs, which are born after a gestation period of nearly 400 days, are covered in white spots and stripes that help them blend in with the dappled light of the forest. Adult tapirs can live over 30 years. Baird's tapirs are named for the U.S. naturalist Spencer Baird, who first observed tapirs in Mexico in 1843. Although tapirs once lived in the forests of eastern North America, they were most likely hunted to extinction after the arrival of early humans. Costa Rica's indigenous Bri Bri believe Tapir is the sister of their creator, Sibú. Because Tapir was stubborn and difficult, however, Sibú allowed the Bri Bri to hunt tapirs on Earth. Today Baird's tapirs are found from southern Mexico to Colombia, though they are classified as endangered due to human hunting and habitat loss. Tapirs were formerly found throughout Costa Rica, but today they are rare outside of a handful of protected areas. Corcovado National Park has the largest tapir population in Costa Rica, with an estimated 200 individuals.

Kinkajou
(Potus flavus)

Kinkajous are nocturnal, tree-dwelling mammals that range from southern Mexico to Brazil. Although rarely seen during the day, they are sometimes spotted wandering along the branches of trees at night. Kinkajous have sharp teeth and they are officially classified as carnivores, but nearly all of their diet consists of fruits and plants. The kinkajou's long tongue extends up to five inches and is used to lick nectar from flowers. Its prehensile tail, which can wrap around branches, helps the kinkajou dangle upside down, while flexible ankle joints allow it to descend trees head-first. Adult kinkajous weigh roughly 2.5 kg (5.5 pounds), measure roughly 50 cm (1.6 feet) long (with an equally long tail) and can live 20–30 years.

Northern Tamandua
(Tamandua mexicana)

The Northern Tamandua is a species of anteater that ranges from southern Mexico to northern Peru. As it wanders through the forest, its pea-sized mouth ejects a long, sticky tongue up to 40 cm (16 inches). The tongue sucks up live ants and termites, which are then crushed by a muscular gizzard in the digestive tract. Large claws help them rip open wood in search of prey. Some studies suggest that tamanduas eat roughly 9,000 insects *each day*, and in certain areas their diet is roughly two-thirds termites and one-third ants. That said, they tend to avoid insects with spiny bodies and harmful chemicals. Tamanduas grow up to 60 cm (2 feet) long and weigh up to 4.5 kg (10 pounds). They are generally seen in remote areas wandering along the forest floor or climbing along the branches of trees.

Central American Squirrel Monkey
(Saimiri oerstedii)

Squirrel monkeys (*mono titi* in Spanish) are the smallest and most endangered monkeys in Costa Rica. Once common in Costa Rica and Panama, most of their former range has been destroyed due to deforestation. Today, squirrel monkeys are found only along Costa Rica's southern Pacific coast with Manuel Antonio marking their northern limit. It is estimated that there are fewer than 3,000 individuals remaining. Squirrel monkeys are omnivores that eat fruits, insects and small lizards, and they can weigh up to 1 kg (2.2 pounds). They travel in troops of up to 70 monkeys, but unlike most monkey species, males stay in the troop where they were born while young females leave in search of mates. Squirrel monkeys live up to 15 years. Their distinctive call is a series of whistles and chirps.

Spider Monkey
(Ateles geoffroyi)

Spider monkeys are the largest monkeys in Costa Rica, growing up to 61 cm (2 feet) long and weighing up to 9 kg (20 pounds). They are famous for their dexterity, with arms that are 25% longer than their legs—the opposite of most mammals—and a powerful prehensile tail that essentially functions as a fifth appendage. Spider monkeys also have unusually long, strong fingers, and their tail has a fleshy pad near the tip that enables better gripping. These adaptations help spider monkeys swing through the trees with ease, seeking out the ripe fruits that form the vast majority of their diet. Females are often mistaken for males due to their exceptionally large clitoris, which is even larger than the male penis. During breeding season females in heat mate 3–4 times daily, with mating sessions lasting up to 23 minutes.

The booming roar of the howler monkey is one of Costa Rica's most memorable sounds. Lasting 4–5 seconds, it is audible from several kilometers away, even through dense jungle. The roar is used to communicate with distant monkeys and is made possible by an unusually large bone in the throat called a hyroid, which amplifies vocal sounds. Despite the power of their roar, howler monkeys are notoriously lethargic. Much of their diet consists of low-nutrient leaves, and howlers spend most of their time napping on branches. They weigh up to 7 kgs (15.4 pounds) and live in troops of up to 45 individuals. The youngest male is often the most dominant member of the troop—an unusual contrast to most other primate species where age determines status. Alpha males proposition females by flicking their tongues, and mating lasts roughly 30 seconds. Howlers are the most common monkeys in Costa Rica.

Howler Monkey
(Alouatta palliata)

White-Faced Capuchin Monkey
(Cebus capucinus)

Named for their resemblance to Italian Capuchin monks, who dressed in dark robes with hoods (*capuccios*), white-faced capuchins are the second-most common monkey in Costa Rica. Although cute, they are considered by many the "devils of the rainforest"—aggressive omnivores that eat everything from flowers and insects to birds and baby coatis. Capuchin monkeys have proportionally large brains, and they are considered the smartest New World monkeys. They can use sticks as weapons and sometimes rub their fur with specific plants, perhaps to benefit from insecticide or fungicide properties. Highly adaptable, they can be found at all but the highest elevations in Costa Rica. Capuchin monkeys grow up to 3 kg (6.6 pounds) and travel in troops of up to 30 individuals.

Bats

Roughly half of Costa Rica's mammal species are bats. At last count, there were 113 bat species in Costa Rica—about 10% of all bat species worldwide and over double the number found in the United States. The most famous are vampire bats, which consume the blood of animals. They are the world's only parasitic mammal species, and all three of the world's vampire bat species are found in Costa Rica. About 50% of the country's bat species are insect-eaters, about 25% are fruit-eaters and about 10% are nectar and pollen eaters (the rest eat a combination of foods). Insect-eaters use echolocation, a kind of biological sonar that uses high-frequency vocalizations to locate insects in flight. Fruit-eaters and nectar-eaters play a critical role in seed dispersal and pollination. The smallest bat species in Costa Rica is the black myotis, which measures just 5 cm (2 inches) long and weighs 5 grams (0.2 ounces). The largest bat species is the spectral bat (also known as the false vampire) with a wingspan up to 1 meter (3 feet). The spectral bat is the world's largest carnivorous bat, and it feeds mainly on sleeping birds.

Greater Broad-Nosed Bat
(Platyrrhinus vittatus)

Northern Ghost Bat
(Diclidurus albus)

Peccaries

These hog-like animals typically weigh 20–30 kgs (44–66 pounds), and they are found only in the Americas. Costa Rica is home to two peccary species. The collared peccary ranges from Texas to Argentina. In Costa Rica it is found at all but the highest elevations. The white-lipped peccary, which is slightly larger, was once common in rainforests throughout the country. Over the past several decades, hunting and habitat loss have confined it to a handful of remote areas, most notably the Osa Peninsula. White-lipped peccaries travel in stampeding herds of up to 300 individuals. They are famous for the pungent odor produced by their anal glands, which is used to mark territory.

Collared Peccary
(Pecari tajacu)

Sloths

These unusual animals are famous for their slow motion lifestyles. Found only in the New World tropics, they spend most of their lives dangling from trees, and they are known simply as *osos perezosos* ("lazy bears") in Spanish.

To conserve energy, sloths have the lowest body temperature of any mammal—as low as 25°C (77°F) in two-toed sloths. Sloths are vegetarians that digest leaves, branches and twigs through a process of bacterial fermentation. Their multi-chamber stomachs, which comprise nearly one-third of their body weight, can take up to a month to digest low-nutrient plant matter. Sloths urinate and defecate roughly once a week, and they climb down from trees to do so. Why they spend so much precious energy to relieve themselves is a mystery.

Sloths have more neck vertebrae than most mammals, allowing them to rotate their head 180 degrees, which helps them scan the surroundings for predators such as jaguars and harpy eagles. Their fur, meanwhile, is an ecosystem unto itself. A single sloth can harbor up to 100 moths and 1,000 beetles. Sloth hair also encourages the growth of algae, which gives many sloths a greenish hue that serves as camouflage.

Two-toed sloths have a gestation period of over 300 days. Newborns weigh as little as 200 grams (8 ounces), and adult sloths can live 20–30 years.

Costa Rica is home to two species of sloth that grow up to 60 cm (2 feet) long and weigh 4–6 kgs (9–13 lbs). In prehistoric times, a giant ground sloth existed that, when standing on its hind legs, measured roughly 6 m (20 feet) tall.

Brown-Throated Three-Toed Sloth
(Bradypus variegatus)

Hoffmann's Two-Toed Sloth
(Bradypus variegatus)

SEA TURTLES

Although sea turtles spend nearly all of their lives swimming in the open ocean, females return to the same beaches where they were born to lay eggs in the sand. Costa Rica's beaches are visited by five of the world's seven sea turtle species: leatherbacks, green, olive ridley, loggerhead and hawksbill.

Leatherbacks are the world's largest sea turtles, growing up to 3 meters (9.8 feet) long and weighing up to 900 kg (2,000 pounds). Their unusually long front flippers measure up to 2.7 meters (8.8 feet). Instead of a hard bony shell, they have a soft, leathery back. They are streamlined, fast and capable of diving 1,200 meters (4,000 feet). Leatherbacks migrate thousands of miles in search of jellyfish, their favorite food, and they are found as far north as Alaska and Newfoundland. Fatty insulation helps them regulate their body heat in frigid sub-Arctic waters. During nesting season, leatherbacks lay clutches of 50–100 eggs the size of billiard balls. The most important leatherback nesting beach in the eastern Pacific is Playa Grande (p.294) on the Nicoya Peninsula. On the Caribbean coast, leatherbacks nest in the Gandoca-Manzanillo Refuge (p.487).

Green turtles are Costa Rica's second largest sea turtles, measuring up to 1.5 meters (5 feet) long and weighing up to 190 kgs (420 pounds). They are named for the green fat beneath their shells. Green sea turtles feed on sea grass, and they migrate thousands of miles in search of food. Tortuguero (p.447), on the Caribbean coast, is one of the world's most famous green sea turtle nesting beaches.

Hawksbill and loggerhead turtles nest in small numbers in Costa Rica. Loggerheads grow up to 1 meters (3 feet) long and weigh up to 200 kgs (440 pounds). Hawksbills measure roughly 0.8 meters (2.6 feet) long and weigh around 80 kgs (180 pounds). In the days before plastic, hawksbills were harvested in large numbers on the Caribbean coast for their beautiful translucent shell, which was used to make combs, eyeglass frames and other decorative items.

Olive ridleys are the smallest sea turtles in Costa Rica, measuring just 0.6 meters (2 feet) long and weighing 30–40 kgs (66–88 pounds). At two beaches in Costa Rica, Playa Ostional (p.308) and Playa Nancite, olive ridleys gather in mass nestings called *arribadas* that last several days. This extraordinary spectacle is believed to be a form of protection against predators. By laying hundreds of

Leatherback
(Dermochelys coriacea)

thousands of eggs, olive ridleys overwhelm predators that feed on eggs. This same strategy protects baby turtles when they hatch en masse.

Although the exact timing varies by species, most sea turtle eggs incubate over a period of 50–70 days. Upon hatching, baby turtles instinctively scamper into the ocean as quickly as possible to avoid predators. Yet even after reaching the water, the vast majority do not survive to adulthood. Fish and

Green Turtle
(Chelonia mydas)

birds represent a constant threat to hatchlings. Those sea turtles that make it to adulthood have no natural predators, but sharks sometimes take a bite out of their flippers. Although sea turtles spend most of their time underwater, they must constantly surface to breath air. They extract freshwater from saltwater and excrete excess salt through ducts near their eyes.

Sea turtles were once abundant throughout the world's oceans, but populations have declined by an estimated 90% over the past century. All five Costa Rican sea turtle species are listed as endangered or critically endangered. Hunting and egg harvesting have taken the heaviest toll. For centuries turtle meat was a staple of coastal diets, and sea turtle eggs are considered an aphrodisiac in Latin America. Although it is illegal to harvest sea turtle eggs in Costa Rica, *hueveros* ("egg poachers") prowl beaches and dig up eggs for sale on the black market.

Although turtle hunting and egg poaching are on the decline, industrial fishing inadvertently kills thousands of turtles each year. In the 1980s commercial fishing boats used giant drift nets that stretched for miles and killed nearly everything in their path. Giant drift nets were internationally banned in 1992, but sea turtles must still contend with longlines that dangle thousands of hooks and can stretch up to a hundred miles. Longlines sometimes snag sea turtles, which often suffocate before they can be set free.

Over the past several decades, Costa Rica has taken many important steps to protect sea turtles. In one recent survey, Costa Rica was ranked third in the world for its sea turtle conservation efforts; only the U.S. and Australia ranked higher. If you'd like to help save sea turtles in Costa Rica, there are a number of excellent volunteer opportunities. The oldest and most famous is run by the Sea Turtle Conservancy (www.conserveturtles.org) in Tortuguero. Earthwatch (www.earthwatch.org) also organizes volunteer programs that help the critically endangered leatherbacks at Playa Grande.

Olive Ridley
(Lepidochelys olivacea)

Arribadas

Costa Rica is home to one of nature's most amazing spectacles: mass sea turtle nestings called *arribadas*. During an arribada, tens of thousands of olive ridley turtles gather at a single beach to lay their eggs at the same time. Scientists believe this unusual behavior is a defense mechanism against predators that eat turtles and turtle eggs. By overwhelming predators with sheer numbers, sea turtles ensure that most of their eggs will hatch. Arribadas only occur at a handful of beaches in the world, and Costa Rica is home to two of them: Playa Ostional (p.308) on the Nicoya Peninsula and Playa Nancite in Santa Rosa National Park.

Playa Ostional

Humpback Whale
(Megaptera novaeangliae)

Humpback whales grow up to 17 meters (56 feet) long and weigh up to 43,500 kgs (48 tons). Found in oceans throughout the world, they spend half the year feeding in cold, nutrient-rich waters, then migrate to warm tropical waters to mate and give birth. Costa Rica's Pacific coast is the only known place in the world that attracts humpbacks from both the northern and southern hemispheres. Northern humpbacks, which visit January–March, come from as far away as California. Southern humpbacks, which visit August–October, come from as far away as Antarctica—one of the longest animal migrations on the planet. While in the tropics, humpbacks eat no food, surviving entirely off accumulated fat reserves.

Hammerhead Shark
(Sphyrna lewini)

Famous for their flat, elongated heads, hammerhead sharks are found in tropical and temperate waters throughout the world. Their eyes, which are located at the far ends of their heads, give them full 360-degree vision. During the day hammerheads swim in large schools close to shore. At night they venture offshore alone to hunt. Isla Del Coco (p.441), off Costa Rica's Pacific coast, is famous for its abundant hammerhead populations. Like all sharks, hammerheads have been severely over-fished in the past several decades. In 2012 Costa Rica banned shark finning, a highly wasteful practice in which sharks are killed only for their fins, which are used to make a popular Asian soup. In 2011, an estimated 400,000 sharks were harvested in Costa Rica for their fins.

Spinner Dolphins
(Stenella longirostris)

These playful dolphins are famous for their love of leaping acrobatically out of the water, performing up to five spinning revolutions or one graceful pirouette in mid-air. "Spinners" measure up to 2 meters (6.6 feet) long and weigh up to 95 kg (200 pounds). They are found in tropical waters throughout the world, and they can dive up to 300 meters (1,000 feet) in search of fish, squid and shrimp. Like all dolphins, they communicate using echolocation, a kind of biological sonar. The waters off Costa Rica's Pacific coast are home to "superpods" of spinner dolphins that number 1,000 individuals or more. Because they often swim with schools of yellowfin tuna, spinner dolphins are vulnerable to accidental capture in industrial fishing nets.

West Indian Manatee
(Trichechus manatus)

These gentle, vegetarian mammals grow up to 3.5 meters (11 feet) long and weigh up to 600 kg (1,300 pounds). Surprisingly agile, they have been observed underwater doing rolls, somersaults and swimming upside down. Manatees are extremely timid, and they will submerge at the slightest disturbance, holding their breath underwater for up to 20 minutes. West Indian manatees are the world's largest manatee species, and they live in shallow coastal areas from the southeastern United States to Brazil. In Costa Rica they were once abundant along the Caribbean coast, including freshwater rivers and lagoons, but hunting and motor boat collisions have drastically reduced local manatee populations. Today Costa Rican manatees avoid humans at all costs, and they are rarely spotted.

Dolphin Superpods

The waters off Costa Rica's Pacific Coast are home to spectacular dolphin "superpods" that feature thousands of frolicking dolphins. These mass congregations appear to be largely social in nature, with superpod dolphins spending much of their time chattering, eating and mating. There are seven species of dolphins that form superpods in Costa Rica. Occasionally, two superpods will merge to form a "megapod." To witness a dolphin superpod firsthand, contact Costa Cetacea (p.404), which offers "Blue Water Safari" tours departing from Drake Bay.

HISTORY

Humans FIRST OCCUPIED Costa Rica around 12,000 BC. These early settlers, descendents of the hunter/gatherers that crossed the Bering land bridge during the last Ice Age, lived largely migratory lifestyles. Around 8,000 BC they began making the transition to sedentary village life, and by 4,000 BC they were practicing agriculture. Yet despite their increased reliance on planted crops, hunting and gathering remained an important part of everyday life.

By 500 AD, small clans had organized into formal hierarchies with groups of villages belonging to a *cacicazgo* ("chiefdom") ruled by a *cacique* ("chief"). Villages consisted of round or oval houses with conical thatched roofs. Some of these structures were enormous, measuring up to 28 meters (92 feet) in diameter and 15 meters (49 feet) tall. The largest houses, which were often built on circular mounds, provided shelter for up to 300 people. Slash and burn techniques were used to clear forest for both agriculture and settlement.

Clothing and physical decoration depended on both region and climate. In warm coastal areas men and women covered their pubic area with a thin cloth. In the mountains they wore a kind of skirt made from bark. Throughout the region men and women wore ornate necklaces and pierced their ears, noses and lips. Body paint and tattoos were common, and some groups intentionally filed their teeth and used flat boards to deform the skulls of young children (p.67).

Separate indigenous groups normally interacted with one another in one of two ways: war or trade. Many villages were defensive in nature, and artifacts depict warriors in battle gear carrying the decapitated heads of their victims. Weapons included axes and long wooden spears tipped with sharp stone or obsidian points. Following battle, surviving victims were either killed, enslaved or subjected to human sacrifice.

When indigenous groups weren't fighting, they were trading. The most valuable items were gold and slaves, but agricultural goods and animal products were far more common. Thanks to the region's diverse ecology, different regions specialized in different resources. Coastal groups harvested fish, shells, salt and sea turtles eggs. They also extracted a vibrant purple dye from a particular species of mollusk. Inland farmers grew maize, beans, cacao, yucca and pejibaye (p.84). Handmade crafts—pottery, cloth, hammocks, woven baskets—were also exchanged, and trade networks reached as far as Mexico and the Caribbean islands. Both jade and obsidian came from present-day Guatemala.

Much of what we know about local indigenous cultures comes from arti-facts made for practical or ceremonial purposes. The most dazzling artifacts are crafted from jade and gold, but there are also beautiful ceramics and stone statues (p.67). Astute observers of the natural world, local artisans often incorporated animals into their designs. Birds, frogs, snakes, monkeys, crocodiles and jaguars were all popular subjects. Although objects made from perishable materials such as wood and animal skins probably made up the majority of everyday items, such objects have long since disintegrated due to Costa Rica's harsh tropical climate.

Local indigenous groups all shared an "animist" religion that imbued humans, animals and natural phenomenon with divine spirits. Communication with the spirit world was the domain of the shaman, who was responsible for diagnosing and curing illness. The shaman was also in charge of human sacrifice, and cer-emonies were probably accompanied by music from flutes and drums.

Located between South America and Mexico, Costa Rica was sandwiched between three of the world's great civilizations: the Maya and Aztec to the north and the Inca to the south. Although never dominated by any of these civilizations, local indigenous groups were plugged into vast trading networks that brought cultural and technological influences from each. In fact, Costa Rica was one of the major crossroads between South American and Mesoamerican cultures. Indigenous groups in northern Costa Rica centered their villages around plazas and grew corn, beans and squash, much like cultures to the north. Indigenous groups in southern Costa Rica grew yucca and pejibaye, chewed coca leaves and followed a matrilineal clan structure, much like cultures to the south.

Although small-scale artistic achievements flourished in Costa Rica, indigenous groups never achieved the vast social complexity of the Inca, the Aztec or the Maya. There was no written language and they left behind no monumental structures. Costa Rica's most famous archaeological site is Guayabo (p.249), near present-day Turrialba. Home to dozens of circular bases that most likely provided the foundation for large houses, Guayabo was occupied for roughly 1,000 years between 500 BC and 1400 AD. At its peak it was probably home to no more than 10,000 people.

But despite the lack of social complexity—or perhaps because of it—indigenous society in Costa Rica was remarkably stable over the long-term. Constant warfare meant no single group achieved complete dominance, and in contrast to larger civilizations, most notably the Maya, local indigenous populations never faced collapse due to over-exploitation of natural resources. Although some archaeologists believe local indigenous groups did over-exploit their resources periodically, they simply faced periods of decline rather than total collapse.

By the 15th century there were probably 500,000 indigenous people living in Costa Rica. Two major *señorios* ("lordships") were located in the Central Valley and northwest Costa Rica, and they oversaw roughly 18 smaller cacicazgos. Although multiple languages were spoken, Huetar, the language used in the Central Valley, was used to communicate among different groups.

These were the conditions that prevailed when indigenous groups encountered a group of strange new arrivals from half a world away.

EUROPEAN CONTACT

IN 1502, on his fourth and final voyage, Christopher Columbus became the first European to visit Costa Rica. Still searching for Asia, Columbus sailed to Honduras and cruised down the east coast of Central America. When he reached Cariari (present-day Limón, Costa Rica), he anchored near an offshore island. Struck by the abundant vegetation, he called the area "the Garden." Later explorers were more interested in reports of gold worn by the natives, and before long Spaniards were calling the region *Costa Rica*, the "Rich Coast."

Although initial Spanish contact was brief, an invisible killer was soon racing through the region: smallpox. This European disease, which until then was completely unknown in the Americas, arrived in Mexico in 1520 and spread through Central America along indigenous trade networks. Unlike Europeans, indigenous people had no natural resistance to the highly contagious virus, which killed up to 50% of its victims.

Europe had suffered smallpox epidemics for centuries, and Europeans often isolated smallpox victims to prevent further spread of the disease. In Central America, indigenous families tended to gather around sick relatives, which further accelerated the spread of the virus. The scope of death was extraordinary. Much of Central America's population—indeed, much of the population of the Americas—was devastated before anyone laid eyes on a Spaniard.

Tragically, smallpox was just the beginning. Measles, cholera, typhus, diphtheria, influenza—all swept through the Americas in wave after wave of death. It has been estimated that previously unknown diseases accounted for up to 95% of indigenous deaths following European contact.

Thus, when Gil González sailed north from Panama in 1522 to explore Costa Rica's Pacific coast, he encountered a region that was, in all likelihood, already devastated by disease. Although González did not know this—Europeans did not realize they had transported deadly microbes to the New World—he was struck by the lack of natives in the region. He did encounter a small indigenous population in present-day Nicoya, where he took 100,000 pesos worth of gold and captured hundreds of slaves to be sold in Panama and Peru. He then continued on foot to Nicaragua, where there were reports of more gold and larger indigenous populations.

Costa Rica's Caribbean coast, meanwhile, was virtually ignored. In the decades following contact, Spain was far more focused on Mexico and Guatemala, where vast amounts of gold had made a handful of conquistadors rich. Both regions were also home to large indigenous populations, which attracted both missionaries (eager to convert souls) and colonists (eager for cheap labor). As a result, Guatemala became Spain's administrative center for all of Central America, including far away Costa Rica.

THE COLONIAL ERA

IN 1560 SPANISH authorities in Guatemala decided it was time to explore and colonize Costa Rica. Juan de Cavallón was dispatched to Costa Rica's Caribbean coast, and he marched his men up the rugged Turrialba Valley to the fertile Central Valley roughly 1,400 meters (4,600 feet) above sea level. Cavallón was followed two years later by Juan Vázquez de Coronado, who founded the colonial capital of Cartago.

The supposed riches of the "Rich Coast" never materialized, however, so colonists focused on exploiting indigenous labor. This was technically illegal—Spain had stopped granting rights to indigenous labor following early abuses in the Caribbean, Mexico and Peru—but colonists simply ignored the law. Under the so-called *encomienda* system, indigenous people were required to provide both goods and labor to the colonists. Because indigenous populations were small and spread out, colonists concentrated them into new villages to make large-scale farming and ranching operations more efficient. Many Spaniards also took indigenous wives because female colonists were in short supply.

Not surprisingly, Costa Rica's indigenous people despised the encomienda system. One European observer noted that when indigenous groups realized the colonists were coming they "burned their houses, cut down the fruits and trees, took the harvest from the fields and destroyed the country; then they immediately fled to the mountains." Many indigenous people fled to the rugged Talamanca Mountains southeast of Cartago.

As new markets for wheat, corn and pack animals opened up in Nicaragua and Panama, Costa Rica's colonists needed additional workers to expand their operations, so they headed into the Talamanca Mountains. In 1610 indigenous warriors staged a violent uprising in protest. The colonists responded by declaring the natives in open rebellion and sending military troops to capture slaves.

In the long run, however, Costa Rica's encomienda system was doomed. As European diseases continued to decimate native populations, the indigenous workforce shrank from a high of 70,000 in 1569 to just 7,000 by 1610. By the end of the 17th century, nearly 70% of colonists in Cartago described themselves as making a living from their own labor.

The encomienda system had collapsed, but Christian missionaries continued to push into the Talamanca Mountains in search of converts. In 1709 Franciscan friars were operating 14 missions in the region when indigenous warriors launched a surprise attack. Led by a cacique named Pablo Presbere, the rebels set fire to churches and freed indigenous "workers" from missions. Troops from Cartago captured Presbere and executed him in public. But the indigenous rebels had made their point. Going forward Spanish colonists largely avoided the Talamanca Mountains, which have remained a remote refuge for indigenous groups to the present day.

INDEPENDENCE

THROUGHOUT THE 1700s, Costa Rica struggled with poverty and irrelevance. In 1723 Cartago consisted of just 70 adobe houses, and nearly everyone lived at the subsistence level. Compared to other Spanish colonies, where conquistadors had acquired vast riches and built impressive cities, Costa Rica seemed like an afterthought.

In an attempt to grow the economy, colonists planted cacao, tobacco and sugarcane. Although a few families grew relatively wealthy, nothing produced widespread economic gains, and colonists' meager profits were heavily taxed by the authorities in Guatemala. At one point, so little silver was in circulation that Costa Rican colonists used cacao beans as currency.

Even the church struggled. Although Costa Rica was officially Catholic, church attendance was notoriously low. In 1711 the nearest bishop, who lived in León, Nicaragua, ordered the construction of three new churches in Costa Rica to boost religious enthusiasm. The colonists were so slow to comply, however, that they were threatened with excommunication.

By 1801 Costa Rica was home to roughly 50,000 people, 83 percent of whom lived in the Central Valley. Living in a remote mountain valley with little to trade, colonists found themselves largely disconnected from the outside world. When Guatemala declared Central America independent from Spain on September 15, 1821, the news didn't reach Costa Rica for a month. Costa Rica was thus taken by surprise when it learned of its own independence.

Following independence, an ideological struggle soon broke out among the Central Valley's four largest towns. Cartago and Heredia wanted to join the new "Mexican Empire" promoted by Mexico, while San José and Alajuela opposed the idea. Representatives from the towns met and agreed to remain neutral "until the clouds of the day disappear." Then, on April 5, 1823, tensions erupted in the Battle of Ochomogo, a one-day confrontation that left 20 people dead. San José and Alajuela emerged victorious, and Costa Rica's capital was moved from Cartago to San José.

Elsewhere in Central America, internal conflicts were even more violent. Nicaragua quickly descended into a bloody civil war following independence, and in 1824 the citizens of its southernmost province, Guanacaste, voted to be annexed by peaceful Costa Rica. Despite many regional tensions, attempts were made to unify Central America. Costa Rica joined the short-lived Federal Republic of Central America, which drafted a federal constitution that proclaimed freedom of thought and abolished slavery.

Costa Rica elected its first head of state, Juan Mora Fernández, in 1824, but within a decade the dictator Braulio Carrillo had come to power. Carrillo declared independence from Central America, abolished many dysfunctional Spanish laws and established a legal code inspired by the French. But his most important contribution was the promotion of a strange new crop: coffee.

REPUBLIC OF COFFEE

AROUND THE TIME Costa Rica acquired its independence, a new crop sprouted up in the Central Valley. No one is sure exactly when the first coffee plants arrived, but they forever altered the course of Costa Rica's history. The "golden grain," as it came to be known, ultimately transformed tiny, poverty-stricken Costa Rica into Central America's most prosperous republic.

Coffee, which grows only at high elevations in the tropics, was first discovered in Ethiopia sometime around the 6th century AD. By the mid-1700s, it had become a fashionable drink in Europe and an important crop in the New World colonies. As luck would have it, Costa Rica's Central Valley offered the perfect conditions for coffee farming: mild temperatures, abundant rainfall and rich volcanic soils. The Central Valley was also home to thousands of small- and medium-sized farms in need of a lucrative crop.

Coffee's potential was huge, but several obstacles stood in the way. Because coffee plants take up to five years to produce beans, poor farmers were reluctant to gamble on the strange new crop. To encourage cultivation, the government offered generous benefits—tax breaks, free land, free coffee plants—to anyone willing to take the chance. The next challenge was finding an export market. On Christmas Day 1843, a British merchant docked his ship in the Pacific port of Puntarenas and took on coffee as cargo. Within two years, 29 ships were transporting coffee to Europe, and England became Costa Rica's largest coffee buyer.

The economic impact was swift and dramatic. By 1853 Costa Rica was shipping seven million pounds of coffee a year—roughly 90% of total exports. As one lawyer put it, coffee made Costa Rica "rich and prosperous in the space of fifteen years, bringing it trade, civilization, population and tax revenues with such increasing rapidity that ... relative to the rest of the Central American Republics, Costa Rica is the one that exports most and so is richest."

Coffee not only enriched Costa Rica, it united the country in a common cause. Prior to coffee, Central Valley towns were constantly bickering over petty disputes. After coffee, everyone focused on *el grano de oro*. Perhaps most important, because Costa Rica's population was small, there was plenty of land to go around. When farmers wanted to plant more coffee, they simply cleared more forest, gradually expanding the frontiers of the Central Valley. In other Central American countries, where populations were large and territory was scarce, land disputes often led to civil war.

Aside from indigenous groups, nearly everyone prospered from the introduction of coffee. But some citizens grew far richer than others. The biggest beneficiaries were the owners of beneficios, large facilities where coffee was processed. Small farmers sold ripe coffee berries to beneficios, where the bean was extracted, dried and packaged for export. Owners of beneficios grew extremely wealthy, creating a small coffee oligarchy—the *cafetaleros*—who effectively controlled the country for the next century.

By the late 1800s, coffee dominated the Costa Rican economy, but nearly all coffee exports were shipped to Europe via the Pacific coast. Because there was no reliable transportation route to the Caribbean coast, coffee was loaded onto wooden ox carts and transported along bumpy dirt roads to the Pacific port of Puntarenas. From there it was shipped to Panama, where it was transported across the isthmus by mule and loaded onto ships waiting on the Caribbean coast. The alternative, sailing all the way around the southern tip of South America, took even longer.

If Costa Rica built a train from the Central Valley to the Caribbean coast, it would dramatically cut transportation costs and boost profits. Unfortunately, a series of steep, treacherous mountains stood in the way. The engineering challenge was far beyond the scope of anyone in Costa Rica, so members of the coffee oligarchy outsourced the job to a U.S. consortium. The railroad that resulted, which came to be known as the "Jungle Train," not only reshaped the history of Costa Rica, it reshaped the history of Central America.

WILLIAM WALKER

& The Battle of Rivas

Although virtually unknown in the U.S., Tennessee native William Walker is one of the most important—and hated—figures in Costa Rica's history. His bizarre attempt to conquer Central America in the mid-1800s made him the original "Gringo Loco" and resulted in Costa Rica's most legendary battle.

Born to a prominent family in 1824, Walker graduated summa cum laude from the University of Nashville at the age of 14. After earning graduate degrees in both medicine and law, he decided on journalism as a profession. He moved to New Orleans, became editor of a liberal newspaper that denounced slavery and married a woman who was deaf and mute. When his wife died in a cholera epidemic, Walker suffered a severe mental breakdown.

Following the Gold Rush to San Francisco, Walker became a wildly popular reporter who exposed corrupt public officials. At one point when a crooked judge jailed him, four thousand citizens gathered to demand his release. But hidden beneath Walker's high moral standards lurked an ominous disposition. Caught up in the expansionist fever that pervaded California (which the U.S. had just acquired from Mexico), Walker hatched a plan to take over Sonora, Mexico.

In 1853 Walker assembled 44 recruits and launched his attack on Sonora. The assault was a disaster. Most of his men died or deserted, and Walker barely made it back with his life. In San Francisco he was brought to trial for violating U.S. law, but he was quickly acquitted by a sympathetic jury. At the time, men like Walker were so common they had a name: "Filibusters"—renegade gringos who tried to conquer land south of the border.

When civil war erupted in Nicaragua in 1854, the 31-year-old Walker smelled opportunity. He offered his support to the citizens of León, who were fighting the citizens of Grenada, and under Walker's leadership León emerged victorious. After the war, Walker became head of the military and took effective control of the country. He confiscated land and declared English Nicaragua's co-official language. Denouncing the label "filibuster," Walker claimed he wanted to "regenerate" Nicaragua by introducing American values and democracy to replace the corrupt vestiges of the Spanish colonial system. Dozens of U.S. newspapers cheered him on. Nicaragua's neighbors, including Costa Rica, were appalled.

Costa Rican President Juan Rafael Mora publicly denounced Walker's actions, claiming the gringo had secret plans to take over all of Central America. Mora pressed his case before the Legislative Assembly, and on March 1, 1856 Costa Rica declared war on Nicaragua. Over 9,000 troops—one in every 12 Costa Ricans—marched towards the border.

When Walker learned of Mora's actions, he launched a preemptive strike in northern Costa Rica. Walker's troops were overwhelmed, however, and they retreated to Nicaragua. The Costa Ricans followed them across the border and on April 11 a battle broke out in the town of Rivas. While Walker's troops were holed up in a building, a Costa Rican drummer boy, Jaun Santamaría, ran over and set fire to the structure. Santamaría was shot and killed, but the fire flushed out Walker's men, who retreated to the capital of Grenada. In the victory celebration that ensued, Costa Rican soldiers threw the bodies of Walker's slain troops into the town's wells. This likely caused a massive cholera outbreak, which forced the Costa Ricans to abandon Nicaragua and head home. Tragically, they brought cholera with them, and over 20% of Costa Rica's population died in the ensuing epidemic.

Walker, meanwhile, faced internal revolt in Nicaragua. In desperation, he held a fraudulent election, assumed the Presidency and repealed the abolition of slavery to gain the support of pro-slavery advocates in the American South. In response, he was chased out of Nicaragua by a coalition of Central American troops backed by Cornelius Vanderbilt, who operated a shipping route through Nicaragua. Walker returned to the U.S., but within a few years he was back in Central America attempting to take over Roatán, Honduras. That attempt also failed, and in 1860 he was executed by a Honduran firing squad.

As the decades passed, the Battle of Rivas took on heroic proportions in Costa Rica. Because the country had effectively gained its independence by mail, Costa Rica lacked a "founding myth" for its citizens to rally around. In the 1880s, savvy politicians promoted the Battle of Rivas as a country-defining event. William Walker became the principal villain of Costa Rican history, and Juan Santamaría, the humble drummer boy, was exalted as a selfless role model for the lower classes.

A century later, in a bizarre twist of fate, a U.S. State Department employee named William Walker became Deputy Assistant Secretary of State for Inter-American Affairs. Walker (no relation to the filibuster) helped administer policy support for the Nicaraguan Contras and was later considered for an ambassadorship in Costa Rica. His name proved too controversial, however, and he was denied the post. Juan Santamaría, meanwhile, became the official name of the international airport in Alajuela—which now welcomes over one million visiting gringos each year.

Juan
Santamaría

COSTA RICA GOES BANANAS

IN 1870 Costa Rica contracted a British company to build a train from the Central Valley to the Caribbean coast. The engineering challenge proved too difficult, however, and the project was abandoned under a pile of debt. In 1884, Costa Rica, still desperate for a train, turned to a U.S. businessman named Minor Keith. In exchange for building the train, Keith was promised a 99-year lease, full control of the port of Limón and 800,000 acres of land alongside the tracks.

The challenges Keith faced were enormous. The terrain was rugged, prone to flooding and—most perilously—plagued with malaria and yellow fever. Keith started out with several hundred Costa Rican workers, but nearly all of them died. He then hired a group of 2,000 primarily Italian workers, but most of them deserted. Next up, a batch of 700 prisoners from New Orleans; only 25 survived. At that point, hardy black workers from Jamaica were brought in and they finally finished the job. By the time the "Jungle Train" was completed in 1890, roughly 5,000 workers had lost their lives during its construction.

To feed his workers, Keith planted bananas alongside the train tracks. To make some extra money he began exporting bananas to the U.S., which turned out to be incredibly lucrative. Within two decades, banana exports equaled the value of coffee exports in Costa Rica, and Keith's banana business had become more profitable than the train itself.

Bananas shook up Costa Rica's economy and its demographics. By 1912 roughly 20,000 English-speaking black Jamaicans had come to Costa Rica to work in the banana industry. Many became small, independent farmers who sold their crop to Keith's United Fruit Company (UFC), which controlled the far more profitable aspects of processing, packing and distribution. Like the coffee industry, the banana industry spawned a small group of wealthy oligarchs. Although the coffee barons welcomed their banana brethren—Keith even married into a wealthy coffee family—tensions flared between banana workers and the UFC.

The first major strike occurred in 1910 to protest, among other things, the UFC practice of paying for bananas in coupons redeemable only at company stores. The stores, which sold imported goods that entered the country tax-free, ensured that virtually none of the banana profits circulated back into the local economy. Labor unrest became a semi-regular occurrence, culminating in a 1934 strike organized by Costa Rican Communists that mobilized 10,000 banana workers.

Despite the problems, banana strife in Costa Rica was far less volatile than in other Central American countries. As U.S. demand for the yellow fruit boomed, banana cultivation spread throughout the region. Jungle was chopped down, bananas were planted and trains were built to transport the crop. Some countries became so dependent on bananas—and so easily manipulated by the United Fruit Company—that they became known as "Banana Republics."

United Fruit Company

Born in Costa Rica in the 1880s, the U.S.-owned United Fruit Company (UFC) became one of the 20th century's most powerful corporations. UFC ships, which transported bananas around the globe, comprised the world's largest private fleet, and UFC hospitals formed the world's largest private health system. But the company's notorious labor practices and government meddling soon made it one of the most detested companies in Latin America.

In Costa Rica, the UFC ruled over the remote Caribbean zone like a feudal lord, inspiring Communist Carlos Luis Fallas to write *Mamita Yunai* ("Mommy United"—as in *Yunai*-ted Fruit). The novel, which portrays the plight of banana workers, is one of Costa Rica's most famous works of literature. As the UFC spread to neighboring countries, so did its notoriety. The term "Banana Republic" was coined by the writer O. Henry in 1905 after he witnessed UFC's political manipulations in Honduras. In 1928 a UFC strike turned deadly in Colombia—a scene dramatized by Gabriel García Márquez in *100 Years of Solitude*. In 1954 UFC encouraged the CIA overthrow of Guatemala's leftist president—an event witnessed by a young Che Guevara. Fidel Castro grew up in a UFC plantation town in Cuba, and in 1961 UFC ships transported Cuban exiles to the Bay of Pigs in an attempt to overthrow him. The UFC became known as *El Pulpo* ("The Octopus") because its tentacles were everywhere. If you've ever wondered about the roots of anti-Americanism in Latin America, the UFC is a good place to start.

Today the former United Fruit Company operates under the Chiquita brand, and in recent years the company has taken many steps to repair its tarnished image. Its Costa Rican bananas are now certified by the Rainforest Alliance, which requires high environmental and labor standards.

COSTA RICA TRANSFORMED

AT THE START of the 19th century, Costa Rica was a poor, self-sufficient country largely ignored by the outside world. By the end of the century, it was exporting millions of pounds of coffee and bananas to Europe and the United States. The export boom not only brought in money, it brought new ideas from Costa Rica's trading partners.

By the mid-1800s, rich coffee oligarchs were sending their children to university in Europe. When the children returned, they brought back new tastes and political ideas. At the same time, many Europeans, fleeing wars and unemployment, moved to balmy Costa Rica to cash in on the coffee boom. Between 1870 and 1920 European immigration represented roughly 25% of Costa Rica's population growth. Costa Rica was happy to accommodate new arrivals, provided they were sufficiently light-skinned; in 1862 Costa Rica passed a law forbidding all non-European immigration.

Meanwhile, the cultivation of bananas brought Costa Rica in close contact with the United States, which was quickly becoming the world's technological and economic leader. In 1884, just two years after New York installed electric streetlights, San José become the first city in Latin America with electric streetlights. Five years later, under the guidance of United Fruit Company owner Minor Keith, San José installed Latin America's first electric streetcar.

As Costa Ricans came into close contact with the outside world, they began to question their own political institutions, which were heavily influenced by the Spanish colonial system. Political reform became a defining feature of 19th century Costa Rica, but it was an incredibly rocky process. Between 1842 and 1871 there were seven coups and six new constitutions. But the *idea* of democracy always remained important, and as the decades progressed the country's democratic institutions gradually strengthened.

Formal education was also introduced in the 19th century. The country's first school opened in 1814, the country's first university was founded in 1843, and the first school for girls opened in 1849. Slowly but surely, education spread throughout Costa Rica. In 1864 the country's illiteracy rate was roughly 90%. By 1892 it had fallen to 65%. Perhaps most notably, the emphasis on schooling coincided with a de-emphasis on the military. By the 1880s the government was spending more money on education than on the military, and there were more schoolteachers than soldiers.

Costa Rica made great strides in the 19th century, but many problems remained. Despite the success of coffee and bananas, the majority of Ticos remained chronically poor. Ironically, Costa Rica developed a typical colonial economy *after* its independence, exporting two basic commodities and importing nearly all manufactured goods. But the international market for commodities was notoriously volatile, as soon became painfully clear.

THE CIVIL WAR OF 1948

BY THE EARLY 20th century, Costa Rica was plugged into the global economy, exporting millions of pounds of coffee and bananas. But exports exposed the tiny country to geopolitical forces beyond its control. As Europe descended into war and the U.S. struggled with the Great Depression, Costa Rica's exports plummeted. Suddenly, the country found itself under severe stress.

Economic turmoil and decreased government spending led to increased social unrest. A series of presidents attempted to establish a progressive income tax, but they were defeated by the powerful coffee oligarchy. The rise of the Soviet Union, meanwhile, inspired the establishment of a local Communist party. (Although in a unique Costa Rican twist, Tico communists denounced class warfare and the suppression of religion.) All of this coincided with the effects of urbanization. By 1927 San José was home to 50,000 people and problems such as crime, prostitution and drug addiction had taken root. Life was changing fast, and many people struggled to cope.

In 1940 Rafael Calderón was elected president. Although born to an elite family, Calderón was a committed social reformer who established social security, founded the University of Costa Rica and increased funding for public housing. Calderón's reforms were loved by the working class and loathed by the coffee oligarchy. After a series of corruption scandals, however, his popular support diminished, pushing him into an alliance with the Communist party. Together they introduced a Labor Code that mandated safe working conditions and guaranteed the right of labor to organize.

But Calderón's Communist alliance, heavy-handed tactics and penchant for corruption alienated much of the country, and in 1948 newspaper publisher Otilio Ulate defeated Calderón for the presidency. In response, Calderón declared the results invalid. His loyalists in the legislature annulled the election, which sent the already polarized country into turmoil.

No one was more outraged than José Figueres, a coffee farmer who had long been one of the president's most vocal critics. Passionate, intellectual and politically savvy, Figueres considered Calderón a dictator and he rallied his countrymen to take up arms in the name of democracy. Figueres had spent years stockpiling weapons at his farm in preparation for armed conflict, and he quickly assembled a rebel insurgency. In response, Calderón's supporters took up arms with the country's 300-man army, vowing to protect the new social reforms.

Significantly, events leading up to the conflict coincided with the start of the Cold War. Figueres recognized this and deftly used it to his advantage by stoking U.S. fears of communism. As a result, the U.S. limited arms sales to Costa Rica and pressured other countries to do the same. When Figueres' forces rose up, the Costa Rican army was ill-equipped, putting Calderón at a strategic disadvantage. In effect, Costa Rica became Latin America's first Cold War battleground.

On March 11, 1948 the first battle erupted in San Isidro del General. Figueres captured the town and immediately sent planes to Guatemala, where the pro-democracy Caribbean Legion (p.156) provided the first of 19 flights supplying weapons and trained militants. With the added support, Figueres won a series of critical battles. By the time a peace agreement was signed on April 19, roughly 2,000 people had died—the deadliest clash in Costa Rica's history.

To calm the raw emotions that lingered after the 1948 election, Figueres was installed as head of a temporary "junta" that ruled the country unilatererally for 18 months. Taking advantage of his sweeping powers, Figueres set to work establishing a "second republic." To the delight of his opponents, Figueres kept all of Calderón's reforms in place. Then he set to work implementing his own reforms.

Figueres gave blacks born in Costa Rica full citizenship and women the right to vote. He nationalized the banks, established state-run public utilities and guaranteed public education for all. To crack down on authoritarian tendencies, Figueres outlawed the Communist party and weakened the power of the executive branch. In a final flourish he abolished Costa Rica's army, taking a sledgehammer to San José's Bella Vista barracks and vowing to turn it into a museum.

By the end of the junta's 18-month reign, it had issued over 800 new laws. Building on a long tradition of pre-existing reforms, José Figueres had seized the moment and reshaped Costa Rican society. By the time Figueres peacefully handed the Presidency to Ulate, Costa Rica had embarked down the brave new path of the "Tropical Welfare State."

JOSE FIGUERES

Considered the most influential President of the 20th century, José Figueres led Costa Rica's 1948 Civil War and served three times in office. "Don Pepe," as he is affectionately known, ushered in the so-called Tropical Welfare State and left his intellectual fingerprints all over modern-day Costa Rica.

The son of Spanish immigrants, José Figueres was born in San Ramón, Costa Rica in 1906. In the 1920s he traveled to the U.S. to study at M.I.T., but he spent most of his time at the Boston Public Library reading books about economics, history and sociology. An admirer of Thomas Jefferson and the U.S. political system, he became a harsh critic of communism, which he felt stifled individual initiative.

When Figueres returned to Costa Rica, he purchased a coffee farm in Tarrazú that he named *La Lucha Sin Fin* ("The Struggle Without End"). Describing himself as a "farmer-socialist," he provided health care and education for all of his workers.

Figueres burst onto the political scene in 1942, when he took to the radio to denounce President Rafael Calderón for allowing his followers to confiscate the property of German and Italian immigrants during World War II. While Figueres was still on the air, police officers stormed into the studio and arrested him. Figueres was exiled to Mexico, where he founded a group called the Caribbean Legion that vowed to overthrow Latin American dictators. Among the group's members were Fidel Castro and Che Guevara, whom Figueres would later part ways with following their embrace of communism in Cuba.

After leading an armed resistance against Calderón in 1948, Figueres came to power in Costa Rica and implemented a series of sweeping social reforms. Many of his ideas seemed crazy. When he abolished Costa Rica's army—an idea inspired by H.G. Wells' *Outline of History*—Figueres declared, "The future of mankind cannot include armed forces." (He then added that police were necessary because "people are imperfect.") Although an ally of the U.S., Figueres frequently spoke out against U.S. support of dictators. With a commanding grasp of both U.S. and Latin American culture, he acted as an intellectual bridge between the two regions and often used his knowledge to outmaneuver U.S. foreign policy in Costa Rica.

Above all else, Figueres was an idealist committed to democracy and social justice. His greatest hope was that his achievements in Costa Rica would someday resonate throughout the region. Towards the end of his life, he stated that Costa Rica's experience offered a deeper and more human revolution than Fidel Castro's Cuba. "This is an exemplary little country," he once told a reporter, "We are the example for Latin America."

THE GOLDEN ERA

FOLLOWING THE CIVIL War of 1948, Costa Rica entered into three decades of nearly uninterrupted peace and growth. After José Figueres stepped down, stable democracy returned and authoritarian tendencies all but vanished from politics. At the same time, the sweeping reforms Figueres initiated delivered impressive results. Large investments were made in education, social security, public health and infrastructure. Hydroelectric dams and rural electrification projects brought cheap power to nearly every corner of Costa Rica.

Figueres' reforms also included a heavy dose of state intervention in the economy. Costa Rica's dependence on two basic commodities—coffee and bananas—made the country extremely vulnerable to external shocks, as the first half of the 20th century had perfectly demonstrated. Poverty, meanwhile, remained stubbornly widespread. Figueres wanted to use state intervention to correct market failures, steering money towards domestic industry to diversify and develop Costa Rica's economy.

The bank nationalizations neatly summed up his philosophy. Instead of private banks reinvesting money in coffee and bananas, which provided the highest returns, a state-run bank would reinvest money in workers and small businesses. This, combined with high taxes on imports to promote Costa Rican products, was the plan to break the cycle of underdevelopment. It was a mixed economy that, in the words of Figueres, tried "to pull together the benefits of [the capitalist and communist systems], and reduce the disadvantages of each."

Things got off to a great start. The 1950s and 60s are fondly remembered as the "Golden Era" of Costa Rica. The millionth child was born in 1956, and a sense of optimism prevailed. Jobs were plentiful, crime was low and living standards were on the rise. By 1960 roughly 30% of the government budget was devoted to education. Exports benefitted from a booming global economy, and the new reforms initiated by Figueres reduced income inequality. Figueres proved so popular that he was elected president in 1953 and again in 1970.

Costa Rica was making great strides, but many politicians grew impatient with the pace of change, so they doubled down on state-led development. Instead of simply nudging the economy in a particular direction, the state became directly involved in a wide range of industries. This strategy, creating state-run businesses to diversify the economy, became popular throughout Latin America.

But there was a fatal flaw in the plan: state-run companies were highly vulnerable to direct political manipulation, and corruption became endemic. Instead of profits the companies generated massive debts, and failing companies were propped up to preserve jobs. In the 1970s government spending increased by a factor of ten while tax revenue remained flat. To cover the growing deficit, Costa Rica took out progressively larger loans from international lenders. It was an unsustainable strategy, and the bill was about to come due.

THE 1980S: A DECADE OF CRISIS

BY THE MID-1970s, Costa Rica's economy seemed to be producing impressive results. Unemployment was low and living standards were improving. On a wide range of social indicators—life expectancy, literacy, infant mortality—Costa Rica outperformed its neighbors. But the economic prosperity was built on an illusion. By 1979 one in five workers was employed by the government, which officially accounted for a quarter of the economy. Others pegged that number closer to 50%. Most troubling, the expansion of government was fueled entirely by debt.

In the 1970s international banks were eager to lend to Latin American countries, whose soaring economies seemed like the wave of the future. By 1980 Costa Rica's foreign debt per capita was among the highest in the world. But when the global economy turned south, creditors grew nervous and stopped lending. Suddenly, Costa Rica could not even pay the interest on its debt.

In 1981 Costa Rica defaulted on its foreign debt. The consequences were swift and dramatic. Inflation topped 100%, the colón lost roughly 70% of its value against the dollar, and the poverty rate swelled to 54%. Large slums popped up around San José, and people covered their houses with metal bars and razor wire. Tragically, Costa Rica's default was just the tip on the iceberg. Throughout Latin America, country after country defaulted on massive debts that had grown in a frenzy of easy lending and state-led development. Economic growth collapsed, and the 1980s became known as Latin America's "Lost Decade."

The debt crisis was mirrored by a political crisis in Nicaragua, Costa Rica's troubled northern neighbor. In 1979 Sandinista revolutionaries overthrew the corrupt dictator Anastasio Somoza, whose family had ruled over Nicaragua for five decades. Somoza's human rights abuses were infamous, and Costa Rica provided critical early support to the Sandinistas. But once in power, the revolutionaries adopted increasingly Marxist and anti-democratic policies. Many inside and outside of Nicaragua grew suspicious of the Sandinistas, who aligned with Cuba and the Soviet Union. In response, a group of Nicaraguan "Contras" formed to overthrow the Sandinistas.

The internal struggle between the Sandinistas and the Contras quickly morphed into a geopolitical struggle between U.S. President Ronald Reagan and the Sandinista's communist/socialist sympathizers. In the eyes of Reagan, a Soviet-aligned Nicaragua was a destabilizing force in the region and a potential beachhead for nuclear weapons. Determined to prevent a "second Cuba," Reagan armed and trained the Contras.

At the same time, leftist insurgencies erupted in El Salvador and Guatemala. As much of Central America descended into a series of bloody civil wars, Costa Rica stood out as an oasis of peace and democracy. It was a powerful example for the troubled region. But with Costa Rica's economy in free fall, U.S. officials worried that it too could fall prey to radicalism and revolution. Costa Rican leaders,

desperate for U.S. cash, deftly played up these fears. To prop up the country as a stabilizing force in the region, U.S. officials bailed out Costa Rica. In 1981 the U.S. gave Costa Rica $20 million in economic assistance. The following year that number jumped to $90 million. And from 1983–1985, the U.S. gave $200 million a year to Costa Rica. These cash infusions stabilized the critically wounded banking system, which had run out of foreign reserves.

At the same time, Costa Rica turned to the International Monetary Fund and the World Bank for emergency loans. These lenders-of-last-resort offered Costa Rica an economic lifeline, but with strings attached. In exchange for emergency loans, Costa Rica was required to reduce the size of government, eliminate trade barriers and privatize government-run businesses. These reforms, which later came to be known as "neoliberal," were a drastic reversal from Costa Rica's previous development strategy. Instead of focusing on limiting foreign imports and developing internally, the neoliberal model pushed for increasing exports through foreign investment in private industry.

Because the new model required drastic changes—particularly a reduction in government and promotion of the private sector—it generated backlash among the left. A few Costa Ricans even accused the U.S., the IMF and the World Bank of intentionally undermining the country's cherished social institutions. Most controversial was the privatization of the banking system. Private banks, it was feared, would not take the necessary steps to diversify the economy away from traditional agricultural exports. But with the flaws of the old model laid bare, Costa Rican leaders supported the new reforms.

RESTORING THE PEACE

AS THE NICARAGUAN war between left-wing Sandinistas and right-wing Contras raged in the 1980s, Costa Rica found itself dragged into the struggle. Although Costa Rica originally backed the Sandinistas, it switched its support to the Contras after the Sandinistas veered away from democracy and towards the Soviet Union. The Contras, who used northern Costa Rica as a staging ground for rebel attacks, were armed by U.S. President Ronald Reagan, who had vowed to remove the left-wing Sandinistas from power.

In 1986 Oscar Arias was elected President on a promise of restoring neutrality and pacifism to Costa Rica's foreign policy. Shortly after taking office, he shut down a secret CIA airfield in northern Costa Rica that was used to aid the Contras. Arias' actions incensed the Reagan administration, which immediately suspended millions of aid payments to Costa Rica. The aid was ultimately restored, but Reagan's problems had only just begun. Within months, Reagan associate Oliver North was caught illegally selling arms to Iran and secretly funneling the profits to the Contras. This circumvented the 1982 Boland Amendment, which barred Reagan from arming the Contras "for the purpose of overthrowing the Government of Nicaragua." The political scandal, known as the Iran-Contra affair, significantly weakened the U.S. President.

The political blow to Reagan opened a window of opportunity for Arias, who had crafted a regional peace plan. The plan called for suspension of aid to the Contras and the recognition of the Sandinistas as the legitimate government of Nicaragua—provided that they hold democratic elections. The Reagan administration, which continued to argue for a military solution, opposed the plan because it legitimized the Sandinistas. Other Central American presidents worried that the Sandinistas might actually win the elections. But Arias stood firm. He was convinced that a democratic solution was the only true path to long-term peace in the region. Against long odds, he convinced Nicaraguan leader Daniel Ortega to accept the proposal.

In August 1987 the leaders of five Central American countries signed the Esquipulas II Accord, which was based on the Arias peace plan. It was a powerful assertion of regional sovereignty. Rather than buckle to pressure from foreign powers, the accord put Central Americans in charge of Central America. Although the plan did not end the fighting immediately, it set in place a broad roadmap for future peace.

For his efforts pursuing the peace accord, Oscar Arias was awarded the 1987 Nobel Peace Prize. When free and fair elections were held in Nicaragua in 1990, the Sandinistas were voted out of power—much to their surprise. And by the mid-1990s, the wars in both Guatemala and El Salvador were finally winding down. By the time the fighting had ended, the Central American civil wars had claimed over 250,000 lives.

OSCAR ARIAS

Over the past fifty years, no Costa Rican president has been more consequential than Oscar Arias. Born to a wealthy coffee family in 1940, Arias studied at the University of Costa Rica and the London School of Economics before entering politics. In 1986, in the midst of an economic crisis and civil war in neighboring Nicaragua, he was elected President of Costa Rica.

Although Costa Rica was heavily dependent on U.S. aid when Arias took office, he stood up to Ronald Reagan's aggressive foreign policy in the region. Arias shut down U.S.-backed Contra bases in Costa Rica and pushed a Central American peace plan that stressed disarmament and democracy. Against long odds, the Arias peace plan prevailed and helped end the bloody wars that plagued Central America in the 1980s. In 1987 Arias was awarded the Noble Peace Prize for his efforts. "This prize," said Arias, "is a recognition of Costa Rica, of the way we are and the way we think, and of what Costa Rica is worth to the whole world." Following his presidency, Arias was elevated to near sainthood in Costa Rica.

In 2003 Arias lobbied to overturn a constitutional amendment barring former presidents from seeking re-election, and in 2006 he was re-elected president. His signature accomplishment was passage of the U.S.-proposed Central American Free Trade Agreement—a move that enraged many on the left. Although a slim majority of Costa Ricans supported the president, anti-Arias graffiti covered San José and his once sky-high popularity was deeply tarnished.

In 2009 Arias gave a speech at a summit of Latin American leaders. After listening to anti-American diatribes by Hugo Chávez and others, Arias chastised the group for blaming the U.S. for "our past, present and future problems." As Arias put it, "Latin Americans did something wrong ... we have an average of 7 years of education ... In our countries taxes cover about 12% of the gross national product and it isn't anyone's responsibility other than ours that we don't charge more to the wealthiest people in our countries ... I ask myself: who is our enemy? ... It's the lack of education. It's illiteracy. It's the fact that we don't spend on our people's health." Arias denounced excessive military spending, then pointed to Asia as a role model. He pointed out that several Asian countries had been poorer than Latin American countries 50 years ago, but after reforming their economies and focusing on education they were now far richer. "While we continue arguing about 'isms' (which is better, capitalism, socialism, communism, liberalism, neoliberalism, sociochristianism?) the Asians found a very realistic 'ism' for the 21st Century ... pragmatism." It was an ideology that Oscar Arias had embodied for decades.

A NEW MILLENNIUM

BY THE YEAR 2000, Costa Rica was a country transformed. In the 1970s it was economically isolated and dependent on a handful of agricultural crops. Following the financial crisis and deep economic reforms of the 1980s, Costa Rica finally achieved what had always eluded it: a diversified economy. Services, tourism and manufactured exports formed the new foundation of the economy.

This dramatic shift was perfectly illustrated when President José Maria Figueres (the son of José Figueres) personally courted tech-giant INTEL to open a factory in Costa Rica. Shortly after the factory opened in 1997, microchips became Costa Rica's number one export. By 2006 Costa Rica was exporting over $1 billion worth of microchips each year—roughly 7% of GDP. Dozens of high tech firms followed INTEL's lead, opening call centers and regional offices to service the growing Latin American market. High-paying tech jobs blossomed, and parts of San José, Costa Rica began to resemble San José, California.

Tourism also boomed. By 1994 tourists were generating more money than coffee or bananas. Particularly important was eco-tourism, which benefitted from Costa Rica's excellent system of national parks. Eco-tourism brought economic opportunity to rural areas that had previously been neglected and fostered a dramatic shift in environmental thinking. Rather than viewing forest as something to be cleared to make way for farms and ranches, many Costa Ricans began viewing forest as something to be protected for future generations.

As steady growth continued throughout the 1990s, lawmakers gradually deepened the economic reforms. But when lawmakers tried to privatize the government-run electric/telecommunication company ICE (prounounced "EEE-say"), massive protests erupted. ICE, which had brought electricity and telephone service to the most remote and poverty-stricken corners of Costa Rica, was a cherished public institution. It was also one of the last remaining symbols of the post-1948 reforms that had ushered in Costa Rica's Golden Era. People took to the streets, and lawmakers scrapped the privatization plans.

Then, in 2005, the U.S. proposed the Central American Free Trade Agreement (CAFTA). The agreement (known as the TLC, *Tratado de Libre Comercio*, in Costa Rica) offered Central American countries permanent duty-free access to U.S. markets. In exchange, Costa Rica would need to offer duty-free access for U.S. products—and allow private companies to compete with ICE.

CAFTA sparked massive protests, polarizing the country and rekindling old intellectual battles. Many felt it was akin to selling out Costa Rica to foreign interests, an updated version of the United Fruit Company. Some feared that small Costa Rican companies would not be able to compete with the potential flood of U.S. products. Others simply did not want more integration with the U.S., which had lost much of its credibility in the region following the onset of the Iraq War.

INTEL Factory

In some ways, however, CAFTA was not such a radical departure from the status quo. Since the 1980s, the U.S. had allowed Central American products to enter the U.S. duty free as a way to encourage economic development in the region. But that access was not guaranteed, and it needed to be periodically renewed. Meanwhile, many Central America countries placed high tariffs on products imported from the U.S., including technology products like computers that helped small- and medium-sized businesses.

Although other Central American nations quickly approved the treaty, Costa Rica held out. The biggest sticking point was ICE. But despite the universal appreciation of the company's past contributions, many people had become fed up with the bloated and inefficient company. As the sole provider of mobile phones, ICE was a government-run monopoly, and its service often reflected that. Although its prices were low, waiting lists and long lines were common.

When Oscar Arias was re-elected president in 2006, he threw his weight behind CAFTA. The support of Arias was critical. No one could honestly accuse the Nobel Prize-winner of being a stooge of the U.S. But despite his endorsement, the treaty repeatedly stalled in the Legislature. In a bold move, Arias put the fate of CAFTA in the hands of the voters by organizing an unprecedented direct referendum. It passed with just 51.6% of the vote. As with his peace accord two decades earlier, Arias gambled on democracy—and won. Although opponents continued to fight CAFTA in the courts, it was ultimately signed into law in December 2008.

COSTA RICA TODAY

IN TODAY'S GLOBALIZED world, Costa Rica is more connected to outside influences than ever before. In 1988 just 29% of the population had a telephone. In 2012 over 90% of homes had a mobile phone, 46% had a computer and 34% were connected to the Internet. Smartphones are quickly becoming ubiquitous, and nearly every young Tico uses Facebook and other social networks. Although people retain a strong sense of what it means to be Tico, life is changing fast.

The rapid technological changes mirror rapid social changes, as Costa Rica shifts from a mostly rural to a mostly urban society. In the 1960s, Costa Rica's Central Valley was covered with coffee farms and the average family had seven children. Today, the Central Valley is covered with shopping centers and the average family has just two children. Along the coast, a large influx of tourists and expats has also caused big changes in some beach towns. Nearly 90% of coastal real estate is owned by foreigners, leading some Ticos to feel like strangers in their own country.

Today, Costa Rica has one of the highest standards of living in Latin America, thanks in large part to the country's long history of economic and social reform. In 2014 the literacy rate was 96%, GDP per capita (PPP) was $12,900 and the average lifespan was 79 years (the same as the U.S.). But despite Costa Rica's many successes, most Ticos hold a surprisingly low view of their government. According to a recent poll, just 40% of Ticos trust the government, and less than 3% are active in political parties. Some of this cynicism can be traced to corruption scandals that landed two former presidents in jail while a third fled to Europe. The scandals, which involved over $12 million in bribes, simply confirmed the suspicions of many Ticos about that their government is rife with corruption.

Suspicion of government was on full display in 2012 when President Laura Chinchilla attempted to raise taxes to cover a gaping hole in the social security fund. The public uproar stopped the plan dead in its tracks and delivered Chinchilla the lowest approval rating of any president in Latin America. Although tax evasion is rampant—by some estimates roughly one-third of taxes go unpaid—most people were loath to throw more money at the public sector, which is widely viewed as a piggybank for the well-connected. Many public sector jobs pay double the salaries of their private sector equivalents, and public sector salaries make up a whopping 50% of the government budget.

Although Ticos are clearly unhappy with some aspects of their government, 68% of Ticos consider Costa Rica "better than other countries." And though just 24% of Ticos report feeling "very satisfied" with democracy, 90% report that "under no circumstances" would they support a military government—by far the highest percentage in Latin America.

In recent years narcotrafficking has become one of the country's most serious concerns. Sandwiched between South America producers and U.S. consumers,

Costa Rica has become a major transit route for the roughly 300 tons of cocaine consumed by the U.S. each year. Authorities now seize several tons of cocaine annually, and cocaine use in Costa Rica is on the rise. In 2010 roughly 3% of Ticos admitted to having tried cocaine, up from 0.5% in 1990.

Narcotrafficking has been a long simmering problem, but a more dramatic shock came from the 2008 U.S. financial crisis. The U.S. accounts for roughly 40% of Costa Rican exports, 50% of tourists and two-thirds of foreign investment. As a popular saying goes, when the U.S. sneezes, Costa Rica catches a cold. Yet in stark contrast to past crises, which often led to social and political unrest, Costa Rica's newly diversified economy proved remarkably resilient.

Of course, some areas were harder hit than others. In the years leading up to the crisis, several popular beach towns experienced a real estate boom that mirrored the bubble in the U.S. As prices in the U.S. skyrocketed, Costa Rica was promoted as an affordable destination for expats and retirees. In some towns, most notably Jacó and Tamarindo, condo towers and gated communities exploded in popularity. But when the bubble burst, everything ground to a halt. Even today many developments remain vacant or half-finished.

In the Central Valley, where most Costa Ricans live, it was an entirely different story. The years following the crisis were marked by a boom in new development. Cranes dotted the skyline and luxury malls expanded in posh suburbs. Condo towers and gated communities flourished. The technology industry continued to expand, with high tech-products (electronics, optics, medical equipment) making up 75% of exports.

The changes in the Central Valley reflect both the promise and the problems of the new Costa Rica. Since the economic reforms of the 1980s, nearly all Costa Ricans have benefitted from economic growth, but the rich and educated have benefitted far more than others. Between 1994 and 2004 rich incomes doubled while poor incomes grew by just seven percent. Large slums are now located a stone's throw from some of the wealthiest neighborhoods in Costa Rica.

Perhaps most alarming, as inequality has risen, public investments in infrastructure, education, health services and security have lagged. While the affluent send their children to good private schools, public schools are chronically underfunded. Today, just 40% of students complete high school. The debt-ridden public health system is plagued with long lines and waiting lists, and homicides have doubled since 1995. In 2011 there were less than 300 police patrol vehicles for the entire country. Not surprisingly, a paltry 15% of Ticos consider public security "good or very good," and 61% believe the country is becoming less safe.

Yet despite these gloomy statistics, it's important to note that Costa Rica has faced many challenges since its independence nearly two centuries ago, and it has generally risen to the occasion. Its strong tradition of democracy and social reform has consistently, if slowly, moved the country forward. That probably explains why a sky-high 88% of Ticos recently reported that they were "satisfied with their lives"—the highest percentage in Latin America.

THE CENTRAL VALLEY

THIS BROAD MOUNTAIN valley is the cultural, economic and political heart of Costa Rica. Home to nearly three million people—about two-thirds of the country's total population—it's a sprawling metropolis centered around San José, the capital and largest city. The Central Valley is also home to Costa Rica's largest international airport, which means the majority of visitors pass through here at some point on their trip.

The Central Valley is bounded by the Talamanca Mountains to the south and a chain of volcanoes—Poás, Barva, Irazú, Turrialba—to the north. The valley, which is roughly 70 km (43 miles) long by 20 km (12 miles) wide, has an elevation of 800–1,500 meters (2,620–4,920 feet). Throughout the year temperatures vary between 17–26°C (63–79°F), resulting in a climate often referred to as "Eternal Spring." The only downside is abundant rain, about 2 meters (6.5 feet) a year, most of which falls between May and November.

The Central Valley is home to four major towns: San José, Heredia, Alajuela and Cartago. A century ago these towns were separated by vast coffee fields, but urban sprawl has long since merged San José, Heredia and Alajuela into one interconnected city. Cartago, which is physically separated from the other towns by a narrow mountain pass, has escaped some of the sprawl, which is why I've included it in the Southern Mountains chapter.

Sadly, the Central Valley has grown with virtually no planning, resulting in a congested maze of unmarked streets. Public infrastructure is inadequate, traffic is bad and getting worse, and crime is a growing problem. As wealthier Ticos have fled the urban core, previously low-key suburbs (most notably Escazú) have become increasingly overdeveloped. No wonder most tourists flee the Central Valley in favor of more scenic destinations.

That said, the Central Valley is home to a handful of worthwhile attractions. In addition to what I call the "Big Three"—downtown San José, Poás Volcano, the La Paz Waterfall Gardens—there are some interesting destinations scattered around Cartago (p.241). And if you're a nature junkie who can't stand the thought of spending your last night in Costa Rica surrounded by urban sprawl, consider one of the ecolodges near La Selva in Puerto Viejo de Sarapiquí (p.188), a small jungle town located two hours from the international airport in Alajuela.

SAN JOSÉ

COSTA RICA'S CAPITAL and largest city is a gritty concrete jungle home to 360,000 people (a number that swells to over one million if you include greater San José). If you've been dreaming of tropical paradise, San José will certainly let you down. The city is dominated by grime, crime, traffic and bad 1970s architecture. These days opinions on San José tend to fall into one of two categories: those who don't like it, and those who insist it isn't nearly as bad as everyone claims.

Yet scattered among the post-modern carnage are just enough museums, parks and historic sites to keep things interesting. Despite San José's bad reputation, you can easily spend an enjoyable day here. And if you've never visited a city in the developing world, San José is an eye-opening experience.

But let's be honest. With so much natural beauty lying *outside* of San José, it's foolish to focus your time in the city. So don't put San José on your "must-see" list. But don't write it off entirely, either. If your schedule leaves you with some extra time in San José, the city is definitely worth checking out. And if you'd rather not explore the congested urban core, there are some great rural attractions— national parks, wildlife centers, coffee tours—on the outskirts of town.

Although San José has recently fallen on hard times, a century ago it was exceptionally lovely. When the great Nicaraguan poet Rubén Darío visited in 1891, he declared that San José was "among the most enchanting of Central American cities." As late as the 1960s, San José was still charming and safe, but as urbanization accelerated new problems popped up that were never fully addressed. During the 1980s, a time of economic and political crisis in Central America, the decline accelerated, and San José never fully recovered. Adding insult to injury, many of downtown's most beautiful historic buildings were torn down to make way for parking lots and strip malls.

As the urban core festered, San José's wealthiest residents fled to the upscale suburb of Escazú, located 6 km (3.7 miles) west of downtown. Today Escazú is jam-packed with expensive condo towers and high-end shopping centers. It's as if, sometime in the 1990s, Costa Rica's elite took one look at downtown San José, shrugged and decided to build an entirely new city in Escazú.

In recent years, however, a glimmer of an urban revival has begun in Bario Amón, a once-grand neighborhood located just north of downtown. Home to wealthy coffee barons in the late 1800s, Barrio Amón has more recently become famous for its large concentration of brothels and transvestite streetwalkers. But artists and hipsters are now moving into the historic buildings, and there are a handful of charming shops, restaurants and boutique hotels.

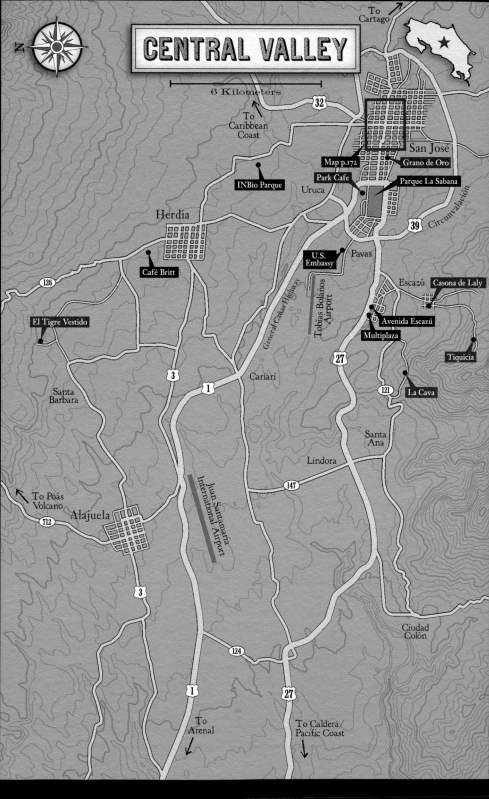

Getting to San José

Nearly all international visitors fly into Jaun Santamaría Airport in Alajuela, located 20 km (12.5 miles) northwest of downtown San José (30-minute drive without traffic). Airport taxis (2221-6865) are orange, and they will take you to downtown San José for $25–35. Both Interbus and Grayline (p.20) offer shuttles from the airport to most hotels in San José for around $15 per person (reservations required). Many hotels also offer airport shuttles. Buses (₡550) depart the bus stop in front of the airport for downtown San José every 10 minutes. (Make sure you get on the bus to San José, not Alajuela.) Both red TUASA buses and tan Station Wagon buses head to Ave 2, Calle 12/14, across from Parque La Merced.

There's also the small Tobías Bolaños airport, which is popular for regional flights, in Pavas, 8 km (5 miles) west of downtown San José (20-minute drive). Pavas can be a sketchy neighborhood, so it's best to take a taxi to/from here.

Getting Around San José

Greater San José is a jumble of unmarked streets (p.21), many of which are one-way. Driving here is extremely challenging, even for people used to aggressive, big city driving. The best way to get around is by taxi. If you hail a taxi on the street, make sure it's an official, licensed taxi (p.20). Although public buses are cheap and reliable, the routes can be confusing. I don't recommend using buses in San José unless you have a good grasp of Spanish and familiarity with navigating cities in Latin America.

San José Hotels

Downtown San José has a wide range of hotels, but due to the gritty nature of downtown, some people prefer staying in the upscale suburb of Escazú, a 15-minute taxi ride away. There's also a wide range of hotels near the airport, but values there are hard to find. If you're looking for value, it can be more cost-effective to stay in San José or an adjacent suburb and take a taxi or shuttle to/from the airport. Visit www.jameskaiser.com for complete San José hotel info.

Staying Safe in San José

During the day, San José is very safe. With the possible exception of pickpockets, there's very little to worry about. At night, however, San José can become dangerous. Do not wander around downtown San José at night, especially if you're alone. At night it's always best to take a taxi to/from your destination.

To avoid pickpockets, don't look like a tourist. First and foremost, don't wear shorts. Very few people wear shorts in San José, and bare legs stand out. Also avoid loud Hawaiian shirts and vibrant fleece/synthetic clothes. Don't wear a big camera around your neck, and don't stare at fold-out maps in the middle of public spaces. Place your wallet in your front pocket and hang on to your purse.

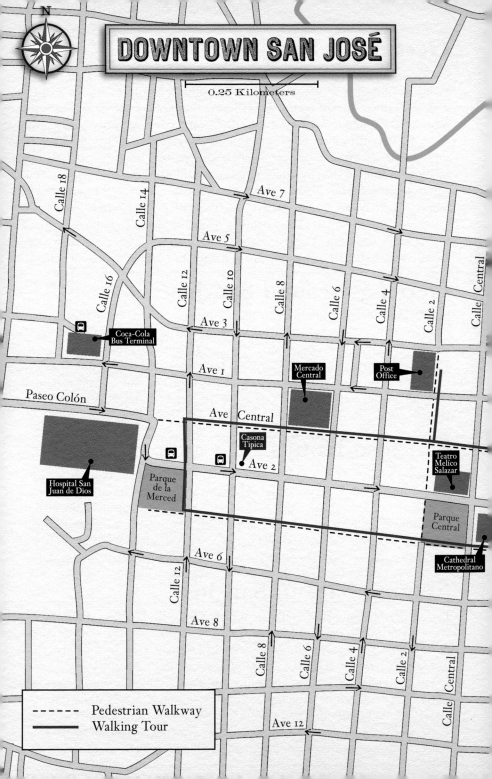

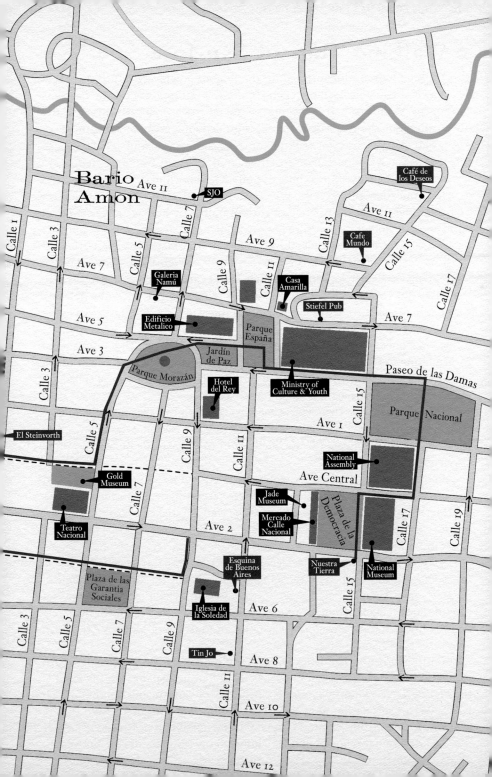

★Walking Tour of San José

This walking tour, outlined in red on the map of downtown San José, covers downtown's highlights. Plan on a half-day for the full route, but if you have less time, focus on the first half of the tour. In the rainy season it's best to start early due to afternoon showers. For an excellent guided tour, get in touch with Stacey Auch, who offers a variety of walking tours, including food and art tours. Cost: $28. (6050-1952, www.toursanjosecostarica.com). Urban Adventures (4000-5730, www.sanjoseurbanadventures.com) also offers walking and culture tours.

Start your tour with a typical breakfast of *chorreadas* or *tamales* at Nuestra Tierra Restaurant (p.182), where rustic decorations pay homage to Costa Rica's agricultural history. Be sure to order a *chorreador* of coffee (p.69).

Next, head across the street to the Plaza de la Democracia, which is overlooked by the imposing yellow National Museum (p.176). The museum is housed in the former Bellavista Fortress, which was once used as an army barracks. It was here that José Figueres abolished the army in 1948 (p.156). Notice the bullet holes on the building's side turrets. These remnants of the 1948 Civil War have been left as reminders of the war's violence and bloodshed. The entrance to the museum is located in front of a space-aged metal and glass sculpture, which houses a giant pre-Columbian stone sphere (p.67). On the northwest side of the Plaza de la Democracia is the modern new Jade Museum, which houses the largest collection of pre-Columbian Jade artifacts in the Americas.

From the Plaza de la Democracia head to Calle Central (aka Cuesta de Moras) and turn right. As you head up the hill, you'll pass the National Assembly, Costa Rica's legislative chamber. The outside wall of this charming building is often covered with angry graffiti.

After passing the National Assembly, turn left and head to Parque Nacional. This lovely park is filled with statues of famous Latin Americans, including Cuba's Jose Martí and Mexico's Miguel Hidalgo. The statue in the center of the park celebrates Costa Rica's defeat of William Walker, a *gringo loco* who tried to conquer Costa Rica in 1856 (p.148).

From the north end of Parque Nacional head down the street called *Paseo de las Damas*, which is named for the *damas* trees that line the street. The name of the tree comes from its long clusters of yellow fruit, which reminded early settlers of the braided blond hair of European women. Head west down the street and you'll pass the entrance to the Costa Rican Museum of Modern Art, which showcases consistently quirky exhibits.

Continue down Paseo de las Damas, but before crossing the bridge, turn right and head down the stairs towards leafy Parque España. On the right is the *Ministerio de Cultura y Juventud* ("Ministry of Culture and Youth"), which is located in a former liquor factory. Take a quick peek inside to see if they're hosting any interesting cultural events. On the north end of Parque España is the *Casa Amarilla* ("Yellow Building"), home to the Ministry of Foreign Affairs.

From the southwest corner of Parque España, head west to the *Jardín de Paz* ("Peace Garden") in front of the *Edificio Metálico* ("Metal Building"). This striking metal building was pre-fabricated in Belgium then assembled in Costa Rica in the late 1800s. Today it's a school for roughly 1,000 local children.

Continue west to Parque Morazán, distinguished by a neoclassical dome in the center. The park is named for Francisco Morazán, a Honduran revolutionary who overthrew Costa Rica's government in 1842 in an attempt to unite Central America. The citizens of Costa Rica revolted against Morazán, however, and he was executed by firing squad in the park that now bears his name. The dome in the center of the park, called the *Templo de Música* ("Music Temple"), is often used as a bandstand for public concerts.

From Parque Morazán, head south down Calle 5 towards the Plaza de la Cultura. Along the way you'll pass a handful of beautiful old buildings, which are sadly uncommon in San José these days. At the Plaza de la Cultura you'll find the Pre-Columbian Gold Museum (p.176) and the National Theater (p.177), both of which are worth a visit.

Next, head west along Ave Central, a bustling pedestrian boulevard. Turn right on Calle 2 and head to the *Oficina de Correos* ("Post Office). After taking a quick peek inside this beautiful building, head back to Ave Central and continue west until you reach Calle 6. At the corner of Calle 6 and Ave Central is the *Mercado Central* ("Central Market"), a covered shopping area filled with small vendors selling produce and knickknacks. There are also some *sodas* (budget restaurants) selling typical Costa Rican food. Note: The Mercado Central is notorious for pickpockets. Be alert!

Continue west along Ave Central, then head two blocks south along Calle 12 until you reach *Parque de la Merced* ("Park of Mercy"). Bounded by the pretty Iglesia La Merced on the east and the Hospital San Juan de Dios to the west, Parque de la Merced is a popular hangout for Nicaraguan immigrants (p.57).

Continue south to the pedestrian walkway along Ave 4, then head six blocks east to Parque Central, distinguished by an imposing arched dome. To the north is the beautiful yellow Melico Salazar Theater, which is a great place to check out a live music or theater performance. To the east is the Cathedral Metropolitana, the largest and most important Cathedral in San José.

Continue east along Ave 4 to the *Plaza de las Garantia Sociales* ("The Plaza of Social Guarantees"). The plaza's name is a reference to the *Caja*, Costa Rica's Social Security System, which is headquartered in the tall, ugly building on the north end of the plaza.

Continue east along Ave 4 to the *Iglesia Señora Nuestra de la Soledad* ("Church of Our Lady of Solitude"), a pretty colonial church alongside Calle 9. The surrounding neighborhood has a substantial Chinese population, and in 2012 it was declared "Chinatown," much to the satisfaction of Costa Rica's new best friend (p.179). As such, it's a fitting place to end this historic walking tour and re-enter the 21st century.

Museums

★ NATIONAL MUSEUM

Located in the Bellavista Fortress (a former army barracks that was converted into a museum after the army was abolished in 1948), the *Museo Nacional de Costa Rica* features an impressive collection of archaeological artifacts, a butterfly garden and some good rotating exhibits. Open 8:30am–4:15pm. Closed Monday. Admission: $8 adults, children under 12 free. Located on the eastern side of Plaza de la Democracia. Calle 15, Ave 2/Central. (2257-1433, www.museocostarica.go.cr)

★ PRE-COLUMBIAN GOLD MUSEUM

The *Museo del Oro Precolombino* displays Costa Rica's largest collection of gold artifacts, including exhibits detailing the gold-shaping process. Open 9:15am–5pm. $11 adults, $8 students, children under 12 free. The museum is located next to the National Theater, under the Plaza de la Cultura. The entrance is accessible from Calle 5, Ave 2/Central. (2243-4202, www.museosdelbancocentral.org)

★ JADE MUSEUM

The *Museo de Jade* showcases the largest collection of jade artifacts in the Americas. In addition to jade, the collection includes some of Costa Rica's most impressive pottery and stone sculptures. Open 8:30am–3:30pm. Closed Sunday. Admission: $9, children under 12 free. Located near the northwestern corner of Plaza de la Democracia. Calle 13, Ave Central (2287-6034, www.portal.ins-cr.com)

The National Theater

Located in the heart of downtown San José, the *Teatro Nacional* is considered the most beautiful building in Costa Rica. Opened in 1897, it is a scale replica of the Opéra Comique in Paris, reflecting Costa Rica's 19th century obsession with all things French. The opulent interior is decorated in Italian marble and Costa Rican tropical hardwoods.

The idea for a grand National Theater was born in 1888, after a powerful earthquake destroyed San José's previous theater. Although new plans were quickly drawn up, construction was delayed until an Italian opera star touring Central America refused to visit Costa Rica because it lacked a suitable venue. Stung by the insult, the Costa Rica government implemented a special coffee export tax to pay for construction of the million-dollar venue. At the time, San José was a city of dirt roads, and shortly after the National Theater opened a foreign visitor described it as a "jewel in a mudhole."

The National Theater is open from 9am–6pm Dec–April, 9am–4pm (closed Sundays) May–Nov. There's a nice cafe on the first floor as well as a small giftshop. Bilingual tours of the theater are available every hour on the hour, except noon ($7 adults, children under 12 free). The best way to experience the theater, however, is to attend a live performance. Tickets often cost less than $12, and the schedule is listed on the theater's website (www.teatronacional.go.cr). The National Theater is located at Ave 2, Calle 3/5. Tel: 2221-1100

Shopping
★ FERIAS

Open-air markets, called *ferias*, are one of the best ways to absorb the local culture. On Saturday mornings there's a great feria in Pavas (10-minute taxi ride from downtown) and the upscale, organic *Feria Verde* in Aranjuez, northeast of Barrio Amón. On Sunday mornings the country's biggest feria is in Zapote (10-minute taxi ride from downtown).

GALERÍA NAMÚ

This fair-trade gallery showcases an impressive collection of handmade crafts from indigenous artisans. Ave 7, Calle 5/7. (2256-3412, www.galerianamu.com)

KIOSCO SJO

To check out Costa Rica's contemporary design scene, head to this trendy boutique in Barrio Amón. Ave 11, Calle 7. (2258-1829, www.kioscosjo.com)

MERCADO CALLE NACIONAL

This crowded street market, located at the western end of Plaza de Democracia, offers a vast selection of tourist souvenirs.

Nightlife
★ JAZZ CAFÉ

The best place for live music—salsa, rock, reggae—in San José. Jazz Café operates two locations, one in the university neighborhood of San Pedro (10-minute taxi ride east of downtown) and one in Escazú (10-minute taxi ride west of downtown). Check their website for upcoming shows. (www.jazzcafecostarica.com)

EL CUARTEL DE LA BOCA DEL MONTE

This longtime favorite, located in Barrio La California, often features live music and is popular with 20- and 30-somethings. Ave 1, Calle 21/23.

STIEFEL PUB

This upbeat, laid-back pub in Barrio Amón features an impressive selection of Costa Rican craft beers, including one you can drink from a glass boot. Food includes burgers and sandwiches. Closed Sunday. Ave 7, Calle 13/15. (8569-5555)

EL STEINVORTH

Located in a renovated historic building, this exposed brick loft attracts legions of urban hipsters. Calle 1, Ave 1/Central. Closed Sun–Tues. (www.elsteinvorth.com)

HOTEL DEL REY

Love it or hate it, you can't ignore this massive hotel/casino filled with hookers and the gringos who love them. One of downtown's most popular destinations. Ave 1, Calle 9. (2257-7800, www.delreyhotel.com)

Parque La Sabana

This park, the largest in San José, is located at the site of the former international airport. In the 1970s the old runway was replaced with soccer fields, jogging trails, an artificial pond and over 5,000 non-native trees. Today the non-native trees are being replaced with native saplings to attract more birds. Parque Sabana, which is located at the western end of Paseo Colón, is a popular place for Ticos to relax and play during the day, but it's considered very unsafe at night.

The eastern end of Sabana is home to the Costa Rican Museum of Art (Open 9am–4pm, Closed Sunday, free admission), which is housed in the former airport terminal. This charming building, built in 1940, is worth a quick peek inside. Be sure to visit the "Diplomat Lounge" on the second floor, which features a 3D mural depicting the history of Costa Rica.

The western end of Sabana is dominated by the new National Stadium, a $100 million sports complex donated by the Chinese government. Why would China be so generous? As of 2006, Costa Rica was one of just 26 countries that maintained diplomatic relations with Taiwan, which China considers a renegade province. Of those 26 countries, half were located in Latin America and the Caribbean. In 2007 Costa Rica ended diplomatic relations with Taiwan and established diplomatic relations with China. Since then, China has lavished Costa Rica with the new stadium, a free trade agreement, 450 new police cars, a $25-million police academy, the purchase of $300 million government bonds and a $500-million investment in Costa Rica's oil refinery. This generosity is presumably designed to persuade other countries to follow Costa Rica's lead.

Escazú

This upscale neighborhood is located 6 km (3.7 miles) from downtown San José. Arriving from the highway, the main entrance to Escazú is marked by a giant Walmart, but don't let that fool you. This is the most exclusive neighborhood in Costa Rica, home to a mix of rich Ticos and expats. Escazú (pop. 62,000) has an architectural style that I like to call "Miami without Zoning," which blends upscale shopping centers with a crumbling infrastructure. The northern edge of Escazú, which lies along Highway 27, is home to the most expensive shops and restaurants in Costa Rica. The most famous destination is Multiplaza, a sprawling indoor mall that sells just about everything. Smaller but more impressive is the ultra-luxe Avenida Escazú, an open-air shopping center that's home to Costa Rica's first IMAX, first Starbucks and a handful of terrific restaurants. There are few tourist attractions in Escazú, but if you're interested in observing rich Ticos in their native habitat, head to Avenida Escazú for lunch or dinner.

Set back from the highway is "downtown" Escazú, which is referred to as San Rafael de Escazú. This area is centered around a congested Y-intersection next to Scotiabank. If you head into the dramatic hills above downtown, you'll pass the traditional neighborhoods of Escazú Centro and San Antonio de Escazú, which have somehow managed to escape the recent development craze. In the past this area was famous for witches, which have become the unofficial symbol of Escazú. Today San Antonio de Escazú is famous for its annual Boyero Parade (p.78) held in mid-March.

Frequent buses to Escazú depart downtown San José just east of the Coca-Cola bus terminal. It's much easier to take a taxi, however, which costs $10–15 from downtown San José.

Heredia

Located 9 km (5.6 miles) northwest of San José on the slopes of the dormant Barva Volcano, Heredia grew rich on coffee in the 19th and 20th century. Today many of the coffee fields have been replaced by call centers and tech companies that employ thousands of ambitious young Ticos, many of whom graduated from the nearby National University of Costa Rica. Not surprisingly, Heredia's infrastructure hasn't kept pace with its growth, and traffic is often congested at the start and end of the workday.

Although Heredia (pop. 140,000) is nicknamed the "City of Flowers," the name comes from the prominent Flores ("Flowers") family, not any high concentration of flowers. Downtown Heredia is similar to San José, but smaller and safer. Its main tourist attraction is *El Fortín*, a strange defensive tower built with concave windows (which funnel bullets *into* the structure). Heredia's top attractions are located on the outskirts of town (see following page). Regular buses to Heredia depart downtown San José from Calle 1, Ave 7/9. Taxis to Heredia from downtown San José cost $15–20.

★CAFÉ BRITT COFFEE TOUR

Costa Rica's most famous coffee company offers Costa Rica's most popular coffee tour. The 2-hour, bilingual tour involves costumed characters explaining every step of the coffee-harvesting process. It's sprinkled with humorous skits, making it a great choice for families with children. The tour ends with a coffee tasting at the factory store and coffee bar. Tour times are 9:30am, 11am, 12:45pm and 3:15pm. Cost: $22 per person, $17 students, $14 kids. Transportation is available from San José hotels for $17 per person. Combo tours with INBioparque (see below) are also available. (2277-1600, www.coffeetour.com)

★INBIOPARQUE

This wildlife park is run by the non-profit National Biodiversity Institute, which promotes biodiversity research in Costa Rica. A network of trails heads through various Costa Rican life zones—rainforest, dry forest, wetlands—filled with Costa Rican wildlife—sloths, iguanas, poison dart frogs and more. Guided tours are offered at 9am, 11am and 2pm ($25 adults, $19 students, $15 kids). Half-day tours, which include transportation and lunch, cost $55. Open Friday 8am–4pm; Sat, Sun 9am–5:30pm. (2507-8107, www.inbioparque.com)

Alajuela

Costa Rica's second-largest city (pop. 290,000) is located 5 km (3 miles) north of the international airport and 20 km (12.4 miles) northwest of downtown San José. Unfortunately, downtown Alajuela offers very little for tourists, but the outskirts of town are home to two of the Central Valley's most popular attractions: Poás Volcano (p.187) and the La Paz Waterfall Gardens (p.188).

Sarchí

This small town, located 30 km (18.6 miles) northwest of downtown Alajuela, is famous for its woodworking shops, which produce furniture, souvenirs and painted oxcarts (p.78). There are dozens of workshops in town, most of which are spread out along the road that twists through the center of town. The most famous workshop in Sarchí is the Chaverri Oxcart Factory (2454-4411).

Other San José Day Trips

La Selva: Gorgeous rainforest outside the city (p.188)

Islas Tortuga: Tropical Islands in the Gulf of Nicoya (p.343)

Río Pacuare: The best rafting in Costa Rica (p.39)

San José Restaurants

★PARK CAFE (Lnch, Din: $32–38)

One of the best restaurants in Costa Rica, Park Cafe serves Old World classics (rabbit, duck, lamb) with modern panache. If you're a foodie looking to splurge, Park Cafe is worth it. Great wine list. Reservations recommended. Open Tues–Sat. Closed Sept & Oct. Sabana Norte, 100 meters north of Rosti Pollo. (2290-6324, www.parkcafecostarica.blogspot.com)

★GRANO DE ORO (Brk: $9–13; Lnch $14–33, Din: $18–35)

Located in the historic Grano de Oro Hotel, this is one of the most elegant restaurants in San José. The mouth-watering menu fuses French, Italian and Costa Rican flavors. Great wines. Paseo Colon. (2255-3322, www.hotelgranodeoro.com)

★LA TERRASSE (Din: $14-28)

This superb all-French restaurant, located in a private house built in 1927, features entrees like baked salmon with pistachio, boeuf bourguignon and veal stew. Reservations are essential; no more than 10 guests are served at a time. Prix fixe menu available. (2221-5742, www.restaurantlaterrasse.blogspot.com)

★ESQUINA DE BUENOS AIRES (Lnch, Din: $15–26)

This delightful Argentinian restaurant is big on 1920s retro charm. The menu features plenty of red meat—including strange, tasty cuts—plus good pasta. Great Argentinian wines. Calle 11, Ave 4. (2223-1909, www.laesquinadebuenosaires.com)

★TIN JO (Lnch, Din: $11–18)

The top Asian restaurant in San José. Tin Jo offers a wide range of delicious classics from China, Thailand, Korea and India, plus a healthy selection of vegetarian options. Good wines. Calle 8, Ave 6/8. (2221-7605, www.tinjo.com)

CAFE MUNDO (Lnch, Din: $12–24)

Located in a beautiful colonial mansion tucked away in Barrio Amón, Café Mundo offers good pasta, pizza and internationally-inspired appetizers. Closed Sunday. Ave 9, Calle 15. (2222-6190)

ALMA DE CAFÉ (Brk, Lnch: $7–12)

Located in the beautiful National Theater (p.177), this charming café serves soups, salads, sandwiches, quiche and delicious espresso drinks. Great for lunch. (2010-1119, www.almadecafe.net)

NUESTRA TIERRA (Brk: $4-7; Lnch, Din: $16–28)

This rustic, Costa Rican-themed restaurant is a great place for breakfast (try the chorreada or tamale), but lunch and dinner are very expensive. Open 24 hours. Located just southwest of the National Museum. (2258-6500)

LUBNÁN (Lnch, Din: $14–20)
Tasty Lebanese & Middle Eastern food, with a happening bar in the back. If you're hungry, try the mezza, a 2–3 person platter filled with bite-sized delicacies. Paseo Colón, Calle 22/24. Closed Mon. (2257-6071, www.lubnancr.com)

CAFÉ LOS DESEOS (Lnch, Din: $6–9)
This funky cafe is popular with young San José hipsters. The menu has sandwiches, wraps and pizzas. Closed Sun, Mon. Calle 15/Ave 11. (2222-0496)

CASONA TIPICA (Brk: $6; Lnch, Din: $6–10)
If you're looking for affordable, authentic Costa Rican food, head to this local favorite. Be sure to order some coffee, which is served in a traditional *chorreador*. Ave 2/Calle 10. (2258-8384)

Escazú Restaurants
★**PRODUCT C** (Lnch, Din: $16-23)
Fresh, sustainable seafood, expertly-prepared, make this my favorite restaurant in the high-end Avenida Escazú shopping center. Good wines and craft beer. (2288-5570, www.product-c.com)

CASONA DE LALY (Lnch, Din: $6–12)
From the food to the ambiance, this is one of the most authentic Costa Rican dining experiences in the Central Valley. The rustic restaurant serves a wide range of affordable classics like casados, ceviche and patacones. (2288-5807)

Heredia Restaurants
★**EL TIGRE VESTIDO** (Brk: $10; Lnch: $13-16; Din: $20-25)
Located at the beautiful Finca Rosa Blanca hotel/coffee plantation, this delicious restaurant combines local ingredients with modern flair. Good wines. 30-minute drive from Juan Santamaría Airport. (2269-9392, www.eltigrevestido.com)

Alajuela Restaurants
★**XANDARI** (Brk: $10-17; Lnch: $11-16; Din: $15–25)
Great food and spectacular views of the Central Vally are the highlights at this boutique hotel. Located in the hills above Alajuela, it's a 20-minute drive from Juan Santamaría Airport. (2443-2020, www.xandari.com)

JALAPEÑOS CENTRAL (Lnch, Din: $7–9)
Located in the heart of Alajuela, this hole-in-the-wall Tex-Mex joint offers hearty portions, speedy service and a pleasant atmosphere. (2430-4027)

Miradors

The nighttime view of San José from the surrounding mountains is one of the highlights of the Central Valley, and several *miradors* (restaurants with a view) have cashed in on that fact. There's no better way to finish a trip to Costa Rica than with dinner at a beautiful mirador. To visit any of the following, take a taxi or use your car's GPS.

★ TIQUICIA (Lnch, Din: $16-25)
Perched above Escazú, this is the all-around best mirador near San José. Tasty, traditional food, plus live music Fri, Sat. Closed Mon. A 15-min drive from downtown San José. (2289-5839, www.miradortiquiciacostarica.com)

LA CAVA (Din: $14–20)
Located in the cellar of a former monastery in Escazú, the ambiance at La Cava is unique, if a bit musty. (2228-8515, www.monastere-restaurant.com)

RAM LUNA (Din: $20–40)
Ram Luna is widely considered the king of the miradors, but it's located in Aserrí, a 45-minute drive from downtown San José. Weds & Thurs feature a two-hour show of traditional music and dance ($40 per person). Reservations essential. (2230-3022, www.restauranteramluna.com)

Poás Volcano National Park

This dramatic volcano, which forms the northwest edge of the Central Valley, is famous for its massive, lake-filled crater. Both the crater and the surrounding cloud forest have been protected as Poás Volcano National Park, which due to its proximity to San José—just 45 km (28 miles) from downtown—is the most visited national park in Costa Rica, with over 300,000 people visiting each year. If you're looking for an accessible, natural escape from the gritty sprawl of the Central Valley, Poás makes a great day trip.

Rising 2,708 meters (8,885 feet) above sea level, the upper slopes of Poás are often covered in clouds, which gives rise to lush cloud forests. But the main attraction is the volcano's massive crater, a barren lunar landscape that stands in stark contrast to the surrounding vegetation. The crater measures 1,320 meters (4,331 feet) across and 300 meters (984 feet) deep. It's often claimed, falsely, that this is one of the largest volcanic craters in the world. Although not true, it does contain one of the most acidic crater lakes in the world. The lake rests upon a cooled column of magma roughly 500 meters (1,640 feet) deep, which in turn rests upon a chamber of molten and semi-molten magma. Volcanic gasses bubble up through the lake, giving the water a temperature of 58-93°C (136-199°F) and a pH of roughly 0.8. Both the depth of the lake and its color vary due to rainfall and changing volcanic conditions. During periods of increased volcanic activity and reduced rainfall, the lake sometimes dries up completely. Poás emits between 40 and 500 tons of CO_2 each day, and other ejected gases generate acid rain and acid fog that have left parts of the volcano's northwest slope barren and lifeless.

Poás has erupted several times in the past two centuries, and the small museum near the park entrance displays photos of recent eruptions. In 1910 an eruption produced an ash cloud 8 km (5 miles) high that deposited roughly 640,000 tons of ash over the Central Valley. The last major eruption was in 1953, which produced an ash cloud 7 km (4.3 miles) high and gave the crater its current shape. Minor eruptions are far more common. On Christmas Day 2009, a minor eruption launched a mixture of ash and water 550 meters (1,804 feet) in the air.

The crater viewpoint, located 1 km (0.5 miles) from the park entrance, is accessible via a paved, wheelchair accessible path. After checking out the crater, consider hiking through the forest to Lago Bruto, a small lake located in the ancient crater of the extinct Bruto Volcano, which last erupted 8,300 years ago. The hike to Lago Bruto takes about 30 minutes round-trip.

Poás Volcano National Park is 26 km (16 miles) from Alajuela (40-minute drive) and 45 km (28 miles) from San José (1-hour drive). The park is open 8am–3:30pm, but it's best to get there as early as possible because the crater is often covered in clouds by late morning.

La Selva

La Paz Waterfall Gardens

This popular tourist destination features 5 waterfalls, 3.5 km (2.2 miles) of hiking trails and a large wildlife refuge filled with over 100 Costa Rican species, including monkeys, sloths, toucans, hummingbirds, frogs and jaguars. Located just 30 km (18.6 miles) from Alajuela, La Paz Waterfall Gardens makes a wonderful day trip if you're looking to get out of the urban jungle and visit the real one. It also makes a great afternoon destination after a morning trip to Poás Volcano, which is a 30-minute drive away. Lunch is also available at their buffet-style restaurant. Open 8am–5pm. Cost: $38 adults, $22 kids. Transportation from San José area hotels available. (2482-2720, www.waterfallgardens.com)

La Selva Biological Station

Ok, this lush nature reserve isn't located in the Central Valley—it's on the Caribbean side of the Central Mountain Range. But because it lies just 75 km (47 miles) from Juan Santamaría Airport in Alajuela (2-hour drive), it makes an excellent day trip from the Central Valley if you're looking for primary rainforest filled with wildlife. Over 100 mammal species and 440 bird species have been identified here, including green macaws. The reserve, which is run by the Organization for Tropical Studies (2766-6565, www.ots.ac.cr), features several kilometers of easy, well-maintained hiking trails. Basic lodging is available, and there are a handful of private ecolodges nearby, making this a great place to stay if you don't want to spend your last night in the gritty Central Valley. La Selva is located near the small town of Puerto Viejo de Sarapiquí (not to be confused with Puerto Viejo de Talamanca, the popular Caribbean beach town).

La Paz Waterfall Gardens

NORTHERN MOUNTAINS

CUTTING DIAGONALLY ACROSS the northwest corner of Costa Rica, this string of lush mountains and dramatic volcanoes is home to some of the country's most famous destinations. From the cool, high elevation cloud forests of Monteverde to the charred slopes of Arenal Volcano, the Northern Mountains offer an incredible diversity of landscapes. And because they've attracted a steady stream of travelers for decades, the Northern Mountains are famously family-friendly.

Two major *cordilleras* (mountain ranges) make up the Northern Mountains: the Cordillera de Guanacaste and the Cordillera de Tilarán, whose highest peaks measure 2,028 meters (6,654 feet) and 1,850 meters (6,000 feet) respectively. They are not the tallest mountains in Costa Rica, but the Northern Mountains are incredibly accessible. Lying between the international airports at Liberia and San José, and just a half day's drive from the beautiful beaches of the Nicoya Peninsula and the Central Pacific, the Northern Mountains are the most popular mountains in Costa Rica.

The most famous destination is Arenal Volcano, located near the eastern base of the Tilarán Mountains. For decades Arenal was one of the most active volcanoes in the world, delighting tourists with its remarkably consistent eruptions. In 2010, however, the volcano entered a period of extended dormancy. Today the area around the volcano is more famous for outdoor adventures—canyoning, canopy tours, whitewater rafting—and an abundance of natural hot springs.

Monteverde, which lies near the crest of the Tilarán Mountains, is home to Costa Rica's most stunning and accessible cloud forest. This chilly, misty landscape shelters an impressive range of plants and animals, many of which are found nowhere else. For many eco-travelers, particularly bird watchers, Monteverde is a must-see destination. In addition to the natural beauty, Monteverde is also home to a wide range of family-friendly activities such as canopy tours, coffee tours and wildlife exhibits.

The only downside to Arenal and Monteverde: big crowds during high season (December to March). If you're looking for more peace and quiet, consider the Río Celeste, a brilliant blue river home to waterfalls and hotsprings, or Rincón de la Vieja, Costa Rica's miniature version of Yellowstone. Both are located alongside volcanoes that rise dramatically from northern Costa Rica's hot, flat plain, and both remain well under the tourist radar.

Arenal Volcano

ARENAL

COSTA RICA IS home to over a dozen volcanoes, but Arenal is the most famous by far. Few volcanos in the world claim such a perfect conical shape, and few have delighted so many visitors. It all started in 1968, when Arenal erupted after lying dormant for nearly 500 years. For the next four decades the volcano spewed out a steady stream of lava and hot rocks, attracting a steady stream of tourists who watched the glowing eruptions safely from afar.

Then, in 2010, Arenal went quiet. The eruptions stopped, and as of this writing it's officially considered "inactive." According to scientists, the last time Arenal stayed inactive for this long, it stayed inactive for several hundred years.

Is the party over? Not necessarily. The volcano could rumble back to life at any moment. But let me be honest: even when Arenal was active, lava watching was a very hit or miss proposition. Clouds cover the volcano for much of the year, so simply catching a glimpse of the erupting peak always required a certain amount of luck. In addition, the glowing lava could only be seen at night (assuming it was a clear night) and only on the volcano's northern or western slope (depending on which way the lava was flowing). Unless you were staying at a hotel with clear views of the lava on a cloudless night, chances are you wouldn't catch a decent glimpse of the eruption. If you did get lucky, however, watching Arenal erupt was one of Costa Rica's most spectacular experiences.

I don't want to call Arenal overrated. It's a fascinating, beautiful place. But if you visit with expectations of dramatic glowing eruptions, you'll likely end up disappointed. So why visit Arenal? Because the region around the volcano is filled with family-friendly eco-adventures. The rugged topography serves up some of the best whitewater rafting and canyoning in Costa Rica, plus canopy tours, waterfall hikes and great wildlife watching. Arenal is also surrounded by a number of beautiful hotsprings, which means you can finish your action-packed day soaking in a naturally heated pool, cocktail in hand.

The downside to all these options? Lots of tourists. La Fortuna, the region's bustling hub, is jam-packed with restaurants, souvenir shops and "tourist information centers." It's half genuine Tico town (there are lots of typical restaurants) and half tourist trap (there's a Burger King). That said, with a rental car or a taxi it's easy to escape the crowds. Just north of Arenal are several luxurious, remote hotels, many of which feature on-site hot springs. A bit further is the small pueblo of El Castillo, which offers dramatic views of Arenal's charred western slope and beautiful Lake Arenal, the largest man-made lake in Central America.

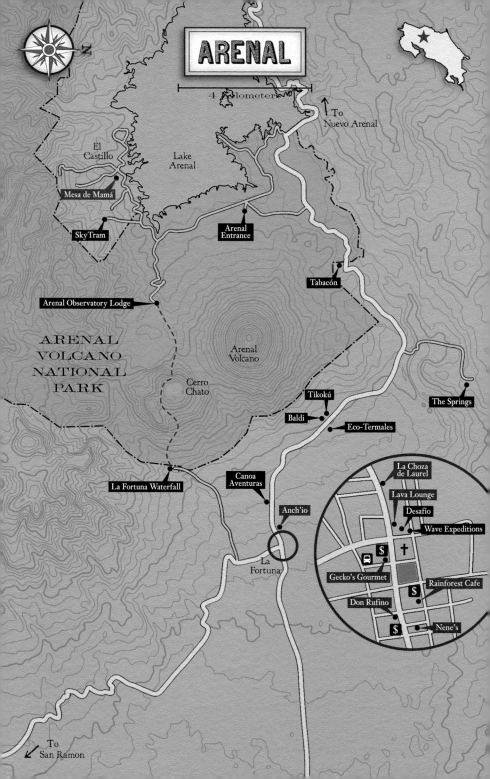

Erupting Arenal (viewed from El Castillo)

Getting To Arenal/La Fortuna

La Fortuna is located 121 km (75 miles) from San José (2.5-hour drive), 141 km (88 miles) from Liberia (3-hour drive), and 66 km (41 miles) from San Ramon (90-minute drive). The airport (10-minute drive east of La Fortuna) is serviced by Nature Air (p.18). Grayline, Interbus and Easyride (p.20) offer shuttle service. Transporte San Carlos buses (2255-4318) depart San José for La Fortuna from Calle 12, Ave 7/9 at 6:15am, 8:40am and 11:30am (₡2,490, 4.5 hours). Return buses depart La Fortuna at 12:45pm and 2:45pm. If you're traveling to/from Monteverde, consider the 3-hour Taxi-Boat-Taxi transfer (aka Jeep-Boat-Jeep) across Lake Arenal offered by Desafío Adventures ($32, 2479-0020, www.desafiocostarica.com) and Red Lava ($25, 8398-9581, www.redlavatouristservicecenter.com).

Getting Around Arenal/La Fortuna

A car is nice to have around Arenal, but by no means necessary. If you're staying in El Castillo or around Lake Arenal, however, you'll definitely want your own transportation. Taxis (2479-8522, 8749-7878) are plentiful in downtown La Fortuna, and most tours offer free rides to/from local hotels. Car rental in downtown La Fortuna is available from Adobe (2479-7202) and Alamo (2479-9090).

Arenal/La Fortuna Hotels

Most budget hotels are located in downtown La Fortuna, and most luxury hotels are located on the road that skirts the northern base of the volcano. If you're looking for peace and quiet, check out the tiny village of El Castillo (p.191) or hotels around Lake Arenal (p.209). Visit www.jameskaiser.com for complete hotel info.

La Fortuna

Lying 5 km (3.1 miles) east of Arenal Volcano, La Fortuna is a small town that's dominated, quite literally, by Arenal. On clear days the volcano's massive cone towers over the western horizon. Viewed from La Fortuna, Arenal's eastern slopes appear lush and green, but the volcano's western slope is burnt to a crisp. Over the past several decades, debris ejected from the volcano has tumbled down the volcano's western slope away from La Fortuna. So even if Arenal is erupting when you arrive, don't expect to see much action from La Fortuna. Also note that, when viewed from La Fortuna, Arenal appears to have a single cone. But look closely and you'll see that the volcano actually has two cones—an older inactive one (left) and a newer more active one (right). These two cones become clear and distinct as you head west towards Lake Arenal.

Prior to 1968, La Fortuna was a sleepy agricultural town. The name *La Fortuna*, "The Fortunate," refers to rich agricultural soils, not the town's fortunate location away from destructive lava flows. In fact, prior to 1968 local villagers didn't even realize that the massive, cone-shaped hill looming above town was a volcano. After Arenal's eruption in 1968, adventurous visitors began trickling in, and over the past two decades the trickle has turned into a flood. Today downtown La Fortuna is jam-packed with hotels and souvenir shops, and the road heading west of town is dotted with private hot springs and luxury hotels. Although most of downtown La Fortuna is cluttered and unattractive, the flower-filled public park is among the loveliest in Costa Rica.

La Fortuna Waterfall

Arenal Volcano National Park

The views of Arenal from La Fortuna are impressive, but if you're interested in the volcano's geology it's worth visiting Arenal Volcano National Park. Located near the western base of the volcano—about a 25-minute drive from downtown La Fortuna (a roughly $25 taxi ride)—the park offers dramatic views of Arenal's charred western slope, which has experienced multiple eruptions since 1968. The national park is open from 8am–4pm, and the park entrance fee is $10 adults, $1 kids 6–12, under 6 free. (2200-4192, www.parquenacionalvolcanarenal.com)

To get to the park entrance, follow the main road north from La Fortuna. About 5 minutes past Tabacón Spa & Resort, you'll reach a junction marked by a blue and white police station on the right. Head left on the dirt road that heads towards El Castillo. The park entrance is located roughly 2.1 km (1.3 miles) down the dirt road on the left.

In addition to dramatic views (on clear days, at least), the park offers 4.8 km (3 miles) of hiking trails. The most popular trail is the 2 km (1.2 mile) Las Coladas Trail, which heads to the remnants of a 1992 lava flow. Walking on top of the cooled black lava is a truly unique experience. At the end of the trail, an elevated viewpoint offers dramatic views of both the volcano and Lake Arenal. When you head back, it's worth taking the 1.8-km (1.1-mile) El Ceibo Trail, which passes by two impressive trees: a giant ceibo and a massive strangler fig. The park also offers a covered viewpoint and the 1-km (0.6-mile) Heliconia Trail.

Local, bilingual guides offer guided tours of the park's trails ($20 per person, prices negotiable.) Although the trails are easy to follow on your own, a guide is worth it if you want to learn about the geologic history of the park. Sadly, the national park doesn't offer any detailed information about the volcano—no visitor center, no interpretive signs, no brochures. Unless you hire a guide, you won't learn much about the volcano.

Another alternative to Arenal National Park is the privately owned Arenal 1968 (8701-6561, www.arenal1968.com). Located just north of the national park entrance, Arenal 1968 offers over 30 kms (18.6 miles) of hiking/biking trails, including trails that pass over the original 1968 lava flow. There's also a trail that passes by Lake Los Patos, which was created after the 1968 eruption. Guided hikes are available, though they are best reserved in advance.

Another great place to check out is the Arenal Observatory Lodge. This private lodge—the only hotel located inside the park—was originally built in 1987 as a Smithsonian Institute scientific research station. It has since been converted into an upscale hotel. Perched safely on a bluff just 2.7 kms (1.7 miles) south of the volcano, it offers stunning views of Arenal. There's a small museum and over 10 km (6.2 miles) of hiking trails, including a trail to a lovely waterfall and a trail to the top of Cerro Chato (p.206). Non-guests can enjoy the hotel's museum and trails for $8 per person. The lodge is about a 10-minute drive past the park entrance. (2290-7011, www.arenalobservatorylodge.com)

Although the exact details of Arenal's inner workings remain a mystery, the volcano is the result of tectonic plate movement. As the Cocos Plate (located off the Pacific Coast) collides with the Caribbean Plate (which includes Costa Rica), underground rocks melt and rise into a magma chamber below Arenal. When pressure on the magma becomes too great, the volcano erupts.

Carbon dating indicates that Arenal is roughly 7,000 years old. It has erupted multiple times, and eruptions seem to follow a somewhat predictable cycle. Small eruptions occur every 300–400 years and large eruptions occur every 600–800 years. No wonder Costa Rica's indigenous Malekus tribe believed the god of fire lived inside the volcano. The Spanish name *Arenal* ("sand pit") is derived from the sandy deposits left by volcanic debris.

On July 29, 1968, Arenal erupted after lying dormant for roughly 450 years. At 7:30am an enormous crater (Crater A) blasted open halfway up the volcano's western flank, resulting in a "pyroclastic flow." Giant rocks whizzed through the air at 500 meters (1,640 feet) *per second*, and a molten ash cloud raced down the slopes at 150 kilometers (93 miles) per hour. The ash cloud, which reached temperatures up to 1,000°C (1,832°F), vaporized everything in its path, including trees, houses and people. Rocks ejected from the volcano landed up to 5 kilometers (3.4 miles) away and left impact craters up to 25 meters (82 feet) in diameter.

Over the next three days Arenal continued to erupt. Two additional craters (B and C) blasted open on the volcano's western flank, and vast quantities of ash and rocks rained down over the region. By the time the volcano settled down, Arenal had destroyed over 1,500 hectares (3,700 acres) and killed nearly 100 people.

Arenal's eruption caught everyone by surprise. Before it exploded, no one realized it was a volcano. There were, however, several ominous signs leading up to the event. In 1967 the temperature of the nearby Tabacón river increased substantially. Then, in April 1968, a series of earthquake "swarms" that lasted through July hit the region. The night before Arenal erupted, over 5,000 detectable earthquakes were measured.

On September 19, 1968, 52 days after the initial eruption, lava began flowing from Crater A. The lava flow lasted five-and-a-half years, at which point lava began flowing from the topmost of the newly blasted holes (crater C), then located at 1,450 meters (4,757 feet). From that point on, crater C became the volcano's main crater. Although Arenal went through periods of inactivity, regular lava flows slowly built up a new western cone, resulting in a "two-headed" volcano.

In 1984 the volcano entered into a "strombolian" phase marked by new types of eruptions. In strombolian eruptions, gas bubbles rise through the magma column and burst at the top of the crater, ejecting lava and volcanic debris in the process. Because strombolian eruptions are relatively mild, they do little damage to the volcano's internal structure and can often last for decades. This is exactly what happened at Arenal. To the delight of tourists and hotel owners, Arenal began producing regular, sustained eruptions of lava and molten rocks that could be viewed safely from a distance.

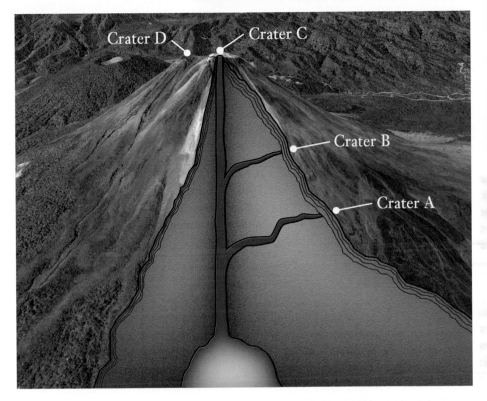

Since 1984 Arenal's strombolian phase has been punctuated by several dozen powerful pyroclastic flows—though none as destructive as 1968. In the late 1990s the volcano entered a period of heightened activity, and during this time it was considered one of the most active volcanoes in the world. By 1997, thanks to the regular lava flows, the cinder cone produced by crater C had risen 300 meters (984 feet) to 1,750 meters (5,741 feet)—117 meters (384 feet) taller than crater D, Arenal's ancient cinder cone.

Then, in October 2010, the eruptions suddenly stopped. The lava stopped flowing, and as of this writing Arenal has not yet rumbled back to life. Is the party over? Not necessarily. Arenal could reawaken at any moment. But even if Arenal has entered a new period of dormancy, future eruptions certainly await.

According to vulcanologist Guillermo Alvarado, Arenal's 1968 eruption contained the force of several atomic bombs. But by historic standards, 1968 was considered a "small" eruption. "Big" eruptions have been up to *ten times* larger. And if past cycles are any indicator, a big eruption could happen sometime within the next 200 years. Ironically, as our scientific knowledge of the volcano's risks has grown, the surrounding tourist infrastructure has grown right along with it. Today dozens of hotels, and the national park itself, are located near Arenal's most dangerous zones along the northern and western flanks. Of course, a future catastrophe could be a long way off. But it's not a matter of *if*. It's a matter of *when*.

★Hot Springs

The upside of being located next to a giant volcano? Abundant thermal hot springs. And there's no shortage of local resorts that have cashed in on this fact. After a long day of adventure tours, there's nothing like soaking in a soothing hot spring. Listed below are Arenal's most famous and popular hot springs, all of which feature man-made pools fed by naturally heated water.

TABACÓN ($60 adults, $10 kids 6–11; $45 adults, $10 kids after 6pm)

This was the first hot spring resort at Arenal, and it's the most luxurious by far. The pools are gorgeous, the landscaping is impeccable and the service is top-notch. In addition to thermal pools, there's a swim up bar and a zen-inspired adult-only area that's great for reading and relaxing. Of course, all this luxury comes at a price. But if you're looking to splurge, Tabacón is worth it. Open 10am–10pm. A 15-minute drive from La Fortuna. (2519-1999, www.tabacon.com)

ECO-TERMALES ($34 adults, $24 kids 5-12)

If you're interested in beautiful hot springs with a lush, natural feel at a reasonable price, this is the place for you. Though not as extensive as other hot springs, Eco-Termales focuses more on simple elegance and a commitment to sustainability. To prevent overcrowding, they limit the number of guests during each of their three visitation periods (10am–1pm, 1pm–5pm, 5pm–9pm). Reservations are required. A 5-minute drive from La Fortuna. Open 10am–9pm daily. (2479-8787, www.ecotermalesfortuna.cr)

THE SPRINGS ($50 per person, two-day pass)

If you like the idea of a large luxury hot spring resort but $60 seems a bit pricey, try The Springs. It features multi-level pools, swim-up bars, lushly landscaped hot springs and some of the most dramatic volcano views in town. Their pass also includes access to the resort's private hiking trails and a wildlife center that features wildcats and monkeys. Open 8am–10pm. A 20-minute drive from La Fortuna. (2401-3310, www.springscostarica.com)

TIKOKÚ ($24 adults, $12 kids 4-12)

If you're just looking to soak your bones in some hot water—ultra-luxe, mega-lush fantasy landscapes be damned—check out Tikokú. These small, classy hot springs are one of the best deals in town. Open 10am–8pm. A 5-minute drive from La Fortuna. (2479-7156, www.hotelarenalkioro.com)

BALDI ($31 adults, $15.50 kids under 7)

Less expensive, and less luxurious, than other hot springs, Baldi focuses on crowd pleasing features like water slides, swim-up bars and flat screen TVs. Open 10am–10pm. A 5-minute drive from La Fortuna. (2479-2190, www.baldihotsprings.cr)

Tabacón

Eco-Termales

The Springs

★La Fortuna Waterfall

This 70-meter (230-foot) waterfall, located just 5 km (3 miles) from downtown La Fortuna (about a 10-minute drive), is one of the most dramatic, accessible waterfalls in Costa Rica. Although there's an entrance fee ($10 per person, kids under 8 free) all proceeds go to the town of La Fortuna. (Now you know why the public park looks so nice). From the entrance, a steep trail descends nearly 600 meters (1,969 feet) to the base of the waterfall, a hike that takes 10–20 minutes depending on your fitness level. There are two observation platforms overlooking the waterfall, and swimmers can take a dip in the lovely, chilly pool. The far side of the pool is off limits due to the possibility of falling rocks. Lifeguards will give you a whistle warning if you get too close. From the lower observation platform a short trail heads to a series of smaller, calmer pools located downstream from the waterfall. The waterfall attracts roughly 300–400 people per day, and during holidays it can attract over 1,000 people per day. If you're looking for peace and quiet, visit early or late. Open 8am–5pm. Note: A free swimming hole, popular with locals, is located just below the bridge crossing the Río Fortuna, just south of the turnoff to the waterfall on the main road.

★Canyoning

Canyoning (aka Canyoneering) involves descending rugged, water-filled canyons using ropes and climbing equipment, and the mountains around Arenal offer some of the best canyoning in Costa Rica. If you're looking for a challenging, adrenaline-soaked adventure, look no further. My favorite local outfitter is **Desafío Adventures** (2479-0020, www.desafiocostarica.com). They lead descents down Lost Canyon, which features four waterfalls ranging from 7–70 meters (23–230 feet). Cost: $95, includes lunch. Another good option is **Pure Trek Canyoning** (2479-1313, www.puretrek.com). They lead descents down El Cacao Canyon, which features four waterfalls ranging from 9–49 meters (30–160 feet). Cost: $98, includes lunch.

Whitewater Rafting

Arenal is the whitewater rafting capital of northern Costa Rica, lying within striking distance of several exciting rivers. The most famous is the Río Sarapiquí, a 2.5-hour 12 km paddle through 40–50 rapids ranging from Class II to Class IV ($89 per person, 12 years minimum age). In the rainy season there's also the Río Toro, a 3-hour paddle that blasts 17 km through 60–80 rapids ranging from Class II to Class IV ($89 per person, 12 years minimum age). A less heart-pounding option that's better for families with kids is the Río Balsa, a two-hour 9 km paddle through 25–35 rapids ranging from Class II to Class III ($70 per person, 8 years minimum age). Lunch is included on all trips. Good local outfitters include **Wave Expeditions** (2479-7262, www.waveexpeditions.com) and Costa Rica Descents (2479-9419, www.costaricadescents.com).

Canyoning

Canopy Tours

SKY TREK

Located in El Castillo (p.208), Sky Trek offers terrific views of Lake Arenal and the western slope of Arenal Volcano. After riding up an open-air tram, you'll zip down the cables at blazing speeds. Ten cables, 3 km (1.9 miles) total length, longest cable: 750 meters (2,461 feet). $77 adults, $61 students, $48 kids. They also offer a Sky River combo tour with rafting. (2479-4100, www.skyadventures.travel)

ECOGLIDE

Ecoglide's emphasis on safety and professionalism makes this a great canopy tour for families with kids. Fifteen cables, 2 km (1.2 miles) total length, longest cable: 430 meters (1,411 feet). Optional Tarzan swing. Cost: $55 adults, $45 kids/students. (2479-7120, www.arenalecoglide.com)

Cerro Chato Hike

It's illegal to climb to the top of Arenal, but lying just southwest is Cerro Chato, an extinct volcano that rises 1,440 meters (4,724 feet) above sea level. Two rugged, challenging trails head to Cerro Chato's lake-filled crater, and it's even possible to swim in the chilly lake. If you're looking for a tough hike, Cerro Chato is the best around. Note: Both approaches pass over private land and require an entrance fee. The eastern approach ($10 per person) starts at the La Fortuna Waterfall (p.204). The western approach ($6 per person) starts at Arenal Observatory Lodge (p.220). Both trails are steep, rugged and take roughly four hours round-trip. If you'd feel safer going with a guide, Canoas Aventuras offers guided hikes for $91 per person. (2479-8200, www.canoa-aventura.com)

Caño Negro Day Trip

If you're a hardcore wildlife watcher or birder, a day trip to Caño Negro Wildlife Refuge should be near the top of your list. Located just south of the Nicaraguan border, marshy Caño Negro is home to over 300 bird species (including the rare jabiru), plus caimans, sloths and three species of monkey. Day trips explore the Río Frío, which borders the reserve. Several companies offer tours, but I like Canoas Aventuras. Cost: $63 per person. (2479-8200, www.canoa-aventura.com)

Arenal Hanging Bridges

This 250-hecatre reserve offers 3.1 km (1.9 miles) of trails, including six hanging bridges that range in length from 48 to 98 meters (157 to 322 feet). This is one of the best birdwatching spots in Arenal (almost 200 species have been spotted here), and birdwatching and natural history tours are offered. Located 20 km (12.4 miles) from La Fortuna. Transportation is available for a fee. Open 7:30am–4pm. Cost: $24 adults, $14 students. (2290-0469, www.hangingbridges.com)

Arenal/La Fortuna Restaurants

★DON RUFINO (Lnch, Din: $15-30)
This is the best restaurant in downtown La Fortuna. The international menu is extensive and pricey, but there are some good, less-expensive options like casados, pastas and sandwiches. A great place to try the traditional Costa Rican soup *crema de pejibaye*. (2479-9997, www.donrufino.com)

GECKO'S GOURMET DELI (Brk: $5–9; Lnch: $8–10)
This small, charming cafe offers tasty breakfasts, great sandwiches and wraps, salads, smoothies and ice-blended coffee drinks. Great for take-out. (2479-8905, www.geckogourmet.com)

LAVA LOUNGE (Lnch, Din: $10–20)
Salads, burgers, pizza, sushi—there's a little bit of everything on Lava Lounge's large, eclectic menu. The laid back atmosphere and party-friendly bar are popular with the young backpacker crowd. (2479-7365, www.lavaloungecostarica.com)

ANCH'IO (Lnch, Din: $11–20)
If you're craving Italian, head to this charming open-air restaurant that specializes in pasta dishes and wood-fired pizzas. Closed Tues. (2479-7024)

LA CHOZA DE LAUREL (Lnch, Din: $10–23)
This large, popular restaurant serves traditional Costa Rican food prepared with an upscale touch. This is a great place to try traditional drinks like *guanabana* and *mora*, and traditional foods like *sopa negra* and *patacones*. The only thing that isn't traditional: the prices. (2479-7063, www.lachozadelaurel.com)

RAIN FOREST CAFÉ (Brk: $4–9, Lnch, Din: $6–11)
Great breakfasts and reasonably priced typical dishes (casados, churrasco, patacones). Free wifi. (2479-7239)

NENE'S (Lnch, Din: $7–16)
Located down a quiet side street, this charming local favorite is worth seeking out if you're looking for quality food at reasonable prices. The menu is a mix of Costa Rican and international influences—rice dishes, pastas, lots of meat and fish options, a very expensive flaming entree, and great ceviche. (2479-9192)

SODA VIQUEZ (Brk: $4–6; Lnch: $6–11)
For inexpensive, traditional Costa Rican food, head to this small, well-kept *soda*, which offers all the classics—*gallo pinto*, *casados*—plus pasta, hamburgers, and some international dishes.

LA MESA DE MAMÁ (Brk: $5–7; Lnch, Din: $7–9)
If your looking for a simple, authentic restaurant serving typical food, look no further. Located in the tiny pueblo of El Castillo. (2479-1954)

El Castillo

The tiny pueblo of El Castillo is the polar opposite of La Fortuna. Lying along the southern shores of Lake Arenal, it's delightfully remote and untouristy. In addition to the four essentials—school, church, *pulpería*, soccer field—there are a handful of nice hotels, most of which provide stunning views of Arenal's charred western slope. (On the off chance that Arenal is erupting when you visit, El Castillo is usually one of the best places to view it at night.) If you're looking to escape the crowds and get in touch with rural Costa Rica, this is the place to be. The downside: Because El Castillo is a roughly 40-minute drive from La Fortuna (half of which is on a bumpy, dirt road) you'll need a car or taxi to get here. And since most tours don't offer free transportation to El Castillo, you'll need to drive to La Fortuna to go whitewater rafting, canyoning, etc.

Fortunately El Castillo has just enough to keep you occupied. It's a 10-minute drive from the national park entrance and a 10-minute drive from the Arenal Observatory Lodge (p.220). El Castillo is also home to Sky Trek (p.206), which offers canopy tours, hanging bridges and tram rides. The Arenal Eco-Zoo (2479-1058, www.arenalecozoo.com) has an impressive collection of snakes, lizards, frogs and insects, and the Butterfly Conservatory boasts one of the largest butterfly collections in Costa Rica (2479-1149, www.butterflyconservatory.org). For upscale food with great volcano views, head to Fusión Grill. For inexpensive, authentic Costa Rican food, head to the tiny *soda* La Mesa de Mamá.

For complete El Castillo hotel info visit www.jameskaiser.com.

Lake Arenal

This beautiful lake, lying just west of Arenal Volcano, is the largest man-made lake in Central America, measuring 30 kms (19 miles) long by 5 kms (3.1 miles) wide. A hydroelectric dam near the eastern end of the lake generates roughly 20% of Costa Rica's electricity—enough to power roughly 200,000 homes. Prior to the construction of the dam in 1979, much of the lake was a broad valley home to the small villages of Arenal and Tonadora. When the dam was built, the villagers were relocated to the town of Nuevo Arenal, which lies above the lake's northwest shore. Today the abandoned villages of Arenal and Tonadora lie submerged at the bottom of the lake, though the town's church steeple becomes visible during low-water years.

The paved road that wraps around the lake's northern shore is home to a handful of hotels and restaurants. Nuevo Arenal, the lake's largest town, is located 46 km (29 miles) from La Fortuna (1-hour drive). My favorite restaurant along the road is Macadamia, which combines healthy, organic food and coffee with terrific views of the western end of Lake Arenal. Macadamia is located west of Nuevo Arenal as you head towards Tilarán.

Lake Arenal is famous for winds that can blow 60+ knots, making it popular with windsurfers, kiteboarders and wind turbine operators. The lake is also home to *guapote* ("the big handsome"), a fighting fish popular with anglers. Captain Ron Saunders can arrange fishing tours (8339-3345, www.arenalfishing.com).

MONTEVERDE

THE CLOUD FOREST is one of the world's most incredible ecosystems, and Costa Rica is home to one of the world's most incredible cloud forests: Monteverde. Located near the crest of the Tilarán Mountain Range, Monteverde's cool, misty forests are home to a stunning range of plants and animals, from the resplendent quetzal to the world's smallest orchid. But Monteverde is more than just biodiversity. The surrounding region has coffee tours, hanging bridges and lots of outdoor adventures. If you're an eco-traveler looking for a family-friendly destination, and you don't mind chilly weather, it's hard to beat Monteverde.

The region's undisputed highlight is the Monteverde Cloud Forest Reserve, a private 4,000-hectare (9,900-acre) reserve that's home to over 400 bird species, more plant species than the U.S. and Canada combined and the highest concentration of orchids in the world. Roughly 13 km (8 miles) of well-maintained hiking trails twist through the lush topography, opening up the wonders of the cloud forest to everyday travelers. Guided morning hikes seek out birds and flowers, while guided night hikes reveal the fascinating world of frogs and insects.

Not far from the Monteverde Reserve is the small town of Santa Elena, which is home to an abundance of private wildlife exhibits featuring frogs, snakes, butterflies and bats. In Santa Elena there's seemingly no end to all the eco-education, which is particularly nice if it's raining (which it often is in the afternoon). The rugged mountains around Santa Elena are also the birthplace of canopy tours, and the country's best canopy tours are still found here.

Thanks to its global fame and family-friendly reputation, the Monteverde Cloud Forest Reserve attracts over 70,000 visitors each year. During peak season (December–March) it can get crowded, but fortunately there are several additional reserves nearby where it's easy to escape the crowds. And all that tourism has an upside: a great selection of hotels and restaurants. You don't have to rough it in Monteverde, no what matter your price range. If avoiding tourists is your main priority, however, consider the cloud forests near San Gerardo de Dota (p.257), which are also beautiful (though not as spectacular as Monteverde).

Visiting the chilly mountains where boots and sweaters replace sandals and bikinis isn't what most people think of when they think of Costa Rica. But experiencing the wonders of the cloud forest is, in my opinion, one of the country's true highlights. Your tan may suffer in the short term, but the beauty of the lush landscapes will probably stay with you for life.

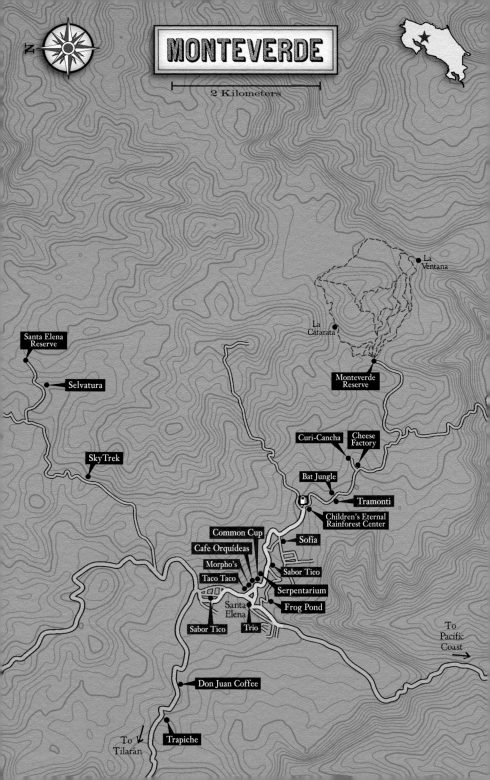

MONTEVERDE

2 Kilometers

N

La Ventana

La Catarata

Santa Elena Reserve

Selvatura

Monteverde Reserve

SkyTrek

Curi-Cancha

Cheese Factory

Bat Jungle

Tramonti

Children's Eternal Rainforest Center

Common Cup

Sofía

Cafe Orquídeas

Morpho's

Sabor Tico

Taco Taco

Serpentarium

Santa Elena

Frog Pond

Sabor Tico

Trio

To Pacific Coast

Don Juan Coffee

To Tilarán

Trapiche

La Catarata in Monteverde Reserve

Getting to Monteverde

Monteverde is 182 km (114 miles) from San José (3-hour drive) and 109 km (68 miles) from Liberia (2.5-hour drive). Roads to Monteverde are often bumpy, so 4x4 is recommended. Shuttle service to Monteverde is offered by Grayline, Interbus and Easyride (p.20). Transporte Tilarán buses (2222-3854) depart San José for Monteverde from Calle 12, Ave 7/9 at 6:30am & 2:30pm (₡2,500, 4.5 hours). Return buses to San José depart Monteverde at 6:30am & 2:30pm. For travel between Monteverde and Arenal, the best option is the Taxi-Boat-Taxi transfer offered by Desafío Adventures ($32, 2479-0020, www.desafiocostarica.com) or Red Lava ($25, 8398-9581, www.redlavatouristservicecenter.com).

Getting Around Monteverde

A car is nice to have in Monteverde, but it's not necessary. A public bus runs from downtown Santa Elena to the Monteverde Reserve at 6:15am, 7:30am, 9:30am (peak season), 1:20pm & 3pm (cost: ₡600). Most private tours offer free transportation. Taxis (2645-6969, 2645-7272) are plentiful in downtown Santa Elena. A taxi from Santa Elena to the Monteverde Reserve should cost around $10.

Monteverde Hotels

Downtown Santa Elena, the commercial hub of the region, is packed with *pensiónes* (hostels) catering to backpackers and budget travelers. The road from Santa Elena to the Monteverde Reserve is lined with more upscale hotels and eco-lodges. Visit www.jameskaiser.com for complete hotel info.

Quakers & Quetzals
The Story of Monteverde

Monteverde is famous for its biodiversity, but the region's human history is equally fascinating. The story began in an unlikely place: Fairhope, Alabama, where in 1948 four young Quakers refused to register for the U.S. military's newly established peacetime draft. The Quakers, whose religious beliefs oppose all forms of violence, were sent to jail for their dissent. Upon their release, they decided to leave the United States.

The Quakers considered moving to Canada (too cold) and Mexico (weak property rights) before finally deciding on Costa Rica. The tiny country offered good weather, cheap land and—most importantly—it had recently abolished its army. The Quakers packed their bags and embarked on a three-month, 3,000-mile journey across Central America. After arriving in Costa Rica, they bought 1,500 hectares (3,700 acres) of cloud forest near the crest of the Tilarán Mountain Range, which they named *Monteverde* ("Green Mountain").

The next step was figuring out how to earn a living. Because Monteverde was isolated and the roads connecting it to the outside world were terrible, they needed a high-value, nonperishable product. So they decided to make cheese. Cloud forest was cleared to create pastures for dairy cattle, but they left one-third of their land untouched to protect the watershed. In 1953 the Quakers opened the Monteverde Cheese Factory.

Monteverde's next big moment came in 1970, when a biologist named George Powell arrived to study birds. Powell was amazed by the biodiversity he encountered, and he began a crusade to permanently protect the Quaker's pristine cloud forest. At first the Quakers opposed Powell's idea, but he ultimately convinced them of its importance. Working together, Powell and the Quakers teamed up with Costa Rica's Tropical Science Center and U.S. environmental organizations to create the Monteverde Cloud Forest Reserve. By the end of the 1980s, the reserve protected over 4,000 hectares (9,900 acres).

Today the Monteverde Cloud Forest Reserve is just one of several private reserves that together protect over 60,000 hectares (148,000 acres) in the Tilarán Mountain Range. Although eco-tourism is now the region's number one industry, the Monteverde Cheese Factory continues producing cheese and dairy products. Tours of the facility are offered daily at 9am and 2pm ($10 adults, $8 children), and a small store next to the factory sells cheese, ice cream and other treats. (2645-7090, www.monteverdecheesefactory.com)

Monteverde Cloud Forest Reserve

This private reserve protects over 4,000 hectares (9,900 acres) of lush cloud forest (p.102) and protects some of the most incredible wildlife in Costa Rica. Located at high elevations in the tropics, cloud forests derive much of their precipitation from passing clouds. Because the temperature is cool year-round—on average 19°C (66°F) in Monteverde—the ecology is markedly different from that found along the hot, humid coast. The chilly, damp cloud forest is draped with ferns, mosses and orchids, giving the landscape a mystical, primordial feel.

Monteverde Cloud Forest Reserve (2645-5122, www.reservamonteverde.com) straddles Costa Rica's continental divide at the tip of the Tilarán Mountain Range. As trade winds blow hot, moist air from the Caribbean up the eastern slope of the Tilarán Mountains, the air cools and condenses, bathing the mountains in thick clouds. These clouds provide abundant mist and rain—Monteverde receives an average of 2.5 meters (8.2 feet) of precipitation annually—which keeps the region lush and green.

The steady moisture also lays the groundwork for incredible biodiversity, which is further enhanced by a rugged topography. Thanks to an abundance of microclimates, six ecological zones are found within the boundaries of the reserve. All told, Monteverde is home to over 3,000 plant species, over 400 bird species, over 100 mammal species and over 150 amphibian and reptile species. Although scientists still aren't sure how many insect species live in Monteverde, estimates run into the tens of thousands.

Not surprisingly, Monteverde lures a steady stream of ecologists and biologists from around the world, but you don't need a PhD to enjoy its wonders. The reserve has 13 km (8 miles) of well-maintained hiking trails that crisscross the lush topography, heading to beautiful viewpoints and a pretty waterfall. The entrance to Monteverde is located roughly 5 km (3.1 miles) southeast of downtown Santa Elena, about a 15-minute drive. At the reserve's entrance there's a ticket office, gift shop, bathrooms, a small restaurant, and a hostel that can accommodate up to 42 guests. Just south of the parking area is a free hummingbird garden next to a private coffee shop/giftshop. The reserve is open from 7am to 4pm daily. Entrance fee: $18 adults, $9 students/kids, under 6 free.

Note: The Monteverde Reserve only permits 240 total visitors at one time. During peak season (Christmas week, Easter week) the reserve often fills up by mid-morning and late arrivals must wait until someone leaves before they can enter. If you're willing to pay for a guided tour (see below), you can make reservations in advance; otherwise the reserve is first-come, first-served. It's best to get there as early as possible. If there are long lines at Monteverde when you arrive, consider visiting one of the other local cloud forest reserves (p.220).

Guided tours of Monteverde's trails are offered at 7:30am, 11:30am and 1:30pm. The tours, which last 2–3 hours, cost $33 per adult and $24 per child (includes entrance fee). I highly recommend paying for a guided tour. Eagle-eyed guides can spot incredible animals that you'd otherwise miss. Without a guide, it's likely you'll end up with a "vegetarian tour"—all plants, no animals. Trust me, a guide is worth the price. Advance reservations are available by calling 2645-5122 or emailing reservaciones2@cct.or.cr. In non-peak season, it's often possible to book a guided tour when you arrive at the entrance. Monteverde also offers guided night tours (p.220) and a special five-hour birdwatching tour that leaves at 6am ($64 per person, includes entrance fee, minimum three people).

Regardless of whether or not you pay for a guided tour, Monteverde is a great place to go hiking on your own thanks to the well-maintained, easy-to-follow trails. Free maps are provided to all visitors. Trail maps are also posted at every junction, so it's nearly impossible to get lost. Note: Because the weather is often misty or rainy, some trails can get muddy. Hiking boots, warm layers and rain gear are *highly* recommended.

One of the most popular hikes in the reserve is to *La Catarata* (p.213), a viewpoint overlooking a small, pretty waterfall. (No swimming allowed.) The hike to La Catarata is about 1.3 km (0.8 miles) round-trip and takes about one hour. To get there follow the *Quebrada Cuecha* Trail to *Sendero El Río*. (Sendero means "Trail" in Spanish.) After 250 meters you'll reach the junction to La Catarata. Bear left and follow the trail 90 meters to the overlook. On your way back, take the *Sendero Tosi*, which passes by an impressive strangler fig tree.

If you're looking for a longer hike, head to *La Ventana* viewpoint, which offers dramatic views of the continental divide. The hike to La Ventana is about 4 km (2.5 miles) and takes roughly two hours round-trip. To get there from the reserve entrance, follow the beautiful *Sendero Bosque Nuboso* 2 km (1.2 miles) to the viewpoint. After soaking in the views (on clear days, at least), head back along *Sendero Camino*. This former road is my least favorite trail in Monteverde, but it will lead you to *Sendero Wilford Guindon*, which is far nicer and crosses a 100-meter (328-foot) suspension bridge that offers superb aerial views of the cloud forest.

Orchids & Air Plants

Monteverde is home to over 500 orchid species—roughly 1/3 of all orchids in Costa Rica and the highest known concentration of orchids in the world. Orchids belong to a group of plants called epiphytes that are notable for growing on top of other plants. Instead of absorbing nutrients from the ground, epiphytes absorb most of their nutrients from dust in the air or water droplets in passing clouds. For this reason epiphytes, which include mosses and bromeliads, are also known as "air plants." Not surprisingly, misty cloud forests such as Monteverde have more epiphytes than any other forest type in the world.

Monteverde Wildlife

Above all else, Monteverde is a birdwatching paradise. There are roughly 430 recorded bird species, including the region's star attraction: the resplendent quetzal (right). Considered one of the most beautiful birds in the world, quetzals (p.108) are found in Monteverde year-round, though they are most common from January to June. Another highlight is the three-wattled bellbird (below), named for its three distinctive wattles (fleshy, dangling "moustaches") and it's booming call, which resembles the metallic clang of a bell. Bellbirds, which migrate throughout Costa Rica, are found in Monteverde from March to July. Both quetzals and bellbirds follow the fruiting cycles of wild avocado trees, of which there are over 100 local species. Other famous birds include the orange-bellied trogon, found only in Costa Rica and Panama, and the emerald toucanet. Roughly 20% of the bird species in Monteverde are long distance migratory birds, including swallow-tailed kites from South America and Baltimore orioles from North America.

Monteverde is also home to over 100 mammal species, the vast majority of which are bats and rodents. There are over 70 bat species in Monteverde,  including false vampire bats with wingspans up to one meter (3 feet) long. The reserve is also home to over 160 reptile and amphibian species and tens of thousands of insects. Among the insect species is the enormous Hercules Beetle, which grows up to 160 mm (6.3 inches) long, as well as the tiny "feather-winged" beetles, which can measure just 0.5 mm (0.02 inches) long. Larger mammals such as monkeys and sloths are occasionally seen, but they generally prefer the warmer temperatures found at lower elevations.

The Golden Toad

In 1964 biologists discovered a brilliantly colored toad in Monteverde. "My initial response," wrote Jay Savage, who first chronicled the toad, "was one of disbelief and suspicion that someone had dipped the examples in enamel paint." For the next two decades, Monteverde's "golden toad" was one of the region's star attractions. During mating season it was possible to see mass gatherings of over one hundred toads. Tragically, the golden toad disappeared in 1988, and it is now officially classified as extinct. Since the late 1980s, roughly 40% of the amphibian species have disappeared from Monteverde. Although scientists have not determined an exact cause, the deadly chytrid fungus, which has devastated amphibian populations worldwide, is among the leading culprits.

★Other Private Reserves

Although Monteverde is the most famous and popular cloud forest in the area, during peak season its nickname, Monteverde "Crowd Forest," is well-deserved. Fortunately, there are several additional private reserves nearby where it's easy to escape the crowds.

SANTA ELENA RESERVE

This 310-hectare (765-acre) cloud forest reserve, administered by the local high school, offers 12.7 kms (7.9 miles) of hiking trails. Because it's located at an elevation of 1,600 meters (5,250 feet), Santa Elena is cloudier and cooler than other reserves. Entrance: $14 adults, $7 students/kids. Guided tours ($15/person) are offered everyday at 7:30am, 9am, 11:30am, 1pm. Located 7 kms (4.3 miles) north of downtown Santa Elena (25 minute drive). Round-trip transportation is available for $4 per person. Open 7am–4pm. (2645-5390, www.reservasantaelena.org)

CURI CANCHA WILDLIFE REFUGE

This private 96-hectare (237-acre) wildlife refuge contains both transitional forest and cloud forest, so there's a better chance to see mammals here than in Monteverde. Curi Cancha, which is located above the Monteverde Cheese Factory, limits the number of visitors to just 45 people at a time. Entrance: $12 adults, $10 kids. Guided tours ($15 adults) are available at 7:30am, 11:10am, 1:30pm, 5:30pm. Open 7am–3pm & 5:30pm–7:30pm. (2645-6915, www.reservacuricancha.com)

CHILDREN'S ETERNAL RAINFOREST

In 1987 a group of Swedish schoolchildren grew alarmed at the deforestation taking place in the tropics. Working together, they raised enough money to purchase 25 acres of forest next to Monteverde. Their idea spread to other countries, and today the *Bosque Eterno de los Niños* ("Children's Eternal Rainforest") protects 22,500 hectares (55,600 acres)—the largest private reserve in Central America. The reserve operates two locations in Monteverde. The Information Center features a gift shop and a short film about the reserve. The Bajo del Tigre Visitor Center (2645-5305, 8am–4pm) offers 4.4 kms (2.7 miles) of hiking trails in transitional forest (not cloud forest) which offers a better chance to see mammals. Entrance: $12 adults, $10 students/kids. Guided tours (which include the entrance fee) are $28 adults, $24 students, $16 kids. Night tours are also available. (2645-5851, www.acmcr.org)

★Night Tours

At night the forest comes alive with amazing insects and frogs not seen during the day, and the symphony of chirps and croaks is not to be missed. Guided night tours are available at the Monteverde Reserve ($17/person, 5:45pm–7:45pm, 2645-5122), Children's Eternal Rainforest ($22 adults, $19 students, $14 kids, 5:30pm–7:30pm, 2645-5305) and Curi Cancha ($14/person, 5:30pm–7:30pm, 2645-6915).

Santa Elena Reserve

★Canopy Tours

Monteverde is the birthplace of canopy tours (p.33), and it still offers some of the best tours in the country. There are basically two types of canopy tours in Monteverde: Classic and Extreme. Classic tours (Original Canopy Tour, Selvatura) are adventurous but not *too* heart-pounding. Extreme tours (100% Aventura, Sky Trek) are all about speed and adrenaline.

THE ORIGINAL CANOPY TOUR

The first canopy tour in Costa Rica is one of the most rugged and adventurous. Fifteen cables, 3.1 km (2 miles) total length, longest cable: 800 meters (2,625 feet). There's also a Tarzan Swing, a rope ladder climb inside a giant strangler fig and great views of the Nicoya Gulf. Tour times: 7:30am, 10:30am, 2:30pm, 5:30pm. Cost: $45 adult, $35 student, $25 kids. (2645-5243, www.canopytour.com)

SELVATURA CANOPY TOUR

At just under 5 km (3 miles) total length, this is one of the longest canopy tours in Costa Rica. Fifteen cables, 4.9 km (3 miles) total length, longest cable: 1 km (2/3 mile). Optional Tarzan swing. Relatively mellow, Selvatura is a good choice for young kids or elderly travelers. Tour times: 8:30am, 11am, 1pm, 2:30pm. Cost: $45 adults, $40 students, $30 kids. (2645-5929, www.selvatura.com)

SKY TREK

SkyTrek offers one of the fastest, most thrilling zip lines in Monteverde. The tour starts with a tram ride that rises 1,736 meters (5,700 feet) through the cloud forest, and on clear days you can see Arenal Volcano. Ten cables, 2.7 km (1.7 miles) total length, longest cable: 750 meters (2,460 feet). A great choice if you're focused on speed and views. Tour times: 7:30am, 9:30am, 10:30am, 12:30pm, 1:30pm, 3pm. Cost: $71 adults, $57 students, $45 kids (2479-4100, www.skyadventures.travel)

100% AVENTURA

This is the best tour for adrenaline junkies. Ten cables, 3 km (1.9 miles) total length. 100% Aventura claims the longest cable in Latin America: 1,590 meters (just shy of 1 mile). There's also a "Fly like Superman" cable and a "Mega Tarzan" Swing. Tour times: 8am, 11am, 1pm, 3pm. Cost: $45 adults, $35 kids. (2645-6388, www.aventuracanopytour.com)

★Selvatura Adventure Park

This private nature reserve is like a cloud forest Disneyland. There's a canopy tour, hanging bridges, butterfly garden, snake and reptile room, hummingbird garden and one of the largest private insect collections in the world. If you're only in Monteverde for a day or two, a trip to Selvatura is a great way to maximize your time. You can pay for activities individually or save money with a combo ticket. (2645-5929, www.selvatura.com)

SkyTrek Canopy Tour

★Trapiche Tour

This two-hour tour focuses on the extraction of sugar from sugar cane using a traditional *trapiche* ("sugar mill"). After walking through a sugar cane field, you'll watch as raw cane juice is extracted, boiled, poured into molds and distilled into *guaro*, the local liquor of choice. Liberal tastings accompany each stage of the process. The tour also includes a brief introduction to coffee growing and processing. Cost: $32 adults, $12 kids. (2645-7780, www.eltrapichetour.com)

★Coffee Tour

There are several coffee tours in Monteverde, but my favorite is the Don Juan Coffee Tour, which takes place at a small, family-owned coffee farm. Every step of the coffee-making process is covered, from planting and harvesting to roasting. You can pick coffee fruit during harvesting season (December–February) or smell the fragrant flowers when the coffee plants are in bloom (March–June). The two-hour tour, which pays plenty of homage to traditional Costa Rican culture, also includes a quick introduction to chocolate making. Tour times: 8am, 1pm. Cost: $30 adults, $12 kids. (2645-7100, www.donjuancoffeetour.com)

Ecology Exhibits

There's no shortage of private ecology exhibits in Monteverde, and any of the following are a great place to spend an hour or so, especially if it's raining. All offer guided tours and none charge admission for children under 6. The most popular is the **Frog Pond** ($13.50 adults, $12 students, 9am–8:30pm, 2645-6320), which is home to over two dozen frog species, including poison dart frogs and the famous red-eye leaf frog, plus a butterfly garden. Another great option is the **Bat Jungle** ($12 adults, $10 students, 9am–7:30pm, 2645-7701), which explores the fascinating world of bats and includes a visit to the "bat cave," a glass-enclosed exhibit featuring seven live bat species. There's also the **Serpentarium** ($13 adults, $11 students, $8 kids, 9am–8pm, 2645-6002), which features snakes and reptiles, and behind Cafe Orquídeas is the **Orchid Garden** ($10 adults, $7 students, 8am–5pm, 2645-5308), home to 450 orchid species.

San Luis Waterfall

A visit to this lovely, remote waterfall is great way to escape the bustling tourism around Monteverde. The waterfall, located above the quaint village of San Luis, is a roughly 40-minute drive from downtown Santa Elena. To get there follow the road towards the Monteverde Reserve and take the first right past Hotel Fonda Vela. A wooden sign should point the way. After following a twisty road down a steep hill, which offers sweeping views of the San Luis Valley and the Gulf of Nicoya, signs will direct you to the waterfall. From the entrance it's a roughly 40-minute hike to the falls. Cost: $10 per person.

Monteverde Restaurants

★SOFÍA (Lnch, Din: $17–23)
One of the most upscale options in Monteverde, Sofía offers "Nuevo Latino Cuisine"—an artful mix of Latin and international styles with lots of traditional Costa Rican ingredients. Great cocktails. (2645-7017)

★TRAMONTI (Lnch, Din: $10–19)
Of all the Italian restaurants in town, Tramonti is my favorite for its of delicious food and warm atmosphere. Homemade raviolis, wood-fired pizza, good wine. (2645-6120, www.tramonticr.com)

★TRIO (Lnch, Din: $9–18)
This chic bistro serves delicious Costa Rican-inspired meals in a modern romantic setting. Although just steps from downtown Santa Elena, the restaurant overlooks a beautiful forest. (2645-7254, www.aborigencr.com)

CABURÉ CAFE (Lnch: $10; Din: $12–16)
This pleasant cafe, located above the Bat Jungle, offers sandwiches, wraps, salads and Argentine specialties. There's also a nice selection of Argentine wines, delicious handmade chocolates and decadent desserts. Closed Sunday. (2645-5020, www.cabure.net)

SABOR TICO (Brk: $5; Lnch, Din: $5–8)
Want authentic, delicious Costa Rican food? This local favorite can't be beat. In addition to *gallo pinto* and *casados*, there are lesser known favorites like *chifrijo* and *arracache*, plus delicious drinks like *horchata* and *resbalada*. Located in front of the soccer field. Cheap, filling and *muy* Tico. Two locations: Up the hill across from the soccer field (2645-5827) and the Centro Comercial Plaza (2645-5968).

ORCHID CAFE (Brk: $6–8; Lnch: $9–11)
The most upscale café in town—a great place to sip espresso drinks and munch on crepes, paninis, salads and delicious desserts. Free wifi. (2645-6850)

THE COMMON CUP CAFE (Brk, Lnch: $7)
Popular with backpackers, this rustic, laid-back café offers good coffee, smoothies and tasty sandwiches. Free wifi. (2645-6247)

TACO TACO (Lnch, Din: $6–8)
Located next to Pension Santa Elena, this simple take-out counter serves the best tacos, burritos and quesadillas in the Northern Mountains. (5018-0525)

MORPHO'S (Lnch, Din: $8–14)
This funky backpacker favorite offers hearty portions in a nice, candle-lit setting. In addition to Costa Rican classics, there's a good range of upscale entrees, many with tropical flair. (2645-7373)

RÍO CELESTE

THIS STUNNING RIVER, located near the base of the Tenorio Volcano, is one of Costa Rica's most beautiful destinations. Its water is tinted brilliant blue by naturally occurring minerals (*celeste* means "sky-blue" in Spanish), and trails alongside the river head to a stunning waterfall and nice views of the volcano's peak. If you're looking for an outdoor destination that's lush, beautiful and off-the-beaten path, it's hard to beat the Río Celeste. Although far less famous than other popular sights in the Northern Mountains, I consider it one of the region's highlights.

The river itself is located in *Parque Nacional Volcán Tenorio* ("Tenorio Volcano National Park"), which surrounds the Tenorio Volcano. The park covers roughly 225 square km (140 square miles), but visitors are only allowed along the Río Celeste corridor, which is flanked by several good hiking trails. There are two entrances to the park. The main entrance, El Pilón, is located 10 kms (6.2 miles) from the town of Bijagua, and the Puesto entrance is located 12 km (7.5 miles) from Bijagua. Both entrances provide easy access to good hiking trails that lead to the same popular sights.

The Río Celeste would be amazing anywhere. But tucked away in this lovely, lonely corner of Costa Rica, it's even more special. The small town of Bijagua, which lies between the Tenorio and Miravalles volcanoes, is about as authentic and quaint a *pueblo* as you can find in Costa Rica. There are no big resorts or mega-hotels here, just a smattering of small shops and restaurants that cater to locals. Although there are a handful of great eco-lodges near the park, the town is nowhere near as developed as Arenal or Monteverde. As of this writing, there isn't even a canopy tour. If you're looking for an authentic slice of rural Costa Rica, Bijagua won't let you down. (If you're looking for great restaurants, luxury spas and endless outdoor adventures, however, it's best to look elsewhere.)

The only downside to the Río Celeste is the short window during which the river is, well, *celeste*. During the rainy season, the river is often muddy and brown. If you want to experience the river's brilliant blue water, it's best to visit during dry season: December–March, with February being the absolute best month to visit. That said, the river can be muddy (or blue) any time of year. It all just depends on the weather. If you do happen to visit Costa Rica during peak dry season, definitely consider a trip to the Río Celeste. And even if the river isn't brilliant blue when you arrive, rest assured that the national park and surrounding scenery remain lovely year-round.

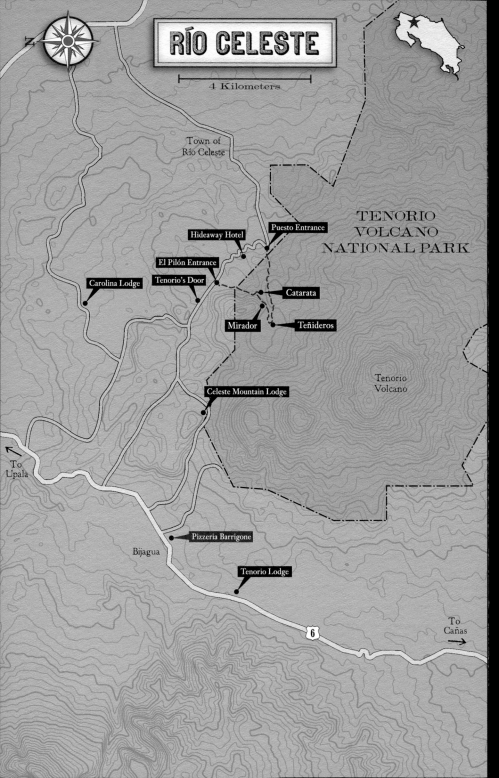

El Teñideros

Getting to Río Celeste

The closest town to the Río Celeste is the small village of Bijagua. To get to Bijagua, drive to Cañas—located 42 km (26 miles) from Liberia (40-minute drive) and 163 km (101 miles) from San José (2.5-hour drive)—then head north towards Upala. Bijagua is located roughly 35 km (21.7 miles) north of Cañas (40-minute drive). It's best to arrive by car, but Autotransporte de Upala buses (2470-0197) depart Cañas for Upala seven times daily and stop in Bijagua. Buses to Cañas depart Liberia from the Local Bus Terminal throughout the day. Another popular way to visit Río Celeste is on a day tour from Arenal. Tour operators include Canoa Aventuras (2479-8200, www.canoa-aventura.com) and Desafío Adventures (2479-0020, www.desafiocostarica.com).

Getting Around Río Celeste

Simply put, it's best to have a car here. The most popular hotels are located several kilometers from the park entrance, so having your own car is pretty much essential. And due to the very bumpy roads, 4x4 is a must.

Río Celeste Hotels

There are about a dozen hotels near the Río Celeste, covering the full spectrum from cheap to luxurious. Most hotels are all-inclusive, providing meals and offering tours, but the vibe is far more eco-boutique than mega-resort. For complete lodging information visit www.jameskaiser.com

Parque Nacional Volcán Tenorio

This beautiful national park protects roughly 13,000 hectares (50 square miles) around the Tenorio Volcano, which rises 1,916 meters (6,286 feet) above sea level. The highlight of the park, however, is the Río Celeste, which is accessible via hiking trails from the park's two entrances. The main entrance, El Pilón, includes a ranger station (2206-5369), bathrooms and a small restaurant. Admission: $10 per person. Open 8am–5pm, but hikers are not allowed into the park after 2pm.

At El Pilón you can talk to the ranger on duty and pick up some useful information about the park. You can also hire professional guides ($20–30) who will explain interesting facts about the park. Some guides can even take you to remote areas where tourists rarely go.

It takes roughly three to four hours to hike the park's trails, but the scenery is so lovely that, weather permitting, you should plan on spending the entire day here. Pack a picnic lunch and enjoy it at one of the beautiful spots along the trail. Also note that the trails are often muddy, even during dry season, so hiking boots are essential. Plan on hiking in shorts and a T-shirt, but also bring plenty of water and a waterproof jacket.

Starting from El Pilón entrance station, the *Misterios del Tenorio* trail heads 1.5 km (1 mile) to the Río Celeste Waterfall. At nearly 30 meters (98 feet) in height, this is the scenic highlight of the park. The base of the waterfall is reached via a steep side trail that branches off the main trail, and metal cables have been strung along the trail to aid in the sometimes slippery descent.

Past the waterfall junction, the *Misterios del Tenorio* trail continues 1.1 km (0.7 miles) to *El Teñideros* ("The Dyer's Shop"), the source of the Río Celeste's unusual blue hue. Along the way you'll pass a *mirador* ("viewpoint") that offers a nice panorama of Tenorio Volcano, which has been inactive for several hundred years. A short distance later you'll pass the "Blue Lagoon," a calm stretch of river where the water is particularly vibrant. The trail then crosses two suspension bridges before reaching El Teñideros. From the trail you can see a small stream pouring into the Río Buenavista, which tumbles down from Tenorio Volcano. Where the two streams meet, the water seems to turn bright blue. The color results from a substance composed of aluminosilicates—a combination of aluminum, silicon and oxygen—that coats the bottom of the river. The substance, which forms where the two streams meet, absorbs all colors except blue, which is reflected back and gives the water a blue appearance. Local lore offers a different explanation: when God was finished painting the sky, he dipped his paintbrush in the river.

As you head back along the trail, keep your eyes out for howler monkeys, agoutis and tapirs. According to park rangers, Tenorio National Park is the second best place to see tapirs in Costa Rica after Corcovado. Tapirs feed on the jícaro danto tree (*Parmentiera valeri*), which is endemic to the Guanacaste Mountain Range. Tenorio Volcano's crater is also home to a small lake called *Lago Las Dantas* where tapirs (*dantas* in Spanish) sometimes drink.

La Cangreja Waterfall

RINCÓN DE LA VIEJA

THIS RUGGED NATIONAL park, located in the northwest corner of Costa Rica, is famous for great hiking trails and unusual volcanic geology. The name *Rincón de la Vieja* literally means "Old Woman's Corner," but in this case it's best translated as "Witch's Hideout." After spending some time in the park you'll understand why. A wide range of unusual volcanic features—bubbling mud pots, sulfurous hot springs, steamy pits—give the park an eerie, haunted feel. This is Costa Rica's version of Yellowstone, providing an unusual glimpse of earth's dirty, smelly inner workings.

Over 40 km (25 miles) of hiking trails crisscross the southern half of the park, providing access to geological oddities, beautiful waterfalls and the crater of the park's namesake volcano, which rises 1,806 meters (5,925 feet) above sea level. Private tour operators offer a wide range of outdoor adventures such as canopy tours, horseback riding and whitewater inner tubing. However you choose to wear yourself out, you can finish the day at one of the soothing thermal pools located just outside the park.

Yet despite all the activities and the fact that the park lies less than an hour's drive from the international airport in Liberia, Rincón de la Vieja remains well under the tourist radar. Surrounded by cattle ranches and wide open spaces, it has an authentic, rustic feel. If you're looking for a rural adventure destination that isn't overrun with tourists, it's hard to beat Rincón de la Vieja.

The geothermal energy that generates mudpots and fumaroles in Rincón de la Vieja was recently tapped to generate something more useful: electricity. In 2011 a $160 million geothermal energy plant opened just outside the park, providing a continuous source of cheap, sustainable electricity. When operating at full capacity, the plant generates 35 megawatts of electricity—enough to power about 100,000 homes. It has been estimated, however, that land within the national park has enough potential to generate over five times that amount. Although national park land is legally off limits to development, the Costa Rican government recently introduced a controversial bill to sidestep that ban.

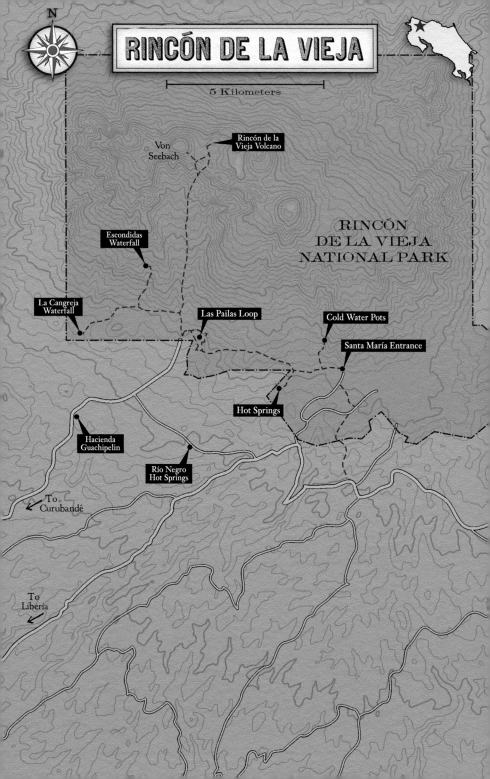

Getting to Rincón de la Vieja

The Las Pailas entrance to Rincón de la Vieja is located 10 kms (6.2 miles) from the tiny village of Curubandé (15-minute drive), 26 kms (16 miles) from Liberia (45-minute drive) and 230 km (143 miles) from San José (4-hour drive). Note: The Las Pailas entrance is only accessible via a private road administered by hotel Hacienda Guachipelin. You'll have to pay a $1.50 per person toll to use this private road. Tranbasa buses (2666-0517) depart Liberia for Curubandé at 6:40am, noon, 5pm (₡860, 40 minutes). Return buses depart at 5:30am, 7:30am, 1:15pm. The Santa María entrance is located 24 km (15 miles) from Liberia (45-minute drive) via the small village of San Jorge.

Getting around Rincón de la Vieja

Rincón de la Vieja is located in a remote, sparsely populated area, so the main issue is getting from your hotel to the park entrance. Many local hotels offer guided tours of the park that include transportation, but having your own car is nice if you want to visit on your own schedule. Due to the bumpy dirt roads (which become muddy in rainy season) 4x4 is definitely recommended.

Rincón de la Vieja Hotels

There are about a dozen hotels near Rincón de la Vieja, covering the full spectrum from cheap to luxurious. Most are all-inclusive, providing meals and offering tours. Visit www.jameskaiser.com for complete hotel info.

Rincón de la Vieja National Park

Protecting over 14,000 hectares (54 square miles), Rincón de la Vieja is a geothermal hotspot that's home to some of Costa Rica's most fascinating geology. The park has two entrances: *Las Pailas* ("The Cauldrons") and Santa María, which are located about 5 km (3.1 miles) apart—a roughly 20-minute drive along bumpy dirt roads. Both entrances provide access to the park's extensive network of hiking trails, but Las Pailas is far more popular due to its proximity to the park's most spectacular sights. If you're only here for a day or two, focus on Las Pailas. Open 7am to 4pm, closed Mondays. Admission: $10 per person.

The most popular hiking trail in the park is the 3-km (1.9-mile) loop located just east of the Las Pailas Ranger Station. The trail passes by the park's most impressive geothermal features, including bubbling mud pots, steamy fumaroles, and an otherworldly lagoon. Hiking the loop takes about two hours.

Another popular trail heads to *La Cangreja* ("The Crab") Waterfall, a 40-meter (131-foot) stunner that tumbles into a lovely pool. This is a great place to relax, swim and eat a picnic lunch. The trail to La Cangreja is 5 km (3 miles) and takes about four hours round-trip. Another option is the 4.3-km (2.7-mile) trail to the Escondidas Waterfalls, a series of four waterfalls 60 meters (197 feet) high. The trail to Escondidas Waterfalls is about four hours round-trip from Las Pailas.

The most challenging trail in the park heads to the lake-filled crater of Rincón de la Vieja volcano. The trail is 8 kms (5 miles) long, rises roughly 1,000 meters (3,281 feet) and takes about eight hours round-trip. As of this writing, however, the trail was closed due to volcanic activity. If the trail is open, I highly recommend going with a guide who can safely lead you to the top. Most hotels can arrange private guides.

Crowds are rarely a problem at Las Pailas, but if you're really looking to get away from it all, head to the Santa María entrance. From the entrance (reached via an unmarked turnoff up a narrow, rugged road), a trail heads 3 km (1.9 miles) to a natural hot spring. Though not as scenic or comfortable as the private hot springs found outside the park, it is definitely more natural.

Hacienda Guachipelin

This large hotel/ranch borders the park and offers a full array of adventure tours including horseback riding, a canopy tour, waterfall canyoning and whitewater inner tubing down the Rio Negro. Individual tours cost $35–55 per person, but there's also a one-day adventure pass ($55 adults, $45 kids, not including $10 park entrance fee) that lets you take multiple tours from 8am to 5pm, including a visit to the Rio Negro Hot Springs ($10 per person without the pass). Hacienda Guachipelin also runs Simbiosis Spa, which offers beauty treatments, massage and thermal pools. (2666-8075, www.guachipelin.com)

SOUTHERN MOUNTAINS

THIS REMOTE, HIGH-ALTITUDE region is overlooked by most tourists, but if you don't mind the chilly climate you'll be treated to some of Costa Rica's most rugged and dramatic scenery. Unlike the far more famous Northern Mountains, which can feel touristy in places, the Southern Mountains remain delightfully authentic. This is a rural region of small farming villages nestled in deep mountain valleys. Although a handful of nice lodges and restaurants have popped up in recent years, for the most part the pace of life hasn't changed in decades.

The region's largest town, Cartago, is situated at the foot of Irazú Volcano, which towers 3,432 meters (11,260 feet) above sea level. Downtown Cartago is a bustling commercial hub that's home to Costa Rica's most famous church, the Basílica de los Ángeles. Within a short drive of Cartago are several interesting destinations, including the beautiful Orosi Valley and Guayabo National Monument, Costa Rica's most impressive archaeological site.

Southeast of Cartago the Pan-American Highway heads up into the rugged Talamanca Mountains—the tallest mountains between Guatemala and Colombia. South of the highway lies the Zona de los Santos, a series of small towns where life revolves around the coffee harvest. This area is also famous for its high concentration of quetzals, one of Costa Rica's most beautiful birds. Beyond the Zona de los Santos the highway passes the chilly *Cerro de la Muerte* ("Hill of Death"), before descending towards San Isidro de El General, a medium-sized town situated in a lovely valley.

Towering above San Isidro is Chirripó, Costa Rica's tallest peak, which rises 3,820 meters (12,533 feet) above sea level. A rugged trail heads to the top of Chirripó, whose summit provides views of both the Caribbean Sea and the Pacific Ocean (on clear days). A rustic shelter near the peak offers overnight lodging, allowing hikers to spend multiple days enjoying the high altitude scenery.

To be sure, the Southern Mountains are not for everyone. If you're dreaming of palms trees and fruity cocktails, this is not the place for you. But if you love mountains and rural authenticity, and don't mind swapping sandals for sweaters, you're going to love it here. After spending some time on the hot, humid coast, the Southern Mountains are a cool breath of fresh air.

CARTAGO

CARTAGO IS THE largest town in the Southern Mountains and one of Costa Rica's most historically important towns. Founded in 1563 by Juan Vásquez de Coronado, it was the country's first Spanish settlement and Costa Rica's original capital. In 1823, shortly after independence, the citizens of San José defeated the citizens of Cartago at the Battle of Ochomogo (p.145) and the capital was moved to San José. Although the hard feelings have long since vanished, Cartago has been overshadowed by San José ever since.

Located just 22 km (14 miles) east of San José, Cartago (pop. 160,000) is technically considered part of the Central Valley. But thanks to the Ochomogo Pass, a narrow mountain pass that separates Cartago from San José and separates the Atlantic and Pacific watersheds, Cartago feels largely disconnected from the Central Valley's urban sprawl. Although the downtown is dirty and congested, the small urban core is surrounded by farms and forests.

Cartago is also noticeably cooler than the Central Valley. Located 1,435 meters (4,708 feet) above sea level—265 meters (869 feet) higher than San José—days in Cartago are often sunny and mild, but temperatures can get chilly at night. Those cool temperatures are what attracted the original Spanish settlers, who found Cartago far more pleasant than the sweltering coast.

Although hardly a tourist highlight, Cartago is home to Costa Rica's most famous church, the Basílica de los Ángeles. Each year on August 2, the Basílica hosts over one million visitors who travel to Cartago on foot from all over Central America. These visitors come to pay their respects to the church's patron saint, *La Virgen de los Ángeles* (aka *La Negrita*).

Once you've gotten your fill of Cartago's gritty downtown, you can check out some of the nice destinations that lie just a short drive away. The most famous is Irazú, an active volcano that towers above the northern edge of town. Irazú's eruptions have periodically terrorized Cartago's citizens, but these days its impressive crater is a popular tourist destination. Lying northeast of Irazú is Turrialba Volcano, which rumbled back to life in 2009 after nearly a century and a half of dormancy.

To the south of Cartago lies the lovely Orosi Valley, famous for coffee farms and Costa Rica's oldest colonial church. If you're looking for an authentic Costa Rican village unaffected by urban blight, Orosi is a great destination. The town is home to several charming B&Bs, and the surrounding scenery is perfect for a scenic drive.

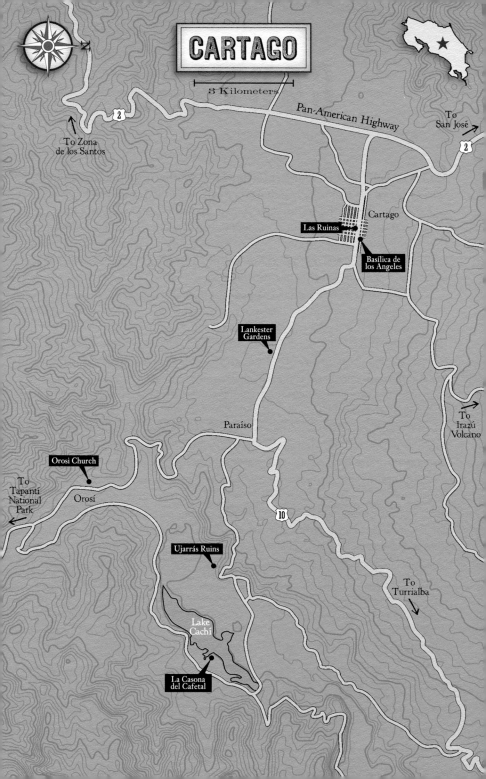

Las Ruinas

Getting to Cartago

Cartago is located 22 kms (14 miles) east of San José (30-minute drive). To drive to Cartago from downtown San José, head east along Avenida 2 until it merges with Highway 2, then follow the highway up and over the windy Ochomogo Pass, which separates Cartago from San José. Shuttle service to Cartago is offered by Grayline (p.20). Lumaca buses (2537-2320) depart San José for Cartago from Calle 5, Ave 10 every five minutes from 5:15am to midnight (₡500, 45 minutes).

Getting Around Cartago

Downtown Cartago's main tourist sights are easily visited on foot. If you're interested in visiting the popular sights outside Cartago—Irazú, Orosi, Guayabo—it's best to have your own car, although it's possible to hire a taxi in downtown Cartago near the Basílica de los Ángeles. It's also possible to travel around by bus, but you'll need a good grasp of Spanish and sense of adventure.

Cartago Hotels

I don't recommend spending the night in downtown Cartago for two reasons: 1. There aren't that many decent hotels, and 2. There are some great hotels in the beautiful countryside outside Cartago, especially in Orosi. For complete hotel info visit www.jameskaiser.com

Basílica de los Ángeles

This beautiful church is the most important religious site in Costa Rica. Officially called *La Basílica de Nuestra Señora de los Ángeles*, its claim to fame revolves around its association with the *La Virgen de los Ángeles* (aka *La Negrita*), a small stone statue discovered by a local indigenous girl in 1635 (p.51). The original church was built in 1639, and the current structure was rebuilt in 1912. The small statue of La Negrita is usually perched above the altar in an ornate golden frame.

Each year on August 2, over one million people walk to the Basílica to celebrate the discovery of the Virgen de los Ángeles. Most of these visitors, called *romeros* ("pilgrims"), walk 22 km (13.7 miles) from San José to Cartago, but some come from as far away as Panama and Nicaragua. The most devout romeros arrive barefoot, and some even approach on their hands and knees. On the morning of August 2, an outdoor ceremony features speeches by religious leaders and the president of Costa Rica.

The Basílica attracts devout worshippers throughout the year, and visitors often show their respect by walking down the center aisle on their knees. Mass is held daily at 6am, 9am, 11am and 6pm. If you step inside the church, please be respectful. When Mass is being conducted, do not wander around and take photos. After you've explored the inside of the church, head outside and follow the path to the grotto behind the church. Here you will find a spring dispensing holy water, and a small museum that includes a representation of the Virgen de los Ángeles and hundreds of *exvotos* (small religious offerings).

Las Ruinas

Seven blocks west of La Basílica de los Ángeles are *Las Ruinas*, "The Ruins," which mark the location of an old, abandoned stone church. According to legend, the site has been cursed since the mid-17th centurys when the priest of the church and his brother both fell in love with the same beautiful girl. When the girl began a relationship with the priest's brother, the priest grew enraged and murdered his brother in the church. Shortly thereafter, the church was destroyed by an earthquake. Although it was rebuilt several times, the church was repeatedly destroyed by earthquakes. The current ruins date to a powerful earthquake in 1910. Ironically, Las Ruinas is now a popular gathering spot for young lovers, though on foggy nights the ghost of the murderous priest is said to wander the grounds. The garden-filled interior, which is normally closed off by iron gates, is open to the public the first Sunday of every month.

Costa Rica Craft Brewing Company

Costa Rica's most famous craft brewer offers guided tours ($10/person) Weds, Thurs at 2:30pm, 3:30pm and 4:30pm; Sat at 1pm and 2:30pm. The entire brewing process is explained in detail, and the tour concludes with a tasting of their beers (including several varieties not commercially available). During the week they're open Mon–Fri 9am–5pm, Sat 1pm–4pm. The brewery is located 3 km (1.9 miles) south of downtown Cartago off the Pan-American Highway. Note: There are plans to move the brewery to Ciudad Colón (west of San José) sometime in 2015; call ahead to confirm their current location. (2573-3724, www.beer.cr)

Lankester Gardens

If you're interested in botany, it's worth visiting these extensive gardens, which feature over 3,000 plant species. The highlights are the 1,000 orchid species, many of which bloom March–May. The gardens were founded by the British naturalist Charles Lankester, and today they are operated by the University of Costa Rica as a research center. Located 4 km (2.5 miles) southeast of Cartago near Paraíso. Open 8:30am–4:30pm. Admission: $8. (2511-7939, www.jbl.ucr.ac.cr)

Restaurants

LA CASONA DE CAFETAL (Lnch: $16–25)
The region's most famous restaurant is located on the shores of Lake Cachí. Surrounded by coffee fields, it serves traditional Costa Rican food. (2577-1414)

LA PUERTA DEL SOL (Brk: $7–9; Lnch, Din: $8–12)
Downtown Cartago's best restaurant is located just north of the Basílica de los Ángeles. The menu offers plenty of Costa Rican classics. (2551-0615)

Irazú Volcano

Towering 3,432 meters (11,260 feet) above sea level, Irazú is the tallest volcano in Costa Rica. Although the origin of the name *Irazú* is unknown, it is most likely derived from indigenous words that mean "earthquake" and "thunder." Over the past 300 years Irazú has experienced over 20 eruptions, most recently on March 19, 1963—a date that coincided with the arrival of U.S. President John F. Kennedy. As the Catholic Kennedy was mobbed by crowds in downtown San José, ash ejected by Irazú rained down over the Central Valley. The ash drifted as far away as Tamarindo, over 200 km (124 miles) distant, and in places the ash layers were 0.5 meters (1.6 feet) thick. These days Irazú's activity is confined to a handful of smoking fumaroles.

Irazú National Park lies 14 km (8.7 miles) northeast of Cartago. A paved road heads 27 km (17 miles) from downtown Cartago and climbs 2,000 meters (6,562 feet) to the rim of the volcano's crater. The drive takes about 45 minutes, and on clear days you'll be treated to spectacular views of the broad valleys below. From the park entrance a path heads to a viewpoint where you can peer into the depths of the lake-filled crater, which measures 1,050 meters (3,445 feet) across and 300 meters (984 feet) deep. On clear days it's possible to see both the Caribbean and Pacific from the top of Irazú, but on most days thick clouds cover the volcano by 10am. Needless to say, it's best to arrive early. Open 8am–4pm, last entrance 3pm. Admission: $10 per person. A bus departs San José for Irazú at 8am from Calle 6, Ave 1/3; the bus departs Irazú for San José at 12:30pm.

Orosi Valley

This beautiful valley, located 10 kms (6.2 miles) southeast of Cartago, is filled with coffee farms and surrounded by lush mountains. It's a terrific destination if you're interested in visiting a traditional Costa Rican village that remains largely unaffected by urbanization. The town (pop. 10,000) is centered around a large plaza with a charming colonial church, la Iglesia de San José Orosi, on the west end. The church was built in 1743 by Franciscan missionaries, and today it's the oldest functioning church in Costa Rica. Inside the church is a small museum with some interesting Spanish colonial objects. Orosi is also home to two hot springs: Los Balnearios (2533-2156) and Los Patios (2533-3009).

Towards the southern end of the Orosi Valley is Tapantí National Park, a rarely-visited park that offers several kilometers of hiking trails and great bird watching. This is one of the wettest areas in Costa Rica, receiving up to 7 meters (23 feet) of rain annually. Open 8am–4pm. Admission: $10 per person.

If you visit Orosi by car, it's worth making a loop around Lake Cachí, a man-made lake that powers a large hydroelectric dam. On the eastern side of the lake is La Casona de Cafetal (p.245), a famous lakeside restaurant surrounded by coffee fields that serves traditional Costa Rican food. Continue around the lake and you'll pass the turnoff for the Ujarrás Ruins, the crumbling remains of Costa Rica's oldest church, built in 1693. The 30-km (18.6- mile) loop that wraps around Orosi and Lake Cachí takes about 45 minutes to drive starting from the town of Paraíso (a 10-minute drive southeast of Cartago).

Turrialba Volcano

Although located just 10 km (6.2 miles) northeast of Irazú Volcano, Turrialba is one of the most rugged and least visited volcanoes in Costa Rica. Reached via a series of bumpy dirt roads, it rises 3,340 meters (10,958 feet) above sea level, and its slopes are surrounded by cool cloud forests and dairy farms. This is where Costa Rica's popular Turrialba cheese is produced. If you're a volcano-lover looking for a rustic destination with no crowds, this is the place to visit. From Cartago it's a roughly 1.5-hour drive.

Turrialba Volcano experienced a major eruption in 1864, ejecting massive amounts of ash over a four-year period. Following that eruption, the volcano stayed quiet for roughly 140 years. Then, in 2009, Turrialba rumbled back to life, belching thick clouds of ash and vapor. In response the government closed Turrialba National Park, and for the most part it has remained closed since then. If the park is open when you visit, a steep, rugged road heads up the side of the volcano towards the crater (four-wheel-drive is necessary). The main crater is about 50 meters (164 feet) deep and filled with smoking fumaroles. Open 8am–3pm. Admission: $10 per person.

In my opinion, the best way to visit the volcano is to spend the night at the Turrialba Lodge (2273-4335, www.volcanturrialbalodge.com), a working cattle farm with impressive views of the volcano. This is the only hotel anywhere near the park, and it offers a variety of guided tours. Bring warm clothes—temperatures often drop below freezing at night.

Guayabo National Monument

Located 7 km (4.3 miles) north of Turrialba, Guayabo National Monument is home to Costa Rica's most impressive archaeological ruins. That said, it's best to arrive with low expectations. Compared to the world-class ruins of the Aztec and Maya, Guayabo seems pretty lackluster. But if you're passing through the area and interested in archeology, it's definitely worth a visit.

Situated between Turrialba Volcano to the northwest and the imposing Talamanca Mountains to the east, Guayabo is located next to the most accessible route between the Caribbean lowlands and the Central Highlands. This strategic position made Guayabo a vital commercial link between the two ecosystems. It was probably founded around 1,000 BC, and it reached the height of its development between 300 and 700 AD. At its peak Guayabo may have been home to as many as 15,000 people. The ancient city's most impressive features are stone roads, retaining walls, petroglyphs and a functioning aqueduct system. A series of large, circular mounds were probably used as foundations for dwellings. Archaeological evidence indicates residents farmed yucca, corn and pejibaye. Although Guayabo thrived for hundreds of years, it was mysteriously abandoned in the 15th century, shortly before the arrival of the Spanish. The first excavation was organized in 1882, and gold figures and ceramic objects excavated here are now on display at the National Museum in San José.

Guayabo National Park is located 60 km (37 miles) from Cartago (1.5-hour drive). Open 8am–3:30pm. Admission: $10.

ZONA DE LOS SANTOS

THE ZONA DE LOS SANTOS ("Zone of the Saints") is one of Costa Rica's most beautiful—and overlooked—destinations. Filled with coffee farms and cloud forests, it's well off the beaten path, but those who venture here are rewarded with stunning landscapes and the slow pace of authentic rural life. Once you've gotten your fill of the beach and the jungle, consider visiting these small, traditional towns, where coffee and quetzals (p.108) dominate the agenda.

The small village of San Gerardo de Dota is the most popular destination in the Zona de los Santos. Famous for quetzals, which migrate to this remote mountain valley to feed on the wild avocado trees, it's a bird watchers paradise. But you don't have to be a birder to enjoy San Gerardo de Dota. The town is also home to a handful of great hiking trails, and trout fishing in the cool Savegre river is also popular. In recent years several charming hotels have opened up, and there are even a handful of upscale restaurants.

West of San Gerardo de Dota lies Santa María de Dota (pop. 4,000), which is just beginning to dabble in tourism. This tidy town might just be the most charming coffee destination Costa Rica. The steep mountains that surround Santa María are covered in coffee farms, and the local cooperative, Coopedota, offers tours of the local processing facility. If you visit during peak harvest, Dec–Feb, you'll get to witness the entire process from picking to packing. But even if you visit in the off-season, you can still take the tour and sample delicious coffee at Coopedota's nice cafe.

East of Santa María de Dota is Copey, a tiny pueblo that's charmingly trapped in time. West of Santa María de Dota lies the *canton* ("county") of Tarrazú, which produces the most coffee in Costa Rica. Due to its rich soils and high elevation, many people consider Tarrazú coffee to be the country's best. Tarrazú's largest town is San Marcos (pop. 9,000), a bustling commercial hub where the population triples during peak harvest season.

Keep in mind that tourist offerings in the Zona de los Santos are sparse and spread out. Don't expect to be overwhelmed with options, and be prepared to practice your Spanish. This isn't a place for the unadventurous, which is exactly the point. If you're looking to step back in time and experience the quiet peace of rural life that long characterized Costa Rica, there's no better place than the Zona de los Santos.

San Gerardo de Dota

Getting to the Zona de los Santos

Santa María de Dota is located 42 km (26 miles) from Cartago (45-minute drive) and 60 km (37 miles) from San José (1.25-hour drive). San Gerardo de Dota is located 46 km (29 miles) from Santa María de Dota (45-minute drive) and 70 km (44 miles) from Cartago (1-hour drive). Both towns are located off the Pan-American Highway, which runs between Cartago and Dominical. If you're driving to/from San José, the most dramatic route is via Frailes and San Marcos de Tarrazú, which takes you through some of the most beautiful coffee scenery in Costa Rica. "Los Santos" buses (2546-7248) to Santa María de Dota (₡1,950, 2 hours) depart San José from the MUSOC Terminal at Calle Central, Ave 20 at 6am, 9am, 12pm, 2:30pm, 3pm, 5pm, 7:30pm.

Getting Around Zona de los Santos

Simply put, you'll want a car. This is a rural area where the attractions are spread out. Although it's possible to get around by bus or taxi, having a car will allow you visit various places on your own schedule.

Zona de los Santos Hotels

Lodging is limited in the Zona de los Santos, and most hotels are small-scale mom-and-pop operations. San Gerardo de Dota has the most luxurious options, and there are handful of simple options in Santa María de Dota and Copey. Visit www.jameskaiser.com for complete hotel info.

Santa María de Dota

Nestled in a gorgeous mountain valley where the hills are covered in coffee farms, Santa María de Dota gets my vote for the most authentic small town in Costa Rica. The pace of life is delightfully laid-back, and during peak harvest (Dec–Feb) indigenous Guaymí migrant workers in colorful clothes stroll around town. Santa María's main attraction is Coopedota, the local coffee cooperative that works with over 700 local farmers to process, pack and ship their delicious harvest around the world.

★ COOPEDOTA

This local cooperative offers one of Costa Rica's best coffee tours. Coopedota was the first cooperative in the world to offer certified Carbon Neutral coffee, and they have taken impressive steps to recycle their waste and reduce their environmental impact (all of which is explained on the tour). A small cafe next to the processing facility sells over 30 coffee drinks, baked goods and bags of excellent fresh-roasted coffee. (2541-2828, www.coopedota.com)

Tarrazú

This 300-square-kilometer (116-square-mile) region produces the most coffee in Costa Rica. Coffee grown at Tarrazú's cool, high elevation, 1,400–1,600 meters (4,600–5,250 feet), takes longer to ripen, producing a harder, higher quality bean. Tarrazú's largest town is San Marcos, located 7 km (4.4 miles) west of Santa María de Dota. Other than driving through the region to get a sense of the scenery, the top attraction is Coopetarrazú, the local coffee cooperative which sells bags of coffee.

Copey & Providencia

The tiny pueblo of Copey, located 8 km (5 miles) east of Santa María de Dota, is home to a charming church, a nice soccer field, a small *pulpería* (corner store) and not much else. Quetzals are common from Feb–April, and local hotels can arrange tours. If you're feeling adventurous, head to the even smaller village of Providencia, located about 13 km (8 miles) southeast of Copey. The bumpy dirt road that heads to Providencia offers gorgeous mountain scenery.

Los Quetzales National Park

This national park opened in 2006, and though the name is exciting it still isn't ready for prime time. There are just a handful of hiking trails, and to be honest it's easier to spot quetzals in San Gerardo de Dota (p.257). Admission: $10.

Guaymí girl picking coffee in Santa María de Dota

San Gerardo de Dota

This remote mountain valley is the best place in Costa Rica to see quetzals (p.108), one of the world's most beautiful birds. But even if you're not a bird-watcher, San Gerardo de Dota is a great destination. The surrounding mountains are protected as Los Quetzales National Park, and despite a sprinkling of tourists not much has changed in decades. If you're looking to experience the beauty of the cloud forest, but don't want to deal with the crowds at Monteverde, San Gerardo de Dota is a great alternative.

A single 9-km (5.6-mile) road descends from the Panamerican Highway to San Gerardo de Dota, and all the town's attractions are located along the road. Lying between 2,000–3,000 meters (6,562–9,843 feet) above sea level, San Gerardo de Dota is a chilly mountain town where average temperatures range from 8–17°C (46–63°F) and jackets or sweaters are required at night. It's not tropical, but a cool night curled up in front of a fire with a cup of *agua dulce* (p.88) can be divine.

Thanks to an abundance of wild avocado trees, quetzals are common throughout the valley, and quetzal watching is the town's top activity. Peak season is Jan–May, though with a good guide quetzals can be spotted any time of year. All hotels can arrange guided tours, and during peak season it's entirely possible to spot quetzals on your own. Birders can also look for emerald toucanets, collared trogons and volcano hummingbirds.

Near the southern end of the valley is the town's most popular hike, an easy 1-km (0.6-mile) trail that follows the Rio Savegre to pretty waterfall. The most challenging hike is the 9-km (5.6-mile) trail that connects San Gerardo de Dota with Cerro de la Muerte (p.259). The trail starts/ends at Savegre Lodge, and several hotels offer guided hikes that descend from Cerro de la Muerte to San Gerardo ($60, 6 hours). The Savegre Lodge also has over 30 km of hiking trails on their property that non-guests can hike for $10/person.

Trout fishing is also popular in the cool, clear Rio Savegre, which flows through the center of the valley. If you didn't bring your own gear, Los Lagos Restaurant has a stocked pond where, for $7, you can easily hook a trout using fishing poles. They will even clean and cook your catch.

★LE TAPIR (Brk: $12; Lnch, Din: $14–21)
The most upscale restaurant in town, located in the chic Dantica lodge. Homemade pasta and Latin-Euro fusion flavors. Reservations necessary. (2740-1067)

KAHAWA CAFE (Lnch, Din: $9–11)
Trout is the specialty at this charming open-air restaurant, which features a great location next to the Savegre River. (2740-1081)

MIRIAM'S (Brk: $6; Lnch, Din: $8)
For delicious homemade meals, visit Miriam, who serves up filling Costa Rican food from her home just up the hill from Dantica. (2740-1049)

Cerro de la Muerte

Towering 3,451 meters (11,322 feet) above sea level, *Cerro de la Muerte* ("Hill of Death") is the country's fourth-highest peak. Located just off the Pan-American Highway, it's reached via a dirt road, and the peak itself is covered in communication towers. At night temperatures can drop below freezing, and Cerro de la Muerte is named for the travelers who froze to death here in the pre-highway days. At the peak of the last Ice Age, roughly 20,000 years ago, Cerro de la Muerte was home to a 5-square-kilometer (1.9-square-mile) glacier.

CHIRRIPÓ

REACHING A MAXIMUM elevation of 3,820 meters (12,533 feet), Chirripó is Costa Rica's tallest mountain and one of the country's most rugged destinations. Its dramatic peak is reached via a 20-km (12.4-mile) trail that rises over 2,200 vertical meters (7,218 feet) from the tiny mountain village of San Gerardo de Rivas. Along the way, hikers pass through cloud forests and *páramos*—a unique ecosystem found only at high elevations in the New World tropics. From Chirripó's summit, sweeping 360-degree views tumble down over graceful valleys and shimmering lakes. On clear days you can see both the Caribbean *and* the Pacific! If you're a strong hiker who doesn't mind frigid temperatures, Chirripó is one of Costa Rica's most rewarding adventures.

Of course, Chirripó is not for the faint of heart. Exceptionally strong hikers can summit and return in a single day, but most mortals spend two to three days hiking the steep mountain. Overnight hikers spend the night at Crestones Base Camp, a rugged lodge located at 3,400 meters (11,155 feet) that's 5.5 km (3.4 miles) from Chirripó's summit. The base camp accommodates up to 60 guests and offers basic features like bunk beds, bathrooms and ice-cold showers. (If you've never had the opportunity to see your breath while showering, Crestones Base Camp will give you that chance.) Daytime temperatures at Crestones range between 4–18°C (40°–65°F), while nighttime temperatures can drop below 0°C (32°F). Although hardly luxurious, the base camp puts Chirripó within the reach of average hikers and makes sunrise summits feasible.

Both Chirripó and Crestones Base Camp are located within the boundaries of Chirripó National Park, which covers over 50,900 hectares (197 square miles) in the Talamanca Mountains. Although the park has dozens of kilometers of hiking trails, most of the hiking highlights are located within a few kilometers of Crestones Base Camp. After successfully summiting Chirripó, you can hike the trail to Ventisqueros, at 3,812 meters (12,507 feet) Costa Rica's second highest peak, or follow trails to beautiful valleys and lakes. Many people stay at least two nights at Crestones Base Camp to take advantage of all the nearby trails. Without a doubt, Chirripó National Park is the hiking capital of Costa Rica.

Although Chirripó National Park is accessible from several entrance points, nearly everyone enters from San Gerardo de Rivas, a quaint mountain village located about 1,400 meters (4,593 feet) above sea level. The trail to Chirripó starts from the upper end of town, and a handful of hotels cater specifically to hikers. If you're looking for an authentic Tico village, San Gerardo de Rivas is hard to beat. Its home to spectacular landscapes and a handful of interesting activities, including tours of local farms and day hikes to beautiful waterfalls.

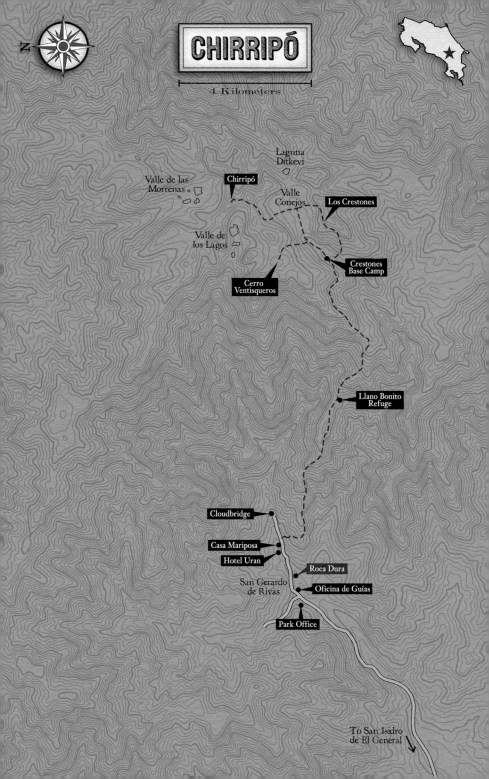

Getting to San Gerardo de Rivas

San Gerardo de Rivas is located 148 kms (92 miles) from San José (3-hour drive) and 20 kms (12.4 miles) east of San Isidro de El General (30-minute drive), the closest major town. The last 10 km of the road to San Gerardo de Rivas is unpaved. Hernandez Solis buses (2771-2314) depart San Isidro de El General for San Gerardo de Rivas at 9:30am, 2pm, 6:45pm (₡1,000, 1.5 hours). Taxis from San Isidro to San Gerardo de Rivas cost around $40.

Getting Around San Gerardo de Rivas

Although San Gerardo de Rivas is small, the landscape is quite steep, and the 2-km (0.6-mile) hike from the town center to the trailhead will definitely make you sweat. Some hotels offer to take you to the trailhead

San Gerardo de Rivas Hotels

There are a handful of hotels in San Gerardo, including two that are steps from the trailhead, and several in "downtown" San Gerardo, which is about 2 km (0.6 miles) from the trailhead. Several of the downtown hotels offer free shuttles to the trailhead and/or camping on their property. There are also several upscale boutique hotels just outside San Gerardo. Visit www.jameskaiser.com for complete hotel information.

San Gerardo de Rivas

Nestled in a beautiful mountain valley, this tiny pueblo survives on a mix of agriculture and Chirripó tourism. Yet despite the steady trickle of hikers, San Gerardo de Rivas feels remarkably authentic and undiscovered. There's a soccer field, a church, a school and a small market with a surprisingly decent selection of backpacking food. The surrounding area has a number of interesting activities—coffee tour, trout farm, cheese factory—but almost none have official schedules; it's best to ask your hotel manager, who will probably know the person to call. About two kilometers east of town is the private Cloudbridge Nature Reserve (www.cloudbridge.org), which protects 700 acres adjacent to Chirripó National Park. The reserve is open to the public, and it has several great hiking trails.

The town's biggest festival is Carrera Chirripó (www.carrerachirripo.com), a 34-km (21-mile) footrace from San Gerardo de Rivas to Crestones Base Camp and back. Held the last Saturday in February, the race features 225 contestants, most of whom are Tico. As of 2014, the men's record, set by Juan Ramón Fallas, was three hours and four minutes and the women's record, set by Andrea Sanabria, an indigenous Bri Bri who walked two days from her remote mountain village to compete in the race, was four hours and 19 minutes!

ROCA DURA (Brk: $6; Lnch, Din: $8–12)
The town's most popular bar/restaurant overlooks the soccer field and serves tasty, filling food like casados and pastas. (2742-5071)

Chirripó National Park

One of the most rugged and remote national parks in Costa Rica, Chirripó is famous for its namesake mountain (the tallest between Guatemala and Colombia) and its impressive network of hiking trails. Many of the current trails follow ancient indigenous paths that once facilitated communication and commerce between the Caribbean and Pacific slopes. At the park's lower elevations cool cloud forests dominate the landscape, providing habitat for amazing animals such as quetzals, tapirs and jaguars. Around 3,400 meters (11,155 feet) the cloud forest gives way to *páramo* (p.105), a unique ecosystem found only at high elevations in Central and South America.

Because Chirripó National Park lies on the crest of the Talamanca Mountains, its climate is influenced by both Caribbean and Pacific weather systems. Conditions can, and do, change rapidly. Days that start off sunny and clear often become cloudy and rainy, and rainy mornings can give way to clear afternoons. The best time to visit is during the dry season, Jan–April, with Feb and March providing the best weather. That said, it can rain at any time of year. *Chirripó* is an indigenous word that means "Land of Eternal Waters," and the park receives up to 3.5 meters (11.5 feet) of rain each year. In October, the rainiest month, the park shuts down entirely. (The park also closes the last two weeks of May for trail maintenance, and the last weekend in February for the annual Chirripó footrace.)

All visitors to Chirripó National Park must purchase entrance permits ($18 per day), and those spending the night at Crestones Base Camp must make reservations ($10 person per night). Reservations are available the first Monday in November for hiking dates Dec–May, and the first Monday in May for hiking dates June–Sept. They are available through the park office (Tel: 2742-5083), which is open from 6:30am to 4:30pm. Chirripó is extremely popular with Ticos, and advance permits often sell out within hours of becoming available, *especially* for weekends and holidays. Even if you do secure a permit, you'll have to transfer money into the park's Costa Rican bank account.

To accommodate travelers who miss out on the initial round of advance permits, the park releases 10 additional permits the day before the hike. These permits, available at the park office in San Gerardo de Rivas, are offered on a first-come first-served basis starting at 6:30am, and some hikers start lining up as early as 4am to ensure a spot. (Tip: try to plan your departure date in the middle of the week when permits are easier to come by.) For more information visit the park website: www.parquenacionalchirripo.com

If you don't feel like hauling up your heavy gear, you can hire porters at the *Oficina de Guías* ("Guide's Office") in San Gerardo de Rivas. During the dry season, horses haul gear up the mountain; during the rainy season, the porters haul it up themselves. Cost is roughly $42 for 14 kg on the way up, $3 for each kg on the way down. The office is open from 11am to 6pm (Tel: 2742-5225), and gear rental and basic food supplies are also available. They can also arrange private hiking guides and cooking services at Crestones Base Camp.

The trailhead to Chirripó is located 2 km (0.6 miles) from the center of San Gerardo de Rivas. Crestones Base Camp is located 14.5 km (9 miles) from the trailhead; average hiking time: 8–10 hours. Visitors are required start their hike before 10am. (The average descent is 5–7 hours, and visitors are required to depart before noon.) The trail starts off steep and rugged, providing a good taste of what's to come. Wooden sign posts mark each kilometer. At kilometer 4 you'll reach the official park boundary. At kilometer 7.5 you'll reach Llano Bonito Refuge, which offers water and bathrooms. Once past the refuge, you'll encounter three of the trail's most challenging sections: *Cuesta de Agua* ("Water Slope"), *Monte Sin Fe* ("Faithless Mountain"), and *Cuesta de los Arrepentidos* ("The Slope of Regret"). As you climb you'll see plenty of burnt trees. Forest fires—some natural, some man-made—have burned in the park nearly every decade since the 1950s.

To get to the summit of Chirripó, head out from Crestones Base Camp to *Valle de Conejos* ("Rabbit Valley"). When you reach the T-intersection, turn left and head up towards the narrow saddle that provides the first dramatic views of Chirripó. The final push to the summit is a steep scramble, but you'll be rewarded with stunning 360-degree views. To the northeast is *Valle de las Morrenas* ("Valley of the Morraines"), home to over half a dozen lakes and the headwaters of the Chirripó Atlantic River, which flows to the Caribbean Sea. To the west is the *Valle de los Lagos* ("Valley of the Lakes"), home to the largest natural lake in Costa Rica and the headwaters of the Chirripó Pacific River, which flows to the Pacific Ocean. Both valleys were sculpted by Ice Age glaciers that flowed down from the sides of Chirripó 20,000 years ago. At their peak, the glaciers covered 35-square-km (13.5-square-miles) and extended as far as Crestones Base Camp.

Chirripó Checklist

• Winter Jacket, Warm Hat, Gloves - Even during the day temperatures can get chilly, and you need to dress accordingly.
• Sunscreen, Sunglasses, Broad Hat - The UV rays at 12,000 feet are even more powerful than the UV rays at the beach.
• Warm Sleeping Bag - Chirripó has the lowest recorded temperature in Costa Rica -9°C (16°F). A warm sleeping bag is essential at Crestones Base Camp.
• Rain gear - Rainstorms are possible any time of year. Be prepared.
• Layers - Average temperatures vary between 0–20°C (32–68°F) and often change rapidly. Dressing in layers helps you adjust quickly and easily.
• Camping Stove and Gas - Essential for hot drinks and warm food at Crestones Base Camp. (Pots, pans and utensils are provided.)
• Hiking Poles or Walking Stick - Especially helpful on the descent.
• Water Bottle and Snacks - You're going to need them.
• First Aid Kit - Just in case.

Overlooking Valle de Conejos

View of Valle de los Lagos from Chirripó

NICOYA PENINSULA

BEACHES, BEACHES AND beaches. Covering most of Costa Rica's northern Pacific coast, the Nicoya Peninsula is home to some of the country's most famous and beautiful beaches—from white sand crescents sheltering sapphire bays to thundering, world-class surf breaks. This region is also home to Costa Rica's driest climate, with nearly six months of steady sunshine from mid-November to April. If you're looking for surf, sand and sun, look no farther.

Unlike the rest of Costa Rica, beaches and beach life are more popular here than wildlife watching and eco-tourism. But there are a handful of world-class eco-highlights. Playa Ostional, located about halfway down the peninsula, is home to spectacular mass nestings of sea turtles. At certain times between July and November, thousands of turtles crawl ashore to lay their eggs in the sand. Farther north at Playa Grande, critically endangered leatherback turtles lay their eggs between November and February.

The Nicoya Peninsula has long been one of the most popular destinations in Costa Rica, but its popularity surged following the opening of Liberia's international airport in 2003. Suddenly, "Sun and Fun" tourists began flooding in at an unprecedented rate. A burst of development ensued in the northern Nicoya (the area closest to the new airport), leaving some backpackers lamenting the crowded, upscale state of a few formerly low-key beaches. The upside is a boom in hotel, restaurant and tour options. Twenty years ago your travel options were limited to rugged and rugged. Today you can choose between rugged, luxurious and everything in between.

When planning your trip to Nicoya, it's best to divide the peninsula into three parts: northern Nicoya, central Nicoya and southern Nicoya. Northern Nicoya—Tamarindo north—is home to stunning beaches, scalloped bays and *lots* of development. Hotels run the gamut from cheap to chic, and great restaurants abound. Some people love all the action, others are put off by the crowds, but a rental car is all you need to access beautiful, secluded beaches. Central Nicoya—Nosara and Sámara—strikes a nice balance between scenery and development. It's great for families, couples and eco-travelers looking for lovely beaches and quiet nights. Southern Nicoya—Santa Teresa to Montezuma—is rugged and remote, attracting a steady stream of backpackers and surfers. The roads are unpaved, the beaches are uncrowded and the travelers are unshaven.

Wherever you end up, keep in mind that during peak dry season (Feb-April) the scenery throughout most of the Nicoya Peninsula is dusty and brown. If you're looking for lush jungle, it's best to head south during the dry season.

Liberia

Although Liberia isn't officially part of the Nicoya Peninsula, the Daniel Oduber International Airport is the main jumping off point for many Nicoya visitors. Liberia is the capital of Guanacaste Province, which covers much of northwest Costa Rica. The town was founded in 1769 when Guanacaste still belonged to Nicaragua, and it quickly became a commercial hub for the cattle ranching industry. On July 25, 1824, the citizens of Guanacaste, fed up with civil war in Nicaragua, voted to be annexed by Costa Rica. Liberia celebrates the annexation each July 25 with a giant fiesta featuring *corridas de toros* (bullfights), *topes* (horse parades), and *Punto Guanacasteco*, the region's traditional dance featuring women in white dresses and *bombas* (p.60).

Although Liberia was once filled with beautiful colonial buildings, most have been torn down to make way for bland, utilitarian shops selling bland, utilitarian items. Fortunately, a handful of old colonial buildings remain. If you want a glimpse of old Liberia, take a stroll down Calle Real (aka Calle Central), where several colonial houses have been reborn as charming hotels and restaurants. (Visit www.jameskaiser.com for complete Liberia hotel info.) Another interesting historic sight is the small, charming Iglesia La Ermita de la Agonía, which was built in 1865.

The international airport is 13 km (8 miles) west of downtown Liberia (10-minute drive). Buses depart from the Terminal Liberia and Terminal Pulmitan. Car rental agencies include Economy (2666-2816), Thrifty (2665-0787), National (2242-7878), Adobe (2667-0608), Avis (2668-1138), Budget (2668-1118), Dollar (2668-1061), Hertz (2668-1048), and Toyota (2668-1212).

Liberia Restaurants

★CAFÉ LIBERIA (Lnch, Din: $9–17)
Located in one of the most beautiful colonial buildings in Liberia, this upscale café is downtown's best restaurant. In addition to great coffee, espresso and baked goods, they offer chic cuisine that blends Costa Rican, Latin American and European flavors. (2665-1660)

TORO NEGRO (Lnch, Din: $9–19)
Housed in a charming colonial building just beyond the main plaza, Toro Negro offers traditional Costa Rican food. Be sure to grab a seat on the large, open-air balcony. Closed Monday. (2666-2456)

★Rincón de la Vieja National Park

Rincón de la Vieja (p.236) is famous for great hiking and geothermal features, and it's just a 45-minute drive from Liberia.

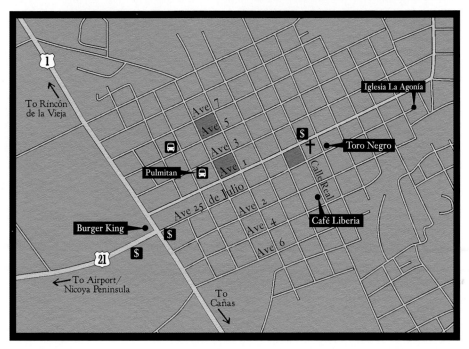

Africa Mía

This private wildlife refuge features free-roaming elephants, giraffes, zebras and other African wildlife. Cost: $30 adults, $18 kids. Jeep safaris are also available ($64 adults, $32 kids). Located 9 km (5.6 miles) south of Liberia. Open 9am–5pm. Closed Mon, Weds. (2666-1111)

Palo Verde National Park

Covering 18,400 hectares (71 square miles), Palo Verde National Park protects 13 different habitats, including rare tropical dry forest p.97, making it one of the most ecologically diverse parks in Costa Rica. The highlight is the wetland, which attracts more aquatic and wading birds than anywhere else in Central America. Nearly 300 bird species have been identified in the park, and peak birdwatching season is during the dry season (Dec–March), when thousands of birds gather at the lagoons to feed and breed. If you're a hardcore birder, Palo Verde should be near the top of your list. The park is open 8am to 4pm. Admission: $10. The turnoff to the park entrance is located across from the gas station in Bagaces, 27 km (17 miles) from Liberia (30-minute drive). From the turnoff it's another hour drive down a dirt road to the entrance. The Organization for Tropical Studies (2524-0607, www.ots.ac.cr) offers overnight lodging in the park. Guided day tours are available from Javier Vargas (8837-1531, www.lovingcostarica.com) and Palo Verde Boat Tours (2651-8001, www.paloverdeboattours.com)

Llanos de Cortés Waterfall

Considered one of the most beautiful waterfalls in Costa Rica, Llanos de Cortés is a broad curtain of water that tumbles into a large, shallow pool. Located just 22 km (13.7 miles) east of Liberia (a 25-minute drive), it makes a terrific trip if you're looking to escape the clutter of downtown. The turnoff, marked by a small wooden sign, is located about 4 km (2.5 miles) west of Bagaces on Highway 1 (The Inter-American Highway). From the turnoff, head 600 meters down the road, turn right at a small gate and drive five minutes to the large parking area. Admission, which benefits the local school, is $2 per person.

Santa Rosa National Park

This rugged national park, which lies just north of the Nicoya Peninsula, protects the largest remaining tract of tropical dry forest (p.98) in Central America. Most of the park is part of the Santa Elena Peninsula, which juts out into the Pacific just south of the Nicaraguan border. Santa Rosa was originally established to protect a historic battle site where Costa Rican troops defeated William Walker (p.148), but these days the majority of visitors are surfers looking to ride the amazing waves at Witch's Rock (*Roca Bruja* in Spanish) and Ollie's Point. Due to the rugged, isolated nature of the park, most surfers arrive by boat from Playa del Coco. If you're interested in a boat trip, get in touch with La Bruja Surf Trips (8835-1098, www.labrujasurftrips.com), which charges $300 for a full day trip (max. 5 people). There's also a basic seaside campground at Playa Naranjo, located just south of Witch's Rock, that's reached via a rugged 13-km (8-mile) dirt road (4x4 required in the dry season, impassible in the rainy season). The road starts at the Santa Rosa entrance station (Tel: 2666-5051), located 35 km (22 miles) north of Liberia off the Pan American Highway. Admission: $10. The campground ($2 per person, per night) has toilets and showers, but no drinking water.

Papagayo Peninsula

This spectacular peninsula, which lies just north of Playa del Coco and frames the western side of *Bahía Culebra* ("Snake Bay"), covers 2,300 acres and spans 15 miles of coastline. It's home to one of the most spectacular resorts in Central America: The Four Seasons Costa Rica, which commands the southern tip of the peninsula. The Papagayo Peninsula is home to a handful of stunning beaches, plus condos, private villas, a marina and an 18-hole golf course designed by Arnold Palmer.

But just because the peninsula is full of *fresas* (p.31) doesn't mean you have to miss out on all the fun. All beaches in Costa Rica are legally open to the public, including the beaches on the exclusive Papagayo Peninsula. To comply with this law, a large parking area has been set up near the entrance to the peninsula (about a 40-minute drive from Playas del Coco), and free shuttles transport visitors between the parking area and the beaches. The most popular and accessible beach is Playa Nacascolo, which draws lots of Tico families on the weekends. There are public bathrooms, showers and a small snack shop near the beach entrance.

The other beaches serviced by the shuttle—Playa Blanca, Playa Virador, Playa Prieta—are largely the domain of Four Seasons guests. Though technically open to the public, non-guests can access them only via a series of long, steep stairways that deter all but the most dogged visitors. (Four Seasons guests simply walk a few meters from the swimming pool.) No doubt about it, you'll have to physically earn these beaches, but they are stunning. If you'd like to visit any of these beaches (I'd recommend either Playa Blanca and Playa Virador), ask the driver to take you to the beach entrance and arrange for a pre-determined pickup time.

Non-guests can also make reservations at the Four Seasons' restaurants. They're pricey, but in addition to terrific food, you'll get an inside look at this stunning resort. Reservations are usually available to the public, though sometimes the restaurants are closed to non-guests during peak season.

★RESTAURANT PAPAGAYO (Brk: $20, Lnch: $18–28, Din: $27–40)

Located next to the Four Seasons swimming pool, this trendy restaurant offers a great selection of traditional Costa Rican food prepared with an upscale touch. In addition to gourmet gallo pinto and casados, the menu includes lesser known specialities such as vigoron and Caribbean rondón. This is the most casual and inexpensive restaurant in the hotel (cocktails are just $12!) as well as the most likely to offer reservations. (2696-0000, www.fourseasons.com)

THE DIVE BAR (Lnch, Din: $10–17)

Located next to the Marina Papagayo, this casual bar is a good option if you don't want to run the gauntlet of security and checkpoints to dine at the Four Seasons. The menu offers sandwiches, burgers and fresh fish (2666-2310).

PLAYA DEL COCO

AT FIRST GLANCE, Playa del Coco seems less impressive than other Nicoya Peninsula beaches. The dark brown beach is hardly among Costa Rica's finest, and the town's main street is cluttered and congested. But the wide, sheltered bay reveals the town's big draw: boats and boating. If you're interested in all things nautical—sailing, sportfishing, scuba diving—Playa del Coco is one of Costa Rica's top destinations.

The waters offshore Playa del Coco are home to some of the most dramatic ocean scenery in Costa Rica. The coastline is dotted with calm bays, tiny islands and dramatic cliffs. The underwater world is home to tropical fish, sea turtles and giant manta rays. Trust me, if you don't get out on a boat while your here, you're missing half the fun. Playa del Coco is home to several excellent sailing and scuba tours, most of which can arrange pick-up or drop-off at the surrounding beaches of Ocotal, Hermosa and Panama.

For decades Playa del Coco was a quiet fishing village that attracted vacationing middle-class Ticos. In recent years there's been a surge in vacationing gringos, and today the town's main street is filled with strip malls and sports bars. Despite some mild congestion, the beach is among the tidiest in all of Costa Rica. It even features a concrete walkway lined with water fountains and showers. Set back from the walkway is a beachfront soccer field that's been hosting local games for generations. The southern end of the beach is more rugged and undeveloped; the northern end is more upscale. The northernmost tip of the beach (about a 20-minute walk from downtown) is delightfully uncrowded. It takes about 45 minutes to walk the entire length of the 3-km (1.8-mile) beach.

Playa del Coco attracts travelers from around the world, but it seems especially popular with Southerners, families and retired expats living out Jimmy Buffett-inspired lifestyles. If you're a 20-something countercultural backpacker, you might feel a bit out of place. Yet much of Playa del Coco remains authentically Costa Rican. On weekends the boardwalk is often filled with local families and street vendors selling typical treats like *granizados* (shaved, flavored ice) and *copos* (shaved, flavored ice mixed with sweetened condensed milk).

Which is not to say that things don't get ritzy around here. Over the past decade there's been a boom in upscale development in Playa del Coco and the surrounding beaches, including the famous Four Seasons Resort on the spectacular Papagayo Peninsula.

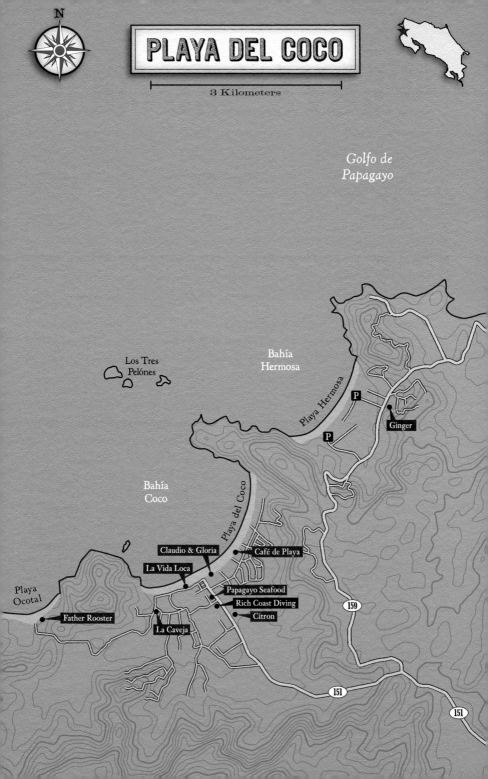

Getting to Playa del Coco

Playa del Coco is 36 km (22 miles) from Liberia (40-minute drive) and 240 km (149 miles) from San José (3.5-hour drive). The closest airport is in Liberia, which is serviced by Nature Air and Sansa (p.18). Shuttles to/from Playa del Coco are available from Grayline and Interbus (p.20). Pulmitan buses (2666-0458) depart Liberia for Playa del Coco every hour 5am–7pm (₡600, 1 hour) from the Pulmitan station; return buses depart every hour 5am–7pm. Pulmitan buses (2222-1650) depart San José for Playa del Coco at 8am, 2pm, 4pm (₡4,150, 5 hours) from Calle 24, Ave 5/7; return buses depart Playa del Coco at 4am, 8am, 2pm.

Getting Around Playa del Coco

Just about everything is within walking distance in Playa del Coco, but if you want to visit the surrounding beaches or the Papagayo Peninsula a car will definitely come in handy. Car rentals are available in Liberia (p.272), and taxis (2670-0408, 2670-1616) are readily available downtown.

Hotels

There are lots of budget hotels in downtown Playa del Coco and a few upscale hotels on the outskirts of town, especially towards the northern end of the beach. The area around Playa del Coco is also filled with condos and time-shares, so don't be surprised if someone attempts to sell you one while you're here. For complete hotel info visit www.jameskaiser.com

★Scuba Diving

Playa del Coco offers some of the best scuba diving on Costa Rica's Pacific coast. Don't expect colorful corals or crystal clear water—visibility usually ranges between 5–20 meters (16–66 feet)—but do expect to see "big game" wildlife such as manta rays, spotted-eagle rays, white-tipped reefsharks and even the occasional whale shark. There are plenty of dive shops in town, but Rich Coast Divers (2670-0176, www.richcoastdiving.com) is my favorite. Another good option is Summer Salt (2670-0308, www.summer-salt.com). The dive sites near Playa del Coco fall into three main categories:

1. Local Dives: There are over 20 dive sites just offshore Playa del Coco, featuring everything from sea horses and pufferfish to spotted eagle rays and the occasional turtle. Cost: About $105 for a two-tank dive.

2. Catalina Islands: Located a one-hour boat ride south, these islands are famous for giant manta rays. Cost: About $135 for a two-tank dive. Note: Scuba trips to the Catalina Islands also leave from Playa Flamingo (p.290).

3. Islas Murcielago ("Bat Islands"): Located 40 kms (25 miles) northwest of Playas del Coco, these islands are famous for bull sharks and the occasional whale shark. Although spectacular, the islands are only visited between May and November (powerful winds prevent boat trips between December and April). The boat ride is 1.5 hours. Cost: About $185 for a two-tank dive. Note: advanced diving experience is required for a trip to Islas Murcielago.

★Sailing

The scenery offshore Playa del Coco is spectacular, and there's no better way to enjoy it than aboard a sailboat. Most sailing tours offer morning snorkel trips or sunset sails for about $70 per person. Private cruises are often available on request. My favorite sailboat tour is aboard the *Sea Bird*, a 45-foot cutter-rigged ketch (8880-6393, www.seabirdsailingexcursions.com). Other recommended cruises include the 47-foot *Kuna Vela* (www.kunavela.com, 2670-1293) and the 43-foot *Spirit of the Ocean* (8707-1837, www.spiritoftheocean.wix.com). There's also the 65-foot catamaran *Marlin* (2653-1212, www.marlindelrey.com), which offers sunset tours ($85).

Sportfishing

The waters offshore Playa del Coco are home to marlin, sailfish and dorado as well as inshore fish like snapper, grouper and mackerel. Local sportfishing is offered by Blue Marlin (2670-2222, 6002-0720, www.sportfishingbluemarlin.com). The most upscale option is Billfish Safaris (8359-9739, www.billfishsafaris.com) based out of the Papagayo Marina that caters to Four Seasons guests.

Playa del Coco Restaurants

★ CAFÉ DE PLAYA (Brk: $9–13, Lnch: $15–30, Din: $26–35)

This elegant beachfront restaurant serves some of the most sophisticated food in Playa del Coco. The menu blends international styles with terrific ingredients. Lunch offers the best views, but dinner is when the menu really shines. Great wine list. Located in the upscale Café de Playa boutique hotel, about a 10–15 minute walk from the soccer field. (2670-1621, www.cafedeplaya.com)

★ LA CAVEJA (Din: $7–11)

This casual, local favorite serves up some of the best authentic Italian food in town. The homemade pasta, pizza and meat dishes are delicious and reasonably priced. Located halfway between Playa del Coco and Ocotal. If you don't have a car, it's best to take a cab. Closed Mondays. (2670-1311)

★ CITRON (Din: $15–23)

Located in the upscale Pacifico shopping center, Citron is the most sleek, modern restaurant in Playa del Coco. The menu fuses Italian, Latin and Asian flavors. Good wine list. Closed Sundays. (2670 0942, www.citroncoco.com)

PAPAGAYO SEAFOOD (Lnch, Din: $12–30)

This long-standing favorite specializes in fresh seafood and old school nautical decor. Fish, shrimp, crab, squid, lobster—plus lots of Cajun options (gumbo, jambalaya, etouffée). If you're in the mood for sushi, there's also Papagayo Sushi Boat next door. (2670-0298, www.papagayo-seafood.com)

DONDE CLAUDIO & GLORIA (Brk: $5–10; Lnch, Din: $10–19)

This laid-back, low-key beachfront restaurant offers one of the best breakfast deals around, plus reasonably priced lunches (sandwiches, burgers, casados) and dinners with fresh seafood options. (2670-0256, www.dondeclaudioygloria.com)

LA VIDA LOCA (Lnch, Din: $7–12)

This beachside bar is a tropical expat's dream, serving up classic American bar food steps from the sea. To get there, cross the rickety wooden footbridge just south of the soccer field (2670-0181, www.lavidalocabeachbar.com).

Best Sunset Cocktails

Cafe de Playa (Classy, beachside cocktails)

La Vida Loca (Cold beer on a barstool with great views)

Playa Ocotal

This small gray beach, located about a 10-minute drive south of Playa del Coco, wraps around a quaint bay filled with small fishing boats and surrounded by steep hills. If you're looking to escape the crowds, Playa Ocotal is a great place to visit. Although the hills overlooking the beach are filled with condos and private houses, the beach itself is rarely crowded, and if the seas are calm you can even snorkel around the rocks offshore. Beachside vendors rent snorkel equipment, and they can also arrange offshore snorkel trips.

⭐ **FATHER ROOSTER** (Lnch, Din: $9–18)
Bursting with ramshackle charm, this funky beachside restaurant is a perfect place for lunch or an afternoon cocktail. There are tables on the wooden porch and tables near the beach, all offering lovely views of the boat-filled harbor. In addition to nachos, salads, burgers and fish tacos, there are big and tasty cocktails. To get there, pass through the entrance gate of the Ocotal Beach Resort, bear right, and turn right at Azul Paraíso. (2670-1246, www.fatherrooster.com)

Playa Hermosa

Playa Hermosa ("Beautiful Beach") is a 10-minute drive north of Playa del Coco. It's remarkably similar to Playa del Coco, but far less developed and crowded. Because it lies alongside the tranquil *Bahía Culebra* ("Snake Bay"), Playa Hermosa is sheltered from the open ocean by the Papagayo Peninsula, so the waves here are almost always gentle and small. The calm water, combined with Hermosa's close proximity to Liberia, makes it very popular with Tico families. There are two main parking areas, both of which are home to unofficial guards who expect a tip. Note: Don't confuse this Playa Hermosa with the Playa Hermosa in the Central Pacific (p.359).

★ **GINGER** (Din: $6–12 tapas, $11–16 mains)
The best restaurant for miles, Ginger serves mouth-watering Asian fusion tapas in a sleek, modern "treehouse" that offers both indoor and outdoor seating. Good wine, great cocktails. Closed Mondays. (2672-0041, www.gingercostarica.com)

Playa Panama

Lying just north of Playa Hermosa, Playa Panama features even fewer visitors and even gentler waves. Even when big swells pound the coast, Playa Panama is often as calm as a lake. There are two popular parking areas: one on the southern end of the beach and one on the northern end of the beach. Both feature impressive views of the Papagayo Peninsula.

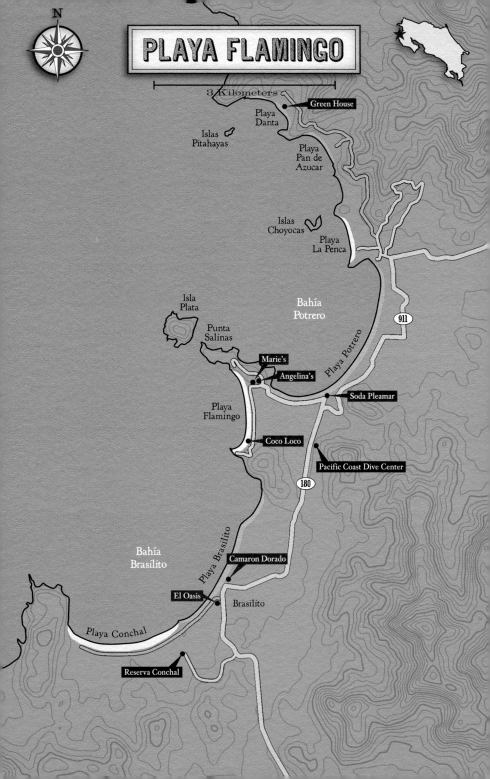

Playa Danta to Playa La Penca

If you're looking for small, isolated beaches where the views are stunning and the crowds are thin, head to this lovely section of coastline just north of Playa Potrero. Playa La Penca has the prettiest, lightest sand, and it's backed by a protected mangrove estuary that's home to parrots and roseate spoonbills. Continuing north along the road, you'll cross a series of hills that offer dramatic views of the coastline before reaching the turnoff to *Playa Pan de Azucar* ("Sugar Bread Beach"), which is accessible via the Hotel Pan de Azucar, a boutique hotel that allows non-guests to park near the lobby and walk to the gray sand beach. If you're looking for peace and solitude, Pan de Azucar is a great choice.

Continue north and soon you'll reach Playa Danta, another gray sand beach fronted by a series of expensive homes, a sport shop that rents sea kayaks and stand up paddle boards and a terrific beachside restaurant: Green House. Just north of Playa Danta is gorgeous, secluded Playa Dantita, which is reached one of three ways: via the beach at low tide, via a steep challenging path or via sea kayak anytime. Low trees offer plenty of shade, and due to its southern exposure Playa Dantita offers a rare glimpse of the rugged mountains set back from the coast.

★**GREEN HOUSE** (Brk: $6–11; Lnch, Din: $11–22)
Located at the Las Catalinas development overlooking Playa Danta, Green House offers healthy seafood prepared with Asian flair. Picturesque ocean views and modern, chic decor make this a great place for a cocktail or a snack. (2654-6150)

Playa Flamingo

Playa Flamingo is considered one of Costa Rica's most beautiful beaches. The powdery white sand slopes gently into the ocean, and its western exposure delivers consistently lovely sunsets. Expensive homes and condos dot the hills on either end of the beach, and the overall vibe is upscale and family-friendly. If words like "hostel" and "counterculture" turn you off, you're going to love Playa Flamingo. Onshore there are great restaurants. Offshore there's great scuba diving, sailing and sportfishing.

Playa Flamingo is located 22 kms (13.7 miles) from Tamarindo (30-minute drive) and 73 kms (45 miles) from Liberia (45-minute drive). Most visitors arrive by car or taxi, but Interbus and Grayline (p.20) both offer private shuttles. Transportes La Pampa buses (2665-7530) depart Liberia for Playa Flamingo at 4:30am, 6am, 8am, 11am and 6pm. For car rental check out Economy (2299-2000) or National (2654-4135). If you're just visiting for the day, parking is available along the road that parallels the beach. For complete Playa Flamingo hotel info visit www.jameskaiser.com)

★Scuba Diving

Lying 10 km (6.2 miles) offshore Playa Flamingo are the Catalina Islands. The waters off these rocky islands are a great place to see giant manta rays (which can grow up to 20 feet across) as well as devil rays, spotted-eagle rays, white-tipped reef sharks and lots of tropical fish. Visibility ranges from 5–20 meters (16–66 feet), but remember, when there's less visibility there are more nutrients and animals in the water. The Catalina Islands are about a 45-minute boat ride away from Playa Flamingo. Local dive shops include Pacific Coast Dive Center (2654-6175, 8827-4525, www.pacificcoastdivecenter.com) and Aquacenter Diving (2654-4141, www.aquacenterdiving.com). A two-tank dive costs about $100.

★Sailing Tours

Playa Flamingo is home to several great sailing tours. Two catamarans, the 34-foot *Lazy Lizard* (2654-5900, www.lazylizardsailing.com, $85 adults, $60 kids) and the 37-foot *Manta Ray* (8320-5317, www.mantaraysailing.com, $65–75 per person) offer morning and afternoon cruises. Private trips, including multi-day voyages, can be booked through Jim McKee (8827-5533, www.flamingobeachcr.com).

Sportfishing

The waters offshore Playa Flamingo are home to sailfish, marlin and dorado, and there's great inshore fishing around the Catalina Islands. If you're interested in sportfishing, contact Oso Viejo, which charters a wide range of boats from 29–58 feet (8827-5533, www.flamingobeachcr.com).

Playa Flamingo Restaurants

★ANGELINA'S (Lnch: $11–21; Din: $16-33)

This hip, high-end restaurant gets my vote for the best meal in town. Lots of Italian and Costa Rican influence, fresh seafood (lobster, mahi mahi) and local ingredients (green papaya salad, pejibaye ravioli). Located on the second floor of the La Plaza shopping center. (2654-4839, www.angelinasplayaflamingo.com)

★COCO LOCO (Lnch, Din: $9–15)

Fresh seafood is the specialty at this casual, beachfront restaurant. Tropical flair, quick service and feet-in-the-sand dining make this the best spot in town to enjoy a cocktail and watch the sunset. (2654-6242, www.cocolococostarica.com)

MARIE'S (Brk: $9–12; Lnch: $8–19; Din: $14–29)

This local favorite, set in a charming open-air space with a giant thatched roof, is your best bet for a reasonably priced meal in Playa Flamingo. The large menu offers everything from fresh seafood to burgers, plus lots of typical Costa Rican options. (2654-4136, www.mariesrestaurantincostarica.com)

PLEAMAR (Lnch, Din: $7–21)

If you've gotten your fill of fancy, expensive dining in Playa Flamingo, head to this simple beachside restaurant, which offers fresh seafood and Tico classics with a view of boat-filled Potrero Bay. (2654-4521)

Playa Conchal

Playa Brasilito

This long, dark sand beach stretches between Playa Flamingo and Playa Conchal. Near the southern end of the beach is the seaside village of Brasilito, which is centered around a palm-fringed soccer field with views of Brasilito Bay and the Catalina Islands beyond. Despite being sandwiched between some of the biggest resorts in Costa Rica, tiny Brasilito retains much of its Tico authenticity, with a handful of shops and *pulperías* clustered around the soccer field. From Brasilito it's only a 3-minute drive (10-minute walk) to stunning Playa Conchal. If you're planning on spending the day at Conchal, consider one of the restaurants in Brasilito for lunch, dinner or sunset cocktails. Brasilito is 17 kms (10.5 miles) north of Tamarindo (30-minute drive) and 62 kms (38.5 miles) south of Playa de Coco (1-hour drive).

CAMARON DORADO (Lnch, Din: $11–28)
This popular beachside restaurant (translation: "Golden Shrimp") is the best place for seafood in Brasilito. The real highlight is the sweeping view, which stretches from Playa Conchal in the south to Playa Flamingo in the north. (2654-4028)

EL OASIS (Brk: $5–10; Lnch: $9–20; Din: $11–24)
This quaint restaurant is your best bet for reasonably-priced, quality food. Though not directly on the beach, it has nice ocean views. Located at the Hotel Brasilito. (2654-5463, www.brasilito.com)

Playa Conchal

In my opinion, this is the prettiest beach on the Nicoya Peninsula. Its powdery white sand, composed of crushed seashells, wraps around a gorgeous turquoise bay that's perfect for swimming or snorkeling. (Beachside vendors often rent snorkel equipment.) Because it's a bit hard to get to—you need to drive or walk along Playa Brasilito then head over a steep, rugged hill—Playa Conchal is overlooked by many visitors. But for those in the know, it's paradise. Not surprisingly, Conchal can get busy on weekends during peak season. Playa Conchal is home to just one hotel: the luxurious Westin Playa Conchal Resort, which features a residential community and an 18-hole golf course designed by Robert Trent Jones. Fortunately, the massive resort is set back from the tree-lined beach, helping Playa Conchal retain a natural feel.

To get to Playa Conchal, head to the village of Brasilito. From the southwest corner of the soccer field, follow the road along the beach until you reach a steep, rugged hill that marks the northern end of Playa Conchal. (Four-wheel drive is recommended.) There's a small parking area just over the hill, and past the parking area the road continues to the southern end of the beach, which is almost always less crowded. Along the way you'll pass vendors and outdoor masseuses catering to the Westin crowd.

Playa Grande

Stretching 4 km (2.5 miles) north from the mouth of the Tamarindo Estuary, Playa Grande is one of the most magnificent beaches in Costa Rica. This long crescent of golden sand offers terrific surfing by day and nesting leatherback sea turtles at night. To protect the critically endangered turtles, which visit between October and February, much of the land surrounding Playa Grande has been declared part of Las Baulas National Park. The creation of the park in 1991 limited development in Playa Grande, keeping it in a far more natural state than its famous neighbor Tamarindo, which suffers from tourist sprawl. Fortunately, you don't have to rough it at Playa Grande. A handful of houses, hotels and restaurants built before the creation of the park offer just enough development to keep things interesting. (Visit www.jameskaiser.com for complete hotel info.) Most hotels and restaurants are located in two main areas: the northern end of Playa Grande, near the national park office, and a southern development known as Palm Beach Estates. Driving time between Playa Grande and Tamarindo is about 30 minutes because you need to drive around the estuary. Another option is to take a boat shuttle (₡500 per person) across the mouth of the estuary. The big waves at Playa Grande make it popular with surfers, but due to powerful riptides swimming here is less safe than at Tamarindo. Just beyond the northern tip of Playa Grande lies Playa Ventanas, a stunning crescent of sand that's more sheltered and better suited to swimming. Beyond Playa Ventanas lies Playa Carbon, a dark sand beach reached by a side trail. Overlooking all of these beaches is dramatic *Cabo Vela* ("Cape Sail"), where *Cerro el Morro* ("Morro Hill") rises high above the landscape.

★Surfing

Due to its western exposure, which catches lots of south-southwest swells, Playa Grande has consistently bigger surf than Tamarindo. Playa Grande is also blessed with offshore winds that shape powerful barrels throughout much of the dry season. In general, the surf at Playa Grande is best from three hours before high tide to two hours after high tide. Peak conditions bring head high to double over-head sets. The best break, "Main Break," is located towards the northern end of the beach in front of Taco Star restaurant. Beginners should stay away from the main break, which is full of experienced locals who don't take kindly to novices.

There are two popular surf shops in town: Frijoles Locos, "Crazy Beans," (2652-9235, www.frijoleslocos.com) and Matos Surf Shop—aka Playa Grande Surf Store—(2652-9227, www.matossurfshop.com). If you're looking for surf lessons, check out Point Break Surf School (8866-4133, www.pointbreaksurf.com), an excellent operation that offers lessons at Playa Grande and will pick you up as far away as the Papagayo Peninsula.

Playa Grande Restaurants

★EL HUERTO (Din: $13–18)

This cozy, hip, pan-Mediterranean restaurant features fantastic wood-fired pizza, delicious steaks and various specialties from southern Spain (the owner is from Cordoba). Good wine list. (2653-1259, www.elhuertodeplayagrande.com)

★GREAT WALTINI (Brk: $9–13; Lnch: $12–18; Din: $19–29)

This ever-popular restaurant, located in the Hotel Bula Bula, offers a wide range of upscale options, from burgers and sandwiches for lunch to fresh seafood and steak for dinner. Dinner reservations recommended. The restaurant also offers free boat rides across the Tamarindo estuary for guests staying in Tamarindo (reservations required). Closed Monday. (2653-0975, www.hotelbulabula.com)

★CANTARANA (Din: $18–22)

Located on the second floor of Hotel Cantarana, this charming open-air restaurant serves a constantly changing menu of creative entrees. Reservations recommended. Closed Monday. (2653-0486, www.hotel-cantarana.com)

UPSTAIRS (Brk: $8–11; Lnch: $11–14; Din: $12–25)

The second story of the Rip Jack Inn, which caters to the surf/yoga crowd, is home to a charming restaurant serving hearty, healthy, upscale meals with lots of seafood options. (2653-0480, www.ripjackinn.com)

KIKES (Brk: $4–6, Lnch, Din: $7–18)

This local favorite is your best bet for budget Tico food in Playa Grande. Look for the large, thatched roof. (2653-0834, www.kikesplace.net)

★Sea Turtle Nesting Tours

Playa Grande is used by a small colony of leatherback sea turtles p.128, which migrate thousands of miles to lay their eggs in the golden sand. Measuring up to two meters (six feet) long and weighing up to 700 kg (1,500 pounds), leatherbacks are the largest turtles on earth. They are also among the most endangered. During Playa Grande's nesting season (late Oct–mid-Feb), turtle tours are offered at night. If you're an eco-traveler visiting during nesting season, don't pass up the chance to take a turtle tour.

Several decades ago leatherback turtles also nested at Tamarindo, but development and light pollution have long since driven the turtles away. These days leatherbacks only nest along Playa Grande, and to protect the turtles strict rules have been established for turtle tours. All visitors must be accompanied by trained guides, all visitors must wear dark clothes and all forms of photography are prohibited. Each night, a maximum of 120 people are allowed on turtle tours—60 from the Playa Grande office and 60 from the Tamarindo office.

Turtle tours involve waiting up to four hours for guides to spot a nesting turtle on the beach. (Be sure to bring a blanket, a book and a snack for the wait.) Once a turtle is spotted, you'll head out to the beach to watch the egg-laying process up close. (Note: Only the egg-laying process is shown; you won't be able to watch the turtle exit or enter the water). It's also important to note that turtle sightings are not guaranteed. Leatherbacks are, after all, critically endangered. Guides claim a 50% success rate during peak season in December and January.

The best place to book the tour is directly through the Playa Grande Local Guide Association (Tel: 2653-0470). Tours cost $25 per person ($15 for the guides, $10 for the park), but if you don't see a turtle, you won't be charged anything. Tours meet at the Playa Grande MINAET office, which features a life-sized model of a leatherback turtle out front. Tours start anywhere from 6pm to midnight, depending on the timing of high tide. (If high tide falls at night, turtles emerge from two hours before high tide to four hours after high tide; if the high tide occurs within two hours of dawn or dusk, turtles emerge throughout the night.) Once a turtle is spotted, guests carpool to the nearest beach entrance then walk a short distance to the turtle.

If you're staying in Tamarindo, you can book a tour through the Tamarindo Local Guides Association (2653-1687, guiaslocalestama@gmail.com). Their office is located in a simple wooden building overlooking the mouth of the Tamarindo Estuary. Tours depart from the office, but in my opinion these tours are less desirable for several reasons: 1) If you don't see a turtle, you won't get a refund 2) to get to Playa Grande, you'll have to cross the estuary by boat, then walk 15 minutes to the waiting area 3.) If a turtle is spotted, you might have to walk another one to two kilometers to get to it and 4.) Once you've seen a turtle, you'll have to walk all the way back to the estuary. Better to book your tour through the Playa Grande office, which is a 30-minute drive from Tamarindo.

Although Playa Grande's leatherbacks are the star attraction, in recent years some guides have begun offering tours between November and April to see nesting Pacific green turtles (aka black turtles) at several beaches north of Playa Grande. Unfortunately, these beaches lie outside the national park, and some guides have taken advantage of the lax regulations by allowing tourists to get extra close and take flash photos, which can result in the turtle abandoning her nest. To go with a respected guide call Annia (Tel: 2653-8500).

Note: This tour is not for everyone

For some visitors a leatherback turtle tour is the highlight of their trip. For others, however, it's a big disappointment. Much of the problem seems to lie with unrealistic expectations, which are often built up by unscrupulous tour promoters. For starters, turtle tours usually involve waiting around for several hours, sometimes well past midnight. And because leatherbacks are critically endangered, there's no guarantee that you'll see one.

Many visitors are also upset by the seeming lack of professionalism that some guides exhibit. While I agree there's always room for improvement, it's important to remember that many of the guides are former egg poachers with little education and limited English skills. By employing former poachers as guides, the park has incentivized them not to dig up turtle eggs, which remains the single biggest threat to the leatherback's survival. Remember, conservation in poor, developing countries poses a unique set of challenges.

Another complaint is that turtle tours seem to interfere with the egg-laying process. Biologists have performed numerous tests and determined that, when conducted properly, turtle tours do not interfere with the egg-laying process. In fact, turtle tours are considered part of the solution because they pay for beach patrols, support scientific research and offer economic incentives for locals to protect (not poach) turtle eggs. If not for the tours, leatherbacks probably would have vanished years ago. At least now they have a fighting chance.

TAMARINDO

TAMARINDO IS THE most popular and developed town on the Nicoya Peninsula. It's home to a big, beautiful beach with great surf, gorgeous views and an abundance (some would say *over*abundance) of hotels, restaurants and bars. The town is also surrounded by Las Baulas National Park, which protects endangered leatherback sea turtles that nest on nearby Playa Grande between October and February. Between the beach life, the nightlife and the wildlife, it's no surprise Tamarindo attracts so many people.

That said, Tamarindo has changed dramatically over the years. In the 1990s it was the remote domain of backpackers and surfers willing to make the bumpy, nine-hour trek from San José. Following the completion of the international airport in nearby Liberia, "Sun-and-Fun" tourists began arriving in droves, and condos and gated communities began popping up around town. Before long, Tamarindo became known as "Tamagringo."

When development ground to a halt after the 2008 financial crisis, concerned locals took the opportunity to pass a law prohibiting large-scale construction close to the beach. By that point, however, cutting edge backpackers and surfers had already decamped to Nosara and Santa Teresa, and today Tamarindo has settled into a mainstream, upscale groove. Although the town now boasts strip malls and traffic jams, rest assured that what originally attracted visitors to Tamarindo—the beach, the surf, the scenery—remain as wonderful as ever. There's a reason why Robert August, one of the stars of the classic surf film *Endless Summer* (and a man who knows a thing or two about amazing surf destinations), decided to make Tamarindo his permanent home.

Yet despite its well-earned reputation for being "too developed," Tamarindo is sandwiched between two big, beautiful, uncrowded beaches: Playa Grande to the north and Playa Langosta to the south. As long as you're willing to wander a short distance away from Tamarindo, you can still experience a place where the waves are uncrowded by day and nesting sea turtles lay their eggs at night. And if you have access to a car, there are plenty of terrific beaches nearby that make a great day trip.

The bottom line is this: If you're looking for a mellow, rustic beach town, Tamarindo is not for you; consider Playa Grande, Nosara or Santa Teresa instead. But if you're looking for a beautiful beach with great restaurants, a thriving nightlife and a bewildering array of activities—everything from sailing to surfing to spa treatments—there's a lot to like about Tamarindo.

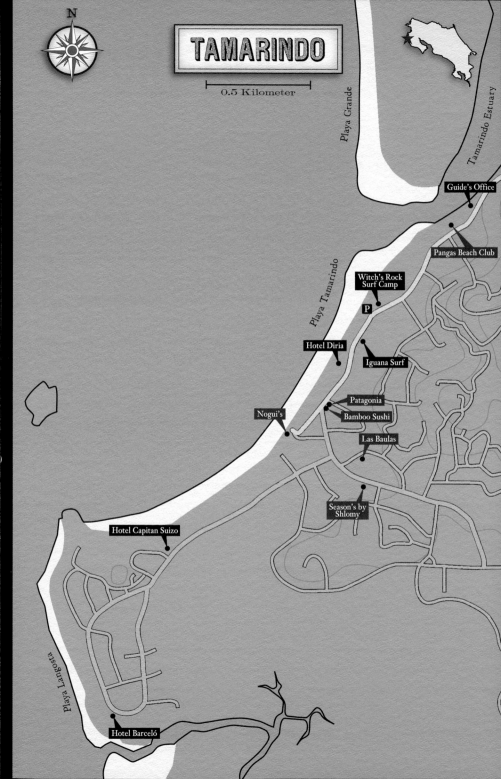

Getting to Tamarindo

Tamarindo is 77 kms (48 miles) from Liberia (1-hour drive) and 253 kms (157 miles) from San José (4-hour drive). The Tamarindo airport, located 3.5 km (2 miles) from downtown, is serviced by Sansa and Nature Air (p.18). Shuttles to/from Tamarindo are offered by Interbus and Grayline (p.20). Tamarindo Shuttle (2653-4444) offers daily shuttles between Liberia and Tamarindo. Transportes La Pampa buses (2686-7245) depart the Terminal Liberia and run between Liberia and Tamarindo (₡1,500, 1.5 hours) throughout the day. Alfaro buses (2222-2666) depart San José for Tamarindo at 11:30am and 3:30pm from Calle 14, Ave 3/5 (₡5640, 5.5 hours). Return buses depart Tamarindo at 3:30am and 5:30am (Mon–Sat), 5:30pm and 1pm (Sun).

Getting around Tamarindo

Tamarindo is a small town that does not require a car. The main reason to rent a car is to visit the beautiful beaches north and south of town. Rental cars are available from Thrifty (2653-0829), Hertz (2653-1358), Euro Car (2653-1809), Budget (2436-2000). Taxis (2653-2728, 8879-3171) are plentiful downtown.

Hotels

There's no shortage of hotels in Tamarindo, from cheap backpacker hostels to expensive luxury resorts. Most budget hotels are located near the center of town; higher end places tend to be located in the hills above town. Playa Langosta, which lies just southwest of Tamarindo, also has several nice hotels as well as houses for rent. Visit www.jameskaiser.com for complete hotel info.

★Surfing

At its heart, Tamarindo is a surf town. Its streets are filled with surf shops, its waves are full of surfers and its fashion sense revolves around Hurley, Billabong and Quicksilver. But hardcore surfers generally avoid the waves here. Due to Tamarindo's northern exposure, it doesn't receive the full blast of south/southwest swells that dominate much of the Pacific coast. As a result, Tamarindo's waves are smaller, gentler and better for beginners. In fact, this is one of the best beginner/intermediate breaks in the country, attracting scores of novices who can be seen falling off their boards and bumping into one another in the lineup.

Tamarindo has two main breaks: El Estero, a river mouth break near the Tamarindo Estuary, and Pico Pequeño, a rocky break in front of Hotel Diriá. Both breaks work best at mid-tide. Low tide is the worst.

The most impressive surf shop in town is Witch's Rock Surf Camp (2653-1238, www.witchsrocksurfcamp.com), which commands a fantastic location in front of the town's best waves. For many surfers, Witch's Rock *is* Tamarindo, providing food, lodging, surf lessons, surf rentals and day trips to nearby surf breaks including (you guessed it) Witch's Rock (p.276). You can even get a surfboard personally shaped by the legendary Robert August here. Other good surf shops include BlueTrailz (2653-1705, www.bluetrailz.com), Iguana Surf Shop (2653-0613 www.iguanasurf.net) and Kelly's Surf Shop (2653-1355, www.kellyssurfshop.com).

If you're a intermediate/advanced surfer looking to avoid all the beginners in Tamarindo, head to Playa Langosta or Playa Grande, which are both within walking distance and offer consistently bigger waves. If you have a car, you can also head south to Playa Avellanas and Playa Negra (p.307), which feature the area's biggest waves.

★Nightlife

Tamarindo is one of the top party destinations in Costa Rica, and for many people the throbbing nightlife is one of the town's biggest draws. There are nearly a dozen watering holes, and the "in" bar shifts nightly throughout the week. It's best to ask around. If you're just looking for a mellow, beachside cocktail, consider laid-back Nogui's or the upscale Pangas Beach Club.

★Catamaran Tours

One of the best ways to enjoy the region's gorgeous shoreline is from the water. Blue Dolphin Sailing (8842-3204, www.bluedolphinsailing.com) runs group tours on their 40-foot catamaran (morning tours: $70 adults, $35 kids under 12; sunset tours: $85 adults, $42.50 kids under 12). Prices include food and open bar. Another popular option is Marlin del Rey (2653-1212, www.marlindelrey.com), a 66-foot catamaran that offers sunset tours ($85 per person).

★Rincón de la Vieja Day Tour

One of the most popular day trips from Tamarindo is the all-day adventure tour offered by Hacienda Guachipelin. Activities include canopy tours, horseback riding, whitewater inner tubing, hot springs and more.

Eco-Tours

Between October and February leatherback turtles lay their eggs at Playa Grande, and nightly turtle nesting tours are offered (p.296). There's also the Tamarindo Estuary, a mangrove-lined waterway filled with fascinating wildlife including monkeys, crocodiles and nearly 200 bird species. Guided boat tours of are offered by Tamarindo Local Guide Association (2653-1687), which has an office overlooking the mouth of the estuary.

Scenic Flights

For breathtaking views of Tamarindo and the surrounding beaches, book a flight in a gyrocopter, an ultralight helicopter that offers spectacular open-air views. Cost: $110/20 minutes, $230/hour. (8827-8858, www.autogyroamerica.com)

Canopy Tours

Although canopy tours near Tamarindo aren't nearly as spectacular as canopy tours elsewhere, there are several local outfitters. I personally like Cartagena Canopy tour. Cost: $35/person. (2675-0801, www.canopytourcartagena.com)

Golf

Just 5 km (3 miles) south of Tamarindo lies the Hacienda Pinilla Golf Course, which offers 18 holes and spectacular ocean views. Rates: $150 for 18 holes, $80 for 9, $75 after 2:30pm. Discounts available for guests staying at Hacienda Pinilla or JW Marriott. (2681-4505, www.haciendapinilla.com)

Sportfishing

The waters offshore Tamarindo are home to sailfish, marlin, tuna and dorado. Charters generally run about $1,000 full-day, $700 half-day. Contact Kingpin Sportfishing (8833-7780, www.kingpin-sportfishing.com) or Yellowfin Guanacaste (8813-9675, www.yellowfinsportfishing.com)

Spa/Massage

The top spa in town is Los Altos de Eros (8850-4222, www.losaltosdeeros.com), which offers a $250 spa package. Less expensive massages are offered along the beach in the shade.

Tamarindo Restaurants

★ SEASONS BY SHLOMY (Din: $15–18)
This stylish, poolside restaurant, located at hotel Arco Iris, offers Mediterranean-inspired food with tropical Asian flourishes. Great for fresh seafood. Good wine list. Closed Sundays. No credit cards. (8368-6983, www.seasonstamarindo.com)

★ PANGAS BEACH CLUB (Brk, Lnch: $8–13; Din: $16–26)
Overlooking the Tamarindo Estuary, this rustic/chic restaurant mixes delicious meats and fresh seafood with beachfront elegance. Great cocktails. (2653-0024)

LAS BAULAS PIZZERIA (Din: $10–15)
The best pizza in Tamarindo. Tasty selection of Italian-style thin-crust pizzas with gourmet toppings like prosciutto and arugula. Great for families (2653-1450)

PATAGONIA (Lnch, Din: $12-23)
Specializing in all things Argentine, this rancho-rustic grill offers mouth-watering steaks, tasty empanadas, homemade pasta and plenty of Malbec. Seafood and veggie options also available. (2653-0612)

BAMBOO SUSHI CLUB (Din: $7-13 per sushi roll)
Great sushi, featuring all the classics plus a large menu of specialty rolls. Although located in the bustling center of town, the interior is peaceful and elegant. (2653-4519, www.bamboosushiclub.com)

JOE'S (Brk: $7–9; Lnch, Din: $10–14)
Located at Witch's Rock Surf Camp, Joe's is the top surfer bar/restaurant in Tamarindo. The reasonably-priced menu includes Tex-Mex, burgers, sushi and craft brews. The open-air balcony offers terrific views of the beach and the waves. Perfect for breakfast, lunch or drinks. (2653-1262, www.witchsrocksurfcamp.com)

NOGUI'S (Brk: $6–10; Lnch, Din: $10–25)
This laid-back, local favorite offers a good selection of grilled meats and fresh seafood mixed with seaside views. Perfect for breakfast or lunch. A good place to sample Tico classics like patacones. (2653-0029, www.noguistamarindo.com)

Best Sunset Cocktails

Pangas Beach Club (Great beachfront cocktails)

Playa Tamarindo (Good western exposure, BYOB!)

Playa Langosta

As you head southwest from Tamarindo to Playa Langosta, you'd be forgiven for thinking you've just wandered into an upscale residential community in California (albeit one with bumpy, unpaved roads). High-end houses, condos and hotels line both sides of the road. But beyond all the private development lies Playa Langosta, one of the region's most beautiful, uncrowded beaches.

Playa Langosta consists of two beaches divided by the mouth of the Langosta Estuary. The northern half of beach is backed by houses and condos, and the shoreline alternates between sand and rocks. Public beach access is marked by small wooden signs next to narrow paths. The best stretch of beach is near the Hotel Barceló, which overlooks the mouth of the estuary. There's a small parking area just before the hotel, and a short shady path heads to the beach. (During high season, beachside massages are often offered along the path.)

The southern part of the beach, which is separated by the river mouth, is far more spectacular—a big, beautiful beach stretching nearly 1.6 kilometers (1 mile) south. There's no development here (the beach is part of Las Baulas National Park), and even during high season it's a great place to escape the crowds. The southern section of Playa Langosta also offers bigger waves than Tamarindo, so it's popular with intermediate and advanced surfers. If you want to explore the southern part of Playa Langosta, you'll need to cross the river mouth, which is best done at low tide.

Local buses run between Tamarindo and Langosta throughout the day.

Playas Avellanas & Negra

Located just 8 km (5 miles) south of Tamarindo, these two beaches are like a time-warp back to the fabled "Costa Rica of 20 years ago." The roads are terrible, the small villages are run-down and the scenery is dominated by farms and forests. The real action lies offshore, where you'll find some of the best surfing in the northern Nicoya. When the swells get big (8 feet or above) and other breaks start to close out, the waves here just get bigger and better. If you're an experienced surfer looking for an undeveloped beach with killer waves, you're gonna love it here. From Tamarindo it's a roughly 30-minute drive to Playa Avellanas, then another 10-minute drive south to Playa Negra. A rental car is definitely recommended here. There are about a dozen hotels scattered between the two beaches, ranging from $15 hostels to more upscale options (visit www.jameskaiser.com for hotel info). Playa Avellanas is the prettier of the two beaches.

LOLA'S (Lnch: $12–16)

Popular with surfers, this famous beachfront restaurant offers cocktails, fresh smoothies, healthy salads, Asian fusion snacks and delicious sand-wiches. Open till sunset, closed Monday. (2652-9097)

Playa Ostional

This dark sand beach, a 20-minute drive north of Nosara, is home to one of nature's most incredible spectacles. Once a month between July and December, thousands of olive ridley sea turtles visit Ostional at the same time to lay their eggs in the sand. This phenomenon, called an *arribada*, lasts 4–7 days, and during this time the beach is covered with hundreds, and sometimes thousands, of turtles. The largest arribadas contain tens of thousands of turtles with each turtle laying roughly 100 eggs.

Arribadas only happen in a handful of places in the world. Although the reason for mass nesting is unclear, scientists believe it is a form of defense against predators. By laying hundreds of thousands of eggs, turtles simply overwhelm predators such as coatis and vultures that feed on the eggs. Although arribadas technically take place all year at Ostional, they are very small from January to June. Large arribadas generally start in July, and they grow progressively larger until they reach their peak in October. The exact timing depends on the moon and the tides, but arribadas often start about a week after the full moon. Equally impressive are the mass hatchings of baby turtles, which take place 45–55 days after an arribada.

One-hour tours ($10 per person) for both arribadas and mass hatchings are available through the local guide association (2682-0428), which has two offices in the village of Ostional. During the largest arribadas, tours are available in the morning, afternoon and night. Hatching tours generally start around 5am. Sámara Adventure Company (2656-0920, www.samara-tours.com) can arrange 4.5-hour turtle tours ($45 per person) that include transportation from Sámara. These days one of the best places to check the status of arribadas is—where else?—Facebook, where the local guide association maintains a page. Search for "Asociacion de Guias Locales de Ostional." In addition to photos and videos, they often post estimated arribada dates and other interesting info.

Biologists first discovered the arribadas at Ostional in 1970. In 1983 Costa Rica established the Ostional Wildlife Refuge, which protects 21 km (13 miles) of beaches and 8,000 hectares (19,800 acres) of ocean. In 1987 a controversial egg-harvesting program was established at Ostional. Although it is illegal to harvest sea turtle eggs in Costa Rica, many Ticos purchase turtle eggs on the black market. (They are eaten both as an appetizer and as a supposed aphrodisiac.) Because the first wave of eggs laid during an arribada are dug up and destroyed by successive waves of turtles, scientists decided a partial harvest at the beginning of the arribada would not harm turtle populations. If a legal, non-destructive harvest were allowed, the thinking went, it would cut down on illegal harvests elsewhere. Unfortunately, the legal harvest at Ostional has provided easy cover for many illegally harvested eggs, which are sold as "eggs from Ostional." In addition, scientists have been unable to determine the long-term impact of the Ostional harvest, which now tops four million turtle eggs annually.

NOSARA

THIS FUNKY BEACH town is best described by two words: surfing and yoga. Nosara's beaches are filled with great waves, and the hills above town are filled with yoga retreats. The only things more common than surfboards and yoga mats are potholes. (The roads are left intentionally terrible to keep development at bay.) All in all, Nosara has a upscale countercultural vibe that attracts global wanderers of all ages, from vacationing backpackers to long-haired retirees who shop at the organic farmers' market and munch on gluten-free food at the town's tasty restaurants. If you're an athletic free spirit looking for a rustic beach town with all the comforts of a Whole Foods, you're going to love Nosara.

In addition to surfing and yoga, Nosara is famous for its proximity to Playa Ostional (p.308), one of the eco-highlights of Costa Rica. This dark sand beach is the world's most important nesting site for olive ridley sea turtles, which arrive once a month during mass nestings called *arribadas*. During peak season between July and November, thousands of turtles arrive and guided tours are available. The Ostional Wildlife Refuge also protects pristine mangroves along the Río Nosara and Río Montaña, which you can explore on boat tours and nearby hiking trails.

Although Nosara technically refers to the small town of Nosara 5 km (3 miles) inland, for most travelers "Nosara" is synonymous with Playa Guiones and Playa Pelada, the region's most beautiful light sand beaches. Playa Guiones attracts surfers from around the world, and its shoreline remains natural and undeveloped thanks to its inclusion within the Ostional Wildlife Refuge. The jumbled maze of dirt roads behind Playa Guiones are home to hotels, restaurants and funky boutiques. Just north of Playa Guiones lies Playa Pelada, a small sheltered beach where fishing boats dot the shore and local families splash in the waves. The southern end of the beach is home to two popular restaurants, but wander north and you'll soon have the beach all to yourself.

For many people, Nosara's beautiful beaches, chilled out vibe and nearby eco-adventures make it one of the top all-around destinations on the Nicoya Peninsula. Although a handful of condo developments have popped up in recent years, Nosara still feels delightfully rustic and off the beaten path. ATVs are the preferred method of transportation for many locals, and the nightlife generally consists of live music at local bars, not all-night dance parties. If you're looking for a healthy, relaxing beach vacation, Nosara is hard to beat.

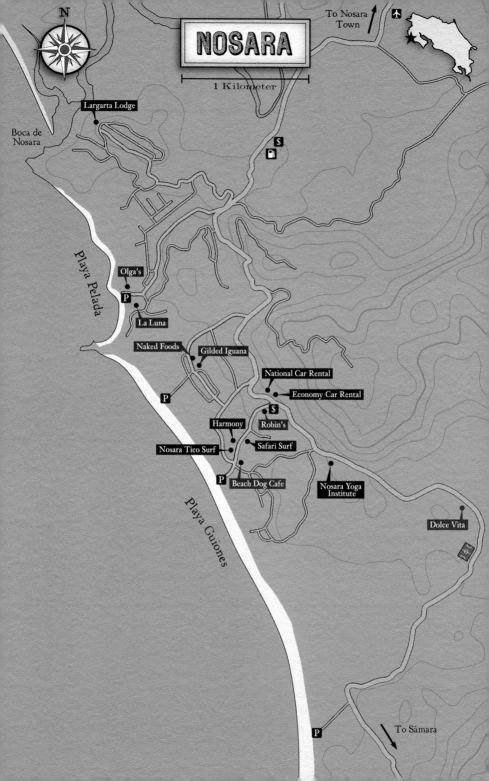

Getting to Nosara

Nosara is 22 km (14 miles) from Sámara (30-minute drive), 127 kms (79 miles) from Liberia (2-hour drive) and 246 kms (153 miles) from San José (5-hour drive). Nosara's airport is serviced by both Sansa and Nature Air (p.18). Alfaro buses (2222-2666) depart San José for Nosara 5:30am from Ave 5, Calle 14 (₡4,805, 6 hours); return buses depart Nosara 12:30pm. Traroc buses (2685-5352) depart Nicoya for Nosara 4:45am (Mon–Sat), 10am, 12:30pm, 3pm, 5:30pm (₡1,870, 2 hours); return buses depart Nosara for Nicoya 5am, 6:30am, 8am, noon, 4pm.

Getting around Nosara

If you're just planning on surfing and doing yoga in Playa Guiones, you can easily get around on foot. If you'd like to check out some of the better restaurants and eco-attractions, a car will definitely come in handy. Both Economy (2299-2000) and National (2682-0052) offer car rentals in Nosara. There are also a handful of taxis in town (8846-3960, 8810-7506), and ATV rentals are available from local tour operators.

Hotels

Despite being relatively small, Nosara has lots of good hotels and several excellent ones. Hotels that cater to surfers and yoga people are generally clustered around Playa Guiones. The hills above Playa Pelada offer more peace and quiet for couples and eco-tourists. Visit www.jameskaiser.com for a complete list of Nosara hotels.

★Surfing

Playa Guiones, the major surf beach in Nosara, is one of the best beginner breaks in Costa Rica and offers consistently good waves for more advanced surfers. Best of all, because the beach is nearly 5 km (3 miles) long, there's usually plenty of room for everyone. Waves are good throughout the year with peak swells often arriving June–September. There's no shortage of surf shops or surf schools in town, but I like Safari Surf School (2682-0113, www.safarisurfschool.com) and Nosara Tico Surf School (2682-4076, www.nosara-surf-school.com).

★Yoga

The most famous yoga school in Nosara is the Nosara Yoga Institute (2682-0071, www.nosarayoga.com), but other popular schools include Costa Rica Yoga Spa (2682-0192, www.costaricayogaspa.com) as well as Pilates Nosara (8663-7453, www.pilatesnosara.com). Although not yoga-specific, the New Age Omega Institute (www.eomega.org) is also popular among the yoga crowd.

★Nosara River Safari

The Ostional Wildlife Refuge, which lies just north of Nosara, protects the Río Nosara and Río Montaña, two mangrove-lined rivers that provide habitat for crocodiles, iguanas and over 270 bird species. This two-hour, guided boat tour cruises through the refuge using a quiet electric motor that doesn't disturb the wildlife. A must for birders. Cost: $35. (2682-0610, www.nosarariversafari.com)

Hiking

Lagarta Lodge offers several kilometers of good hiking trails on their 35-hectare (86-acre) reserve, which boarders the Ostional Wildlife Refuge. You can explore the trails on your own ($6 per person), but guided tours ($15 per person) are highly recommended. My favorite guide is Gabriella, who specializes in plants. Her two-hour tour is offered daily at 6:30am, though later tours are sometimes available. Call for reservations (2682-0035).

Canopy Tour

Miss Sky Canopy claims to have the longest canopy tour in the world with 21 cables stretching over 11 km (6.8 miles). Two tours daily at 8am and 1:30pm. Cost: $70 adults, $45 kids under 13. (2682-0969, www.missskycanopytour.com)

Nosara Wildlife Rescue

This non-profit rescue center rehabilitates wounded wildlife, especially monkeys electrocuted on power lines. If you'd like to learn more about their work and get up close and personal with some amazing animals, sign up for a tour of their facilities. Cost: $50 per person. (2682-1474, 2682-5049, www.nosarawildlife.com)

Nosara Restaurants

★DOLCE VITA (Din: $11–21)

Homemade pasta and ravioli, sumptuous seafood, delicious pizza—all in a rustic jungle setting. A 10-minute drive south of town, but definitely worth the trip. No credit cards. (2682-0107)

★HARMONY HOTEL (Brk: $7–14; Lnch: $13–20; Din: $18–28)

You don't have to be a guest at the super stylish Harmony Hotel to enjoy the top-notch restaurant—a gourmet mix of Tico, Asian and European influences. Lots of organic and vegetarian options. (2682-4114, www.harmonynosara.com)

★LA LUNA (Lnch, Din: $14–20)

This hip restaurant/lounge in Playa Pelada serves tasty food and cocktails right on the beach. The Greek/Mediterranean menu has plenty of delicious choices, and the location is divine. (2682-0122)

ROBIN'S (Brk: $6–8; Lnch: $6–9)

This small cafe/ice cream shop offers healthy soups, salads, wraps and sandwiches, with lots of vegan and gluten-free options. (2682-0617, www.robinsicecream.com)

BEACH DOG CAFE (Brk: $7–10; Lnch: $911, Din: $16–18)

If you're a surfer, you'll probably end up at this open-air cafe at some point on your trip. The menu ranges from Mexican classics to hearty sandwiches, plus tasty dinners with savory, tropical flavors. No credit cards. (2682-1293)

GILDED IGUANA (Brk: $7–10, Lnch, Din: $8–17)

This laid-back bar/restaurant is a local expat favorite, serving up plenty of surfer-friendly comfort food (Tex-Mex, burgers, pasta), plus fresh fish for dinner. (2682-0259, www.thegildediguana.com)

OLGA'S (Brk: $7; Lnch, Din: $9–15)

If you've gotten your fill of vegan, gluten-free food, head to this rustic beachfront restaurant in Playa Pelada for Tex-Mex and *cervezas*.

NAKED FOODS

Fresh squeezed natural juices and organic/vegan treats. (8712-4463)

Best Sunset Cocktails

Sunset Bar at Lagarta Lodge (Terrific ocean views)

La Luna (Hip beachside bar)

SÁMARA

THIS LARGE, LIGHT gray sand beach has long been one of the Nicoya Peninsula's most popular destinations among vacationing Ticos. Its relative proximity to San José—the first big beach on the Nicoya Peninsula serviced by decent roads—lures a steady stream of middle- and upper-class Costa Rican families on weekends and holidays.

Unlike many beaches on the Nicoya Peninsula, there's no single activity or superlative that defines Sámara. No "must-see" reason to visit. Instead, Sámara offers a little bit of everything—swimming, snorkeling, sea kayaking, nightlife—in a beach town that remains true to its Tico roots. There are no mega-resorts dominated by foreigners here, just a number of small-scale hotels, bars and restaurants scattered along the palm-fringed beach. All in all, the town remains charming in a scruffy kind of way. If you're looking for luxury, look elsewhere. But if you're looking for a reasonably-priced, family-friendly beach that isn't overdeveloped—yet still has plenty to do—Sámara is a good bet.

The beach itself is nearly 4 kilometers (2.5 miles) long and slopes gently into the ocean. At low tide, the beach is absolutely huge. At high tide, it's barely there. The graceful crescent bay is sheltered by Isla Chora, the large island just off the southern tip of the bay, as well as a long strip of offshore rocks. Taken together, Isla Chora and the offshore rocks limit powerful waves and riptides, making Sámara one of the Nicoya's safest swimming beaches.

"Downtown" Sámara is located just south of the Lagarta River, which flows into the ocean near the western end of the bay. East of the Lagarta River, the shoreline is packed with beachside hotels and restaurants, many of which practically spill out onto the beach. Continue east and the development gradually tapers off. West of the Lagarta River is a quiet stretch of beach backed by palm trees and a large open field. Because the beach is so big, there's always enough space for everyone, even on busy weekends and holidays.

For me, one of the best things about Sámara is its proximity to some beautiful, undeveloped beaches nearby. Playa Carrillo, located just south of Sámara, is smaller, prettier and less crowded than Sámara. Carrillo is very popular with families, who picnic under the shady palms. Six kilometers west of Sámara lies Playa Barrigona, one of the most beautiful, uncrowded beaches in Costa Rica, but accessible only via a rugged 4x4 road.

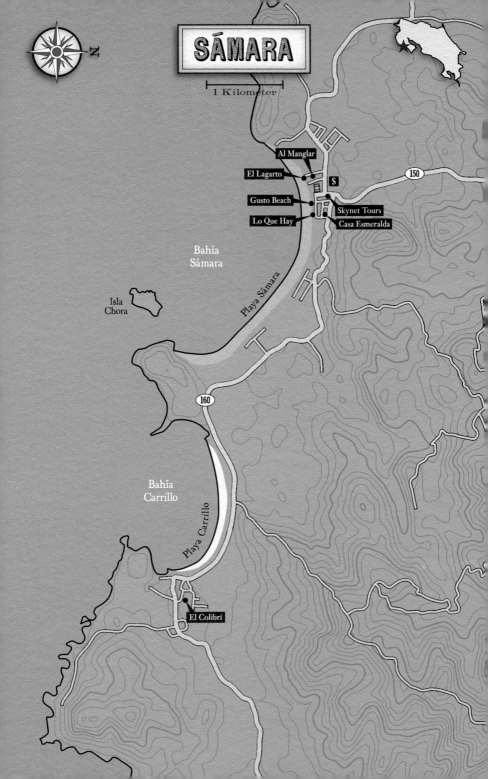

SÁMARA

1 Kilometer

N

Al Manglar
El Lagarto
Gusto Beach
Lo Que Hay
Skynet Tours
Casa Esmeralda
$
150

Bahía
Sámara

Playa Sámara

Isla
Chora

160

Bahía
Carrillo

Playa Carrillo

El Colibrí

Getting to Sámara

Sámara is 36 kms (22.3 miles) from Nicoya (40-minute drive), 115 kms (71 miles) from Liberia (2-hour drive) and 234 kms (145 miles) from San José (4-hour drive). Sansa (p.18) offers flights to the small airport just outside of town. Shuttles to/from Sámara are offered by Interbus (p.20). Alfaro buses (2222-2666) depart San José for Sámara at noon and 5pm from Avenida 5, Calles 14/16 (₡4,470, 5 hours); return buses depart Sámara at 4am and 8am. Traroc buses (2685-5352) run between Nicoya and Sámara throughout the day (₡1,300, 1 hour).

Getting Around Sámara

If you're staying in downtown Sámara, nearly everything is within walking distance. If you want to explore nearby Playa Carrillo, a car will definitely come in handy, although you can also get to Carrillo by taxi or public bus. If you want to check out Playa Barrigona, you'll definitely want a car with four-wheel-drive. Alamo (2656-0958) rents cars from their downtown office.

Hotels

Sámara is full of small hotels clustered around the downtown area. There's a good selection of budget and moderate hotels, plus a few high-end B&Bs. There are also a handful of small hotels in the hills above Playa Carrillo. For a complete list of Sámara and Carrillo hotels visit www.jameskaiser.com

★Sea Kayaking

One of the most popular activities in Sámara is sea kayaking to Isla Chora, the offshore island near the eastern tip of the bay. Kayak trips last about two hours and include a snorkel around the island's reefs. Locals rent kayaks on the beach ($10/hour), or you can get a professional tour from Skynet Tours (2656-0920, www.samara-tours.com). Cost: $50 per person.

★Scenic Flights

There's no better way to appreciate the Nicoya Peninsula's breathtaking scenery than from the seat of a gyrocopter—an ultralight, ultramodern helicopter that offers spectacular open-air views. Flying Crocodile, a German-owned operation, offers flights from their private airstrip, located 5 km (3 miles) west of Sámara at the Hotel Flying Crocodile. Cost: $110/20 mins, $150/30 mins, $230/hour. (2656-8048, www.autogyroamerica.com)

Hiking

Alvaro at Sámara Trails offers a 2.5-hour guided hike through his grandfather's 168-hectare (415-acre) property in the hills above Sámara. The moderate hike passes through beautiful scenery and includes lots of information about tropical dry forests. Tours are offered at 7am (better for wildlife watching) and 3pm (includes sunset at an overlook high above Sámara Bay). Cost: $35 adults, $15 kids, including transportation and a snack. (8835-9040, www.samaratrails.com)

Sportfishing

Kingfisher (2656-0091, 8358-9561, www.costaricabillfishing.com) is one of the most established sportfishing operations in town, offering half-day trips for $800 and full-day trips for $1,250. Peak fishing season is December through April, with marlin most common in January and February.

Other Adventures

Horseback riding on the beach, canopy tours in the forest, snorkeling, scuba diving, offshore dolphin watching—all of these tours can be arranged through Skynet Tours in Sámara (2656-0920, www.samara-tours.com) or Carrillo Adventures in Playa Carrillo (2656-0606, www.carrilloadventures.com). Both companies offer about a half-dozen popular tours.

Sámara Restaurants

★**EL LAGARTO** (Lnch, Din: $17–32)
This laid-back, beachfront restaurant is famous for its wood-fired grill and its delicious steaks (their cattle, raised near Lake Arenal, are free of hormones and antibiotics). The menu includes plenty of grilled seafood options, plus grilled chicken, pork and veggies. (2656-0750, www.ellagartobbq.com)

★**GUSTO BEACH** (Brk: $6–9; Lnch: $9–14; Din: $10–19)
This hip, beachfront lounge offers sweeping views of Sámara Bay. Tables and beanbags are nestled under shady palms, making it great for breakfast, lunch and trendy cocktails served late into the night. No credit cards. (2656-0252)

LO QUE HAY (Brk: $4–6; Lnch, Din: $8–16)
Beachfront, table-in-the-sand dining makes this a great place to enjoy Mexican favorites (tacos, burritos) and pizza. (2656-0811)

EL COLIBRI (Din: $8–17)
This delicious Argentinian restaurant serves delicious grilled steaks and meats. Located in Cabinas El Colibri behind Hotel Esperanza above Playa Carrillo. Closed Mondays. (2656-0656, www.cabinaselcolibri.com)

AL MANGLAR (Din: $10–20)
The ambiance of this Italian restaurant is simple and unfancy, but the homemade gnocchi and ravioli are delicious. There's also pasta, meat dishes, and thin-crust pizzas. No credit cards. (2656-0096)

CASA ESMERALDA (Lnch, Din: $9–17)
This local favorite offers consistently good Italian-inspired food with some cheaper Costa Rican options for those on a budget. Pasta, seafood, steaks and the best *casado* in town. Go with the chef's recommendations and you won't go wrong. Closed Sunday. (2656-0489)

Best Sunset Cocktails

Gusto Beach (Hip beachfront bar)

Playa Carrillo (BYOB)

Playa Carrillo

Playa Carrillo

Follow the main road about 4 km (2.5 miles) southeast of Sámara and you'll soon reach one of Costa Rica's most beautiful, undeveloped beaches: Playa Carrillo. This graceful half moon bay is a near carbon copy of Sámara, but smaller, with lighter sand and with far fewer people. Instead of hotels and restaurants dotting the shore, there are only palm trees swaying gently in the breeze. Carrillo is about as authentically Costa Rican as you can get. The visitors are overwhelmingly Tico families picnicking under the shady palms, and local street vendors sell *pipas* (coconut water), *granizados* (shaved, flavored ice) and *copos* (granizados mixed with powdered milk and sweetened condensed milk) from push carts along the side of the road. Although popular on weekends, Carrillo is big enough that finding an uncrowded spot is rarely a problem. The western end of the beach is usually less crowded, but the eastern end offers better sunset views. A handful of small hotels are scattered among the hills overlooking the beach, and public buses (₡600) run between Sámara and Carrillo throughout the day.

LA SELVA WILDLIFE REFUGE

This private refuge is home to over 30 species of Costa Rican wildlife, including monkeys, wildcats, birds and reptiles. A guided tour is $20 adults, $14 kids. Wooden signs point the way from Playa Carrillo. (2656-2236)

Playa Barrigona

Playa Carrillo is big, beautiful and easily accessible from Sámara. But if you're *really* looking to get off the beaten path, check out Playa Barrigona, which lies 6 kms (3.7 miles) west of Sámara (20-minute drive). This small beach is a hidden gem—powdery light sand, turquoise water, shady trees, dramatic rock cliffs. The best part: because it's poorly marked and only accessible via a bumpy 4x4 road that requires a river crossing, it's almost always deserted. If you're looking to escape the crowds and play castaway, welcome to paradise. To get to Barrigona from Sámara, follow the signs to the Flying Crocodile Hotel until you reach *Ferretería El Coyote*. Instead of turning left to the Flying Crocodile, continue straight for another kilometer or so. Look for a small wooden sign on the left that marks the turnoff to Playa Barrigona, then follow the bumpy dirt road to a small parking area. From the parking area a small trail heads to the beach. During the rainy season, a small waterfall tumbles down the rocks on the southern end of the beach.

SANTA TERESA

LOCATED JUST NORTH of the southern tip of the Nicoya Peninsula, Santa Teresa is home to a series of big, beautiful beaches that offer some of the most consistent surfing in Costa Rica. Yet due to its remote location at the end of a series of bumpy dirt roads, Santa Teresa still feels mellow and low-key. Unlike many beaches in the northern Nicoya, which have become cluttered with condos and mega-resorts, the vibe here remains rugged, rustic and natural.

But Santa Teresa is no longer flying under the radar. The town is now a top destination for trend-setting surfers and backpackers, and a handful of celebrity homeowners—Gisele Bündchen, Mel Gibson—ensure that Santa Teresa regularly lands in the tabloids. The downside: Santa Teresa is no longer a secret. The upside: It's no longer a barren outpost. These days there are a number of charming hotels, excellent restaurants and great yoga studios. For the moment, Santa Teresa exists in a Goldilocks state of development: not too little, not too much.

The name "Santa Teresa" has come to refer to the beaches of Malpaís, Playa Carmen, Santa Teresa and Playa Hermosa—all of which are connected by a bumpy, unpaved road set back about a block from the beach. If you're arriving via Cóbano (as nearly everyone does), you'll know you're in town when you hit *El Cruce* ("The Crossing"), a prominent intersection along the main road. To the south (left) is Malpaís, a small fishing village that's home to a seaside soccer field and a handful of nice hotels. To the north (right) is Playa Carmen, where the main road is crowded with shops and restaurants.

Head north on the main road and things start to mellow out as Playa Carmen transitions into Santa Teresa. Stretching 2.5 km (1.5 miles) north of Playa Carmen, Santa Teresa is the biggest and most beautiful beach in the area, home to a wide range of hostels, hotels and restaurants. North of Santa Teresa is Playa Hermosa, a beautiful, uncrowded beach that's a roughly 8 km (5 miles) from El Cruce (about a 20-minute drive).

Wherever you end up, you'll undoubtedly spend a lot of time at the beach, and at night there's usually a good party somewhere. If you're looking for more than just sun, surf and *cerveza*, Santa Teresa also makes a good jumping off point to explore some of the natural highlights of the southern Nicoya, including Cabo Blanco and the Montezuma Waterfall. ATV rentals are one of the most popular ways to get around.

Note: An unusually high percentage of local businesses, including the gas station, do not accept credit cards here. Fortunately, there are a handful of ATMs in Playa Carmen.

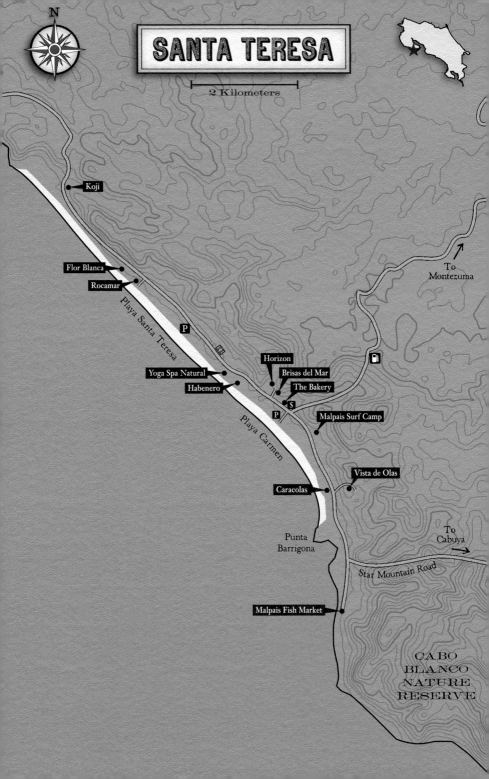

Getting To Santa Teresa

Santa Teresa is 11 km (6.8 miles) from Cóbano (30-minute drive), 57 km (35 miles) from Paquera (1.5-hour drive), 227 km (141 miles) from Liberia (4-hour drive). From San José it's 97 kms (60 miles) to Puntarenas (1.5-hour drive), where you can catch the Paquera ferry (p.340). Note: the road between Playa Carrillo and Santa Teresa is in bad condition and should be avoided. The closest airport is Playa Tambor, 28 km (17.4 miles) from Santa Teresa (1-hour drive), serviced by Sansa and Nature Air (p.20). Shuttles are available from Montezuma Expeditions (2640-0898, www.montezumaexpeditions.com). Transportes Cóbano buses (2221-7479) depart San José for Malpaís from Terminal Atlántico Norte (Calle 12, Ave 7/9) 6am, 2pm (₡6,800, 5 hours); return buses depart 5:30am, 2pm.

Getting Around Santa Teresa

A single 9-km (5.6-mile) dirt road runs parallel to the beaches, offering easy access to just about everything in Santa Teresa. Many hotels offer bicycle rentals, and taxis (8822-0660, 8510-7728) are also available. Rental cars are available from Alamo (2640-0526), Budget (2640-0500), Toyota (2640-0993). ATV rentals (p.328) are also popular.

Santa Teresa Hotels

From $15 surf hostels to $900/night luxury villas, there's a wide range of options here. Visit www.jameskaiser.com for complete Santa Teresa hotel info.

★Surfing

Santa Teresa is home to some of the best beach breaks on the Nicoya Peninsula, and surfing is by far the town's most popular activity. This is a great place for intermediate surfers, and big swells give advanced surfers plenty to brag about. Waves are consistently good year-round, though the best conditions are often found during small to medium swells at low tide. The most popular breaks are at Playa Santa Teresa near Llora Amarilla and Rocamar. Playa Carmen also has some fun waves—and, more importantly, it's a great place to see and be seen. In Malpaís hardcore wave junkies can search out the fun reef-points at Punta Barrigona and Los Suecos.

There are nearly a dozen surf shops along the main road, all of which offer board rentals. Shop around and compare prices. For surf lessons check out:

Costa Rica Surf & SUP (2640-0328, www.costaricasurfandsup.com)

Del Soul Surf School (8878-0880, www.surfvacationcostarica.com)

Malpaís Surf Camp (2640-0031, www.malpaissurfcamp.com)

★Yoga

Yoga is a way of life in Santa Teresa, and there are several great studios that offer group classes to the public.

Horizon Yoga Hotel - A beautiful, hillside studio with incredible ocean views. $12/class, $40/4 classes, $60/8 classes. (2640-0524, www.horizon-yogahotel.com)

Yoga & Spa Natural - Charming beachside studio with great views of the waves. $12/class, $40/4 classes, $64/8 classes. (2640-0402, www.yogaspanatural.com)

Flor Blanca - Terrific yoga instructors at one of the most luxurious hotels in Santa Teresa $12/class, $55/5 classes. (2640-0232, www.florblanca.com)

ATV Rentals

Due to all the dirt roads, ATVs are a great way to get around Santa Teresa and explore the surrounding area. Nearby highlights include the Montezuma Waterfall (p.337), a 45-minute ride, and Cabo Blanco (p.330), a 1-hour ride. Quad Point (2640-0965) in Playa Carmen rents ATVs by the hour (8 hours $50) or by the day (1 day $60, 3 days $150, 7 days $350). Prices are slightly lower in the off-season (May–November). Tip: Before returning the ATV, fill up the tank at the gas station up the hill from El Cruce.

Spa/Massage

Both Horizon Yoga and Yoga & Spa Natural (see Yoga above) offer spa treatments and massage. Pura Vida Bodyworks (8722-1362) also offers massage. Prices generally run $60–75 per hour.

Restaurants

★ BRISAS DEL MAR (Brk: $6–10; Din: $16–21)

Perched on a hill with great ocean views, this creative fusion restaurant offers terrific dining in Playa Carmen. The menu changes, but expect lots of fresh seafood and local ingredients. Good wine, great cocktails. Arrive early to enjoy the sunset. Located at hotel Buenos Aires at the end of a *very* steep hill—best to drive or take a taxi. Closed Mon. No credit cards. (2640-0941, www.buenosairesmalpais.com)

★ KOJI (Din: $7–16 per roll)

Chef Koji serves up some of the best sushi in Costa Rica. Though located in distant Playa Hermosa, if you're a sushi lover, this charming restaurant is definitely worth the drive. Closed Sun–Tues. No credit cards. (2640-0815)

HABANERO (Lnch, Din: $16–24)

Upscale Mexican cuisine in a relaxed, beachfront setting. Great margaritas. No credit cards. (2640-1106)

VISTA DE OLAS (Din: $11–24)

They provide the meat, you grill it. Or just show up for sunset cocktails. Either way, you'll be treated to one of the best views in Santa Teresa. Bring your swimsuit to enjoy the infinity pool. (2640-0183, www.vistadeolas.com)

ROCAMAR (Lnch, Din: $15–19)

If you're looking for a mellow, rustic beach bar, you'll love Rocamar. A great place for beers, cocktails and tasty food. No credit cards. (2640-0250)

THE BAKERY (Brk: $5–11; Lnch, Din: $8–13)

This hip, happening bakery/cafe in Playa Carmen offers delicious sandwiches, paninis, pasta and pizza, plus fresh juices, smoothies and terrific desserts. No credit cards. (2640-0560)

CARACOLAS (Lnch, Din: $8–16)

This charming, beachside restaurant in Malpaís serves traditional Costa Rican food with an upscale touch. Closed Thursday. (2640-0525)

Best Sunset Cocktails

Vista de Olas (The best sunset view in town)

Brisas del Mar (Terrific views, terrific cocktails)

Rocamar (Laid-back beachside bar)

Cabo Blanco Reserve

Cabo Blanco ("White Cape") is located at the southern tip of the Nicoya Peninsula, which is the only part of the peninsula that stays green year-round. Unlike the rest of the Nicoya, which is covered in tropical dry forest p.98, Cabo Blanco is home to tree species from the humid tropical rain forest that don't shed their leaves in the dry season.

Lying just offshore Cabo Blanco is Isla Cabo Blanco, a barren, rocky island that's an important nesting site for seabirds such as pelicans, frigate birds and brown boobies. (The island, which is covered with white bird droppings, gave rise to the name "Cabo Blanco.") Both the island and the southern tip of the peninsula are part of the *Reserva Absoluta Cabo Blanco* ("Cabo Blanco Absolute Nature Reserve"), which now protects 1,200 hectares (4.6 square miles) of land and 1,700 hectares (6.6 square miles) of ocean. The reserve was the brainchild of Olof Wessberg and his wife Karen Mogensen, a Danish-Swedish couple who moved to the southern Nicoya in 1955. Amazed by the abundant wildlife at the tip of the peninsula—and disturbed by the massive deforestation taking place at the time—they lobbied to buy the land and protect it. With the help of the Sierra Club and The Nature Conservancy, they bought five hectares, and in 1963 Cabo Blanco became the first protected area in Costa Rica.

There are two strenuous hiking trails in the reserve. The longest, *Sendero Sueco* ("Swedish Trail"), heads 4.5 kms (2.8 miles) from the park entrance to Playa Cabo Blanco and Playa Balsita, two beautiful beaches on either side of Cabo Blanco. The hike to the beaches is about four hours round-trip. If you're looking for a shorter hike, consider the loop that follows Sendero Sueco, then loops back along *Sendero Danés* ("Danish Trail"). This hike takes about one hour, and there are impressive tree species along the way. Keep in mind that the trails can get muddy during the rainy season (May–Nov).

Cabo Blanco is open Weds–Sun, 8am–4pm (2642-0093). Cost: $10 adults, $1 kids. To drive to Cabo Blanco head to Cabuya, where signs point to the entrance. Shuttle buses run between Cabo Blanco and Montezuma throughout the day.

Cabuya

This small village, located 6 km (3.7 miles) southwest of Montezuma and 2 km (1.2 miles) east of the entrance to Cabo Blanco, is famous for its cemetery, which is located on a small island just offshore. At low tide the island connects to the mainland, and you can walk across and explore it. (Be sure to head back before the tide comes in.) The crossing point is located a block south of Panadaría Cabuya, a nice bakery that serves breakfast, lunch and dinner. Tip: If you're coming from Santa Teresa and you have four-wheel-drive, you can take the Star Mountain road, a 11-km (6.8-mile) dirt road that requires multiple stream crossings in the rainy season.

Cabo Blanco

MONTEZUMA

THIS SMALL SEASIDE village, located just east of the southern tip of the Nicoya Peninsula, is famous for pretty beaches, a stunning waterfall and a funky, countercultural vibe. Although lots of beaches attract hippies in Costa Rica, none attracts as many as Montezuma. The town's main drag is filled with dread-locked vendors selling earthy jewelry, and most visitors have an abundance of hair, tattoos and conspiracy theories. There's even a local fire dancing school. The town's reputation is firmly established in its Spanish nickname: *Montefuma* (*fuma* is derived from the verb *fumar*, "to smoke").

But even if you're not pierced and tattooed in dozens of unlikely places, Montezuma still has a lot to offer. Unlike most beaches on the Nicoya Peninsula, which are generally big and long, Montezuma's beaches are small and separated by a series of rocky outcrops, giving them a more secluded feel. And when the waves are too big for swimming, you can always head to the nearby Montezuma Waterfall, the biggest, most spectacular waterfall on the Nicoya Peninsula. Another nearby waterfall, El Chorro, tumbles off a cliff onto a rocky beach a few kilometers east of town. Montezuma is also a great jumping off point for day trips to Cabo Blanco and Islas Tortugas.

Another nice aspect of Montezuma is its size. Small and compact, virtually all of the town's attractions are located within a short walk of "downtown," which essentially consists of a T-intersection near the main beach. Spread out from the intersection are several seaside hotels and hostels, while pricier ecolodges dot the shoreline and the hills outside of town. Wander northeast along the shore and you'll pass a seemingly endless series of pretty, uncrowded beaches. The farther you go, the more isolated and deserted the beaches become, and topless sunbathing is not uncommon.

As with most hippie destinations, Montezuma has several great restaurants and virtually all of its businesses have a small mom-and-pop feel. If you're looking for a rustic refuge from the strip malls and corporate resorts found in the northern Nicoya Peninsula, Montezuma won't let you down. And though the majority of visitors are young backpackers from North America and Europe, there are plenty of white-haired travelers here, too. I should also mention something not too common here: all-night dance parties. Although a few bars stay open late, people here are more interested in hammocks than house music. In Montezuma, it's all about maximum relaxation.

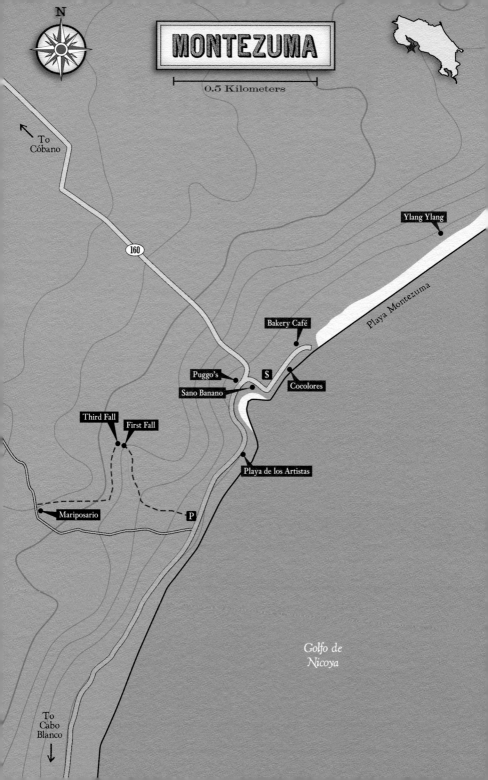

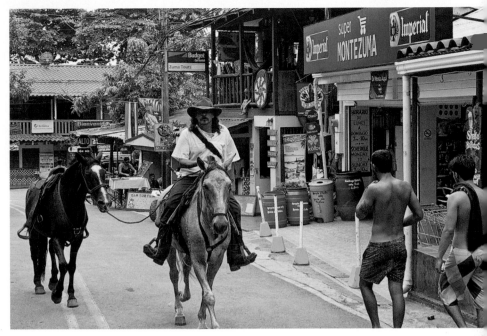

Getting To Montezuma

Montezuma is 200 km (124 miles) from Liberia (3-hour drive), 35 km (22 miles) from Paquera (1-hour drive), and 17 km (11 miles) from Playa Tambor (30-minute drive). The closest airport is at Playa Tambor, which is serviced by Nature Air and Sansa (p.18). Shuttles are available from Montezuma Expeditions (2642-0919, www.montezumaexpeditions.com). If you're driving from San José, the fastest route is through Puntarenas (p.349), where you can catch a ferry to Paquera (p.340). Another option is driving around the Gulf of Nicoya via the Amistad Bridge. Transportes Cóbano buses (2221-7479) depart San José for Montezuma (₡7,190, 5 hours) from Terminal del Atlántico Norte (Calle 12, Ave 7/9) at 6am and 2pm; return buses depart Montezuma at 6:30am and 2:30pm.

Getting Around Montezuma

Montezuma is a very small town, and unless you're staying in one of the high-end hotels outside of town, just about everything is within walking distance. Both taxis (8825-6008, 8818-3895) and ATV rentals are available downtown.

Hotels

Downtown Montezuma has several budget hotels and hostels with dorm rooms, and there are even some seaside bargains to be found. More upscale hotels are located in the hills above town and the beaches outside of town. For complete Montezuma hotel info visit www.jameskaiser.com

★Montezuma Waterfall

This stunning waterfall is Montezuma's most famous attraction, and with good reason. Big and beautiful, it tumbles down a rocky cliff in three tiers, with each tier plunging into a lovely pool that's perfect for swimming. Best of all, the waterfall is located just a short stroll from the center of town.

To get to the base of the waterfall (aka First Fall), walk west on the main road from downtown Montezuma. After about 10 minutes you'll cross a short bridge in front of La Cascada Restaurant/Hotel. Just past the bridge is a parking area on the right (₡1,000 to park). From the parking area a rugged trail follows the western side of a stream that flows from the base of the waterfall. The trail is rocky and sometimes slippery, so it's best attempted with water shoes, though sandals will suffice. After the first major rock outcrop, it's best to cross to the eastern side of the stream, though exactly where will depend on the level of the river. Use your judgement. From the start of the trail, it takes about 15 minutes to reach the base of the waterfall. If you lose the trail (not uncommon), just stay close to the river and keep following it until you reach the 30-meter (98-foot) waterfall. Although the pool here is said to be 15 meters (49 feet) deep, no one has ever survived a jump from the top of the waterfall (and several people have tried).

If you'd like to reach the upper tiers of the waterfall, you have two options. The first, and most dangerous, is to follow the rugged path set back from the base of First Fall. I do not recommend this due to the trail's steep, crumbling condition. A better option is to head to Sun Trails, located about 300 meters past Montezuma Gardens (p.338). If you don't have a car, you can hire a taxi or walk (it's about a 25-minute walk up the steep hill past the turnoff to First Fall). Sun Trails charges a ₡2,000 entrance fee at the front desk to access their well-maintained trail system, which features several hanging bridges and informative signs about local flora and fauna. Follow the trail along the river until you exit Sun Trail's private path and enter the public trail near the top of the Third Fall. Plan on about 20 minutes hiking time from the Sun Trails entrance to the top of the Third Fall. Third Fall is about 3.5 meters (11.5 feet) high, and its pool is said to be 6 meters (20 feet) deep. The rocks here are fun to jump off, and there's a rope swing to the right.

On the far side of Third Fall's swimming pool is the top of Second Fall, which is 15 meters (49 feet) high and is said to be 8 meters (26 feet) deep. Use caution if you choose to jump from Second Fall. I've been told that one person died here after slipping during his jump.

If all this seems a bit complicated/intimidating, you can always sign up for Sun Trail's Waterfall Canopy Tour, which includes a guided trip to Third Fall.

Note: During the depths of the rainy season (September to mid-November) it is not safe to visit the upper tiers of the Montezuma Waterfall.

El Chorro Waterfall

★Islas Tortuga

Montezuma is a one-hour boat ride away from Islas Tortuga (p.343), and Zuma Tours (2642-0024, www.zumatours.net) offers day trips to the island that include snorkeling. Tours depart at 9:15am and return at 4pm. Cost: $55 per person.

Waterfall Canopy Tour

This 9-cable canopy tour zips over the river that feeds the Montezuma Waterfall. Halfway through the tour you'll descend to the Third Fall and enjoy a swim in its beautiful pool. Cost: $40. Tours are offered at 9am, 1pm and 3pm. (2642-0808, www.montezumatraveladventures.com)

El Chorro Waterfall

Located 6 km (3.7 miles) northeast of Montezuma at Playa Cocolito, El Chorro tumbles down from a seaside cliff into a rocky tide pool. Both the waterfall and the nearby beaches are best explored around low tide. Coco Zuma Traveler (2642-0911, www.cocozumacr.com) offers horseback trips to El Chorro. You can also visit the waterfall via Hotel Tango Mar, a 20-minute drive from Montezuma.

Montezuma Gardens

This lovely butterfly garden, located about 1.5 km (1 mile) west of the town center, is a great place to learn about tropical insects and butterflies, including the famous blue morpho. Open 8am–4pm. Cost $4, under 5 free (2642-1317).

Montezuma Restaurants

⭐**PLAYA DE LOS ARTISTAS** (Lnch: $11–17; Din: $15–23)
This charming seaside restaurant offers ocean views and romantic candle-lit dinners. The menu changes daily, but Mediterranean cuisine is their specialty and the seafood is superb. Great cocktails. Dinner Mon–Fri, lunch Sat only, closed Sunday. Reservations recommended. No credit cards. (2642-0920)

⭐**YLANG YLANG** (Brk: $8–11; Lnch: $12–20; Din: $15–22)
The most elegant restaurant in town, located in the upscale Ylang Ylang hotel. The extensive menu draws on Asian and tropical flavors, plus sushi, vegan and raw options. Good wine list. Dinner reservations required before 1:30pm. Note: Ylang Ylang is a 10-minute stroll northeast along the beach, but if you make reservations they offer a free shuttle. (2642-0636, www.ylangylangbeachresort.com)

SANO BANANO (Brk: $5–10; Lnch, Din: $13–18)
Specializing in healthy, hearty meals, *Sano Banano* ("Healthy Banana") has lots of vegetarian and vegan options, plus dishes with fish and hormone-free chicken. No red meat (eco-unfriendly). A tasteful blend of Latin and European flavors, plus sushi. Free movies shown every night at 7:30pm. (2642-0325)

PUGGO'S (Din: $10–28)
This tasty Israeli restaurant offers Middle Eastern classics (hummus, falafel, kebabs) with some Italian and Asian options. Open-air and latern-lit, it's suffused with a chilled out hippie vibe. No credit cards. (2642-0308)

BAKERY CAFE (Brk: $6–8; Lnch, Din: $7–13)
One of the better budget restaurants in town, the Bakery Cafe offers a wide range of options, including Costa Rican, Italian, Indian and Thai dishes. Great fruit juices. (2642-0458)

COCOLORES (Din: $10–20)
This laid-back, seaside restaurant offers a nice selection of international options: pasta, fajitas, kabobs, coconut curry mahi mahi, orange vodka chicken. Good cocktails. Closed Monday. No credit cards. (2642-0348)

Best Sunset Cocktails

Playa de los Artistas (Great drinks, terrific seaside views)
Ylang Ylang (2 for 1 drinks 3pm–6pm everyday)

Playa Tambor

Playa Tambor

Playa Tambor is a big, brown beach that's home to the southern Nicoya's largest airport and the all-inclusive mega-resort Barceló. Although Tambor is nice, nearby Montezuma and Santa Teresa are far nicer.

Paquera

This small port is the departure point for a passenger/car ferry that runs between Paquera and Puntarenas (p.349). The crossing takes 1.5 hours, as opposed to the 4-hour drive around the Gulf of Nicoya. The ferry departs Paquera at 5:30am, 9am, 11am, 2pm, 5pm, 8pm daily. Cost: $2 adults, $1 kids, $25 cars. If you're arriving by car, try to arrive at least 1.5 hours early, especially for the 2pm and 5pm Sunday crossings. A ferry employee instructs you where to park and gives you a voucher. Bring the voucher to the ticket counter, purchase your ticket, then return to your car and wait to be ushered onto the ferry. (2661-2084, www.navieratambor.com)

Playa Naranjo

Located 14 km (8.7 miles) north of Paquera, Playa Naranjo offers another passenger/car ferry that runs to/from Puntarenas. Keep in mind that the 24-km (15-mile) dirt road between Naranjo and Paquera is extremely rugged and bumpy; plan on a 1-hour drive. The ferry departs Playa Naranjo at 8am, 12:30pm, 5:30pm, 9pm. The ferry departs Puntarenas at 6:30am, 10am, 2:20pm, 7:30pm. Cost: $2 adults, $1 kids, $25 cars. (2611-9011, www.coonatramar.com)

Isla San Lucas
"The Island of Lonely Men"

From 1873 to 1991 Isla San Lucas, which lies just off the eastern shore of the Nicoya Peninsula, was home to Costa Rica's most notorious prison. Its horrible conditions were chronicled in the bestselling memoir *La Isla de los Hombres Solos* ("The Island of Lonely Men"), written by former inmate José León Sánchez. Born in 1929 to a prostitute mother and unknown father, Sánchez ended up in an orphanage after his mother tried to trade him for a bag of salt. In 1950 Sánchez was wrongly accused of a murder/robbery at the Basílica de Los Ángeles in Cartago and tortured into confession. He was then sentenced to 45 years at Isla San Lucas, where, in his words, "human beings had absolutely no value."

Sánchez was illiterate when he entered prison, but he learned to read and write from a fellow inmate. Over the course of a decade, he wrote *La Isla de los Hombres Solos* on leftover paper from cement bags. In 1974 his memoir was made into a Mexican film, and the book soon became an international bestseller. In 1998 the Costa Rican Supreme Court reviewed Sánchez's case and declared him innocent of all charges. To date *La Isla de los Hombres Solos* has sold over two million copies, and it is now considered one of Costa Rica's most important works of literature.

Tours of the island, including the prison, are offered by Bay Island Cruises 2258-3536, www.bayislandcruises.com, $95 per person).

Islas Tortuga

The "Turtle Islands," which lie just south of the eastern tip of the Nicoya Peninsula, are two uninhabited islands home to turquoise water, white sand beaches and palm trees swaying gently in the breeze. For many people this is the definition of tropical paradise, although in recent years the beach has become popular and crowded. Boat trips to Islas Tortugas from Montezuma are offered by Zuma Tours. Day trips to Islas Tortugas from San José, which involve a 1.5-hour drive to Puntarenas then a 75-minute boat trip across the Nicoya Gulf, are offered by Calypso Cruises (2256-2727, www.calypsocruises.com, $139 per person) and Bay Island Cruises (2258-3536, www.bayislandcruises.com, $115 adults, $95 students). All trips include food and snorkeling.

INLAND NICOYA

The Nicoya Peninsula's inland attractions are far less spectacular than its beautiful beaches, but if you're looking for authentic Tico culture unblemished by tourism, you'll certainly find it here. A drive down Highway 21, which runs through the heart of the peninsula and passes by the towns of Santa Cruz and Nicoya, provides an interesting dose of local flavor.

Santa Cruz

This bustling Tico town, located 35 km (22 miles) east of Tamarindo, offers little of tourist interest besides bus transfers. If you find yourself passing through around mealtime, however, check out La Venus Del Diriá (Lnch, Din: $9–16), which serves typical food *a la leña* (wood-fired) plus strange regional drinks like *chan* and *linaza*. Located three blocks south of the stoplight on the main highway.

Diriá National Park

Located 14 km (8.7 miles) south of Santa Cruz, Diriá National Park protects over 5,400 hectares of forest. Located at one of the highest points on the Nicoya Peninsula—parts of the park are 980 meters (3,215 feet) above sea level—Diriá includes the headwaters of four local rivers. Over 130 species of birds are found here as well as howler and white-faced monkeys. There are two hiking trails in the park: El Escabel and El Venado, both of which head to the Brazil waterfall. The park also rents out a basic cabin if you'd like to spend the night. No public transportation is available. If you want to visit the park, you'll have to drive or take a taxi from Santa Cruz. Open 8am–4pm. Admission: $10. (8358-4742)

Guaitíl

This small village, located 12 km (7.5 miles) east of Santa Cruz, is famous for its pottery, which features indigenous Chorotega designs. Guaitíl pottery is sold in gift shops throughout Costa Rica, but if you're looking for the best prices and selection you'll definitely find them here. Several workshops surround the town square, and many offer free pottery making demonstrations.

Nicoya

Nicoya is an authentic Tico town that most travelers pass through on their way to Sámara or Nosara. Downtown Nicoya is a congested maze of one-way streets filled with basic shops and restaurants. Although much of the town is bland and run-down, the Iglesia de San Blas is a pretty 17th-century church that overlooks a peaceful town park where the town's citizens gather to chat and relax.

Each year the town of Nicoya hosts two impressive celebrations: Día de Guanacaste (July 25) and the Festival de La Virgen de Guadalupe (December 12). Día de Guanacaste celebrates the transfer of Guanacaste Province, which includes much of the Nicoya Peninsula, from Nicaragua to Costa Rica in 1824. The Festival de La Virgen de Guadelupe, which combines traditional Catholic and indigenous Chorotega beliefs, includes a parade where a statue of the Virgin is walked through the streets while citizens play indigenous music and drink *chicha*, a fermented corn beverage.

★DIRIÁ COFFEE TOUR

The rugged mountains that rise up from the Nicoya Peninsula are high enough to support coffee farming, and the Diriá Coffee Tour explains the entire process from seed to sack. After learning about the life cycle of a coffee plant, you'll take a tour of the local processing facility where coffee beans are extracted from ripe coffee fruit. This is definitely one of the better coffee tours in Costa Rica. Located just east of the town of Hojancha, 13 km (8 miles) from Nicoya. Cost: $20 adults, $10 kids. (2659-9130)

Barra Honda National Park

This small national park, located 26 km (16 miles) from the town of Nicoya (30-minute drive), protects Costa Rica's most impressive cave system, a series of more than 40 caverns that descends 249 meters (817 feet) below ground. Although most of the caves are off limits to non-spelunkers, guided tours of the impressive Terciopelo Cave are offered. After attaching a safety harness and descending a 19-meter (62-foot) metal ladder, you'll squeeze through tight crevices and enter dark chambers filled with impressive stalactites and stalagmites in this 62-meter (203-foot) deep cave. After emerging from the cave, be sure to hike to the dramatic *mirador* ("lookout"), which offers sweeping views of the valley below Barra Honda and the head of the Nicoya Gulf. Tours of the Terciopelo Cave last 3–4 hours and cost $25 per person (plus $10 park entrance fee). Guides can be reserved at the Barra Honda entrance station (2659-1551), but cave tours are only available from 8am to 1pm. Harnesses, helmets and headlights are provided. Be sure to wear closed-toe shoes and cool clothes—it gets surprisingly hot in the caverns.

Uvita

CENTRAL PACIFIC

LOCATED LESS THAN 120 kms (75 miles) from San José, the Central Pacific has long been one of Costa Rica's most popular destinations. But its proximity to the nation's capital isn't the only reason for its popularity. The combination of beautiful beaches, abundant wildlife and lush mountains offers some of the most dramatic coastal scenery in Costa Rica.

The Central Pacific lies in an ecological transition zone. To the north are the tropical dry forests of the Nicoya Peninsula, which turn brown and dusty during the region's long dry season. To the south are the lush, humid rainforests of the Osa Peninsula, which are green (and rainy) year-round. Between these two extremes lies the Central Pacific, which in many ways combines the best of both worlds: beautiful, sunny beaches with lush jungles and abundant wildlife. National parks and eco-adventures abound, and nearly everything is conveniently spread out along the Costanera Highway that parallels the coast. If you're looking for a beach destination that offers more than just sun, surf and *cerveza*, the Central Pacific is a great choice.

In general, the Central Pacific gets less developed the further south you go. Jacó, the closest nice beach to San José, saw a burst of development in the years leading up to the 2008 financial crisis. Although the beach is nice and the surf is good, Jacó's current defining characteristic is a cluttered downtown surrounded by condo towers. Just north of Jacó is Playa Herradura, a sportfishing mecca home to the luxurious Los Sueños marina/golf resort. Just south of Jacó, meanwhile, are several uncrowded beaches that seem a world away from Jacó's chain restaurants and nightclubs.

The most famous destination in the Central Pacific is Manuel Antonio, a dramatic stretch of coastline that's home to Manuel Antonio National Park. Renowned for stunning beaches and abundant wildlife, Manuel Antonio was one of Costa Rica's original eco-highlights. As its fame grew, the lush hills outside the park filled up with hotels and restaurants, which means lots of choices, lots of luxury and lots of tourists.

South of Manuel Antonio lies the *Costa Ballena* ("Whale Coast"), so named for migrating humpback whales that visit August–October and January–March. This relatively undeveloped stretch of coast is home to big, uncrowded beaches surrounded by dramatic hills. The Costa Ballena includes Dominical (a hippie/surf town), Uvita (home to great beaches protected by a national park), and Ojochal (a tiny village filled with great restaurants). If you're looking to escape the crowds, but still want a sprinkling of creature comforts, any of these towns will treat you right.

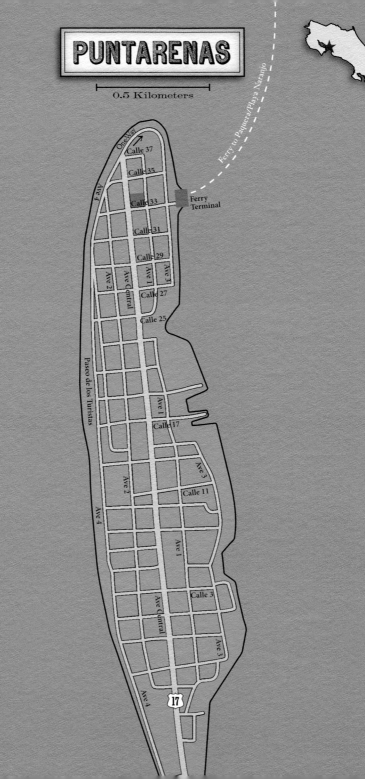

PUNTARENAS

0.5 Kilometers

N

Ferry to Paquera/Playa Naranjo

One Way

Calle 37

Calle 35

Calle 33

Ferry
Terminal

Calle 31

Calle 29

Ave 3

Ave 1

Ave 2

Ave Central

Calle 27

1 Ave

Calle 25

Paseo de los Turistas

Ave 1

Calle 17

Ave 3

Ave 2

Calle 11

Ave 4

Ave 1

Calle 3

Ave Central

Ave 3

Ave 4

17

Puntarenas

This run-down port town offers little of interest for most travelers. But Puntarenas is the departure point for two car/passenger ferries that make regular runs across the 11-km (6.8-mile) wide Gulf of Nicoya to the eastern side of the Nicoya Peninsula. By riding the ferry, which takes about 1.5 hours, you'll spare yourself the 4-hour drive around the Gulf of Nicoya and enjoy dramatic views from the water. But the ferries only really make sense if you're traveling to the southern Nicoya (Montezuma, Cabo Blanco, Santa Teresa). If you're traveling to the central Nicoya (Sámara, Nosara) or northern Nicoya, it makes more sense to drive around the Gulf of Nicoya, crossing at La Amistad Bridge.

The most popular ferry runs between Puntarenas and Paquera (p.340), which provides the fastest access to the southern Nicoya Peninsula. The drive from Puntarenas to Paquera is four hours, so taking the ferry saves you roughly 2.5 hours of travel time. The ferry departs Puntarenas at 5am, 9am, 11am, 2pm, 5pm, 8:30pm daily. The ferry departs Paquera at 6am, 9am, 11am, 2pm, 5pm, 8pm daily. Cost: $2 adults, $1 kids, $25 cars. (2661-2084, www.navieratambor.com).

Another ferry runs between Puntarenas and Playa Naranjo (p.340), which is located about 24 km (15 miles) north of Paquera (about a 1-hour drive along a very bumpy dirt road). The ferry departs Puntarenas at 6:30am, 10am, 2:20pm and 7:30pm. The ferry departs Naranjo at 8am, 12:30pm, 5:30pm and 9pm. Cost: $2 adults, $1 kids, $25 cars. (2611-9011, www.coonatramar.com)

Although both ferries are prompt and functional, boarding them can be a bit confusing, especially if you're driving a car. The process goes like this: drive counterclockwise around the western tip of the Puntarenas Peninsula until you reach the ferry terminal or until you reach a line of cars waiting to reach the ferry terminal. (Note: do not leave your car unattended, especially if it's filled with luggage; theft is always a possibility here.) When you reach the ferry terminal, drive up to the yellow gates on the left and a parking attendant will show you where to park and give you a ticket. Take this ticket across the street to the *Boleteria* ("Ticket Office") located inside the Musmanni Bakery. The longer line on the right is for passengers without a car, the shorter line on the left is for passengers with a car. After purchasing your tickets, return to your car. When the cars start boarding, drive up to the ramp and an attendant will take your ticket and wave you on. Another attendant will then tell you exactly where to park on the ferry. Lock your car and head up to the higher decks where there's a snack shop, a bar and benches with open-air views.

Puntarenas is located 73 km (45 miles) from Jacó (1-hour drive), 98 km (61 miles) from San José (1.5-hour drive), 130 km (81 miles) from the town of Nicoya (2-hour drive) and 136 km (185 miles) from Liberia (2-hour drive).

Tárcoles River

This muddy brown river is famous for crocodiles, which can be seen from the large concrete bridge spanning the river 2 kms (1.5 miles) north of Carara National Park. The crocodiles, which can grow up to 4.5 meters (15 feet), are among the biggest in Costa Rica, and it's usually possible to see over a dozen at one time. (The most I've counted is 37!)

The only thing more frightening than the toothy crocodiles is the bridge itself, which has a dangerously narrow walkway, broken railings and lots of traffic. Be careful. Also note that the makeshift parking areas on either side of the bridge are notorious for break-ins. Unless a police officer or parking attendant is present, it's best not to leave your car unattended. Remember to tip the parking attendant.

As you stare at the murky water below the bridge, contemplate the fact that the Tárcoles is one of the most polluted rivers in Central America. The river's 2,100 square-kilometer watershed drains much of metropolitan San José, where most sewage and wastewater is dumped *untreated* into rivers that ultimately flow into the Tárcoles. Although Costa Rica has done many wonderful things for the environment, it's been estimated that over 90% of the country's blackwater (sewage) is dumped back into the environment without any treatment whatsoever. Crocodiles supposedly thrive in polluted waters, which may be one of the reasons they are so numerous in the Tárcoles River. Having said that, tours of the river, are surprisingly worthwhile. They include up close encounters with crocodiles and terrific birdwatching. See Río Tárcoles Tour (p.356).

Carara National Park

This often-overlooked national park, located 2 km (1.2 miles) south of the Tárcoles bridge and 23 km (12.4 miles) north of Jacó, is far less famous than Manuel Antonio or Marina Ballena farther south. But Carara's virgin forest, good hiking trails and lack of crowds make it a great place for wildlife watching. Birders in particular will like the park, which is one of just two places in Costa Rica that supports a healthy population of scarlet macaws. (The other is the Osa Peninsula.) Today there are about 450 scarlet macaws living in and around the park, up from about 230 in the 1990s. Other bird species include parakeets, mot mots, manakins, hummingbirds, woodpeckers, trogons and roseate spoonbills. There are also capuchin monkeys, howler monkeys, two-toed sloths, three-toed sloths and Costa Rica's largest population of crocodiles (found in the swamps alongside the Tárcoles River). As always, the best wildlife watching is in the morning.

All told, Carara protects 5,240 hectares (20.2 square miles) and contains more primary rainforest than Manuel Antonio. Because Carara is situated between the tropical dry forest, found in the northern pacific, and the humid rain forest, found in the southern Pacific, it lies in an ecological transition zone that's home to over 1,400 plant species. The park is open 8am to 4pm daily. Hiking boots and insect repellent are definitely a good idea here.

Note: Scarlet macaws regularly visit the small beachside village of Tárcoles, located a short distance from the park. In the morning, it's sometimes easier to spot macaws in Tárcoles than in Carara National Park.

Playa Jacó

JACÓ & HERRADURA

Located JUST 120 km (75 miles) from San José, Jacó and Herradura are two of the most developed beach towns in Costa Rica. Playa Jacó is a gray sand beach famous for good beginner surf and congested streets packed with shops, bars and restaurants. *Playa Herradura* ("Horseshoe Beach") is a brown sand beach sheltered in a lovely horseshoe-shaped bay. The northern end of Herradura is dominated by Los Sueños Resort and Marina, a massive golf course/marina/condo development that's ground zero for luxury sportfishing in Costa Rica.

Not long ago, both Jacó and Herradura were sleepy seaside towns that catered mostly to Ticos. But all that changed in 2001 with the arrival of Los Sueños Marina & Resort. When this massive luxury development opened its doors—or rather, closed its gates—the risky venture exceeded all expectations and made its backers a giant pile of *dinero*. Other developers took notice, and a tsunami of new construction washed over Jacó and Herradura. Although the 2008 financial crisis brought everything to a halt, the character of both towns was forever changed, resulting in two wildly divergent opinions among travelers. Allow me to sum up the most extreme versions.

Among backpackers and eco-travelers, Jacó and Herradura are like Soddom and Gomorrah. Jacó: A symbol of tourism gone awry. A formerly quaint beach town filled with condos, fast food chains and prostitutes. Herradura: A once sleepy fishing village overrun by a mega-resort catering to rich foreigners who came all the way from their gated communities in the U.S. to visit a gated community in Costa Rica.

Among sportfishermen and fun-in-the-sun travelers, Jacó and Herradura are nothing but a good time, baby. Jacó: An action-packed beach town with good surf and a vibrant nightlife, full of bars and free of smelly backpackers in Che Gueverra T-shirts. Herradura: Home to the most beautiful development in Costa Rica—a place where the roads are good, the lawns are manicured and rules and regulations are actually enforced.

In short, whether you'll like Jacó or Herradura depends a great deal on who you are. Just be aware that these towns tend to draw extreme reactions from people. My advice: If you think you'll like Jacó or Herradura, you probably will. If you think you won't like Jacó or Herradura, you probably won't. Trust your instincts on this one.

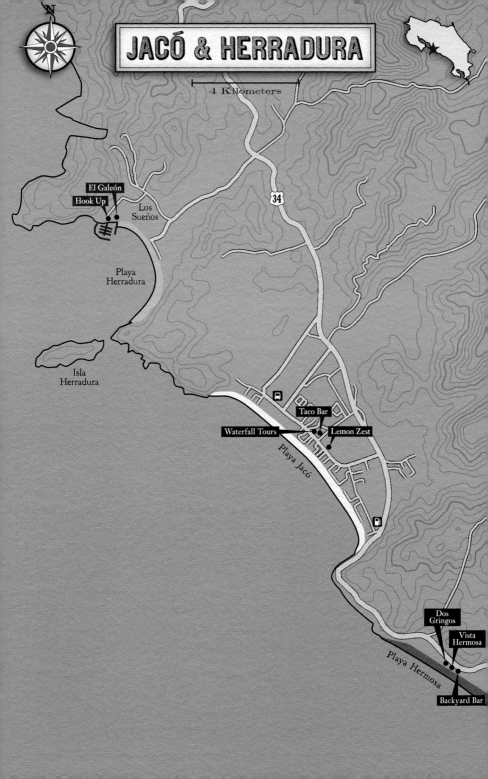

Los Sueños Marina

Getting to Jacó & Herradura

Jacó is 120 km (75 miles) from San José (1.5-hour drive) and 70 km (43.5 miles) from Puntarenas (1-hour drive). Playa Herradura is 9 km (6 miles) north of Jacó (10-minute drive). The closest airport is at Manuel Antonio/Quepos. Shuttles are available from Interbus, Grayline and Monkey Ride (p.20). Transportes Jacó buses (2223-1109) depart San José from the Coca Cola Terminal (Calle 16, Ave 1/3) at 6am, 7am, 9am, 11am, 1pm, 3pm, 5pm, 7pm (₡2,365, 2.5 hours). Return buses depart Jacó for San José at 5am, 7am, 9am, 11am, 1pm, 3pm, 5pm. Buses to Jacó also stop at the turnoff to Playa Herradura, 1 km from the beach.

Getting Around Jacó & Herradura

Jacó is a very walkable town, and the only reason you'd want a car would be to shuttle back and forth between Jacó and Playa Herradura or to visit attractions like the Tárcoles River, Carara National Park or Playa Hermosa. Taxis are plentiful in Jacó (2643-2020). Rental cars are available from Budget (2643-2665), Economy (2643-1098), National/Alamo (2643-1752).

Jacó & Herradura Hotels

Jacó is home to a wide range of budget and moderate hotels and a few upscale options. If you're looking for luxury, head to Playa Herradura, where Los Sueños Marina is located. Although Los Sueños is the big draw, there a few other luxury hotels nearby. For complete hotel info visit www.jameskaiser.com

★Costa Rica Waterfall Tours

This outdoor adventure company offers guided tours of the Central Pacific's best waterfalls, "From the serene to the extreme!" In addition to waterfall tours, they offer canyoning and a wide range of other adventures. (2643-1834, www.costaricawaterfalltours.com)

★Río Tárcoles Tour

The Tárcoles River (p.356) and adjacent mangrove estuary are home to terrific wildlife watching, especially birds and crocodiles. Jungle Crocodile Safari offers 2-hour boat trips at 8:30am, 10:30am, 1:30pm and 3:30pm. Cost: $30 adults, $20 kids under 13. (2637-0656, www.junglecrocodilesafari.com)

Surfing

When conditions are right, Jacó is home to some of the best beginner waves in the Central Pacific. Serious surfers head to nearby Playa Hermosa (p.359). For surf lessons check out Del Mar Surf Camp (2643-3197, www.delmarsurfcamp.com) or Tortuga Surf School (2643-3348, www.tortugasurfcamp.com)

Sportfishing

All local sportfishing revolves around Los Sueños Marina, which is one of the top sportfishing destinations in Costa Rica. Costa Rica Dreams Sportfishing, which has an office next to the marina, offers sportfishing trips ranging from $1,195/day for a 32-foot boat to $2,395/day for a 50-foot boat. Although half-day trips are also available, it takes a full day to motor 20 miles offshore where the sailfish and marlin are caught. (2637-8942, www.costaricadreams.com)

Canopy Tours

Vista Los Sueños is the top canopy tour near Jacó/Herradura. The tour features 14 cables, 3.5 km (2.2 miles) total length, longest cable: 732 meters (2,400 feet). Tours are offered every hour from 8am–3pm, except noon. Cost: $65 per person. (2637-6020, www.canopyvistalossuenos.com)

Rainforest Aerial Tram

This open-air aerial tram glides over the forest canopy offering great views of the surrounding scenery. Cost: $60 adults, $30 students/kids. A tram/canopy combo is also available for an extra $15. (2257-5961, www.rainforestadventure.com)

Golf

Los Sueños Resort and Marina is home to La Iguana, an 18-hole, par 72 golf course designed by Ted Robinson. Non guests: $150 per player. (2630-9151)

Jacó Restaurants

★ADVENTURE DINING (Din: $105)

Perched on a hill high above Jacó, this open-air restaurant offers spectacular views of the surrounding scenery, including Bijagual Waterfall. It's pricey, but if you've got the cash, this all-inclusive dining experience is amazing. Located at Pura Vida Gardens, about a 40-minute drive north of Jacó. Transportation available. Reservations essential. (8352-9419, www.adventurediningcostarica.com)

★ LEMON ZEST (Din: $17–24)

The top restaurant in downtown Jacó offers a delicious menu filled with French, Asian and tropical fusion cuisine. Try to grab a seat on the balcony, which offers good views of main street. (2643-2591, www.lemonzestjaco.com)

TACO BAR (Brk: $6–7; Lnch, Din: $9–14)

This funky taco bar is great for a quick, delicious, inexpensive meal. Fish tacos are the specialty, but the menu also includes salads, burritos, pitas and smoothies. The tacos are tasty, and the swing seats are great. (2643-0222, www.tacobar.info)

Herradura Restaurants

★ANFITEATRO (Brk: $11–13; Lnch, Din: $16-30)

Perched on a hill overlooking Herradura Bay and the Gulf of Nicoya, Anfiteatro offers stunning ocean views. The menu includes gourmet sandwiches, delicious salads, Angus beef, fresh seafood and great cocktails. Located at the opulent Hotel Villa Caletas. (2630-3000,www.hotelvillacaletas.com/anfiteatro)

★ EL GALEÓN (Din: $18–32)

This open-air restaurant, located in front of the marina, is the top restaurant in Los Sueños Resort. The menu features fresh seafood, burgers, sandwiches and $40 Angus steaks. (2630-4555)

★ THE HOOK UP (Lnch, Din: $13–21)

This beautiful bar/restaurant overlooks Los Sueños Marina and caters to the sportfishing crowd. Even if you didn't hook a marlin, you can still sip a cold microbrew while gazing over the multi-million dollar yachts. (2630-4444)

Best Sunset Cocktails

Anfiteatro (Incredible views of the Nicoya Gulf)

Playa Hermosa

Playa Hermosa ("Beautiful Beach") lies just 3 km (1.9 miles) south of Jacó, but this tiny surf village feels like it's a world away. There are only a handful of small hotels set back from the black sand beach, which, despite its Spanish name, is hardly among the most beautiful in Costa Rica. But all that matters to the surfers are the terrific waves offshore. Playa Hermosa is one of the most consistent and powerful breaks in Costa Rica, picking up nearly any swell that passes through. The waves break on most tides, and because the beach is over 5 km (3 miles) long, crowds are rarely a problem.

If you're a hardcore surfer, this is one of the top destinations in Costa Rica. Keep in mind, however, that Playa Hermosa's powerful waves and shallow sand bars are notorious for breaking boards. If you're a beginner surfer, you should probably stick to the smaller waves at Jacó. And if you don't surf, well, you might feel a bit out of place in Playa Hermosa, where virtually everything revolves around the waves.

For food check out the Backyard Bar (Brk: $6–8, Lnch: $10–16), a beachfront surfer favorite with great views of the waves and a menu full of Tex-Mex, burgers and sandwiches (2643-7011); Jungle Surf (Brk: $5–7; Lnch, Din: $6–14) is another popular spot offering hearty casados, seafood and Mexican favorites. Vista Hermosa (Brk: $6–7; Lnch, Din: $7–16), offers great smoothies and a wide-ranging menu filled with Asian, Mexican and Costa Rican influences (2643-6215).

Important note: There are two Playa Hermosas in Costa Rica, this one and Playa Hermosa in the northern Pacific, which has absolutely no surf (p.343).

Playa Esterillos & Playa Bejuco

Though located between Jacó and Manuel Antonio—two of the most developed beach towns on the Pacific Coast—Playa Esterillos and Playa Bejuco are delightfully uncrowded. These long, gray sand beaches are set back from the Costanera Highway, so they've managed to remain low key despite the recent development boom. The beaches are located roughly 20 km (12.4 miles) south of Jacó and 40 km (25 miles) north of Manuel Antonio. Playa Esterillos is over 9 km (5.6 miles) in length and divided into three sections: Esterillos Oeste ("West"), Esterillos Centro ("Center") and Esterillos Este ("East"). Playa Bejuco is located southeast of Esterillos. Both are best visited at low tide when the beach is enormous.

Despite the lack of development, there are a handful of beachfront hotels that cover the full spectrum from luxury to budget. (For complete hotel information visit www.jameskaiser.com). Esterillos Oeste offers some fun surf, but other than surfing and relaxing in a hammock there's not much else going on—which is exactly why some people love these beaches. If you have a car, which is pretty much a necessity here, it's easy to get to Jacó (about a 20-minute drive) or Manuel Antonio (about a 40-minute drive).

For food check out the swanky Alma del Pacifico (Brk: $10; Lnch, Din: $12–20), which offers an upscale mix of traditional Costa Rican food and Mediterranean dishes (Tel: 2778-7070). Just down the beach from Alma del Pacifico is the laid-back Hotel Pelicano (Brk: $6; Lnch, Din: $12–20), which offers sandwiches, burgers and vegetarian options (Tel: 2778-8105).

African Palm Plantations

South of Playa Esterillos, the highway passes through a vast expanse of African palm plantations. The palms, which are native to West Africa, produce large bunches of fruits that are harvested and processed into palm oil, a common ingredient in cosmetics, cooking oils and biofuels. Each fruit bunch weighs up to 25 kg (55 pounds), and one hectare (2.5 acres) of palms can yield over 3,000 kg (6,600 pounds) of palm oil annually. In the 1930s the United Fruit Company (p.152) operated vast banana plantations here, but after a banana blight destroyed the crops in the 1940s African palms were planted. Today the palm plantations are owned by the Costa Rican company Palma Tica.

Working in the palm plantations is physically demanding, and today most workers are poor Nicaraguans who earn roughly $2 per hour. (Ticos prefer less taxing, higher paying work). Palm workers live in company villages that consist of a series of simple, colorful houses surrounding a soccer field. During the day, workers trim the trees, harvest the fruit, and transport the harvest to the processing facility by tractor or oxcart. Because palm plantations are prime habitat for the deadly fer-de-lance (p.116), workers are also required to kill snakes with poison or machetes.

MANUEL ANTONIO

THIS GORGEOUS STRETCH of coastline has long been one of Costa Rica's most popular destinations. Its main attraction, Manuel Antonio National Park, is home to stunning beaches, lush jungle and three species of monkey, including the adorable (and endangered) squirrel monkey. Just outside the park, dramatic hills are filled with upscale hotels and restaurants, many with incredible views. In addition, there's seemingly no end to all the outdoor adventures: sailing, sport-fishing, canopy tours, whitewater rafting. If you want a beach destination that combines eco-tourism with creature comforts, it's hard to beat Manuel Antonio.

These days there's only one drawback to Manuel Antonio: the crowds. Twenty years ago, Manuel Antonio was only accessible via a long, bumpy dirt road, which kept out all but the most determined eco-travelers. Today the road is paved, and now it's jam-packed with hotels and restaurants. While some tourists love all the action and variety, hardcore eco-travelers are avoiding Manuel Antonio in favor of more remote destinations.

Is Manuel Antonio "too touristy"? It depends. By Mexican mega-resort stan-dards, Manuel Antonio is still charming and quaint. But by Costa Rican stan-dards, it's one of the most developed beach towns in the country. That said, if you're a city slicker feeling squeamish about eco-tourism, Manuel Antonio is a great place to dip your toes in the water. The outdoor adventures aren't particu-larly rugged, and a fruity cocktail is never far away. And if you're traveling with kids, "touristy" isn't necessarily a dirty word. There's a wider range of activities here than just about anywhere else on the Pacific Coast.

Keep in mind, however, that Manuel Antonio's popularity has led to ever increasing prices. If you're looking for Third World discounts, you're not going to find them here. Local taxi drivers and street vendors have become experts at inflating their prices, so you'll probably have to employ your bargaining skills.

Despite these hassles, Manuel Antonio remains one of Costa Rica's most beau-tiful destinations. It's one of the northernmost points on the Pacific coast where you can experience the lush tropical rainforest in all its verdant beauty. And as long as you don't visit during the peak months (Dec–March), you won't be over-whelmed by the crowds.

Note: "Manuel Antonio" technically refers to the small village just outside the national park, but people commonly refer to the entire area between Quepos and the park as Manuel Antonio. The small, seaside town of Quepos serves as the main commercial hub of the area. Towards the southern end of town, a busy road rises up into the hills and heads 7 km (4.3 miles) south to Manuel Antonio National Park, passing dozens of hotels and restaurants along the way.

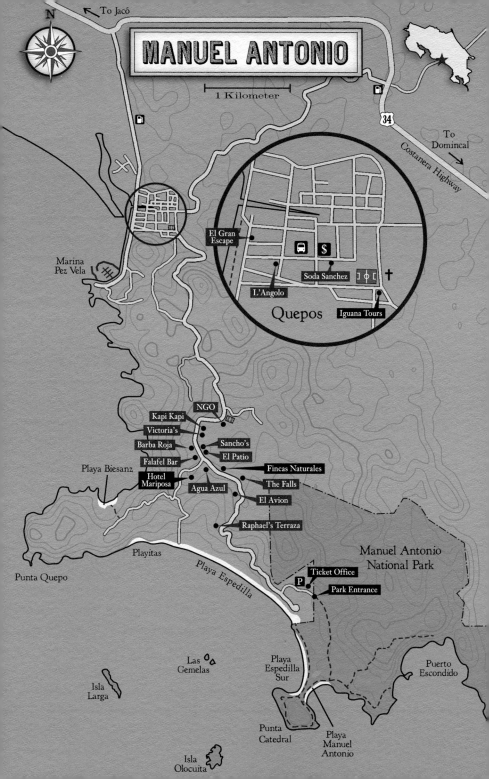

Getting to Manuel Antonio

Manuel Antonio is 132 km (82 miles) from San José (about a 2.5-hour drive) and 71 km (44 miles) from Jacó (about a 1-hour drive). Quepos, the small town located just outside Manuel Antonio, has an airport serviced by Sansa and Nature Air (p.18). Shuttle service is available from Interbus, Grayline and Easyride (p.20). Tracopa buses (2221-4214) run between San José and Quepos throughout the day; depart Calle 5, Ave 18/20 in San José (₡4,520, 3.5 hours).

Getting Around Manuel Antonio

The majority of Manuel Antonio's hotels and restaurants are spread out along the 7-km (4.3-mile) road between Quepos and the national park. Taxis (2777-3080, 2777-0425) and public buses are the best ways to get around. Taxis are easy to flag down on the main road, but many refuse to use meters and charge highly inflated prices. A taxi from Quepos to the national park should cost $9–10 (remember to agree to the price *before* you get in). A cheaper option is the public bus that runs along the road every 15–20 minutes (5:30am to 9:30pm, ₡285), making multiple stops along the way. Car rentals are available from Adobe (2777-4242), Alamo (2777-3344), Economy (2777-5260) and Hertz (2777-3365).

Manuel Antonio Hotels

Quepos has several good budget hotels, but most visitors prefer staying on the scenic hill between Quepos and the national park. The road that crosses the hill is full of hotels ranging from ultra-budget to ultra-luxury. For complete hotel information visit www.jameskaiser.com

Quepos

This bustling town (pop. 14,000) is located at the base of the hill that leads to Manuel Antonio National Park. Whereas the rest of Manuel Antonio caters primarily to tourists, Quepos is a Tico town full of banks, churches, fried chicken joints and shops selling *Ropa Americana* ("American Clothes"). There are also a handful of hotels and restaurants catering to tourists, and the new Pez Vela Marina is ground zero for local sportfishing.

The town itself is named for the Quepoa indigenous tribe, which lived in the area during the pre-Columbian era. The Quepoa fell victim to European diseases during the colonial era, and by the late 1800s their population had collapsed. The modern town of Quepos was built by United Fruit Company (p.152) in the 1930s after the company moved its banana operations from the Caribbean coast to the Pacific coast. Banana executives built houses in the hills above Quepos in an area known as the "American Zone." The company then cleared and drained a low lying mangrove swamp, laid out a street grid and built a barrier along the shore to keep the ocean at bay. Today the ocean barrier, which was once topped with train tracks, is topped by a paved road, and if you stand on it during high tide you can see that downtown Quepos is actually located *below* sea level. Following a banana blight in the 1940s, banana plants were replaced with African palms (p.356) to produce palm oil. Because palm oil is easily transported overland by truck, Quepos declined as a shipping port, and since the 1980s tourism has been the main economic driver of the town.

Playa Biesanz & Punta Quepo

About halfway between Quepos and Manuel Antonio National Park, a long, slender peninsula juts out into the cobalt sea. Known as Punta Quepo, it's home to some of the best views (and most expensive hotels) in the area. Several decades ago, Punta Quepo was home to a large farm and cattle ranch. At that time, much of the peninsula was completely devoid of trees. Today tourism, not farming, is the peninsula's main draw, and the fast-growing jungle has reclaimed much of its former territory.

Although most of the peninsula is private and off-limits, there is a beautiful public beach, Playa Biesanz, near the tip of Punta Quepo. This powdery white sand, which is nestled in a sheltered cove on the north side of the peninsula, is one of the best kept secrets in Manuel Antonio. While most tourists flock to Playa Espadilla or the beaches in Manuel Antonio National Park, quiet Playa Biesanz is a great place to escape the crowds. It's best visited at low tide, when the beach is bigger and sandier. There's even some decent snorkeling, but don't expect anything too spectacular.

To get to Playa Biesanz, follow the 2-km (1.2-mile) paved road that branches off the main road just past El Patio restaurant (look for signs pointing to Hotel Mariposa and Parador Resort). The entrance is located on the north side of the road, between Pacific Souss and Parador Resort. Antonio, an older local man, will direct you to a parking space and charge you $4 to guard your car. A 150-meter (500-foot) trail heads down to the beach from the road.

Playa Espadilla

Just north of Manuel Antonio National Park is Playa Espadilla, a gorgeous 2-km (1.2-mile) beach that, in terms of visitation, is far more popular than the national park. The reason: Access to the park is $10; access to Playa Espadilla is free. Not surprisingly, Playa Espadilla is most popular with backpackers and local Ticos. The busiest stretch of beach is located in front of a small plaza of shops and restaurants. The southern limit of Playa Espadilla is defined by a series of jagged rocks, which mark the boundary of Manuel Antonio National Park.

If you're looking to get away from the crowds, head north along Playa Espadilla and things will quickly start to mellow out. A five-minute stroll usually results in an uncrowded stretch of sand. At the far northern end of Playa Espadilla is La Playita, a small beach accessible only at low tide. La Playita is famous for two things: good surf and gay naked sunbathing, though both depend on local conditions.

The best way to get to Playa Espadilla is by bus or taxi. If you arrive by car, self-styled parking attendants will insist on watching your car for a fee. Feel free to bargain down the price *before* you park. Regardless, never leave anything valuable in your car, and never leave anything valuable unattended on the beach. Playa Espadilla is extremely safe, but petty theft is a problem. Towards the southern end of Playa Espadilla, plastic chairs with umbrellas are available for rent (price negotiable, but expect to pay around $8 per day). As you work on your tan, local vendors often stroll by selling beer and *agua de pipa* (coconut water) straight from the coconut.

If you're feeling hungry, there are a handful of restaurants set back from the beach that offer average food at above average prices. In my opinion, these places are best for a snack and a drink. If you're looking for good food at reasonable prices, take a taxi up the hill towards the better restaurants (p.378). Otherwise check out Marlin, which is one of the better restaurants near the beach.

Lying just offshore Playa Espadilla are a series of rocky islands that buffer big swells, making the beach more swimmable. The large island furthest to the north (right) is *Isla Larga* ("Long Island"). Many locals, however, simply refer to Isla Larga as *Isla Elephante* ("Elephant Island") because at low tide the southern tip of the island appears to stretch out like a long elephant trunk. Just south of Isla Larga/Elephante are two small rocky islands known as *Las Gemelas* ("The Twins"), and just south of Las Gemelas is large *Isla Olocuita*, which is home to nesting seabirds including frigates and brown boobies. "Olocuita" is supposedly an indigenous word that means "guano," and indigenous groups supposedly harvested the guano there and used as a skin cream.

Even further south of Isla Olocuita (not visible from Playa Espadilla), is *Isla Mogote*. This island, which lies near the mouth of the Naranjo River, was supposedly home to an indigenous shaman, and a cave on the island was used to perform ceremonies to ensure abundant fishing.

Manuel Antonio National Park

Manuel Antonio is one of Costa Rica's most popular national parks, and there's a good reason for that. The combination of spectacular beaches, calm turquoise water, lush rainforest and abundant wildlife is truly world-class. This was one of the original beach destinations that made Costa Rica famous, and as you lie on the powdery white sand watching monkeys swing through the trees you'll understand why. For many, this is the definition of tropical paradise. Perhaps most astounding, all this pristine natural beauty is incredibly accessible—the best beaches are just a 25-minute stroll from the park entrance.

At 1,983 hectares (7.7 square miles), Manuel Antonio is one of the smallest national parks in Costa Rica, but it shelters an impressive range of biodiversity. The park is home to over 100 mammal species, including three of the four monkey species found in Costa Rica, and over 180 bird species, including the fiery-billed aracari and mangrove hummingbird. The park also protects rare primary rainforest, which can be explored on a series of well-maintained hiking trails.

If there's a downside to Manuel Antonio, it's the mid-morning crowds. But arrive first thing in the morning or after lunch, and you'll probably wonder what all the fuss is about. In order to reduce crowding, a daily limit of 600 people has been established by the park, so during peak season (Christmas, Easter), you'll want to arrive as early as possible. The park is open 7am–4pm. Closed Mondays.

The main park entrance is set back about a block from the southern end of Playa Espadilla. It's best to take a taxi or the bus to the park entrance, but parking ($4–6) is available at the traffic circle at the end of the road or near the park entrance. (Note: If you drive, when you arrive at Playa Espadilla expect to be hassled by men wearing official-looking shirts informing you that there's no parking near the park entrance. Ignore these hustlers, who have no affiliation with the park, and continue driving towards the park entrance to see for yourself.)

Tickets to enter the park are sold from the Coopealianza building. After purchasing your tickets, prepare to be swarmed by guides offering their services. Should you hire a guide? If you're just interested in seeing monkeys, you can easily do that on your own. White-faced monkeys are very common, and it's usually easy to spot squirrel monkeys and howler monkeys, too. (Just look for the people looking at the monkeys.) If you're fascinated by wildlife and interested in harder to spot animals—sloths, birds, snakes, insects—an eagle-eyed guide is worth it. Good guides carry powerful spotting scopes and know amazing facts about the park's wildlife. The going rate for 2–3 hours is about $25 per person, though groups can often negotiate a lower rate. Before hiring a guide, make sure they have an official ICT card, or, better yet, book a guide ahead of time through your hotel. (Hotels often have relationships with the better guides.)

Also, if you're going to spend the day at Manuel Antonio, consider bringing a picnic lunch. But do not leave your food unattended; the monkeys will steal it.

After entering the park, follow the wide path 2.2 km (1.4 miles) to Playa Manuel Antonio, the loveliest beach in the park. This gentle crescent of sand wraps 400 meters (1,312 feet) around a calm bay surrounded by lush vegetation. A series of offshore rocks shelters the beach from powerful waves, making this a great place for swimming and snorkeling. If Playa Manuel Antonio is too crowded, cross the narrow strip of jungle to Playa Espadilla Sur, another beautiful beach that's almost always less crowded.

Lying at the southwest tip of Playa Manuel Antonio and Playa Espadilla Sur is *Punta Catedral* ("Cathedral Point"). This large rocky outcrop protects both beaches from powerful waves and, in fact, is the reason the beaches exist at all. As offshore waves wrap around Punta Catedral, they sweep sediments in from both sides. Long ago Punta Catedral was an offshore island, but over time the accumulated sediments formed the narrow spit of land that now connects it to the mainland. The scientific term for this type of formation is "tombolo."

A beautiful 1.4-km (0.8-mile) hiking trail wraps around Punta Catedral, passing impressive trees and offering dramatic views of the rocky islands offshore. These islands, which provide shelter for nesting seabirds, are also part of the national park, which includes 55,000 (212 square miles) of marine habitat. Just before reaching Playa Manuel Antonio, the trail passes *La Trampa* ("The Trap"), a circular stone trap, visible at low tide, once used by indigenous people to catch sea turtles. The entire trail takes about 45 minutes round-trip.

If you're up for even more hiking, you can check out the two trails that head east of Playa Manuel Antonio. There's the 1.6-km (1-mile) trail that heads *Playa Puerto Escondido* ("Hidden Port Beach"), a remote beach that's best visited at low tide, and the 1.3-km (0.8-mile) trail that heads to a *Mirador* ("Lookout") with elevated views of Puerto Escondido. Neither trail is a park highlight, but they're both good for wildlife watching and exercise.

When you decide to exit the park, follow the trail along Playa Espadilla Sur north to the park exit. There's an estuary near the exit, which can be shallow or deep depending on the tides. If the water is too deep for your comfort level, a boatman can take you across for about $1.

Today Manuel Antonio is one of Costa Rica's most beloved national parks, but its beautiful beaches nearly ended up in private hands. Although all beaches in Costa Rica are legally considered public property, Manuel Antonio was transferred to the United Fruit Company in 1939 as part of a government orchestrated land swap. In the early 1970s, after the land had been sold to private investors, plans were drawn up to build a large marina/resort. A gate was built to keep out the locals, who responded by destroying the gate. Locals pleaded with the government to turn the beaches into a protected area, and in 1972 Manuel Antonio National Park was established. Its former owner was paid $700,000 in compensation.

Squirrel Monkey

Manuel Antonio National Park

★Sailing Tours

Manuel Antonio boasts one of the most beautiful coastlines in Costa Rica, and one of the best ways to experience it is from the water. There are two companies that offer morning and sunset boat tours, both of which feature snorkeling and wildlife watching. Keep in mind, however, that the snorkeling is just OK due to poor visibility, and animals like dolphins are only occasionally spotted. The real highlight is the scenery. **Sunset Sails** (2777-1304, www.sunsetsailstours.com) offers tours on a 54-foot sailboat that accommodates up to 25 people. Cost: $75 adults, $40 kids. **Planet Dolphin** (2777-1647, www.planetdolphin.com) operates three catamarans ranging in size from 37 to 70 feet. The largest, the *Tom Cat II*, accommodates up to 110 people and has a waterslide. Due to the ample space and steady sailing of a catamaran, this is my top choice for families with young kids. Cost: $80 per person, kids under 6 free.

★Isla Damas Mangrove Tour

This mangrove tour is one of my favorite eco-experiences in Manuel Antonio. Mangroves (p.97) are one of Costa Rica's most fascinating ecosystems, and Iguana Tours offers terrific boat tours and kayak tours of the beautiful mangrove estuary lying just north of Quepos. Tours are available only during high tide, so times change daily and are offered during the day and at night. My favorite is definitely the night boat tour, when animals rarely spotted during the day become active and bioluminescent algae glows in the water. Cost: $65 per person. (2777-2052, www.iguanatours.com)

★Villa Vanilla Spice Tour

This two-hour tour of an organic spice farm is great for foodies or anyone curious about where tropical spices come from. After learning about spices such as vanilla, cocoa, cinnamon and pepper, you'll walk through the farm and taste the finished product at a beautiful viewpoint. A wide range of homegrown spices are also available for purchase. Tours are offered at 9am and 1pm daily. Cost: $35 per person. (2779-1155, www.rainforestspices.com)

Canopy Tours

The lush rainforest and rugged topography near Manuel Antonio are great for canopy tours. There are several local operators, but I like MidWorld the best. Their multi-activity adventure park offers canopy tours, high ropes course, and—their claim to fame—the longest "Superman" line in Costa Rica. Imagine the team challenges on *Survivor* and you've got a pretty good idea of what MidWorld is all about. Individual tours are $75 per person. The Super Combo Tour (canopy tour, Superman line) is $129 per person. (2777-7181, www.midworldcostarica.com)

Canyoning

Quepo Canyoning offers a combo adventure tour that combines tree climbing, three canopy cables, a "monkey drop" and a rappel down a 90-foot waterfall. Cost: $85 per person. (2779-1127, www.quepocanyoning.net)

White Water Rafting

A handful of fun rivers are located within driving distance of Manuel Antonio. During the rainy season (May–November), the Rio Naranjo and Rio Savegre offer class III/IV rapids. During the dry season (November–April), the heart-pumping Rio Chorro offers class IV/V rapids. Quepoa Expeditions is my favorite outfitter in town. Cost: $65–90 per person. (2777-0058, www.quepoaexpeditions.com)

Sportfishing

Quepos is one of Costa Rica's top sportfishing towns, and there's no shortage of boats that can take you offshore. If you want to go 20-35 miles offshore in search of big sailfish and marlin, expect to pay $950–1,800. Half-day inshore trips in search of roosterfish and snapper are $600–750. For a full list of Quepos charters, contact Marina Pez Vela (2774-9000, www.marinapezvela.com).

Fincas Naturales Wildlife Refuge

This private, 25-acre wildlife refuge has over 1.3 km (0.8 miles) of hiking trails that pass through butterfly gardens, crocodile ponds and dense jungle. Guided tours are available, including a two-hour night hike that focuses on frogs. Cost: $20   39 per person. (2777-0850, www.wildliferefugecr.com)

Kids Saving the Rainforest

Since 1999 this nonprofit, which was started by local children, has been working to save the endangered titi monkey and other rainforest animals. They run a wildlife rescue center for injured animals, and to date they've installed over 130 rope "monkey bridges" to help monkeys safely cross the busy road between Quepos and Manuel Antonio. Tours of their Wildlife Sanctuary, which is home to over two dozen monkeys, are offered at 9am Mon, Weds, Fri, Sun. $40 adults, $25 kids. (2777-2592, www.kidssavingtherainforest.org)

Surfing

Although advanced surfers will be much happier at Playa Hermosa or Dominical, there are some fun waves in Manuel Antonio. The most consistent break is La Playita on the north end of Playa Espadilla. For surf lessons check out Manuel Antonio Surf School (2777-4842, www.manuelantoniosurfschool.com).

Manuel Antonio Restaurants

★EL PATIO DE CAFÉ MILAGRO (Brk: $8–12; Lnch: $8–13; Din: $15–23)
This charming bistro/cafe offers a sophisticated menu filled with Latin-inspired dishes and traditional Costa Rican ingredients. They also roast their own local coffee, making this one of the best breakfast spots in Manuel Antonio. (2777-4982, www.elpatiobistrolatino.com)

★KAPI KAPI (Din: $21–30)
One of the most elegantly hip restaurants in Manuel Antonio, Kapi Kapi combines Asian flavors with Costa Rican ingredients. Both the food and the ambiance are sophisticated. Great cocktails. (2777-5049, www.restaurantekapikapi.com)

★AGUA AZUL (Lnch: $11–15; Din: $18–22)
This open-air restaurant is my favorite lunch spot in Manuel Antonio. The ocean views are terrific and the menu is full of tasty comfort food, including Mexican favorites and outrageously large burgers. Dinner offers sophisticated options with Asian and tropical flavors. Closed Weds. (2777-5280, www.cafeaguaazul.com)

★FALLS GARDEN CAFE (Brk: $8–10; Lnch: $7–11; Din: $12–21)
Located in the Falls Hotel, this upscale restaurant fuses European and Latin cuisine with a tropical flair. The menu is creative, the food is delicious and the prices are very reasonable for Manuel Antonio. Be sure to indulge in the great cocktails. (2777-1332, www.fallsgardencafe.com)

RAPHAEL'S TERRAZA (Lnch: $11–13; Din: $13–26)
Seafood (tuna, mahi mahi, shrimp, lobster) is the specialty at this open-air restaurant with nice ocean views. The menu also includes grilled meats, pasta and hamburgers. Great cocktails. 2 x 1 happy hour 4pm–6pm. (2777-6310)

VICTORIA'S ITALIAN (Din: $16–24)
This popular Italian restaurant serves up tasty pasta and seafood, plus thin crust pizzas featuring upscale ingredients (pesto, caramelized onions, Gorgonzola) in a charming setting. (2777-5143, www.victoriasgourmet.com)

EL AVION (Lnch, Din: $11–18)
Fashioned out of the actual Fairchild C-123 cargo plane that was used to smuggle supplies to Nicaraguan Contras in the 1980s, this open-air restaurant offers the most unique dining experience in Manuel Antonio. The menu ranges from burgers to seafood to Tex-Mex, and some tables have nice ocean views. Even if you're not hungry, be sure to grab a drink at the Contra Bar, located *inside* the plane's cargo hold. A great choice if you're traveling with kids. (2777-3378)

FALAFEL BAR (Lnch: $6–8)
Healthy, reasonably-priced Mediterranean and Israeli dishes. The service is quick
and friendly and the charming open-air patio is adorned with comfy bean-bag
chairs. No credit cards. (2777-4135)

BARBA ROJA (Din: $12–20)
Perched on a hill overlooking the Pacific, this open-air bar/restaurant has one
of the best sunset views in Manuel Antonio. The menu ranges from seafood and
sushi to Mexican and BBQ. (2777-0331, www.barbarojarestaurant.com)

NGO (Lnch, Din: $5–7)
This simple Asian restaurant is great if you're looking for a reasonably priced meal.
Vietnamese sandwiches, Singapore noodles, seared dumplings, delicious smooth-
ies. Great for take-out. (2777-6821)

SANCHO'S MEXICAN (Lnch, Din: $7–10)
Tasty and reasonably priced, this simple Mexican burrito and taco joint is great
for a quick meal or take-out. Delivery available. (2777-0340)

Quepos Restaurants

★**EL GRAN ESCAPE** (Lnch, Din: $13–24)
If you're a sportfishermen, you'll definitely end up at El Gran Escape at some
point during your trip. The menu is full of fresh, delicious seafood, and the bar is
perfect for swapping fish tales. Closed Tues. (2777-0395, www.elgranescape.com)

L'ANGOLO (Lnch, Din: $7–14)
This tasty Italian deli, located near the bus station in Quepos, makes the best
sandwiches in town, plus good pasta dishes. One of the best values in Quepos.
Great for take-out. Closed Sunday. (2777-4129)

SODA SANCHEZ (Brk: $5–6, Lnch, Din: $6–12)
This small soda offers the best budget food in Quepos. The standard menu (gallo
pinto, casados) also includes some Mexican favorites. (2777-7273)

Best Sunset Cocktails

Hotel Mariposa (The best view in Manuel Antonio)

Barba Roja (Great views & great cocktails)

Playa Matapalo

Looking for a big, beautiful beach with a handful of small seaside hotels scattered along a bumpy dirt road? Playa Matapalo won't let you down. A 20-minute drive south of Manuel Antonio and a 10-minute drive north of Dominical, Playa Matapalo lies within striking distance of some of the most popular destinations in the Central Pacific—yet it's barely developed and devoid of crowds. You can even stay at a reasonably priced hotel right on the beach and listen to the waves crash at night. (Visit www.jameskaiser.com for complete hotel info.) For a tasty meal, check out the basic, beachfront El Coquito ($10–15).

DOMINICAL

THIS RUSTIC SURF town is famous for great waves, beautiful waterfalls and a funky, party-friendly vibe. But despite its popularity, Dominical has managed to preserve its small town charm. The roads are unpaved, businesses are small mom and pop affairs, and there are still plenty of budget hotels just a short walk from the beach. If you're a surfer in search of a genuine surf town that offers more than just waves, Dominical is a great choice. And if you're a backpacker in search of a laid-back beach town that isn't too touristy (yet still offers yoga and vegan food), Dominical is also a great choice.

For surfers, Dominical's consistent waves are the town's main draw. Even when the rest of the Pacific is small, there's usually good surf here. On big days the powerful waves are best left to advanced surfers, but beginners can take advantage of several good surf schools, which head to less threatening breaks on big days. And if you're looking for surfer-oriented nightlife, Dominical is one of the Central Pacific's top destinations.

If there's one drawback to Dominical, it's the dark, pebble-strewn beach, which is hardly among the loveliest in Costa Rica. You should also be aware that Dominical's powerful waves bring powerful riptides that can make swimming here dangerous. There have been several drownings over the years (see Swimming and Rip Currents, p.25), leading locals to start a private lifeguard program. That said, it's easy enough to head 4 km (2.5 miles) south to Dominicalito, which is home to a lovely, sheltered beach, or Uvita just 19 kms (12 miles) south of Dominical. The mountains above town are also blessed with several terrific waterfalls, offering plenty of freshwater action.

Dominical is also a good jumping off point for some terrific nearby eco-adventures, including Hacienda Barú, a private nature preserve that offers great adventure tours and wildlife watching, and the Nauyaca Waterfall, the most dramatic waterfall in the Central Pacific.

If you're driving to Dominical, the turnoff to the beach is easy to miss. Heading south along the Costanera Sur highway, you'll pass a T-intersection with the Interamericana (which heads to San Isidro de General and San José), then cross a bridge that spans the Baru River. Just past the bridge the turnoff to Dominical is marked by a blue sign that says "Playa Dominical Bienvenidos." The layout of the town essentially consists of two dirt roads. One is set about a block back from the beach that's home to the majority of the shops and restaurants. The second is a long dirt road that parallels the beach.

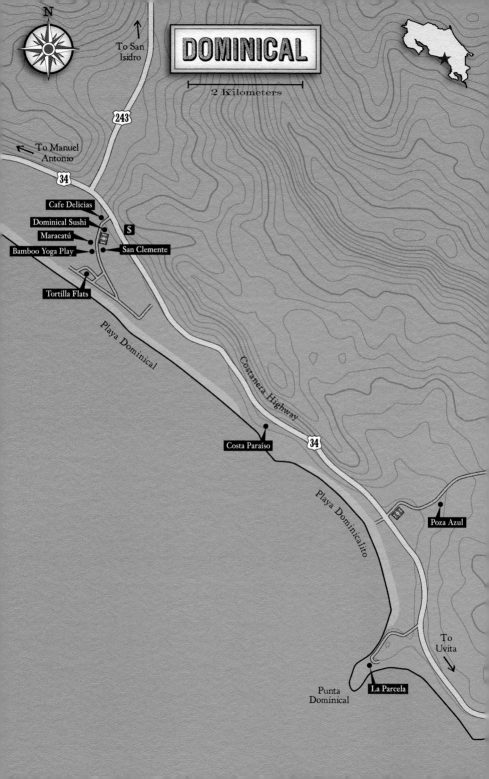

Getting To Dominical

Dominical is 158 km (98 miles) from San José (3-hour drive), 31 km (19 miles) from San Isidro de El General (30-minute drive) and 44 km (27 miles) from Quepos/Manuel Antonio (30-minute drive). The closest airport is in Quepos/Manuel Antonio, which is serviced by Sansa and Nature Air (p.18). Private shuttles to Dominical are available from Grayline, Easyride and Monkey Ride (p.20). Tracopa buses (2221-4214) to Dominical depart San José from Calle 5, Ave 18/20 at 6am and 3pm (₡4,000, 7 hours). Buses to San José depart Dominical at 5:30am and 1pm. Buses from Quepos/Manuel Antonio to Dominical depart 5:30am, 6:30am, 9:30am, 11:30am, 3:30pm, 5:30pm (₡2,000, 1.5 hours).

Getting Around Dominical

If you're just planning on surfing and hanging out in the village of Dominical, there's no need for a car. If you're planning on making Dominical a base for exploring the rest of the coast, however, a rental car will definitely come in handy, though taxis (8317-4089) can usually be found near the soccer field.

Hotels

Due to the large numbers of surfers and backpackers, Dominical has plenty of budget/mid-range hotels in the village, including some right on the beach. In recent years a handful of high-end hotels have popped up in the hills above town, and there are several nice hotels just south of town along the coast. For complete hotel info visit www.jameskaiser.com

★Surfing

Dominical's consistent, powerful waves deliver good rides even when much of the Central Pacific coast is flat. When the swell picks up and the tide is rising, advanced surfers enjoy big, heavy, hollow tubes. The biggest waves are found towards the northern end of the beach; the southern end is better for intermediates. When the swell *really* picks up, Dominical is quick to close out, at which point many surfers decamp to Dominicalito, just south of Dominical.

Note: Even on average days here the waves are heavy and the currents are strong. This is not a good place to learn to surf on your own. That said, there are several good surf schools that can teach you the basics during smaller swells or take you to some mellow beginner breaks.

Costa Rica Surf Camp (8812-3625, www.crsurfschool.com)
Dominical Surf Adventures (2787-0431, www.dominicalsurfadventures.com)
Dominical Waverider Surf Camp (8311-8950, www.dominicalwaverider.com)
Sunset Surf Dominical (8917-3143, www.sunsetsurfdominical.com)

★Poza Azul Waterfall

This beautiful jungle waterfall is a great (and free) place to swim and splash in freshwater. The turnoff to the waterfall is directly across from the turnoff to Playa Dominicalito (look for the sign to Escuela Dominicalito). After crossing a small creek, head up a steep hill roughly 250 meters (800 feet). A short trail heads to the waterfall on the right. Note: Do not leave valuables in your car, theft is common.

★Hacienda Barú

This 345-hectare (853-acre) wildlife refuge, located just north of Dominical, is a former cattle ranch that has been allowed to revert back to its natural state. Over 60 mammal species, 70 reptile species and 300 bird species have been identified here. There are birdwatching tours and nature hikes ($25–35), a 15-platform canopy tour ($40) and a tree climbing tour ($40). Self-guided hiking tours are also available ($7). (2787-0003, www.haciendabaru.com)

Parque Reptilandia

Located 7 km (4.3 miles) northeast of Dominical on highway 243, this impressive reptile park is home to 71 reptile species and 4 amphibian species, including poison dart frogs and deadly venomous snakes. Friday is feeding day. Open 9am–4:30pm. Cost: $12 adults, $6 kids. (2787-0343, www.crreptiles.com)

Yoga

Bamboo Yoga Play is the town's top yoga studio, offering "A Creative Vinyasa flow fusion inspired by Anusara, Hatha and Tantra Yoga." They also offer massage and artful warrior coaching. (2787-0229, www.danyasa.com)

Dominical Restaurants

★ **¿POR QUE NO?** (Brk: $6–8; Lnch: $10–12; Din: $14–25)
Located at the seaside Costa Paraíso Hotel (five-minute drive south of Dominical) this charming restaurant offers great views, terrific wood-fired pizza, delicious *bocas* (appetizers) and decadent deserts. Reservations recommended. (2787-0025, www.cpporqueno.com)

★ **LA PARCELA** (Brk: $13; Lnch, Din: $12–20)
Perched on the lush peninsula just south of Dominicalito, this open-air restaurant serves Costa Rican food from a stunning location. Come for lunch or sunset, when you can enjoy the gorgeous ocean views. (2787-0016, www.laparcelacr.com)

DOMINICAL SUSHI (Lnch, Din: $9–13)
This popular sushi restaurant serves all the classics (miso, tuna rolls, salmon rolls) plus a good selection of creative specialty rolls (8826-7946)

TORTILLA FLATS (Brk: $6; Lnch, Din: $7–14)
This beachside bar/restaurant is a surfer's delight, offering reasonably priced sandwiches, burgers and Tex-Mex. Even if you're not hungry, this is a great place for drinks after a long day at the beach. (2787-0033)

MARACATÚ (Lnch, Din: $10–14)
This funky hippie lounge offers tasty vegetarian/pescatarian food with focus on local, sustainable ingredients. The large menu covers a wide range of ethnic flavors, from Mexican to Middle Eastern. (2787-0091, www.maracatucostarica.com)

CAFE DELICIAS (Brk: $7; Lnch: $8–10)
This charming cafe offers Dominical's best coffee, espresso drinks, smoothies, sandwiches, delicious baked goods and desserts. (2787-0097)

SAN CLEMENTE BAR & GRILL (Lnch, Din: $7–9)
Surfers flock to this laid-back bar/restaurant for its cheap, tasty, filling food and its party friendly vibe. Tex-Mex, burgers, and sandwiches dominate the menu. Daily specials are offered for those on a budget. (2787-0055)

Best Sunset Cocktails

Por Que No? (Beer, wine, crashing waves)

La Parcela (Charming sunset deck above the waves)

Nauyaca Waterfall

This spectacular waterfall is nestled in a lush valley 6 km (3.7 miles) northeast of Dominical. Two-tiered Nauyaca tumbles down 65 meters (215 feet) into a large pool that's perfect for swimming, and guided tours of the waterfall are offered by Don Lulo's, a local family that owns the surrounding property. The tour, which involves a 20-minute horseback ride, starts at 8am, finishes around 1pm, and includes both breakfast and lunch. Cost: $60 per person. Round-trip transportation is available from Dominical, Uvita or Manuel Antonio for a fee. Reservations necessary, no tours Sunday. (2787-0541, www.cataratasnauyaca.com)

Uvita's Whale Tail

UVITA

AT FIRST GLANCE Uvita doesn't seem very inviting. The center of town consists of a series of strip malls along the main highway, and the bumpy dirt roads veering off the highway seem destined for little more. But venture off the asphalt and you'll discover some of the Central Pacific's best kept secrets. Uvita's beaches are beautiful, the lush hills above town are home to some elegant boutique hotels, and there are some terrific outdoor adventures. Add in a handful of great restaurants and there's really just one thing missing from Uvita: crowds. If you're looking for a beautiful beach destination that's far less developed than Manuel Antonio, Uvita is a terrific alternative.

The highlight of Uvita is Marino Ballena National Park, which protects a series of beautiful beaches along the coast. The name *Marino Ballena* ("Marine Whale") refers to two things: the famous sandy "Whale Tail" that stretches out from the shore at low tide and the migrating humpback whales found offshore for much of the year. Boat tours set out in search of humpbacks during whale season, and even in the off-season there's good dolphin watching and fun snorkeling among the park's rocky offshore islands.

Set back from Uvita's beautiful coastline are a series of dramatic, lush hills that shelter pristine rainforest and beautiful waterfalls. The area's natural beauty has long attracted hippies and counterculturalists, but for years Uvita was largely overlooked by mainstream travelers due to the bumpy dirt road between Manuel Antonio and Dominical that prevented easy access. These days the road is paved, and families and couples are showing up in increasing numbers. That said, the town's countercultural vibe is still going strong. Each February Uvita hosts Envision, a "Costa Rican Burning Man" that attracts thousands of psychedelic revelers (www.envisionfestival.com).

Uvita also makes a great base for exploring Dominical, just 20 km (12 miles) north, or the tiny town of Ojochal, just 15 kms (9 miles) south. Home to a funky colony of French-Canadian expats, tiny Ojochal is home to some of the best restaurants in the Central Pacific. Ojochal also provides easy access to Playa Ventanas, a small beach famous for its sea caves.

In short, if you've got a rental car and a willingness to explore, the area around Uvita has plenty to offer. There are beautiful beaches, great outdoor adventures, amazing wildlife, delicious restaurants—and limited crowds. What's not to like?

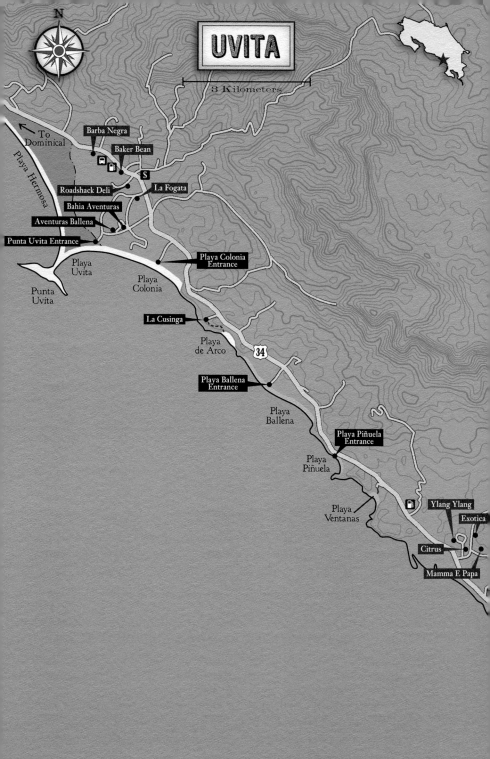

Getting to Uvita

Uvita is 165 kms (103 miles) from San José (3.5-hour drive), 65 kms (40 miles) south of Quepos/Manuel Antonio (50-minute drive) and 20 km (12 miles) south of Dominical (20-minute drive). The closest airports are in Quepos/Manuel Antonio and Palmar Sur, both of which are serviced by Sansa and Nature Air (p.18). Private shuttles to Uvita are available through Grayline, Easyride and Monkey Ride (p.20). Tracopa buses (2221-4214) to Dominical depart San José from Calle 5, Ave 18/20 at 6am and 3pm (₡5,340, 7 hours). Return buses to San José depart Uvita at 5:30am and 1pm.

Getting Around Uvita

Uvita's top attractions are relatively spread out. If you want to take advantage of the best that Uvita has to offer, it's good to have a car. If you're planning on staying in Ojochal, 15 kms (9 miles) south of Uvita (about a 15-minute drive), a car is even more important. That said, Uvita has a dependable taxi service (8791-5680, 8855-3830). Car rentals are available from National (2743-8528) and Alamo (2743-8072).

Uvita Hotels

When it comes to hotels, Uvita has a split personality. The lush hills above town are home to a handful of terrific (and expensive) boutique hotels, while the town itself has mostly budget options. The small village of Ojochal, just south of Uvita, is also home to several good mid-range hotels and a few upscale options. Visit www.jameskaiser.com for complete hotel info.

Marino Ballena National Park

Marino Ballena ("Marine Whale") National Park is famous for its beautiful beaches, its giant sandy Whale Tail and its warm offshore waters that attract migrating humpback whales. Given all the humpback imagery splashed around town, you'd be forgiven for thinking that Uvita is the whale capital of Costa Rica. In fact, humpbacks are most abundant around the Osa Peninsula, about 60 km (37 miles) south of Uvita. Regardless, this entire stretch of coastline is the only known place in the world that draws humpback whales from both the southern and northern hemispheres. Southern humpbacks, which come from as far away as Antarctica, visit from August to October, while northern humpbacks, which come from as far away as California, visit from January to March. During these months whale watching tours are available (p.396).

Created in 1989, Marino Ballena National Park was Costa Rica's first national marine park. Today it protects 5,375 hectares (13,280 acres) of land and 171 hectares (423 acres) of marine habitat. Its beaches are used by nesting olive ridley and hawksbill sea turtles, which visit from July to December. The park also includes several offshore islands, including *Piedra Ballena* ("Whale Rock") and the three rocky islands known as the *Las Tres Hermanas* ("The Three Sisters"). These islands are important nesting sites for seabirds such as frigates and brown boobies, and the surrounding waters are home to coral reefs. Pacific spotted dolphins and bottlenose dolphins are also found in the waters offshore.

To visit the park's beaches you'll need to purchase an entrance pass ($6 per person, per day) from one of the park's four entrance stations: Punta Uvita, Playa Colonia, Playa Ballena and Playa Piñuela, which are open from 7am to 4pm. The entrance pass grants you access to any of the park's beaches for one day. Regardless of where you enter, it's best to visit at low tide when the beaches are big and beautiful. At high tide some beaches are virtually nonexistent. Also be aware that petty theft is rampant. Never leave your items unattended, even for a few minutes.

The park's top beaches are Playa Uvita and Playa Hermosa, which lie on opposite sides of Uvita's famous Whale Tail. This iconic landmark, a naturally occurring combination of sand and rocks that stretches out from Uvita's coast, is visible only at low tide. At high tide the Whale Tail (officially called Punta Uvita) is almost fully submerged and only the rocks that form the tip of the tail are visible above the water. The scientific term for this type of formation is *tombolo*, an Italian word derived from the Latin *tumulus* ("mound"). Tombolos form when waves wrap around a small offshore island—in this case the rocks that make up the tip of the tail—and sweep sediments in from both sides. Over time the sediments accumulate to form a narrow spit that connects to the mainland.

Playa Uvita, Playa Hermosa and the Whale Tail are accessible via the Punta Uvita entrance station. If you only have time to visit one part of the park, this is the place to visit. At low tide you can walk to the tip of the Whale Tail, which provides stunning views of Uvita's dramatic, mountainous coastline. Because the rocky tail provides shelter from offshore waves, the inside of the tail is also a great place to swim and a good place to snorkel.

Just south of Playa Uvita is Playa Colonial, a big sandy beach that stretches 2.5 km (1.6 miles) south to the jungly bluffs of Punta Quebrada Grande. Playa Colonial is accessed via the Playa Colonial Entrance Station, and you can park your car under the palm trees next to the beach. Playa Colonial is especially popular with vacationing Ticos, who bring cars stuffed with picnic supplies.

The two major beaches south of Playa Colonial are Playa Ballena and Playa Piñuela, which are a mix of brown sand and cobblestones, but neither compares with the beauty of the park's northern beaches. Their main attraction is that they're usually deserted. Interestingly, each year between January and February the indigenous Boruca tribe visits Playa Piñuela during the waning moon to extract a blue dye from marine snails found among the rocks.

But wait, there's more! Marina Ballena National Park is also home to a hidden, secret beach: Playa de Arco, a stunner that's sandwiched between the southern headlands of Playa Colonial and the northern headlands of Playa Ballena. Playa de Arco is only accessible at low tide, and there are only two ways to get there. If you're staying at La Cusinga ecolodge, a short trail heads directly from the hotel to the beach. Otherwise you can access Playa de Arco via the northern end of Playa Ballena, where a short, steep trail heads up and over the forested hill to Playa de Arco.

★Whale Watching Tours

Migrating humpback whales visit the waters offshore Uvita from Dec-March and Aug-Oct, and during these months whale watching tours are offered. The best month to see whales is September, but even in off-months the tours, which include snorkeling and dolphin watching, are a terrific way to soak in Uvita's spectacular coastline. Two respected boat tour companies are Ballena Aventura ($70 per person, 2743-8473, www.ballenaaventuracostarica.com) and Bahia Aventuras ($85 per person, 2743-8362, www.bahiaaventuras.com).

If you happen to visit Uvita in September, be sure to check out the annual Whale and Dolphin Festival (www.festivaldeballenasydelfines.com), which features whale and dolphin tours, music, food and much more.

★Canyoning/Waterfall Rappelling

If you're looking for adrenaline-soaked outdoor adventure, contact the folks at Costa Canyoning. Their action-packed tour descends a gorgeous, waterfall-filled canyon using a combination of scrambling and rappelling. The highlight: Rappelling down a series of six waterfalls that range in height from 5 to 25 meters (15 to 75 feet). Snacks and photos are provided. Tours run daily at 9am. Cost: $100 per person, no credit cards. (8309-3747, www.costacanyoning.com)

★Playa Ventanas

This "hidden" beach is famous for twin caves on the northern end of the beach, which are best explored at low tide. The turnoff to Playa Ventanas is 12 km (7.5 miles) south of Uvita, 3 km (1.9 miles) north of Ojochal. Parking is available on private property ($2/car, $1/person) and a short trail heads to the beach.

Snorkeling

At low tide the southern inside half of Uvita's Whale Tail offers some fun snorkeling. Although promoted as "coral reef," it's best to lower your expectations—the vast majority of the scenery is algae-covered rocks. That said, there are some fun tropical fish, so underwater enthusiasts won't be let down. You can rent snorkel equipment from local shops just outside the Playa Uvita park entrance. A even better option is the whale/dolphin tour (above).

Surfing

While advanced surfers flock to the powerful waves at Dominical, beginners will find more to love about the smaller waves along Uvita's coast. For surf lessons check out Uvita 360 (8586-8745, www.uvitasurfcamp.com) or Bodhi Surf School (2743-8453, www.bodhisurfschool.com).

Uvita Restaurants

★EL GECKO (Lnch: $20 Din: $25)
Located at La Cusinga Ecolodge, which has an incredible view of Uvita, El Gecko specializes in upscale meals prepared with local, organic ingredients. Reservations are required for non-guests. Arrive before 5pm to enjoy the sunset. (2770-2549)

★BARBA NEGRA (Lnch, Din: $10-17)
A great place for Mediterranean-Italian fusion food. Seafood, meat, pasta, pizza and more. Closed Saturdays. (2743-8468)

ROADSHACK DELI (Lnch: $9-10)
Classic sandwiches with a gourmet twist. Made with healthy, local ingredients. Salads and smoothies are also available. (8629-8663)

BAKER BEAN (Brk: $5; Lnch, Din: $5-15)
This small bakery/cafe serves bagels and breakfast sandwiches in the morning, pizza and empanadas later on. (2743-8990)

LA FOGATA (Lnch, Din: $9-16)
Thin crust pizza and fresh roasted chicken are the specialties at this local favorite. Closed Tues. (2743-8224)

Ojochal Restaurants

★EXOTICA (Din: $24-28)
One of the top restaurants in the Central Pacific, Exotica offers a mouth-watering melange of French, Asian and Costa Rican flavors. Extensive drink menu. Decadent desserts. Closed Sunday. Reservations recommended. (2786-5050)

★CITRUS (Lnch, Din: $15-27)
If it wasn't for Exotica, Citrus would offer the best food for miles. The menu at this hip creekside restaurant features a wide range of French/Latin fusion cuisine, plus great cocktails. Closed Sunday. (2786-5175)

★YLANG YLANG (Din: $25)
This open-air Indonesian restaurant offers a changing menu, but expect delicious chicken and beef dishes artfully prepared with ingredients such as galangal, lemon grass, coconut milk and chilies. Open Weds–Sat. (2786-5054)

★MAMMA E PAPA (Lnch, Din: $13-17)
This authentic Italian restaurant features homemade pizza and pasta, plus delicious steak and seafood dishes influenced by the flavors of Naples and Puglia. The atmosphere is charming, and the open-air dining room has nice rainforest views. Closed Monday. (2786-5336, www.mammaepapa.com)

Corcovado National Park

SOUTH PACIFIC

COSTA RICA'S SOUTH PACIFIC is a wild paradise home to some of the top eco-adventures in the country. Unlike the Central Pacific and the Nicoya Peninsula, where some beaches are filled with condos and mega resorts, the South Pacific remains rugged and undeveloped. This is partly due to isolation—it's one of the most remote parts of the country—and partly due to the weather—the region is drenched with up to six meters (20 feet) of rain each year, *four times* more than Costa Rica's north Pacific coast. But all that rain has an upside: lush, natural scenery. If you're looking for pristine rainforests filled with wildlife, it doesn't get any better than Costa Rica's South Pacific.

The undisputed highlight of the region is the Osa Peninsula, 40% of which is protected as Corcovado National Park. Considered the crown jewel of Costa Rica's National Park system, Corcovado boasts the most extensive Pacific Coast rainforest in Central America. This world-class park shelters thousands of species, including healthy populations of rare animals such as tapirs, peccaries and scarlet macaws. Corcovado's stunning biodiversity makes it one of the top wildlife watching destinations in the Western Hemisphere.

Corcovado is accessible from two major destinations: Drake Bay, located near the northern tip of the Osa Peninsula, and Puerto Jiménez, located near the peninsula's southern tip. Drake Bay is a remote seaside village accessible by boat or by plane. Puerto Jiménez, by contrast, is an authentic Tico town serviced by public buses and favored by backpackers and budget travelers. Although the town itself is a bit run-down, Puerto Jiménez serves as the jumping off point for the southern Osa, a rugged wilderness home to some of the top ecolodges in the country.

Lying just east of the Osa Peninsula is the region's other natural wonder: the Golfo Dulce. One of just four tropical fjords in the world, the waters of the Golfo Dulce support dolphins, sport fish and seasonal populations of whale sharks and humpback whales. Its lush shores are home to some of the most deserted beaches in Costa Rica, including Pavones, a surfing mecca that boasts the second-longest left pointbreak in the world.

The wild, natural beauty of the Osa Peninsula and the Golfo Dulce attracts a special kind of traveler—rugged, adventurous, outdoorsy. The kind of person who doesn't mind stepping out of his or her comfort zone for the chance to experience something unique. For those who fit that description, the South Pacific is one of the true highlights of Costa Rica.

DRAKE BAY

LOCATED NEAR THE northern tip of the Osa Peninsula, Drake Bay is one of the wildest, most remote places in Costa Rica. Nearly all visitors arrive by plane or boat, and once you're here you're largely disconnected from the modern world. Of course, that's exactly the point. Lying between stunning Corcovado National Park to the south and gorgeous Isla de Caño to the east, Drake Bay is an eco-traveler's paradise.

Although the tiny village is humble and unassuming, the surrounding coastline does not lack for luxury. In fact, Drake Bay is home to some of the top ecolodges in the country, some of which charge upwards of $1,000 a night. But Drake Bay is also home to several excellent mid-range hotels and some good budget options. So don't let the town's famously posh ecolodges scare you away. But do be aware that many of the town's top adventures (boat trips to Corcovado National Park, scuba diving at Isla de Caño) cost $70-120 per person. If those prices don't scare you off, welcome to paradise. You could easily spend a week here and not run out of incredible adventures. Even if you're on a budget, you can always just hike along the gorgeous coastline in search of monkeys, parrots and nearly deserted beaches.

Another important thing to consider: Drake Bay is about as mellow and peaceful as it gets. Public electricity only arrived in 2005, and the center of town consists of two small grocery stores and a handful of budget restaurants. Nearly everyone gets up early to go on eco-tours, and nearly everyone is in bed by 10pm. In other words, Drake Bay is far more popular with families, couples and wildlife watchers than backpackers in search of late night *fiestas*.

Drake Bay—*Bahía Drake* ("Bah-hee-ah Drah-Kay") in Spanish—is named for Sir Francis Drake, who dropped anchor here in 1579. The English privateer had been working his way up the Pacific Coast of South America, plundering Spanish treasure ships as he went. Shortly before arriving in Costa Rica, Drake captured the *Nuestra Señora de la Concepción*, a Spanish galleon filled with 80 pounds of gold and 26 tons of silver. Not surprisingly, there are plenty of buried treasure legends floating around Drake Bay.

The real treasure, of course, is the region's staggering abundance of wildlife—on the ground, in the sea and in the air. Even in Costa Rica, few places offer so much biodiversity packed into such a small area, which is why so many people, myself included, consider Drake Bay one of the highlights of Costa Rica.

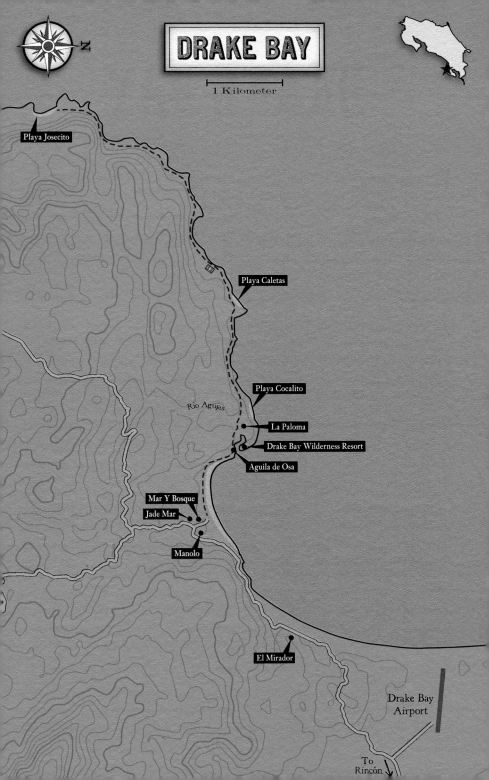

Getting to Drake Bay

There are three ways to get to Drake Bay: by boat, by plane or by car.

By boat: This is my favorite way to get to Drake Bay, involving an hour-long boat ride through the Térraba-Sierpe Delta—the largest remaining mangroves on the Pacific Coast of Central America. Boats depart from Bar Las Vegas and La Perla del Sur Restaurant in the town of Sierpe, 14 km (9 miles) from Palmar Norte, 122 km (76 miles) from Manuel Antonio, and 218 km (136 miles) from San José. Shuttles to Sierpe are offered by Grayline, Easyride and Monkey Ride (p.20). Tracopa buses (2221-4214) to Palmar Norte depart San José from Calle 5, Ave 18/20 throughout the day between 5am and 4:30pm (6 hours, ₡6,000), and from Palmar Norte you can catch the bus to Sierpe or take a taxi ($15–20). You can also drive to Sierpe and leave your car at one of the town's overnight parking lots ($6 per night at Bar Las Vegas, $2 per night at Soda Sierpe). Boats depart Sierpe for Drake Bay at 11:30am ($16 per person) and 3:30pm ($20 per person). Try to arrive early to ensure a seat on the boat (and bring a rain jacket just in case).

By plane: This is the easiest way to get to Drake Bay. There's a runway just north of town serviced by both Nature Air and Sansa (p.18). Alfa Romero Aero Taxi (2735-5178, 2735-5353) also offers chartered flights to Sirena Ranger Station, Carate and Puerto Jiménez.

By car: This is the longest and most difficult way to get to Drake Bay. First you'll have to drive to Rincón, 277 km (172 miles) from San José, then turn north and drive through the rugged dirt roads that cut across the northern Osa Peninsula. The scenery is a mix of cattle farms, tiny pueblos and dense jungle. Multiple river crossings make this road particularly challenging (and sometimes impossible) during rainy season. Trust me, it's better to take the boat or fly.

Getting Around Drake Bay

If you're staying at a budget/mid-range hotel in the center of Drake Bay, every-thing is within walking distance. If you're staying at a remote ecolodge, they will be able to handle all transportation for you.

Drake Bay Hotels

Choosing a good hotel is especially important in Drake Bay, where many hotels are remote and isolated and will thus largely define your experience. "Downtown" Drake Bay is home to a handful of budget hotels and a few mid-range options. Deluxe ecolodges are spread along the coastline southwest of Drake Bay. Note: Due to Drake Bay's remote location, you should definitely have a hotel booked before you arrive. Visit www.jameskaiser.com for complete hotel info.

★Corcovado Boat Trips

Early morning boat trips to Corcovado National Park (p.411) are one of the highlights of a visit to Drake Bay. In fact, many people come to Drake Bay specifically to visit Corcovado by boat, which is one of the easiest and most cost-effective ways to visit the park. Boat trips head to Sirena Ranger Station, leaving around 6am and arriving around 7:15am. After spending the morning hiking Sirena's trails in search of wildlife, you'll eat lunch then return to Drake Bay around 2 or 3pm. Cost: $80-90 per person. With advance planning, you can also arrange overnight boat trips to Sirena Ranger Station, which offers bunk beds and a restaurant (p.414). A separate Corcovado tour heads to San Pedrillo Ranger Station (30-minute boat ride from Drake Bay, $60-80 per person), which is home to some lovely primary rainforest. That said, the wildlife at San Pedrillo is not nearly as spectacular as the wildlife at Sirena. In my opinion, the Sirena trip is much better. Any hotel can arrange these tours, but it's best to book as far in advance as possible, especially during peak season (Dec–April) since daily park visitation is limited. Corcovado tours can also be arranged through Corcovado Expeditions (8846-4734, www.corcovadoexpeditions.net).

★Costa Cetacea Ocean Safaris

If you're interested in seeing dolphins, whales, turtles and other ocean animals in their native habitat, get in touch with Shawn Larkin, the half-man/half-dolphin biologist who specializes in "Blue Water" wildlife safaris. Shawn's trips head 20–30 miles offshore, where the water is brilliant blue and visibility often tops 100 feet. Humpback whales can be seen from Dec–March and July–November, but the real highlight is encountering a superpod of 2,000 dolphins! The waters off the Osa Peninsula are the only place in the world where dolphin superpods are known to exist year-round. Without a doubt, this is one of the most incredible wildlife experiences in Costa Rica. Shawn's tours fill up fast, so book them as far in advance as possible. Cost: $150 per person, 4 person minimum, or $600. (8702-1248, www.costacetacea.com)

★Rainforest Night Tour

If you're fascinated by bugs, spiders and frogs, don't pass up a chance to go on the Night Tour with Tracie "The Bug Lady." Nighttime is the best time to view some of the rainforest's most remarkable creatures, and Tracie is a walking encyclopedia of weird and wonderful knowledge. Although several copycat tours have popped up—many of which are quite good—Tracie's 2.5-hour tour is still the best. Book this tour as soon as possible—space is limited and fills up fast. Cost: $35 per person. Note: Due to logistical issues, this tour is not available to guests staying at remote lodges far away from the village. (8701-7356, www.thenighttour.com)

Spinner Dolphins, Costa Cetacea Safari

★Isla de Caño

Isla de Caño (p.408), located 40 minutes by boat from Drake Bay, is home to one of the healthiest marine ecosystems in Costa Rica. There are seven established dive sites around the island, with depths ranging from 6 meters (20 feet) to 25 meters (80 feet). A two-tank dive generally costs $120–150 per person. Snorkel trips ($70–80 per person) are also offered. Any hotel in Drake Bay can set up a scuba/snorkel trip, but if you're looking to get certified, check out Caño Divers. (2234-6154, www.canodiverscostarica.com)

Coastal Hiking

A beautiful public hiking trail heads southwest from Drake Bay and traces the shoreline 20 km (12.4 miles) to San Pedrillo Ranger Station, the northern entrance to Corcovado National Park. The trail passes a series of rocky coves, deserted beaches and dense rainforest filled with monkeys and scarlet macaws. If you like hiking, this is a great way to spend the day. The trail's most popular destination is Cocalito Beach (about a 30-minute hike from Drake Bay), a charming small brown sand beach good for sunbathing and relaxing. Strong hikers can head to San Josecito Beach (about a 2-hour hike from Drake Bay), a light sand beach sheltered by several small, rocky islands. San Josecito is good for swimming and snorkeling. No matter how far you hike, be sure to bring plenty of water and sunscreen. The trail starts near the western end of Drake Bay Beach, passes by two hotels (Jinetes de Osa and Aguila de Osa), then crosses a narrow suspension bridge above the Río Agujas. From there the trail heads up some tree root stairs, follows a concrete path, then descends to Cocolito Beach. Past Cocolito, the trail alternates between beach and rainforest as it parallels the coast. Shortly before reaching San Josecito, you'll need to cross the Río Claro, which is best done at low tide. On the far side of the river lives Ricardo, who offers canoe/waterfall tours along the Río Claro ($15).

Sportfishing

The waters off the Osa Peninsula are home to some of the best sportfishing in Costa Rica; over 40 records have been set within 80 miles of Drake Bay. Charters are available from Aguila de Osa Inn (2296-2190, www.aguiladeosa.com) and Tranquilo Lodge (8868-7385, www.thetranquilolodge.com). For cheaper inshore options, contact Shawn Larkin (8702-1248) or Craig Harrison (8996-9987).

Canopy Tour

Drake Bay is home to the best canopy tour on the Osa Peninsula: Corcovado Canopy Tour, which features 14 platforms and cables ranging from 190 meters (623 feet) to 400 meters (1,300 feet) in length. Cost: $60 per person. (8810-8908, www.corcovadocanopytour.com)

Playa San Josecito

Kayaking the Río Agujas

A great budget option is renting kayaks from Aguila de Osa ($15/3 hours) and exploring the Río Agujas, a beautiful tidal river best paddled at high tide.

Drake Bay Restaurants

In Drake Bay most lodges are scattered in remote locations away from the center of town, so visitors generally eat all meals at their lodge. (Another reason why you should pick your lodge carefully.) There are, however, a handful of inexpensive restaurants catering to backpackers and budget travelers. Although hardly gourmet, they're good if you're looking to save cash.

JADE MAR (Din: $10–17)
This is the best of the town's budget restaurants, offering an extensive menu full of Costa Rican classics plus seafood, pasta and burgers.

MAR Y BOSQUE (Brk: $6; Lnch, Din: $8–14)
The setting is simple and rustic, but the food is filling and cheap. Typical Costa Rican dishes. No alcohol.

MANOLO'S (Brk: $6; Lnch, Din: $8–9)
This small restaurant has perhaps the nicest atmosphere in town. The menu offers some Mexican favorites, but it's best to stick to the Tico classics.

Isla de Caño

Lying 16 km (10 miles) off the northwest tip of the Osa Peninsula, Isla de Caño is a tropical paradise that offers some of the best scuba diving and snorkeling in Costa Rica. Its tropical waters are home to some of the healthiest corals on the Pacific Coast, supporting 15 coral species and a thriving ecosystem of tropical fish, seahorses, sea turtles, manta rays, stingrays, sharks and even the occasional whale shark. Scuba and snorkel trips are best arranged through dive shops or hotels in Drake Bay (40 minutes by boat), Dominical/Uvita (1.5 hours by boat), or Manuel Antonio (3 hours by boat). Although most famous for its underwater offerings, the island's interior is filled with intrigue. Archaeologists have discovered pre-Columbian spheres (p.67) on the island, and legend has it that Sir Francis Drake dumped silver here to make room for more gold on his ship. In addition, the island receives more lightning strikes than almost any other place in Central America.

CORCOVADO NATIONAL PARK

CORCOVADO NATIONAL PARK is considered the crown jewel of Costa Rica's national park system, which is a remarkable statement when you think about it. Taking up 40% percent of the Osa Peninsula, Corcovado protects the largest remaining expanse of primary rainforest on the Pacific coast of the Americas. Not surprisingly, its biodiversity is off the charts. The Osa Peninsula contains over 250,000 species—*half* of Costa Rica's total—and endangered animals rarely seen in much of the country—scarlet macaws, squirrel monkeys, tapirs—are common, everyday sights in Corcovado. *National Geographic* famously called it "the most biologically intense place on Earth."

Corcovado's main destination is Sirena Ranger Station (p.414), a rustic lodge located halfway down the Osa Peninsula's rugged coast. Surrounded by virgin rainforest, this remote outpost is the best place to see wildlife in Costa Rica. Visitors arrive on foot, by boat or by plane for both day and overnight trips. Spending the night at Sirena is one of Costa Rica's top eco-experiences, but even day trips leave visitors marveling at the towering vegetation and sheer quantity of wildlife. For many travelers, a visit to Sirena is the highlight of their trip.

If you'd like to visit Sirena Ranger Station, your most important decision is how to get there. If you're interested in hiking (it takes a full day to hike to/from Sirena), you'll want to start your trip from Puerto Jiménez (p.423) or Carate (p.427). If you're interested in arriving by boat, a boat trip from Drake Bay (p.404) is your best bet. If you'd like to arrive by plane (the fastest and most expensive option), you can fly to Sirena from Puerto Jiménez, Drake Bay or Carate (p.415).

No matter how you get to Sirena, you'll need permits to enter Corcovado and reservations to spend the night. Hotels near the park and private tour companies can take care of these details for you, or you can contact the park directly. Note: For years it was possible to visit Corcovado on your own, but as of 2014 you are not allowed to enter the park without a certified guide.

To be sure, Corcovado isn't for everyone. It's one of the most remote national parks in Costa Rica, and even day trips to this hot, humid park involve a certain level of discomfort. But if you like wildlife watching, this is one of the most amazing destinations on the planet.

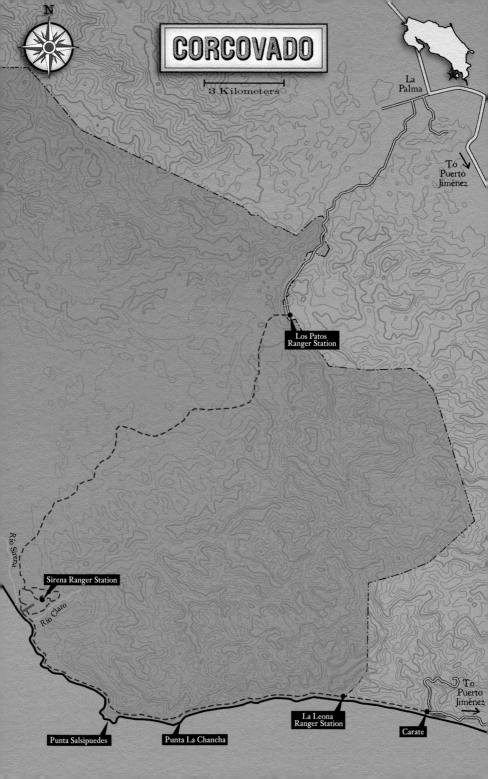

Permits & Reservations

All visitors to Corcovado must have permits, which cost $15 per person, per day. As of 2014, all visitors must also be accompanied by a local guide accredited by the ICT (Costa Rican Institute of Tourism). Prior to 2014 it was possible to visit the park without a guide, but the rules were changed to reduce accidents. If you do not have a permit and a certified guide, you cannot enter the park.

Even when it was possible to visit the park on your own, however, I always recommended hiring a guide. Corcovado can be rugged and confusing. A good guide will keep you safe and point out amazing plants and animals you would otherwise miss.

The easiest way to plan a trip to Corcovado is to book a tour through a local hotel or tour company. They will handle all the logistics (guide, permits, reservations at Sirena Ranger Station), which is no small feat. Although it's possible to handle the logistics on your own, the complexity of the process leaves many foreigners bewildered. If you are interested in handling the logistics on your own, send an email to the park's Puerto Jiménez office (pncorcovado@gmail.com) and ask for the relevant information.

Corcovado Tour Companies

TOUCAN TRAVEL
Offers 1–3 day guided hiking tours, plus boat and plane day trips. With two-day guided tours as cheap as $165 per person, this is one of the best values around. Located in downtown Puerto Jiménez. (2735-5826, www.toucan-travel.com)

OSA AVENTURA
In addition to three-day hiking tours ($350–545 per person), they offer overnight tours that arrive/depart by boat or plane. They also offer "boat and hike" and "fly and hike" combo tours. (2735-5670, www.osaaventura.com)

SURCOS TOURS
Offers day trips and three-day hiking tours ($250–360 per person) starting from either Los Patos or Carate. (8603-2387, www.surcostours.com)

CORCOVADO INFO CENTER
Located in Drake Bay, Corcovado Info Center offers two day Corcovado trips for $270 and three day trips for $500. (2775-0916, www.corcovadoinfocenter.com)

Private Guides

Most guides operate out of Puerto Jiménez, and the park office there has a list of certified guides. I've personally had great experiences with Alvaro Montoya (8705-0046, tamanduaecotour@hotmail.com). Another recommended guide is Rodolfo Gutierrez (8701-6266, rodolfosaenz@hotmail.com)

Sirena Ranger Station

Located halfway down the Osa Peninsula, Sirena Ranger Station is a sprawling complex of wooden buildings that includes offices, dorms, bathrooms, a dining hall, a cooking area and a camping platform—all connected by covered walkways. Accommodations are rustic. The four-person rooms consist of two bunk beds (no sheets), the shared bathrooms have cold water showers and electricity is only available a few hours each day. In front of the ranger station is a large field that's notorious for *garrapatas* ("ticks"). Between the field and the beach is a small grass landing strip used by airplanes. Seven trails radiate out from the ranger station, twisting through dramatic primary rainforest between the Río Claro, to the south, and the Río Sirena, to the north. Overnight lodging at Sirena Ranger Station is $8 per person per night, and camping is $4 per person per night. Meals at the lodge are $20 for breakfast, $26 for lunch, $26 for dinner, or you can bring your own food.

Getting to Sirena Ranger Station
ON FOOT

There are two trails to Sirena Ranger Station, both of which are long and rugged. I personally think the ultimate Corcovado adventure is a multi-day trip starting at Los Patos, spending two or more nights at Sirena and then finishing at Carate. But this trip should only be undertaken by strong, capable hikers. Also keep in mind that the rainy season (May-September) presents special hiking challenges due to slippery trails and swollen rivers; the upside is hiking in cooler temperatures. In October, the rainiest month, the park is closed to visitors.

Carate to Sirena: The trail from Carate to Sirena is 19.5 km (12.1 miles) and takes 6–8 hours. Monkeys and scarlet macaws are common sights along the trail, and it's possible to see tapirs and anteaters. The trail parallels the coast, alternating between trails through the rainforest and hiking on the beach. Beach hiking is very challenging due to the soft sand and open exposure to the sun. Guides generally like to start this hike around 4am to reduce exposure to the midday sun. It's also vital to time your hike so that you reach the Río Claro, located just south of Sirena Ranger Station, within two hours of low tide. At high tide the ocean connects with the river, and the only way to cross it is to wade or swim across the river, which is home to crocodiles and bull sharks. Three km (1.9 miles) north of Carate is La Leona Ranger Station, which marks the southern boundary of Corcovado National Park. Hikers can camp at La Leona, and just south of the ranger station is La Leona Lodge, a private ecolodge that's only accessible by foot. Camping at La Leona Ranger Station or spending the night at La Leona Lodge is a good way to break up the long, challenging hike from Carate to Sirena. The 3-km (1.9-mile) hike from Carate to La Leona Ranger Station takes place entirely along the beach, and it's much more difficult at high tide. If you'd like to drive your own car to Carate, the small *pulpería* next to the airstrip will guard your car

Sirena Ranger Station

for $5 a day. Otherwise you can ride the public *collectivo* bus (p.425) to Carate from Puerto Jiménez.

Los Patos to Sirena: The trail from Los Patos to Sirena is 20 km (12.4 miles) and takes 8–9 hours. Although it generally has less wildlife than Carate-Sirena, Los Patos-Sirena is a better overall trail since there are no long slogs along the beach. The first 7 km (4.3 miles) of the trail involve a bit of up and down elevation change, but the trail flattens out after crossing the Sedral River. To get to the Los Patos trailhead, you'll need to take a taxi from Puerto Jiménez, which takes 1.5–2 hours and costs $70–80.

Note: The 25-km (15.5-mile) trail from San Pedrillo to Sirena has been closed indefinitely to protect sensitive wildlife.

BY BOAT

Arriving by boat is the most popular option for those who don't want to spend 6–9 hours hiking through the jungle. Boats to Sirena Ranger Station depart daily from Drake Bay (p.401), and the trip takes a little over one hour. Toucan Travel and Osa Aventura (p.414) can also arrange boat tours to Sirena from Puerto Jiménez, but the trip takes about two hours.

BY PLANE

There's a dirt landing strip next to Sirena Ranger Station, and Alfa Romero Aero Taxi (2735-5178, aerocorcovado@racsa.co.cr) offers private flights (up to five people) from Puerto Jiménez (15 minutes, $390), Carate (10 minutes, $390) and Drake Bay (20 minutes, $490).

Llorona Waterfall

Baird's Tapir

Osa Wildlife

Above all else, the Osa Peninsula is famous for its abundant wildlife. There are 140 mammal species, 370 bird species and over 10,000 insect species. Even more impressive, many species that have disappeared from much of Central America have healthy populations on the Osa. Baird's tapir is the most famous example. Because tapirs require large tracts of undisturbed forest, they have disappeared from much of their former range. But tapirs are one of the most commonly spotted large mammals in Corcovado National Park. The Osa is also home to Central America's healthiest population of scarlet macaws, which thrive here thanks to the abundance of beach almond trees. White-lipped peccaries, which are now extinct in much of Costa Rica, are also abundant on the Osa, forming groups of up to 300 individuals that stampede through the forest.

The Osa is home to five of Central America's six feline species— jaguar, puma, ocelot, margay, jaguarundi—all of which are endangered. Although jaguars are rarely spotted, they are the undisputed kings of the jungle. Other mammals include tamanduas, an anteater with a 16-inch tongue, and coatis, a raccoon-like animal that scavenges everything from crabs to bird eggs. Both two-toed and three-toed sloths are found in the trees, as are all four Costa Rican monkey species (howler, spider, white-faced capuchin, squirrel).

The waters offshore the Osa are home to 23 species of marine mammals including superpods of spinner dolphins and migrating humpback whales from both the northern and southern hemispheres. Bull sharks patrol the coastline while rivers are home to caimans and crocodiles. Four sea turtle species—olive ridley, Pacific green, leatherback, hawksbill—lay their eggs on the Osa's beaches at night. During the day, those same beaches are teeming with thousands of hermit crabs. Back in the forest, land crabs are so numerous that they often number more than 4,000 per acre. The Osa is also home to the black spiny-tailed iguana—the world's fastest lizard, with speeds topping 22 miles per hour.

Bird life on the Osa is also remarkable. In addition to scarlet macaws there are crimson-fronted parakeets, red-lored Amazon parrots, Baird's trogons, fiery billed aracaris, 10 woodpecker species, 15 tanager species and 20 hummingbird species. Harpy eagles, the largest and most powerful raptors in the Americas, have also been spotted here.

The Osa Peninsula is home to many species considered endemic (found nowhere else in the world). These include birds such as the yellow-billed cotinga and black-cheeked ant-tanager, the deadly black-headed bushmaster snake and the Golfo Dulce poison dart frog. Perhaps most remarkable, because much of the Osa Peninsula remains unexplored by scientists, thousands of new species undoubtedly await discovery.

Osa Flora

Although the Osa Peninsula is most famous for wildlife, its abundant vegetation is what forms the foundation of the peninsula's staggering biodiversity. All told, the Osa is home to 13 major ecosystems, including lowland rainforest, mangroves, prairie forest, freshwater lagoons and coastal lagoons. At the Osa's highest point, 780 meters (2,560 feet) above sea level, there is even a small cloud forest.

The abundance of plants is due to plentiful sun and rain. Parts of the Osa receive up to 6 meters (20 feet) of rain each year—more than any other place on the Pacific Coast of Central America. Although most of Central America's coastal rainforest was chopped down over the past 50 years, the Osa Peninsula was spared much of this destruction due to its remote location. As a result, it's one of the last places in the Americas where virgin rainforest touches the sea. It also contains the most extensive mangrove forests in Costa Rica.

The Osa Peninsula is home to over 2,600 plant species, including 67 species that are endemic (found nowhere else in the world). There are over 700 tree species—more than in any forest north of Panama—including the tallest tree in Central America, a massive 77-meter (250-foot) kapok. Several South American tree species reach their northern limits on the Osa Peninsula, and 30 of Costa Rica's 50 fig trees are found here. Because the soil is surprisingly nutrient-poor, most trees rely on enormous buttressed roots for support instead of deep root systems.

PUERTO JIMÉNEZ

PUERTO JIMÉNEZ IS the largest town on the Osa Peninsula and the southern gateway to Corcovado National Park. Unlike Drake Bay, which is essentially a remote eco-tourist paradise, Puerto Jiménez is an honest-to-goodness Tico town, full of dirt roads and dilapidated buildings. Although a bit rough around the edges, the town is not entirely without charm. It commands dramatic views of the beautiful Golfo Dulce, lies next to a beautiful mangrove estuary, and its trees are filled with scarlet macaws.

West of Puerto Jiménez, a bumpy dirt road parallels the coast for 45 km (30 miles) as it heads towards the southern boundary of Corcovado National Park. After 17 kilometers (11 miles) you'll reach Cabo Matapalo, which marks the southern tip of the Osa Peninsula. Here you'll find luxury ecolodges, beautiful waterfalls and great surf. Past Cabo Matapalo the road veers north towards the small village of Carate, the last outpost of civilization before entering Corcovado National Park. If you're planning an overnight hiking trip in Corcovado, Carate is the most popular starting/finishing point.

As a general rule, Puerto Jiménez attracts more backpackers and budget travelers than Drake Bay. It's easier to get here on the cheap, and it's easier to visit Corcovado National Park on the cheap. That said, things can—and do—get pricey here. The road between Puerto Jiménez and Carate is home to some of the top ecolodges in Costa Rica. Most were built with wealthy wildlife watchers in mind, but many have recently become popular for upscale yoga retreats. The area also attracts its fair share of adrenaline junkies due to its surfing (the best on the Osa) and sportfishing (the best on the Osa).

If you want to hike into Corcovado National Park, you'll need to start and finish your trip in Puerto Jiménez (or from one of the ecolodges in Cabo Matapalo or Carate). The park headquarters are located in Puerto Jiménez, and it's worth stopping there to ask questions, pick up permits and take care of last minute details. Most Corcovado hiking guides are also based in Puerto Jiménez, so if you're looking to hire a good guide, it's worth spending some time here. Finally, Puerto Jiménez is the last refueling stop in the southern Osa, home to the region's only gas station, banks and grocery stores. So fill up your tank and load up on supplies—the wild southern Osa awaits!

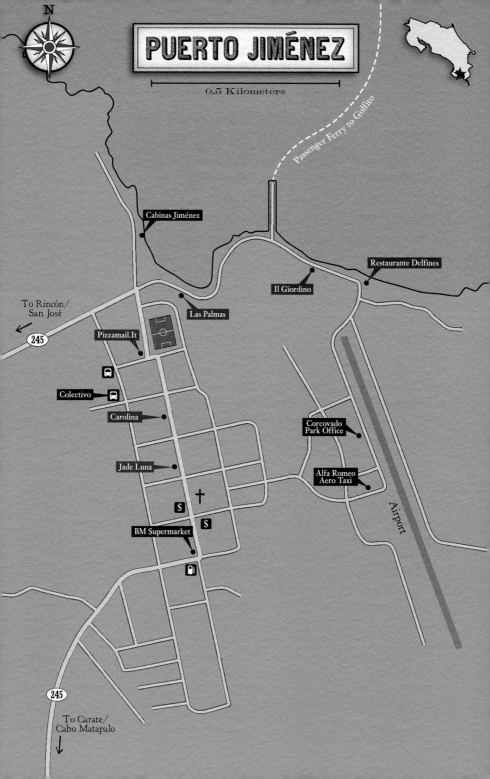

Getting to Puerto Jiménez

Puerto Jiménez is 311 km (193 miles) from San José (6-hour drive). Transportes Blanco buses (2257-4121) depart San José for Puerto Jiménez at 8am, noon from Calle 14 Ave 9/11 (₡7,465, 8 hours). Return buses depart Puerto Jiménez at 5am, 9am. Shuttle service is available from Monkey Ride (p.20). There's also a small airport in Puerto Jiménez that's serviced by both Nature Air and Sansa (p.18). Boat taxis are also available between Puerto Jiménez and Golfito (p.436).

Getting Around Puerto Jiménez

Puerto Jiménez is easy to get around on foot. If you're looking to visit Cabo Matapalo or Carate, you'll have to drive your own car, hire a taxi in Puerto Jiménez or catch the *collectivo* bus (₡4,500, 2.5 hours), which departs Puerto Jiménez for Carate at 6am and 1:30pm; return buses depart Carate for Puerto Jiménez at 8:30am and 4pm. Car rentals are available near the airport from Solid Car Rental (2735-5777), Alamo/National (2735-5175) and Toyota (2735-5295).

Puerto Jiménez Hotels

Downtown Puerto Jiménez has many budget and mid-range options, and there are even a few upscale places on the outskirts of town. The 42-km (27-mile) road between Puerto Jiménez and Carate, meanwhile, is home to some of the best ecolodges in the country, ranging from mid-range to *very* expensive. For complete lodging info visit www.jameskaiser.com

Puerto Jiménez

Although small (pop: 6,000), Puerto Jiménez is the largest town on the Osa Peninsula, comprising about 15 dusty square blocks alongside the beautiful Golfo Dulce. About two dozen small fishing boats are anchored offshore, and the town's run-down main street is lined with shops, restaurants and budget hotels. Although tourists are common, most businesses are budget stores catering to locals, making Puerto Jiménez one of the most authentic Tico towns on the Pacific Coast. Towards the west end of town are two banks, a gas station and the large BM grocery store. If you need to load up on supplies before heading west towards Cabo Matapalo or Carate, this is your last chance to do so.

Originally settled by Panamanian immigrants in the mid-1800s, Puerto Jiménez was home to 1,195 people by 1927. A decade later gold was discovered on the Osa Peninsula, and Puerto Jiménez became a regional boomtown. Although the boom went bust decades ago, some stores continue to offer cash for gold, which is still found in small quantities in nearby rivers.

These days tourism is the main economic driver of Puerto Jiménez, offering a lifeline to what has historically been one of the poorest regions in Costa Rica. Most visitors are hikers and eco-travelers heading to or from Corcovado National Park. The park's main office (Open Mon–Sat 8am–4pm, Sunday 8am–3pm) is located near the airport, and the park's two major trailheads, Carate and Los Patos, are both a roughly two-hour drive from Puerto Jiménez. Local 4x4 taxis charge about $70–100 to go to either of the trailheads.

Cabo Matapalo

Puerto Jiménez to Carate

West of Puerto Jiménez, a bumpy dirt road heads 42 kms (27 miles) around the southern tip of the Osa Peninsula on its way to Carate, a tiny village near the southern edge of Corcovado National Park. The rugged road requires multiple river crossings; four-wheel-drive and high clearance are necessary, even in the dry season. (In October, the rainiest month, several large streams are completely impassable.) If you don't have a car, you can ride in the back of the *collectivo*, a no-frills truck that shuttles people between Puerto Jiménez and Carate (p.425).

Heading out from Puerto Jiménez, you'll pass a series of cattle ranches before reaching the dense jungle of Cabo Matapalo. Located 18 kms (11 miles) west of Puerto Jiménez (40-minute drive), Cabo Matapalo is the southernmost point of the Osa Peninsula. It's home to a handful of spectacular ecolodges, some nice waterfalls and the region's best surf. To check out the shoreline, cross the river past Buena Esperanza Restaurant, then take a downhill left just past the "bus stop" (really just a simple bench) on the left side of the road. Continuing straight takes you to Playa Pan Dulce. Turning right through the stone columns takes you towards Backwash Bay (0.8 kms past the columns) and Playa Matapalo (1.9 kms past the columns).

Past Cabo Matapalo the road continues 24 kms (15 miles) to Carate (1.5-hour drive), a tiny seaside village that's home to a landing strip, a handful of ecolodges and a tiny *pulpería* selling drinks and snacks. For complete lodging info for Carate and Cabo Matapalo, visit www.jameskaiser.com

★Waterfall Rappel/Tree Climb

If you're looking to combine adrenaline with natural history, look no further than Psycho Tours (8353-8619, www.psychotours.com). Located in Matapalo, they offer rappelling tours down a 14-meter (45-foot) waterfall and the 30-meter (100-foot) King Louis Waterfall ($85 per person), as well as tree climbing up a massive 60-meter (197-foot) strangler fig ($55 per person). Combo tours are $120 per person. All tours are led by Andy Pruter, a highly knowledgeable and entertaining naturalist who points out interesting plants and animals along the way.

★Golfo Dulce Boat Tour

The beautiful Golfo Dulce (p.433) is one of the natural wonders of Costa Rica, and there's no better way to experience it than by getting out on the water. Toucan Travel (2735-5826, www.toucan-travel.com) offers a Golfo Dulce boat tour ($60 per person) that combines dolphin watching and snorkeling. Depending on the season, you can sometimes see humpback whales (December, August) or whale sharks (April, October). Cabinas Jiménez (2735-5090) offers a similar boat tour ($65 per person) that also includes a visit to the remote Osa Wildlife Sanctuary (www.osawildlife.org), a rehabilitation center that's home to monkeys, sloths, peccaries and other rainforest animals.

Kayak Mangrove Tour

Just east of Puerto Jiménez the Platanares River supports a beautiful mangrove forest. Aventuras Tropicales (2735-5195, www.aventurastropicales.com) offers guided kayak tours ($45 per person) through the weird, wonderful scenery. Tours are only available during high tide, so tour times change daily. If the mellow mangrove tour isn't enough for you, Aventuras Tropicales also offers a 3-day kayaking/camping tour around the Golfo Dulce.

Finca Köbö Chocolate Farm

If you've ever wondered where chocolate comes from, Finca Köbö will reveal the entire process. Their 2-hour tour of a working organic cacao farm is filled with fascinating info and ends with a delicious tasting. Finca Köbö (*köbö* means dreams in the indigenous Guaymí language) is located 16 km (10 miles) northwest of Puerto Jiménez (about a 20-minute drive along the main road). Cost: $32 per person. No credit cards. (8398-7604, www.fincakobo.com)

Canopy Tour

Aventuras Bosquemar, the only canopy tour in the southern Osa, features five platforms, five zip lines, and over 500 meters (1,640 feet) of cables through primary rainforest. (8846-6673)

Surfing

Cabo Matapalo, located at the southern tip of the Osa Peninsula, is home to some great surf. The area is famous for its right point breaks, which are long and fast with a strong southern swell. On really big days waves can be triple overhead. Due to its remote location—and the expensive prices of most nearby lodges—crowds are usually minimal. But keep in mind that some locals can get territorial. Also note that there are no surf shops nearby, so you'll have to bring your own equipment. If you're interested in surf lessons, check out Pollo's Surf School (8366-6559, www.pollosurfschool.com).

There are three popular breaks at Cabo Matapalo (p.427). **Playa Pan Dulce:** Great rights that can go 200 yards on a good swell. Best on a medium to high tide. **Backwash Bay:** Great right point break but only works at low tide. When conditions are just right, the right at Backwash Bay connects with the right at Playa Pan Dulce. **Playa Matapalo:** A good reef break, mostly rights, that picks up lots of swell and delivers consistently good waves.

Sportfishing

Both the Golfo Dulce and the deep waters offshore are home to some of the best sportfishing in Costa Rica. With a private dock and a fleet of over 40 boats, Crocodile Bay Resort (2735-5631, www.crocodilebay.com) is the region's premier sportfishing operation.

Puerto Jiménez Restaurants

★ IL GIORDINO (Lnch, Din: $11–20)

This charming, seaside Italian restaurant serves up the best food in Puerto Jiménez—homemade pasta, fresh seafood, delicious pizza. Although much of the menu is upscale, there are some terrific lower-cost options as well as fresh seafood and BBQ. No credit cards. (2735-5129, www.ilgiardinoitalianrestaurant.com)

★ BUENA ESPERANZA (Lnch, Din: $12–15)

This funky bar/restaurant, located on the main road near Cabo Matapalo, serves up delicious food in a wild, remote location. The menu changes daily, but there's usually a good mix of seafood and vegetarian options. On Friday nights the bar hosts the best party on the Osa. No credit cards.

★ PEARL OF THE OSA (Lnch: $9; Din: $12–14)

Located in the oceanfront Iguana Hotel, 4 km (2.5 miles) west of Puerto Jiménez on Playa Plantares, Pearl of the Osa offers the area's most upscale dining experience. The menu covers a wide range of flavors, from classic to tropical, with lots of Mexican influence. (8848-0752, www.thepearloftheosa.com)

PIZZAMAIL.IT (Din: $8–12)

This simple, no frills Italian restaurant is located next to the town post office (hence the name) and serves filling pizza made with fresh dough and ingredients. Takeout available. No credit cards. (2735-5483)

LAS PALMAS (Lnch, Din: $12–18)

This simple waterfront restaurant offers great harbor-front views. The menu is a mix of Tico, Gringo and Mexican favorites. No credit cards. (2735-5012)

CAROLINA RESTAURANT (Brk: $6; Lnch, Din: $7–10)

This longtime backpacker favorite serves up tasty, filling Costa Rican food (casados, rice dishes, seafood) at reasonable prices. A great place to try Tico favorites like *patacones* and *sopa negra*. Free wifi. (2735-5185)

RESTAURANTE DELFINES (Brk: $7; Lnch, Din: $8–12)

If you're looking for a simple beachfront restaurant that serves typical Costa Rican food, look no further. In addition to casados, rice dishes and seafood, the menu includes some American and Mexican fast food options. (2735-5083)

JADE LUNA ICE CREAM ($4)

If you've got a sweet tooth, don't pass up Jade Luna's delicious, home-made ice cream. Flavors range from classic (vanilla, coffee, rum raisin) to exotic (orange olive oil walnut, bacon walnut dark chocolate). (8500-4733)

Pavones

GOLFO DULCE

THE GOLFO DULCE ("Sweet Gulf") is one of Costa Rica's most beautiful—and overlooked—natural wonders. Separating the Osa Peninsula from mainland Costa Rica, it's one of just four tropical fjords in the world. Its waters, which reaching frigid depths of up to 215 meters (704 feet), are home to dolphins, whales and dozens of other sea creatures, and its jungle-fringed shores are home to some of the most deserted beaches in Costa Rica.

For me, the best part about the Golfo Dulce is its wild, undeveloped nature. If you're looking for the fabled "Costa Rica of 30 years ago," you'll find it here. The beaches are uncrowded, the unpaved roads are bumpy and stray horses still wander the small *pueblos*. Although the beaches aren't as lovely as their northern counterparts (more dark sand than light sand), they are far more rugged and wild. Mega-resorts and timeshares are completely unknown in these parts.

For surfers, the highlight of the region is Pavones, a world famous point break home to the second-longest left in the world. Just north of Pavones is Playa Zancudo, one of the most remote, laid-back beaches in Costa Rica, and north of Zancudo is Golfito, a former banana town located alongside a stunningly beautiful bay. The town itself is gritty and run-down, but the location is terrific for boaters and sportfishermen.

Despite its remote location, the Golfo Dulce has not remained entirely untouched. By the mid-2000s, shrimp trawlers, which drag large nets over the ocean floor, had overfished the rich waters here. In response, a group of local fishermen and conservationists worked out a deal to ban trawlers from the Golfo Dulce. In 2010 the 75,000-hectare (290-square-mile) gulf was declared a "marine area of responsible fishing," and today the Golfo Dulce is the largest responsible fishing zone in Central America.

Six species of dolphin inhabit the Golfo Dulce year-round, and giant manta rays can sometimes be seen gliding through the water. Whale sharks, which grow up to 40 feet long, often visit in March, and migrating humpback whales visit between Jan-March and Aug-Oct. In fact, the Golfo Dulce is one of the only areas in the world visited by humpback whales from both the northern and southern hemispheres. On land, over 14,000 hectares (34,600 acres) of lush rainforest have been permanently protected as Piedras Blancas National Park along the Golfo Dulce's eastern shore. Although rugged and largely inaccessible, Piedras Blancas provides vital habitat for some of Costa Rica's most endangered species.

Given its remote location and lack of amenities, the Golfo Dulce is not for everyone. But if you're willing to trade luxury and convenience for uncrowded tropical beauty, Costa Rica's "Sweet Gulf" won't let you down.

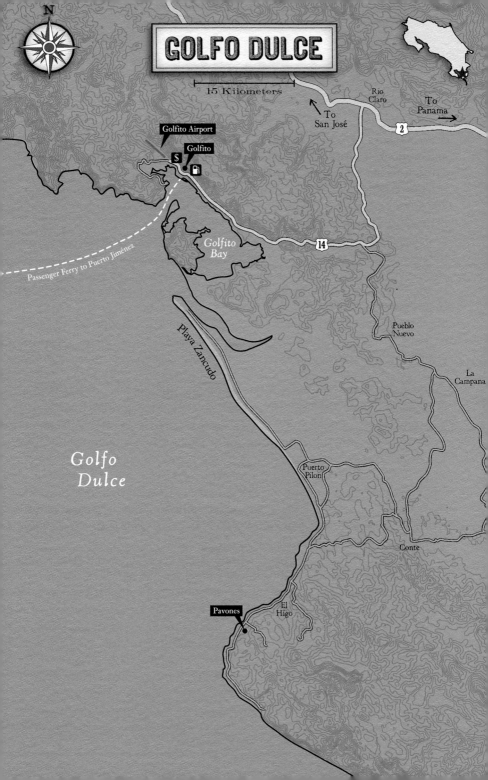

Getting to the Golfo Dulce

Golfito, the bustling hub of this remote region, is located 291 km (181 miles) from San José (6-hour drive). Golfito is home to an airport serviced by Sansa and Nature Air (p.20). Boat taxis depart Puerto Jiménez for Golfito at 6am, 8:30am, 11am, 1pm, 3pm (30 mins, ₡3,000). Private water taxis between Golfito and Zancudo can be arranged ($60, 2776-0012). Tracopa buses (2221-4214) to Golfito depart San José from Calle 5, Ave 18/20 at 7am and 3:30pm (₡7,340, 8 hours); return buses depart Golfito at 5am and 1:30pm. Buses to Pavones depart Golfito at 10am and 3pm (₡2,000, 2 hours).

Getting Around the Golfo Dulce

There are plenty of taxis in Golfito, but Playa Zancudo and Pavones are remote areas where transportation options are extremely limited. That said, both Zancudo and Pavones are small, walkable villages. Rental cars are available in Golfito from Solid Car Rental (2775-3333) and CR Save Rent-a-Car (2227-6464).

Golfo Dulce Hotels

This remote region has mostly budget and mid-range hotels, but there are a handful of nice hotels and even a few high-end ecolodges. Visit www.jameskaiser.com for complete hotel info.

Golfito

This bustling port, the largest town on the shores of the Golfo Dulce, is famous for two things: sportfishing and duty free shopping. If you're in search of marlin, sailfish or low-cost appliances, you're going to love Golfito. Otherwise, it's best to spend your time elsewhere.

Established in 1938 by the United Fruit Company (p.152), Golfito survived off banana exports for decades. Then, in 1985, the company permanently shut down its operations, leaving the town economically devastated. In 1990 the Costa Rican government established a duty-free shopping zone to help revive the local economy. Although duty free shopping has helped slow the decline, Golfito remains a shadow of its former self. These days the town attracts a motley collection of discount shoppers, drug smugglers and expats. But Golfito has tremendous potential. Its harbor is one of the loveliest in Costa Rica, and the dramatic hills that surround town are covered in lush rainforest. There are even some beautiful old houses from the banana era that add a bit of historic charm. For sportfishing, kayak rentals or waterfront meals check out Banana Bay Marina (2775-0255, www.bananabaymarinagolfito.com).

Just north of Golfito is Piedras Blancas National Park, which protects 12,000 hectares (46.3 square miles) of primary rainforest along the Golfo Dulce. Since there are no visitor facilities, the park is best explored through the adjacent Esquinas Rainforest Lodge (2741-8001, www.esquinaslodge.com) or Playa Cativo (2200-3131, www.playacativo.com)

Playa Zancudo

Stretching 10 km (6 miles) south of the Río Coto, Playa Zancudo is a combination of soft brown sand, turquoise water and tremendous views of the Golfo Dulce. It might just be the most laid-back beach in Costa Rica—a place where palm trees and hammocks dominate the daily agenda and your only real worry is falling coconuts. If you're looking for maximum relaxation on a vast beach with no crowds, Zancudo is hard to beat.

Although it takes some effort to get here, you'll be rewarded with some of the best values in Costa Rica. Beachfront cabinas can be rented for under $50 a night (visit www.jameskaiser.com for hotel info), and there are a handful of nice restaurants. My favorite places to eat are Sol y Mar, a beachside bar/restaurant with a tropical expat vibe, Colosos, a charming cabin with an eclectic menu, and Oceano, which serves an international assortment of tasty food.

Zancudo Boat Tours (2776-0012, www.loscocos.com) offers motorboat and kayak trips, as well as a private boat taxi to/from Golfito and Puerto Jiménez. They also offer surfboard and Stand Up Paddleboard rentals. Zancudo Lodge (2776-0008, www.zancudolodge.com) offers both inshore and offshore sportfishing trips.

Playa Zancudo is 314 kms (195 miles) from San José (7-hour drive), and 53 kms (33 miles) from Golfito (1-hour drive). If you don't want to drive, you can fly to Golfito, then hire a private water taxi to Zancudo.

Pavones

This tiny pueblo, located near the southern entrance of the Golfo Dulce, is a surfer's paradise. Pavones is home to a 1.1 km (2/3 mile) long point break that's considered the second longest left in the world (the longest, in Chicama, Peru, is 2 km). Pavones' legendary wave requires a strong southern swell, and the best swells generally arrive during rainy season (April–November). When things really get going, surfers from around the world descend on Pavones, eager to experience rides that can last over two minutes!

Despite Pavones' fame among globe-trotting surfers, the village remains small and uncrowded due to its remote location (7-hour drive from San José, 2-hour drive from Golfito). But when big swells kick up, the waves can get very crowded. There are only a handful of hotels and restaurants in town, as well as a few upscale ecolodges on the road towards Punto Banco, just south of Pavones. Although a few hotels accept reservations, budget places tend to be first-come, first-served. (Visit www.jameskaiser.com for hotel info.)

Buses to Pavones depart Golfito at 10am and 3pm (₡2,000, 2 hours). Return buses depart Pavones at 5am and 12:30pm. If you're driving to Pavones, you'll definitely want 4x4 for the bumpy dirt roads, especially during the rainy season. Note: Although the closest gas station is over an hour away, the local hardware store sells gas by the gallon.

Río Claro ("Clear River") (2776-2016, 8629-2508) rents surfboards and kayaks. Sea Kings Surf Shop rents surfboards and offers lessons (2776-2015). For yoga there's Shooting Star Studio (www.yogapavones.com) or Yoga Farm (www.yogafarmcostarica.org).

Local restaurants include La Bruschetta (La Piña) (Lnch, Din: $16), a charming Italian restaurant serving homemade pizza and pasta on the way to Punta Banco, Café de la Suerte (Brk: $8; Lnch: $8), which serves tasty smoothies and vegetarian food, and Jolly Roger (Lnch, Din: $10–14) which offers a nice mix of Italian, Spanish and Mediterranean food. There are also several inexpensive *sodas* serving typical Costa Rican food. Note: Most places do not accept credit cards, and the closest ATM is in Golfito. Be sure to bring plenty of cash.

ISLA DEL COCO

THIS SPECTACULAR ISLAND, located 540 km (335 miles) off Costa Rica's Pacific coast, is a remote paradise of lush jungle, dramatic waterfalls and world-class underwater scenery. A 36-hour boat ride from the mainland, the island's pristine waters are filled with 18 coral species, over 300 fish species and vast concentrations of schooling hammerhead sharks. Not surprisingly, it's considered one of the top scuba destinations on the planet. Jacques Cousteau famously called it "the most beautiful island in the world."

Isla del Coco (aka "Cocos Island") is a volcanic island that rises roughly 3,000 meters (10,000 feet) from the ocean floor. It's part of a chain of underwater volcanoes that stretches all the way to the Galapagos Islands. The island's highest point, 634 meters (2,080 feet) above sea level, is home to a small cloud forest, and the rugged coastline has cliffs up to 180 meters (590 feet) high. The 8 km by 3 km (5 mile by 2 mile) island receives over 7 meters (23 feet) of rain each year, and it's home to over 200 waterfalls, many of which tumble directly into the ocean. It's home to 235 plant species, 30% of which are endemic (found nowhere else in the world). There are 27 endemic fish species, 64 endemic insect species and three endemic bird species: the Coco Island cuckoo, Coco Island flycatcher and Coco Island finch.

Isla del Coco was first discovered in 1526 by the Spanish explorer Joan Cabezas. In the 17th and 18th century it was regularly visited by pirates, and rumors of buried treasure abound. Over 500 treasure hunts have taken place here, but nothing more than a few doubloons has ever been found. Although it's often claimed that Isla del Coco was the real-life inspiration for Treasure Island, scholars dispute this. It was, however, the inspiration for Jurassic Park's Isla Nublar.

In 1869 the Costa Rican government organized an official treasure hunt on Isla del Coco, which produced no treasure but established the country's official claim to the island. In 1978 Costa Rica made the island and 1,000 square-km (386 square miles) of surrounding water a national park. Although officially protected, illegal shark finning has become a serious problem in recent years. Today conservation organizations such as MarViva are working to correct this problem.

These days most people visit uninhabited Isla del Coco on multi-day scuba diving trips. Unless you have a private yacht, you'll need to visit Isla del Coco with a licensed liveaboard vessel. The two main liveaboard vessels are Okeanos Aggressor (800-348-2628, www.aggressor.com) and Undersea Hunter (800-203-2120, www.underseahunter.com). Both offer 8–12 day diving trips departing from Puntarenas. Prices range from $4,500–6,000 per person.

CARIBBEAN COAST

ALTHOUGH OFTEN OVERSHADOWED by the famous beaches on the Pacific, the Caribbean coast is one of the jewels of Costa Rica. Its beaches are stunning, its wildlife is incredible (even by Costa Rican standards) and its Afro-Caribbean culture spices up the food and the nightlife. The Caribbean coast also remains relatively undeveloped, giving it a more rustic, small-scale feel.

The best way to picture the Caribbean coast is to divide it into two parts: the northern Caribbean and southern Caribbean. The northern Caribbean, which lies north of the port city of Limón, is home to swampy lowlands crisscrossed by rivers and canals. The landscape here is too wet for roads, so people travel by boat, earning the region the nickname "The Amazon of Costa Rica." The top destination is Tortuguero, a stunning national park that protects the most important green sea turtle nesting site in the Western Hemisphere. The northern Caribbean is also home to a handful of remote, world-class sportfishing villages located at Barra de Colorado and Parismina.

The southern Caribbean (aka the Talamanca Coast) is famous for beautiful beaches and the largest coral reefs in Costa Rica. The small, laid-back village of Cahuita offers jungle hiking and great snorkeling in adjacent Cahuita National Park. Just south of Cahuita lies Puerto Viejo, which is home to some of the country's top beaches and a vibrant social scene. Puerto Viejo also lies adjacent to the Gandoca-Manzanillo Wildlife Refuge, a rugged destination home to stunning rainforests and amazing animals. Set back from the coast are the formidable Talamanca Mountains, which rise up thousands of feet and shelter Costa Rica's largest indigenous villages. The southern Caribbean's mix of landscapes and ethnicities is incredible. This is the most ethnically diverse region in Costa Rica, home to indigenous BriBris, Cabécars and Kéköldi, as well as Afro-Caribbeans, Latinos and a recent influx of Europeans and North Americans.

The biggest downside to the Caribbean coast is the weather, which varies between rainy and not-so-rainy. Unlike the rest of Costa Rica, which enjoys a pronounced dry season from January to April, the Caribbean has no true dry season. September and October are the two driest months, and February and March are relatively dry. But keep in mind that the abundant rain is what makes the region so incredibly lush. The lack of pronounced seasons also means that sunny days can be found year-round. It all just depends on the weather.

CARIBBEAN COAST HISTORY

In 1502, on his fourth and final voyage to the Americas, Christopher Columbus sailed south along Costa Rica's Caribbean coast. After dropping anchor at Uvita, a small island just offshore of present-day Limón, Columbus named the area "The Garden" due to its lush vegetation. He then headed south towards Panama and continued his search for Asia.

For the next three centuries, Costa Rica's Caribbean coast remained largely ignored by Europeans. Spanish settlers preferred the high, temperate Central Valley to the humid, disease-ridden jungles. In addition, there was no easy route through the steep, rugged mountains that divide the Caribbean from the rest of Costa Rica. As a result, this isolated region developed independently from the rest of the country, forging a unique history and culture.

The Caribbean was originally home to several indigenous tribes, including the Bribris and Cabécar. Then, around 1750, turtle hunters began arriving from Panama and Nicaragua. These hunters, a mix of Afro-Caribbeans from Panama and Miskito Indians from Nicaragua, visited between May and September to harpoon green and hawksbill turtles for their meat and dig up turtle nests for their eggs. They set up temporary camps on the coast and planted crops to be harvested the following year.

In 1828 a Panamanian turtle hunter named William Smith moved to Cahuita, becoming the region's first permanent Afro-Caribbean settler. Smith brought his family from Bocas del Toro, and over the next several decades they were joined by other English speaking Afro-Caribbean settlers from Panama, Nicaragua and San Andrés Island. Over time farming became more important than fishing, and the most important crops were coconut and cacao. (Prior to the arrival of Afro-Caribbeans, coconut palms did not exist on the Caribbean coast.)

In the late 1800s, the history of the Caribbean coast forever changed when a new railroad linked San José to the port of Limón. The "Jungle Train" finally allowed Central Valley coffee to be exported to Europe via the Caribbean, rather than the much longer Pacific route. To build the train, the Costa Rican government contracted an American businessman named Minor Keith. When he first began work on the railroad, Keith hired Costa Rican workers, but most fell victim to tropical diseases. So Keith recruited more rugged workers from Jamaica. On December 20, 1872 a boat carrying 123 Jamaicans arrived in Limón, and within a year 1,000 more had arrived. Hard working and resistant to tropical diseases, the Jamaicans finished the railroad. They also brought Jamaican music, cooking and English sports like cricket (at the time Jamaica was a British Colony).

Next, Keith set to work creating a vast banana empire. In exchange for completing the railroad, Keith was granted a 99-year lease on the railroad and 800,000 acres of land alongside the tracks. Within a decade he had created enormous banana plantations that employed thousands of Jamaican workers. In 1899 Keith merged his holdings with another company to create the United Fruit Company, (p.152) which soon became one of the most powerful and notorious companies in Latin America. Between 1900 and 1913, an additional 20,000 Jamaicans came to Costa Rica's Caribbean coast in search of work.

In the early 20th century, the United Fruit Company ruled Costa Rica's Caribbean coast like a feudal lord. As its power grew, so did its abuses. During the Great Depression, United Fruit shifted its losses onto small banana farmers and workers using highly questionable practices. Around the same time, a deadly fungus called Panama disease swept through the region and devastated the banana crops. In response, the United Fruit Company moved its banana operations to Costa Rica's Pacific Coast, but the Costa Rican government passed a law prohibiting United Fruit from hiring "noncitizen" (i.e. Afro-Caribbean) workers in the new Pacific plantations. The law was a racist attempt to confine blacks to the Caribbean, trapping them in a region with a depressed economy following the United Fruit Company's departure.

The next big change came in the aftermath of Costa Rica's 1948 Civil War. Prior to 1948, Afro-Caribbean citizens had been ignored at best and exploited at worst. Many were not even recognized as full citizens or allowed to vote. Following the Civil War, Afro-Caribbeans were granted full citizenship, the right to vote and the right to travel beyond the Caribbean coast. The reforms were welcome, but more unification with Costa Rica meant more cultural change. In Afro-Caribbean communities, Spanish began to replace Creole English, Catholicism began to replace Protestantism and soccer replaced cricket.

Changes also came in the form of infrastructure. In the late 1960s, the government dug four large canals in the northern Caribbean, opening up a navigable route to Tortuguero and other small coastal villages. In 1976 a paved road connected Limón to the southern beaches for the first time, allowing cash crops out and cash-carrying tourists in.

Tragedy struck in 1991, when a 7.6 magnitude earthquake rocked the Caribbean coast. The earthquake killed 48 people, destroyed five bridges, and permanently shut down the famous Jungle Train. By that point, however, most commerce was traveling along Highway 32, which connects San José to Limón. Today the highway carries three-quarters of all national commerce.

Although much has changed in Costa Rica's Caribbean, it still remains home to several enormous fruit plantations. Costa Rica is currently the world's largest fresh pineapple exporter and the world's second largest banana producer. But things have greatly improved since the days of Minor Keith. In 1986 EARTH University was founded near Limón to teach sustainable, responsible agriculture to a new generation of students. Today EARTH University is considered one of the top agricultural universities in Latin America.

TORTUGUERO

IN 1953 AN American sea turtle researcher named Archie Carr traveled to the remote village of Tortuguero ("Place of the Turtles") to investigate reports of a large turtle nesting ground. He was amazed by what he saw. Tortuguero, Carr realized, was the most important green sea turtle nesting ground in the Western Hemisphere. Each year between June and October, tens of thousands of green sea turtles returned to the dark sand beach to lay their eggs. Recognizing the region's ecological importance, Carr alerted the Costa Rican government and in 1975 over 35 km (22 miles) of beach were set aside as Tortuguero National Park.

Since the national park was established, sea turtle populations have declined worldwide, but nestings at Tortuguero have actually increased by nearly 500%. Today roughly 20,000 green turtles nest here each year—the largest colony of nesting green turtles in the world. The turtles attract a steady stream of eco-tourists, who come to watch the turtles lay their eggs at night. But Tortuguero is more than just sea turtles. Lying just beyond the beach are a handful of serpentine rivers that reach deep into the jungle, opening up a lush wilderness filled with wildlife. You can explore the rivers by motor boat, kayak or canoe in search of monkeys, sloths, parrots, crocodiles, caimans and dozens of other animals. All told, Tortuguero is home to 60 mammal species, 57 amphibian species, 111 reptile species, over 300 bird species, over 400 tree species and over 2,000 plant species! With so much biodiversity, it's no wonder Tortuguero is the Caribbean coast's top eco-destination and Costa Rica's third-most visited national park.

The visitation statistics are even more impressive when you consider how remote Tortuguero is. Located in the swampy northern Caribbean, it's one of the least accessible areas in the country. Roads can take you to within 32 kms (20 miles) of Tortuguero, but from there it's at least a one-hour boat ride through the jungle. The other option is flying (there's a paved runway north of town), which is spectacular but pricey. But no matter how you get to Tortuguero, it's an adventure you'll never forget. The combination of paddling the jungly waterways during the day and watching sea turtles lay their eggs at night is one of Costa Rica's most magical experiences.

Note: If you're looking for a fun-in-the-sun beach vacation, Tortuguero is not the place to visit. The dark sand beach is far less impressive than other beaches, and the waters offshore are home to dangerous rip-tides. Furthermore, Tortuguero is one of the wettest places in Costa Rica, receiving over 6 meters (20 feet) of rain each year. This is an eco-travelers destination, pure and simple—which is exactly why so many people love it.

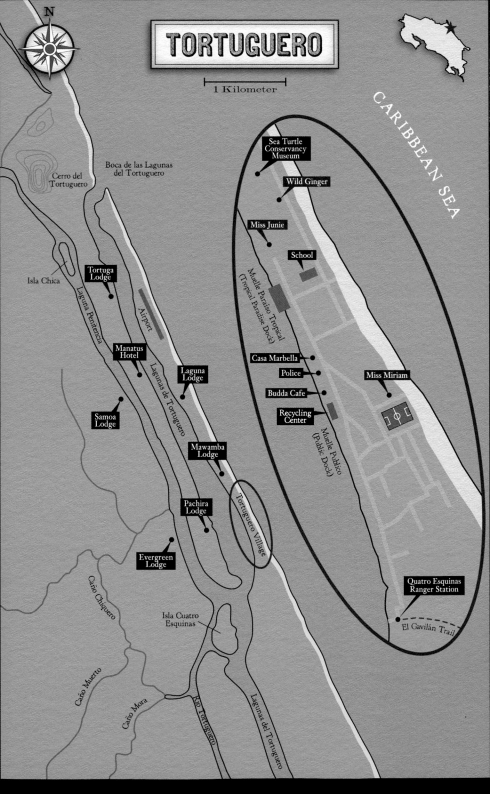

Getting to Tortuguero

There are only two ways to get to Tortuguero: by boat or by plane. Most visitors arrive by boat after a three-hour bus ride from San José. Boats leave from the docks at Cariari, Caño Blanco, Moín and La Pavona, then cruise through the jungle at high speed—a truly unique experience. The flight to Tortuguero from San José is about 35 minutes and offers soaring views of mountains, volcanoes and vast banana plantations. If you can afford it, I highly recommend arriving by boat and departing by plane, which will give you a remarkable view of the landscape. Flights are offered by both Nature Air and Sansa (p.18).

Most hotels offer multi-day packages that include transportation to and from San José. You simply make a reservation and the hotel takes care of all the travel connections for you. Package tours are by far the easiest option, and the majority of visitors choose to go this route. If you want to visit Tortuguero from Puerto Viejo or Cahuita (or vice versa), you can arrange package tours through Exploradores Outdoors (2222-6262, www.exploradoresoutdoors.com).

If you're cheap and adventurous, you can arrange your own transportation to Tortuguero via public buses and private boats. First, head to the small town of Cariari, 22 kms (13.7 miles) north of Guápiles. Grupo Caribeños buses (2222-0610) depart San José for Cariari from the Terminal del Caribe (Calle Central, Ave 15) at 9am, 10:30am (₡1,660, 2 hours). After arriving at the *estación nueva* ("New Station") in Cariari, head four blocks east to the *estación vieja* ("Old Station") and purchase a bus ticket to La Pavona (Rancho la Suerte)—buses (8976-4302, ₡1,000) depart at 6am, 11:30am, 3pm. At La Pavona pick a boat and buy a ticket (₡2,000). Detailed travel info is also available at www.tortuguerovillage.com.

Getting Around Tortuguero

If you're staying at an all-inclusive hotel, your hotel will arrange all local transportation for you. If you're staying in the village of Tortuguero, shoes or boots are all you need to get around. If you do need to cross the waterways independently, water taxis are available in Tortuguero Village at the public dock.

Tortuguero Hotels

There are two types of hotels in Tortuguero: hotels along the banks of the canals, which are generally all-inclusive places that offer their own meals and tours, and hotels in the village of Tortuguero, which cater more to the budget and back-packer crowd. The village of Tortuguero is a bit run-down, but if you're looking for local flavor, it's the place to be. Visit www.jameskaiser.com for a complete list of all hotels in Tortuguero.

IMPORTANT: There are no banks or ATMs in Tortuguero. Upscale hotels and restaurants accept credit cards, but it's best to bring all the cash you'll need.

Turtle Time in Tortuguero

GREEN TURTLES nest from June through mid-October, with peak nesting in August and September. Green turtles are by far the most common turtles at Tortuguero, laying up to 180,000 nests each year. Incubation time: 7 to 10 weeks.

LEATHERBACK TURTLES nest from March through July. Leatherbacks are critically endangered, and nestings have fallen 85% since 1995 to fewer than 300 nests each year. Incubation time: 8-10 weeks.

HAWKSBILL TURTLES nest from June through October. Hawksbill turtles are critically endangered, and fewer than two dozen nests are reported each year. As a result, nesting hawksbill turtles are not shown to tour groups. Incubation time: 7–9 weeks.

LOGGERHEAD TURTLES nest from May through September. Although not as endangered as leatherbacks or hawksbill turtles, loggerheads are rarely seen in Tortuguero, with only occasional nestings observed. Incubation time: 7 to 10 weeks.

For more info on sea turtles, see page 128.

★Sea Turtle Tours

Turtle watching in Tortuguero is all about timing. If you visit during the wrong time of year, you will not see any turtles (see left). Tortuguero is the Western Hemisphere's most important green turtle nesting ground, and if you visit during peak green turtle season (July, Aug, Sept), you'll almost certainly get to see a green turtle lay her eggs at night. But the other turtle species that visit Tortuguero are much less common, so there's no guarantee that you'll see them, even if you arrive during peak nesting season.

If you want to see a turtle lay her eggs at night, you must sign up for a guided tour. Turtles are sensitive creatures, and their nesting is easily disrupted if certain precautions are not taken. For this reason, all visitors must go with trained guides who know the rules of appropriate turtle-watching behavior. (It is illegal for visitors to explore the beach alone at night.) All night tours, which last up to two hours, take place between 8pm and midnight. Cost: $20 per person, $4 of which goes to a sticker that helps pay for turtle protection programs. All visitors must wear dark clothes to remain hidden from the turtles, and no cameras or flashlights are allowed. Shoes or boots (not sandals) are recommended.

Here's how the tour works: When a female sea turtle emerges from the sea, she crawls up the beach above the high tide mark, digs a nest and lays roughly 100 eggs. During the actual egg-laying, it's OK to approach the turtle without disturbing her. But if a turtle is disturbed prior to constructing her nest, she may return to the ocean and dump her eggs. To prevent this, trained turtle spotters wander the beach in search of egg-laying females. When a female is spotted and safe to approach, your guide will be notified via walkie talkie. You will then be taken to the beach to watch the egg-laying process up close.

Nighttime turtle tours are best arranged through your hotel, but they are also offered by tour companies in the village. If money is no object, there's also a high-end turtle tour offered exclusively by Tortuga Lodge (2521-6099), one of the top hotels in Tortuguero. The tour includes a private dinner at Jaloba Ranger Station, located about 40 minutes south of Tortuguero village by boat. The dinner is followed by a private turtle nesting safari on a remote beach. It's expensive ($200–370 per person), but it's spectacular.

Finally, many hotels and tour companies offer turtle hatching tours in the morning. Watching newly hatched turtles scamper out to sea is spectacular (I personally find it more amazing than egg-laying), but it's all about luck. There's simply no good way to determine when a nest will hatch. An eagle-eyed guide can help, but you might have just as much luck wandering the beach on your own. Turtles hatch only when temperatures are sufficiently cool, so you'll have the most luck in the early morning, late afternoon or on cloudy/rainy days. (Note: Touching hatchlings is illegal and can threaten their survival.)

★Boat Tours

Jungle boat tours are the most popular daytime activity in Tortuguero. Unlike turtle watching, boat tours can be enjoyed year-round, and you're pretty much guaranteed to see incredible wildlife. Although it's possible to rent a canoe or kayak on your own, I highly recommend going with a guide. The waterways can be confusing, and experienced guides will be able to spot animals you would otherwise miss. Most hotels can arrange guided boat tours, coordinating pick-up and drop-off from your hotel's dock if you're staying outside the village. Tours run 2–3 hours and cost around $20 per person. If you'd rather book a tour on your own, I recommend contacting Canadian naturalist Daryl Loth (2709-8011) or German biologist Barbara Hartung (2709-8004).

★Sea Turtle Conservancy Center

The Sea Turtle Conservancy (formerly the Caribbean Conservation Corporation) was the driving force behind the creation of Tortuguero National Park. Their welcome center and museum, located just north of Tortuguero Village, is the top attraction in town. The museum displays interesting exhibits on turtles and other wildlife, and a free movie is shown about sea turtles and the legacy of Archie Carr (p.456). There's also a small gift shop as well as information about volunteer opportunities to help sea turtles in Tortuguero. Open 10am–noon, 2pm–5pm. Cost: $2 per person. (2709-8125, www.conserveturtles.org)

Tortuguero Village

The small, car-free village of Tortuguero isn't fancy, but it's definitely worth checking out if you have some free time. A patchwork of sandy trails make up the village "streets," most notably a central trail that runs parallel to the Laguna del Tortuguero and is lined with shops, restaurants and tour companies.

Tortuguero was originally settled by turtle hunters from San Andrés Island in the Caribbean. In 1945 a logging company arrived, and before long the town's population had swelled to 200 families. When the logging company left in 1964, the town's population dwindled to 30 families. But after the national park was established in 1970, tourists began arriving in increasing numbers. Today most of the town's 1,000 or so residents are directly or indirectly employed by tourism. In recent years, many Nicaraguans have come to Tortuguero in search of relatively high paying jobs. Although the town is often bustling and noisy at night, a dense strip of vegetation alongside the beach prevents most of the town's lights and sounds from interfering with the turtle nesting process.

Start your tour of the village at the Cuatro Esquinas ("Four Corners") Ranger Station at the southern end of town. The ranger office is located in an old park patrol boat named *La Tortuga Vigilante* that once prowled local waters in search

Life-sized model of a nesting green turtle at the Sea Turtle Conservancy Center

of illegal turtle poachers. A nearby kiosk offers some basic information about the park, and the 2-km (1.3-mile) El Gavilán hiking trail heads into the rainforest south of the ranger station (p.451).

Continue north along the main trail past the *Muelle Publico* ("Public Dock"), and on your left you'll notice a colorfully painted concrete wall. Behind the wall is the town's impressive recycling center, which recycles over one ton of garbage each day. Before the recycling center was constructed in the late 1990s, garbage was everywhere in Tortuguero. Today all garbage is brought to the recycling center and sorted by hand into plastic, glass, metal and organic material. The organic material is used to create fertilizer for local gardens, and the sorted garbage is loaded onto boats to be recycled. Tortuguero is the only town in Costa Rica that recycles all of the garbage that it generates.

As you continue north, notice the old, rusting machinery strewn about the village—an unintentional monument to Tortuguero's logging days. You'll soon pass the town's police station, and if you happen to wander by around 5:15pm, you might be treated to hundreds of oropendolas returning to their nests in the tree above the station. It is a sight—and a sound—to behold.

Continue past the *Muelle Paraiso Tropical* ("Tropical Paradise Dock"), marked by two giant, cartoonish bird sculptures, and take a right towards the public school. Between the school and the beach is a small dirt path that heads north to the Sea Turtle Conservancy Center, which is the perfect place to wrap up your tour of the village.

Tortuguero Wildlife

Tortuguero's lush jungles, lazy rivers and sandy beaches are jam-packed with biodiversity, making it one of Costa Rica's top wildlife watching destinations. The most famous animals are sea turtles, but other reptiles include freshwater turtles, iguanas and brilliant green basilisk lizards (aka Jesus Christ lizards). The jungles are home to three species of monkeys—howler, spider, white-faced—as well as three-toed and two-toed sloths. Over 300 bird species have been recorded here, including green macaws, toucans and 14 types of heron. Tortuguero is also one of the best places in Costa Rica to spot jaguars, which prowl the beaches and feast on turtles during nesting season. The waters around Tortuguero are home to bull sharks and a small population of West-Indian manatees, but both species are rarely spotted.

Hiking

The 2-km (1.3-mile) El Gavilán Trail starts at the Cuatro Esquinas Ranger Station (located at the southern end of town) and heads south through the rainforest to the beach. Another option is the 2.5-km (1.6-mile) Jaguar Trail. As you hike, look for monkeys and other wildlife. The trail is well-marked but frequently muddy. Boots are required, and they can be rented nearby. Entrance fee: $10.

The most rugged hike is *Cerro de Tortuguero* ("Turtle Hill"), which rises 119 meters (390 feet) and offers good views of the surroundings. You'll need a guide and a boat to get to the trailhead, which starts north of Tortuga Lodge. If your hotel doesn't offer a tour, check with private tour companies in the village. And be prepared for a muddy, slippery hike.

Sportfishing

The waters off Tortuguero are home to terrific snook and tarpon fishing. Captain Eddie Brown offers half-day ($375) and full-day ($600) tours from Tortuga Lodge (2521-6099, www.tortugalodge.com). A less expensive option is Elvin Gutierrez (2709-8115, www.tortuguerosportfish.com).

Restaurants

★MISS JUNIE'S (Brk: $6; Lnch, Din: $14–22)

The oldest and most famous restaurant in Tortuguero. For over seven decades Miss Junie and her family have been serving authentic Afro-Caribbean food. The restaurant, which is located at the northern end of the village, is clean and spacious, with canal views and historic photos on the walls. Reservations recommended in high season. (2709-8029)

★BUDDA CAFE (Lnch, Din: $8–10)

The hippest restaurant in town, with a sleek, modern interior and delightful canal-front dining. The tasty menu runs the gamut from salads to pizzas to crepes, with plenty of vegetarian options and the town's best cocktails. A great place for dinner. Closed Monday. (2709-8084, www.buddacafe.com)

★WILD GINGER (Lnch, Din: $11–21)

This hidden gem, tucked away on a lonely dirt path between the village school and the Sea Turtle Conservancy Center, offers high-end gringo (hamburgers, filet mignon) meets traditional Tico (patacones, black bean dip) with tropical flair (coconut shrimp, ginger chicken salad). (2709-8240, www.wildgingercr.com)

MISS MIRIAM (Brk: $6; Lnch, Din: $10–16)

This tiny, simple restaurant is famous for delicious fall-off-the-bone Caribbean chicken. Other options include steak, pork chops and shrimp casados. A great place for lunch, when you can sit outside next to the village soccer field and watch a pickup game. (2709-8002)

Saving Sea Turtles
ARCHIE CARR

Tortuguero is the most important green sea turtle nesting site in the Western Hemisphere, but without the efforts of biologist Archie Carr, its turtle population would have disappeared long ago. Carr's ground-breaking research led to the creation of Tortuguero National Park, and his remarkable story inspired the modern sea turtle conservation movement.

Born in Mobile, Alabama in 1909, Carr attended the University of Florida, where he became the first student to earn a doctorate in biology. After becoming a professor, he directed his attention to the study of sea turtles. At the time, virtually nothing was known about sea turtles, so Carr began systematically exploring the Caribbean in search of answers. By the time he arrived in Tortuguero in 1953, Carr realized that many sea turtle populations had been decimated due to overharvesting. Although the green sea turtle population at Tortuguero remained large and healthy, local villagers were harvesting vast quantities of eggs and harpooning adult turtles offshore. If the situation continued unchecked, he concluded, the turtles would soon be gone.

In 1956 Carr wrote *The Windward Road*, a collection of essays that described the remarkable lives of sea turtles, the people who harvest them and the decline of turtle populations throughout the Caribbean. The book was a popular success, and it inspired the formation of the Brotherhood of the Green Turtle, later renamed the Sea Turtle Conservancy (www.conserveturtles.org). The organization's work led to the establishment of Tortuguero National Park in 1975 and a national ban on harvesting sea turtle eggs in Costa Rica. Carr's groundbreaking research continues today, and the conservation efforts he pioneered have produced a nearly 500% increase in nesting green sea turtles at Tortuguero since the 1970s.

Among Carr's most lasting influences was his insistence on working with local populations to promote turtle conservation. Carr realized that no long-term conservation plan could succeed without local support, even though many locals felt turtle meat and turtle eggs were their birthright. Rather than take a confrontational approach, Carr spent decades educating local communities about the importance of sea turtle conservation—an ethos that has guided efforts ever since.

In 1987 Archie Carr died at his home in Florida. Over the course of his life, he had become the world's foremost authority on sea turtles. His research uncovered much of what we know about sea turtles today, and his tireless conservation efforts saved several species from extinction. Today he is considered one of the 20th century's great environmental heroes.

Tarpon Fishing in Parismina

Barra de Colorado

This remote village, located just south of the Nicaraguan border, is famous for world-class sportfishing. Tarpon and snook are the highlights, but there are also guapote, mojarra and machaca. The most famous outfitter is the Río Colorado Lodge (2232-4063, www.riocoloradolodge.com), which has been hosting anglers since 1971. Barra de Colorado is a 1.5-hour boat ride from Puerto Lindo and a 2-hour boat ride from Tortuguero, but most people arrive by plane.

Parismina

This tiny, isolated village, located about halfway between Limón and Tortuguero, is of little interest to anyone except sportfishermen, sea turtle volunteers and travelers determined to visit an authentic seaside village that's almost completely unaffected by tourism. Most visitors come for the sportfishing, which revolves around tarpon and snook. The top fishing outfitter is the Río Parismina Lodge (800-338-5688, www.riop.com), an all-inclusive hotel with a small fleet of boats. Parismina is also home to ASTOP (2798-2220, www.parisminaturtles.org), an environmental nonprofit that works with volunteers to help protect nesting sea turtles. Boat shuttles to Parismina depart from Caño Blanco three times daily, and the ride takes about 15 minutes. There are a handful of budget hotels in town and one restaurant: Iguana Verde. Visit www.jameskaiser.com for Parismina lodging options.

Carnaval in Limón

Limón

Home to 60,000 people, Limón is the largest town on the Caribbean coast. A century ago it was a charming port town, shipping bananas and coffee to the U.S. and Europe. Although the nearby port of Moín continues to ship fresh fruit abroad, in recent years downtown Limón has fallen on hard times. The city center is gritty and run-down, and crime is a persistent problem. As a result, most visitors avoid Limón in favor of more beautiful destinations.

These days the top reason to visit Limón is to check out the town's annual Carnaval celebration, which coincides with Columbus Day (known locally as *Día de la Raza*, "Day of the Race") on October 12. It's a week-long celebration featuring music, dancing and parades spiced up with lots of Afro-Caribbean culture, particularly reggae and Calypso Limonense (p.55).

Limón's main tourist destination is Parque Vargas, a leafy park near the water's edge. A few blocks west is the town's most famous building: the Black Star Line (Ave 5, Calle 5). This charming building, used in the 1920s by Jamaican activist Marcus Garvey, is home to a nice restaurant serving classic Caribbean food (for a refreshing drink try the agua de sapo). Just offshore Limón is Isla Uvita, the largest island off Costa Rica's Caribbean coast, where Christopher Columbus dropped anchor in 1502. A few kilometers north of town is Playa Bonita, Limón's most popular beach.

Limón is located 100 km (62 miles) from San José (3-hour drive) and 58 km (36 miles) from Puerto Viejo (1-hour drive).

CAHUITA

FOR TRAVELERS IN search of lazy days and mellow nights, the tiny village of Cahuita won't disappoint. Located next to beautiful Cahuita National Park, it combines user-friendly eco-tourism with a laid back Afro-Caribbean vibe. If you're looking for an authentic, chilled-out destination away from the hustle and bustle of trendy Puerto Viejo, Cahuita is the place to be.

Cahuita's main attraction is Cahuita National Park, a prominent peninsula that lies east of the village. Established to preserve a large coral reef just offshore, it was one of Costa Rica's first protected areas. A 9-km (5.6-mile) trail wanders along the perimeter of the peninsula, passing by beautiful beaches and lush jungles filled with monkeys, sloths and other amazing wildlife. The offshore scenery is equally impressive, with dozens of tropical fish species swimming among the colorful coral reef. Not surprisingly, snorkeling is one of Cahuita's most popular activities.

Just north of the village is Playa Negra, a dark sand beach that's big and delightfully uncrowded. A leisurely bike ride along the long dirt road that parallels Playa Negra is a nice way to spend an afternoon, including lunch or cocktails at one of the charming open-air restaurants along the way. The farther you go, the less developed it gets.

If you visit Cahuita, plan on staying at least two days, which will give you enough time to visit the national park and get a sense of the town. If you find the slow pace of life relaxing and the dirt roads charming, you can stay longer. If you find Cahuita a little *too* mellow for your taste, you can always head south to more lively Puerto Viejo.

Cahuita was the first Afro-Caribbean settlement on the Caribbean coast. Its modern history began in 1828, when a turtle hunter from Panama named William Smith built a home at Cahuita Point. The town grew to about 15 houses by the end of the 1800s, with most people living in what's now Cahuita National Park. In 1915 the president of Costa Rica shipwrecked off Cahuita Point, and he spent the night in a local home. To repay the hospitality he experienced, he bought the land where present-day Cahuita is located for 500 colones, laid out the present road system and gave each local resident a titled piece of land. Tourists began arriving in the 1980s, but even today the town feels delightfully authentic. Dreadlocked Rastas wander the dirt roads, and live calypso music often fills the air on the weekends. If you're looking to experience Costa Rica's Caribbean culture, there's no better place than Cahuita.

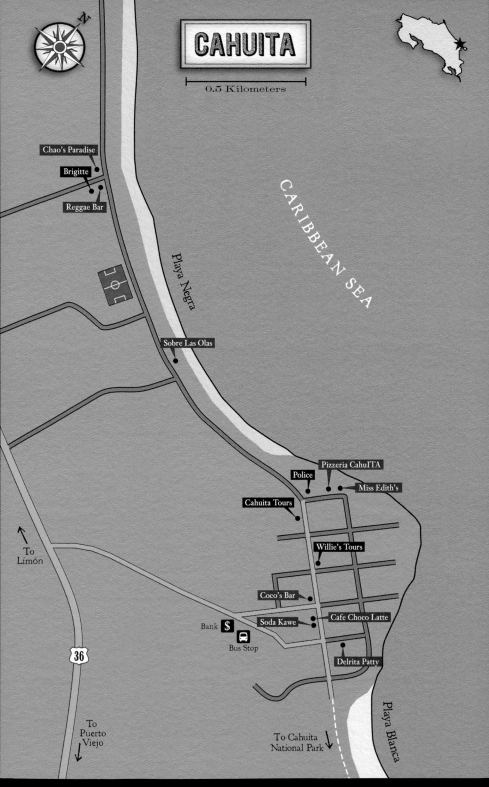

CAHUITA

0.5 Kilometers

N

CARIBBEAN SEA

Chao's Paradise
Brigitte
Reggae Bar

Playa Negra

Sobre Las Olas

Pizzeria CahuITA
Police
Miss Edith's
Cahuita Tours
Willie's Tours
Coco's Bar
Cafe Choco Latte
Soda Kawe
Bank $
Bus Stop
Delrita Patty

Playa Blanca

To Limón

36

To Puerto Viejo

To Cahuita National Park

Playa Vargas

Getting to Cahuita

By road, Cahuita is 200 km (124 miles) from San José (3.5-hour drive), 44 km (27 miles) from Limón (45-minute drive), and 17 kms (11 miles) from Puerto Viejo (15-minute drive). If you drive from San José, be sure to avoid Highway 32 at night due to dense fog, poor visibility and reckless truck drivers. Shuttles to/from Cahuita are offered by Interbus, Grayline and Easyride (p.20). Mepe buses (2750-0023) to Cahuita depart San José from the Terminal del Caribe (Calle Central, Ave 15) at 6am, 10am, noon, 2pm, and 4pm (₡4,670, 4 hours). Return buses depart Cahuita for San José at 7am, 8am, 9:30am, 11:30am and 4:30pm. Buses between Cahuita and Puerto Viejo (₡740) depart throughout the day.

Getting around Cahuita

Flip flops are all you really need to get around Cahuita, unless you want to explore the far reaches of Playa Negra, in which case you can rent bicycles from Brigette or Dr. Bike in Playa Negra. Local establishments can also arrange taxi rides. Most taxis are unmetered, so be sure to negotiate the price *before* you get inside.

Cahuita Hotels

"Downtown" Cahuita is home to most of the budget and mid-range hotels with more upscale hotels scattered along Playa Negra north of town. For complete Cahuita hotel info visit www.jameskaiser.com

★Snorkeling

Cahuita's offshore coral reef is one of the largest in Costa Rica, and snorkeling is the town's most popular adventure. (Scuba is not allowed, nor is it necessary due to the shallow depth of the reef.) Although the corals have been damaged in recent years (p.466), they are still beautiful and filled with dozens of species of tropical fish. If you're lucky, you can also see sea turtles, stingrays, lobsters and nurse sharks. To protect the reef, all snorkelers are required to go with a guide. Good guides charge around $30 per person, and they are best booked through your hotel, Willie's Tours (2755-1024) or Cahuita Tours (2755-0000).

★Hiking

Cahuita National Park is home to an easy 9-km (5.6-mile) hiking trail that wraps around the peninsula, passing by lovely beaches and lush jungle. The most popular hiking destination is Cahuita Point, which lies 3.5 km (2.2 miles) from the Kelly Creek Ranger Station (about an hour one-way). If you're up for a longer hike, follow the trail an additional 5.5 km (3.4 miles) to the Puerto Vargas Entrance Station, which takes about two hours. Just outside the entrance station is an open-air restaurant called Boca Chica that offers showers and a swimming pool. After refreshing yourself there, catch the public bus back to Cahuita, which passes by every half hour (₡500). Guided hikes ($25 per person) are great if you'd like to see wildlife such as sloths and pit vipers. Book a guide through your hotel, Willie's Tours (2755-1024) or Cahuita Tours (2755-0000).

Sloth Sanctuary

Located 10 km (6.2 miles) northwest of Cahuita, the non-profit Sloth Sanctuary nurses injured sloths back to health. Over the past two decades, they've released over 90 sloths back into the wild. Guided tours of the sanctuary ($25 per person) include a movie, a canoe tour through the surrounding jungle, and—best of all—a cuddly sloth show and tell. If you don't have a car, take the bus towards Limón and ask the driver to stop in the village of Penhurst at the *Sanctuario de Peresozos*. (Look for the 20-foot tall replica of a Megatherium sloth—a giant species that went extinct 35 million years ago). The sloth sanctuary is also one of the premier bird watching locations in the southern Caribbean, and birding tours are available. Open 8am–2pm. Closed Mon. (2750-0775, www.slothsanctuary.com)

Tree of Life

This charming wildlife rescue center, located past Playa Negra, features 10 acres of lush gardens and a wide range of animals, including monkeys, sloths, coatis and much more. Guided tours are available. Cost: $20 per person. Closed Monday. (8610-0490, www.treeoflifecostarica.com)

Cahuita Restaurants

★ SOBRE LAS OLAS (Lnch, Din: $13–23)

This restaurant (Spanish for "Over The Waves") has terrific ocean views in front of Playa Negra, just north of town. If you're looking for charming seaside ambiance, look no further. Seafood is their specialty, but their Mediterranean style chicken, steak and pasta dishes are also tasty. Closed Tues. (2755-0109)

★ CAFE CHOCO LATTE (Brk: $4–9; Lnch: $7–10)

This charming Swedish bakery offers upscale breakfast and lunch. A great place for coffee, baked goods and healthy sandwiches on homemade bread. No credit cards (2755-0010)

★ PIZZERIA CAHUITA (Lnch, Din: $12–20)

This Italian-run restaurant is famous for its extensive selection of wood-fired pizzas, but they also offer fresh seafood, tasty beef dishes and delicious pasta. Closed Thurs. (2755-0179)

COCOS BAR & RESTAURANT (Lnch, Din: $7–12)

Cocos is the most happening place in town, offering a wide range of bar food, from Tex-Mex to Tico classics. If you'd like some food with your drinks, this is the place to go. Live reggae and Calypso Limonense (p.55) are often offered on the weekends. (2755-0437)

SODA KAWE (Brk: $5; Lnch, Din: $6–8)

This local favorite is the best budget option in town, serving up basic Tico classics like gallo pinto and casados, but with a fabulous home-cooked flavor. The secret? All food is cooked *a la leña* (using firewood). (2755-0233)

MISS EDITH'S (Brk: $6–9; Lnch, Din: $8–20)

For years this was Cahuita's most famous restaurant, serving an extensive menu of traditional Caribbean classics in a rustic, seaside atmosphere. In recent years the quality has been hit or miss, and the service is often painfully slow. But if you're a hardcore foodie in search of authentic Caribbean flavors, Miss Edith's is worth checking out. (2755-0248)

DELRITA PATTY ($2–4)

Looking for authentic Caribbean food? Visit Delrita, who sells her famous patty (p.86) and other homemade goods from the shack next to her house on the weekends. On Tues and Thurs her family wanders the town selling her baked treats.

Cahuita National Park

This beautiful national park protects the lush peninsula just east of Cahuita. It's home to great beaches, dense jungles and fascinating wildlife. In many ways, Cahuita National Park reminds me of Manuel Antonio (p.363), but with a coral reef and a fraction of the crowds. All in all, this is probably one of the most underrated national parks in Costa Rica.

There are two entrances to the park: Kelly Creek Ranger Station, located at the eastern end of Cahuita's "Main Street," and Puerto Vargas, located near the eastern base of the peninsula. A 9-km (5.6-mile) trail wraps around the perimeter of the peninsula, connecting the two ranger stations and offering great hiking (p.464). A 1,000 "donation" is highly recommended at Kelly Creek Ranger Station. A $10 fee is charged at the Puerto Vargas Ranger Station. The park is open 8am–4pm (2755-0461).

The park's most beautiful beach is Playa Blanca, which stretches south from Kelly Creek. Playa Vargas, which is located on the far side of the peninsula, is also beautiful and usually crowd-free. If you're interested in wildlife watching, I highly recommend hiring a guide to point out hard-to-spot animals that you would otherwise miss. Although there are often locals hanging around the entrance offering guide services, good guides are best hired through your hotel or a local tour company such as Willie's Tours or Cahuita Tours.

Lying just off the tip of the peninsula is one of the largest coral reefs in Costa Rica. Although beautiful, the 240-hectare (787-acre) reef has suffered some damage over the past several decades. At last count, only 27 of the reef's original 34 coral species still survived. Many people blame the damage on increased silt and pesticides washing into the ocean from nearby banana plantations. For the moment, the worst of the damage appears to be done, and the reef may even be recovering. But rest assured there's still plenty to see among the colorful corals. Snorkeling remains a highlight of a visit to Cahuita National Park.

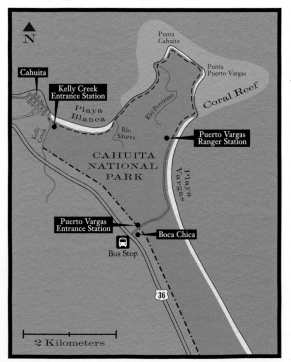

Playa Blanca

PUERTO VIEJO

INCREDIBLE BEACHES, DELICIOUS food and a dread-locked, tropical Rasta vibe. Welcome to what many backpackers consider the top destination in Costa Rica. For those looking to get away from corporate resorts and package tours, Puerto Viejo is a countercultural breath of fresh air. A place where bicycles outnumber cars, hammocks are more important than air-conditioning and yoga is a way of life. Though most popular among 20- and 30-somethings, there are plenty of middle-aged wanderers and white-haired hippies too.

Beaches and social life are Puerto Viejo's main draw, but there are *plenty* of additional activities. Surfing, snorkeling, boat trips, wildlife sanctuaries, chocolate tours, day trips to indigenous communities—you could easily spend a month here and not run out of things to do. Of course, much depends on the weather, which is always prone to rain. But if you do find yourself here during a stretch of beautiful sunny days, you might just quit your day job and join Puerto Viejo's tight-knit community of international expats, many of whom came here on vacation and never left.

The layout of the area is simple—virtually everything lies along a 13-km (8-mile) road. Although people often refer to the entire stretch of road as Puerto Viejo, the name technically refers only to the town of Puerto Viejo, which wraps around a sandy, palm-fringed point that's jam-packed with restaurants, shops and bars. Set back from the hustle and bustle is a quiet residential community. If you're looking for parties and nightlife, Puerto Viejo is the place to be. If you're looking for someplace more peaceful, keep heading southeast along the road. The further southeast you go, the less developed it gets.

Following the road southeast from Puerto Viejo, you'll pass a series of beautiful beaches—Cocles, Playa Chiquita, Punta Uva—before ending up at Manzanillo, a tiny Afro-Caribbean village that's delightfully trapped in time. Spread out along the road to Manzanillo are dozens of hotels and restaurants. Once past Punta Uva, dense jungle becomes the dominant feature on either side of the road, and beyond Manzanillo lies the Gandoca-Manzanillo Wildlife Refuge, a protected area home to virgin jungles and pristine coastline.

For most of the 20th century, Puerto Viejo was largely disconnected from the outside world. These days, the secret is out, and Puerto Viejo has quickly become one of Costa Rica's most popular backpacker destinations. But despite all the changes, it still remains delightfully low-key, which is why so many people keep coming back.

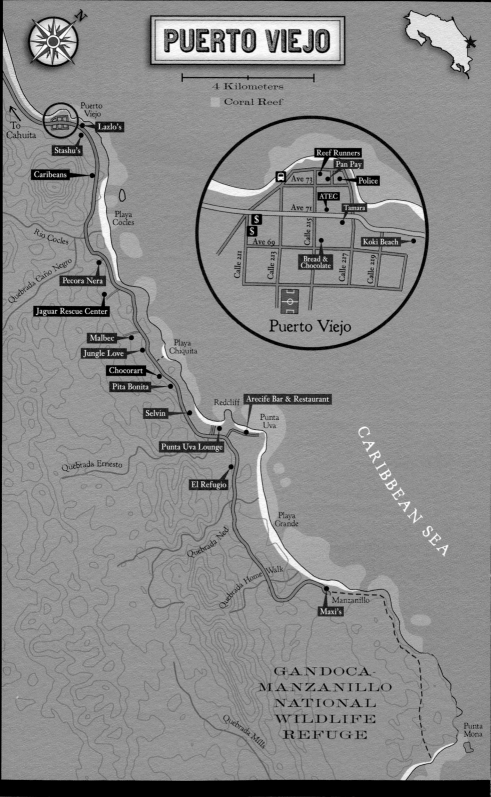

Getting to Puerto Viejo

Puerto Viejo is 225 km (140 miles) from San José (4-hour drive), 59 km (37 miles) from Limón (1-hour drive) and 17 kms (11 miles) from Cahuita (15-minute drive). If you drive from San José, be sure to avoid Highway 32 at night due to dense fog, poor visibility and reckless truck drivers. Mepe buses (2257-8129) to Puerto Viejo depart San José from the Terminal de Caribe, Calle Central, Ave 15 at 6am, 10am, noon, 2pm and 4pm (₡5,480, 4.5 hours). Make sure you take the bus to Puerto Viejo de Talamanca, not the bus to Puerto Viejo de Sarapiquí. Buses depart Puerto Viejo for San José at 7:30am, 9am, 11am and 4pm. Shuttle service is offered by Interbus, Grayline and Easyride (p.20).

Getting Around Puerto Viejo

The area's attractions are spread out along a 13-km (8-mile) road that stretches from Puerto Viejo to Manzanillo. The road is flat, paved and good for leisurely biking. Many hotels rent bikes to guests, and there are bike rental shops in downtown Puerto Viejo (plan on spending about $5 per day). Taxis (2750-2073, 2750-0439) wait in front of the bus stop in Puerto Viejo. At night, taxis are definitely the safest way to get around. Most taxis are unmetered; be sure to negotiate the price *before* you get in the cab. Public buses depart Puerto Viejo for Manzanillo throughout the day (₡610, 30 minutes).

Puerto Viejo Hotels

Although a few hotels in the area have luxuries like pools and AC, most cater to a more rustic, eco-concious crowd. Hotels and hostels in downtown Puerto Viejo are geared towards younger, budget-concious travelers. Hotels in Playa Cocles, Playa Chiquita and Punta Uva are generally nicer and more expensive, though you can still find some bargains. Manzanillo has a handful of budget options. Visit www.jameskaiser.com for complete info on Puerto Viejo hotels.

Staying Safe in Puerto Viejo

These days, nothing bothers Puerto Viejo residents more than the town's bad reputation for crime. Although locals admit that crime happens, they insist that the reputation is based more on racial stereotypes than actual statistics. Personally, I don't think anyone should stay away from Puerto Viejo because of it's reputation for crime, which is overblown and does have a racial element. But crime *is* more of a problem here than in other Costa Rican beach towns, so you do need to be careful. Never leave your valuables unattended, don't wander around lonely streets at night (especially in downtown Puerto Viejo) and don't walk the jungle path between Puerto Viejo and Cocles, where theft is common. When you arrive, ask your hotel about current conditions. Follow that advice, and you should have a safe and wonderful vacation at one Costa Rica's best beach towns.

★Jaguar Rescue Center

This non-profit wildlife rescue center is an amazing place to get up close and personal with some fascinating animals. Run by two Spanish biologists who once worked at the Barcelona Zoo, the Jaguar Rescue Center nurses injured animals back to health for release back into the wild. The center began when locals started bringing the biologists injured animals, and today your visit helps pay for the cost of wildlife rehabilitation. Although their collection of animals is constantly changing (depending on which injured animals are brought in), monkeys, sloths, wildcats, tropical birds and reptiles are common. Guided tours (1.5 hours, $15 adults, kids free) are offered at 9:30am, 11:30am. Volunteer opportunities are also available. Closed Sunday. No credit cards. (2750-0710, www.jaguarrescue.com)

★Chocolate Tours

Cacao has been harvested in the jungles around Puerto Viejo for centuries, and today the area is home to some fantastic chocolatiers that offer guided tours of their operations. If you're even a slight fan of chocolate, these tours are an eye-opening experience. My favorite is Caribeans' Chocolate Forest Experience, located up the hill from OM Yoga in Playa Cocles. Their 3-hour "Bean to Bar" tour ($26 per person) includes a walk through a cacao forest, a chocolate tasting at a stunning viewpoint and an inside look at the chocolate making process. Caribeans also works closely with local indigenous communities to promote organic and fair-trade harvesting (8836-8930, www.caribeanschocolate.com). Another good option is Chocorart in Playa Chiquita, a Swiss-run operation that offers guided tours ($24 per person) Mon, Weds, Fri at 2pm (2750-0075).

★Gandoca-Manzanillo Refuge

This 5,000-hectacre (19.3-square mile) wildlife refuge (p.487) protects a stunning range of forests, wetlands and coastline stretching from Punta Uva to the Panamanian Border. It's the ecological highlight of the southern Caribbean, home to hundreds of animal species. Due to the rugged nature of the refuge, however, it can be difficult to explore on your own. Fortunately, ATEC (p.475) offers guided trips. Options include hiking tours, boat tours, and hiking/boat tours where you hike to a distant point, then return by boat. (Note: Boat trips are fantastic if the weather is good and the seas are calm—but not so great if it's rainy and choppy.) Turtle watching tours are also offered from March–July, when leatherback turtles nest on Gandoca Beach. In the heart of the reserve, 7 km (4.4 miles) south of Manzanillo, there's an organic farm that offers overnight lodging and organic meals at Punta Mona (www.puntamona.org).

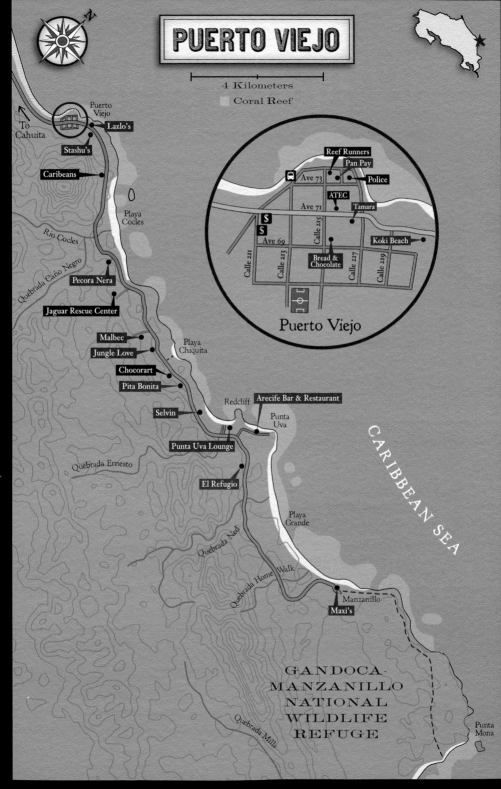

Volunteering at the Jaguar Rescue Center

Snorkeling & Scuba Diving

The waters just offshore Puerto Viejo, Punta Uva and Manzanillo are home to several kilometers of beautiful coral reefs. If you visit Puerto Viejo when the seas are calm and the water visibility is clear, grab a mask and some fins—a spectacular underwater world awaits! Scattered among the brain coral and elkhorn coral are angelfish, parrotfish and dozens of other colorful species. If you're really lucky, you can see turtles, rays and nurse sharks. Visibility varies between 3–30 meters (10–100 feet), depending on recent rain and runoff. The calmest seas are usually found in April, May, September and October.

The best snorkeling is at Punta Uva and Manzanillo, but there are some nice reefs off Puerto Viejo, too. Snorkel gear can be rented at Reef Runners in Puerto Viejo (www.reefrunnerdivers.com, 2750-0480) and Punta Uva Dive Center at Punta Uva (2759-9191, www.puntauvadivecenter.com). Although Puerto Viejo isn't known for its scuba diving, if you're an underwater junkie, it's definitely worth checking out. Most dive tours head to Punta Uva, which has some great underwater walls. Reef Runners and Punta Uva Dive Center both offer both scuba tours and instruction.

Surfing

When conditions are right, Puerto Viejo is home to the Caribbean coast's most legendary wave: Salsa Brava. This powerful freak of hydrology is located just offshore downtown Puerto Viejo in front of Salsa Brava restaurant. It's an expert-only wave that breaks over a shallow reef known for shredding skin and breaking bones. As such, it should be treated with the utmost respect. As Puerto Viejo resident Craig "Tequila" Schieber told the *Tico Times*, "When the waves are good here, it's comparable to Hawaii." Schieber, who won a gold medal at the 2011 World Masters Surfing Championship, has said his two perfect waves are Salsa Brava and Hanalei Bay in Kauai, Hawaii. Salsa Brava works best with a strong easterly swell, and the best surf months are December through March (particularly January and February), with another uptick in June and July.

Non-expert surfers can check out the beach break at Playa Cocles (p.478). Although finicky and temperamental, it's your best bet for less punishing waves. For a good surf instructor call Hershel at Caribe Surf (8357-7703).

Yoga

OM Yoga (2756-8434, www.ompuertoviejo.com), located near the eastern end of Playa Cocles, is one of the most popular Yoga studios in the area. Up the hill from OM is Manú Yoga Village (8326-7048, www.manuyogavillage.com), which offers a spectacular yoga studio surrounded by rainforest. The famous Treehouse Lodge in Punta Uva (2750-0706, www.costaricatreehouse.com) also offers yoga classes to the public.

Salsa Brava, Puerto Viejo's famous wave

Tour Operators

⭐**ATEC** (Talamancan Association of Eco-tourism and Conservation)
This community-based non-profit offers over a dozen tours in the Puerto Viejo area. Open since 1989, ATEC works with local guides to promote socially responsible eco-travel that ensures tourist dollars benefit the community. Their offerings include boat tours, guided hikes, kayaking trips, wildlife watching, visits to indigenous villages, farm tours, Caribbean cooking classes and much more. Their office, located in downtown Puerto Viejo across from Tamara restaurant, also features a small store with books, local music CDs, crafts and internet access. (2750-0191, www.ateccr.org)

EXPLORADORES
This is a good option for rafting tours along the Pacuare River (p.39) (2750-2020, www.exploradoresoutdoors.com)

TERRAVENTURAS
If you're interested in a canopy tour, contact Terraventuras. Cost: $55 adults, $27.50 kids. (2750-0750, www.terraventuras.com)

GANDOCA TOURS
This company specializes in tours in the Gandoca-Manzanillo Refuge (p.487). (8762-8848, www.gandocatours.blogspot.com)

Puerto Viejo Restaurants

★STASHU'S CON FUSION (Din: $11–19)
Specializing in "World Fusion Cuisine," Stashu revels in refined, tropical flavors from Asia, Latin America and the Caribbean. The menu is inventive, eclectic and absolutely delicious. Closed Weds. (2750-0530)

★BREAD & CHOCOLATE (Brk: $6; Lnch: $6–9)
From breakfast waffles to sandwiches on homemade bread, it's hard to find anything on the menu that isn't delicious. Their obsession with quality is legendary—even the peanut butter is homemade. Closed Mon. No credit cards. (2750-0723)

LAZLO'S (Din: 14–15)
Fresh fish, caught daily by Hungarian owner Lazlo, is the only thing on the menu at this laid-back, ramshackle restaurant. The fish changes depending on the catch (snapper, tuna, seabass) but it's always served with homemade french fries and grilled veggies. (8703-6185)

TAMARA (Brk: $6–7; Lnch, Din: $8–12)
For three decades Tamara has served traditional Caribbean food in downtown Puerto Viejo. Rice and beans, rondón, pan bon—all the classics are available in this charming, rustic restaurant. (2750-0148)

KOKI BEACH (Lnch, Din: $13–30)
This hip, open-air restaurant/lounge serves delicious seafood in a relaxed atmosphere that's great for people-watching and some nice ocean views. Two for one happy hour 5pm–7pm. Closed Mon. (2750-0902)

PAN PAY (Brk: $4–7; Lnch, Din: $5–10)
This tasty bakery is Spanish-owned, but after two decades it's a Puerto Viejo institution. Great for a breakfast of coffee and croissants. (2750-0081)

DREADNUT CAFE (Brk, Lnch, Din: $6–8)
Located in front of the bus stop, this Rastafarian-inspired cafe offers tasty espresso drinks plus smoothies, sandwiches and baked goods. Closed Weds. (8703-9993)

Playa Cocles Restaurants

★PECORA NERA (Din: $16–26)
The best Italian cuisine in Puerto Viejo. Pecora Nera combines authentic flavors with a classy tropical atmosphere. Home-made gnocchi and ravioli, delicious spaghetti, great pizza. Their sister restaurant, Gatta Ci Cova, located on the main road, features similar food with slightly cheaper prices. Closed Mon. (2750-0490)

Playa Chiquita Restaurants

★JUNGLE LOVE (Din; $12–17)
This small, open-air restaurant offers excellent fish, pasta and pizza in a delightfully chilled-out atmosphere. As the name implies, this is a great place for a date. Closed Tues. (2750-0162, www.junglelovecafe.com)

MALBEC (Din; $12–21)
This cozy Argentinian steakhouse is a carnivore's delight, offering excellent steaks plus strange, succulent cuts like kidney and sweetbreads. Closed Sun. (2750-0581)

PITA BONITA (Lnch, Din: $10–16)
Middle Eastern classics like hummus, falafel, shakshok and homemade pita bread. Closed Sunday. (2756-8173)

Punta Uva Restaurants

★EL REFUGIO (Din: $15–22)
Nestled in a quiet corner of the jungle just west of Manzanillo, El Refugio serves terrific Argentinian-inspired food and great wine in a charming atmosphere. If you're looking for a romantic dinner, El Refugio is worth the trip. (2759-9007)

★SELVIN (Lnch, Din; $10–20)
The best place for authentic Caribbean food in Puerto Viejo—and possibly the entire Caribbean coast. Their rondón is legendary, and their seafood is always fresh. Open Thurs–Sunday. (2750-0664)

PUNTA UVA LOUNGE (Lnch, Din: $8–12)
Located just off Punta Uva's western beach, this small open-air restaurant serves tasty food and terrific cocktails. A perfect post-snorkel destination. They also offer legendary all night parties every month or so. (2759-9048)

ARRECIFE BAR & RESTAURANT (Lnch, Din: $9–16)
This charming restaurant serves up a mix of traditional Caribbean food and gringo favorites like tacos, fajitas and burgers. Located steps from Punta Uva's eastern beach, it's the perfect place for lunch or an afternoon cocktail. (2759-9200)

Manzanillo Restaurants

MAXI'S (Lnch, Din: $7–16)
This long-time favorite serves traditional Caribbean food right next to the beach. Try the fresh fish with rice and beans. The second floor offers the best view in town. (2759-9073)

Playa Cocles

Located just 1.5 km (0.9 miles) east of Puerto Viejo, Playa Cocles is one of the area's most popular beaches. Its wide crescent of light sand stretches nearly a mile to the east, attracting a steady stream of surfers, backpackers, people watchers and party people recovering from the night before.

The western end of Cocles is the most accessible and popular part of the beach. Lying just offshore is a small island called Pirripli Key. According to local legend, Pirripli Key is home to a buried pirate treasure, but think twice before setting off in search of the booty. As the story goes, when the treasure was buried the pirate captain asked for a volunteer to guard it until he could return. The sailor that stepped forward was killed, and his soul now guards the island.

The beach in front of Pirripli Key is a popular surf break that, while finicky, is far kinder than Salsa Brava. Locals rent surfboards on the beach (feel free to employ your bargaining skills), and across the road are a handful of laid-back restaurants perfect for a snack or a drink. Tasty Waves, located near the western end of the beach next to OM yoga, is a fun surf bar that draws a younger crowd. Farther east you'll find Hotel La Isla and Totem.

The eastern end of Cocles is more mellow and secluded. If you're looking to get away from the crowds, this is a good place to go. There are also two beachfront hotel bars open to the public: laid-back Lapalapa (part of Hotel Camarona) and swanky Numu (part of hotel Le Chameleon); both serve food and drinks.

Note: Cocles is home to some of the strongest riptides in the area. Although lifeguards are sometimes stationed on the beach, you should always use caution. Also, in recent years the jungle path between Puerto Viejo and Cocles has gained a reputation for robbery. It's better not to travel alone there.

Playa Chiquita

This is the area's least well-known beach, which is exactly why some people love it. If you're looking to get away from the crowds and you require only a patch of sand and some palm trees, this is the beach to visit. As the name implies, Playa Chiquita is a relatively small beach. It features a series of exposed coral reefs that were uplifted in 1991, when a 7.6-magnitude earthquake rocked the Caribbean coast. Although the reefs prevent broad expanses of sand from forming, they form protected pools perfect for wading. Even though Playa Chiquita is off the beaten path, there are lots of terrific restaurants nearby.

Playa Chiquita is located about 5 km (3.1 miles) south of Puerto Viejo, and the entrance is very easy to miss. Look for "Equilibrio" on the right, just east of Shawandha Hotel. Across from Equilibrio is a small concrete frame that marks the entrance to Playa Chiquita. Follow the path beyond the concrete frame, and you'll soon come to a lovely stretch of beach.

Playa Cocles

Volunteering at the Jaguar Rescue Center

Punta Uva

The two beaches at Punta Uva are, in my opinion, two of the best beaches in Costa Rica. Golden sand, turquoise water, coral reefs, palm trees, monkeys, green macaws, beachside cocktails—ahhh, paradise.

Located 7 km (4.4 miles) east of Puerto Viejo, Punta Uva ("Grape Point") is home to two beaches separated by a rocky headland that most locals call Punta Uva, but which is actually called Red Cliff. (Punta Uva is the sandy point farther east.) Draped in luxuriant jungle, Red Cliff has a rugged hiking trail that connects the two beaches and offers great views along the way. The best viewpoint, located at the very tip, veers off the main trail near an old gravestone. Be careful if you hike here, the trail is often muddy and slippery.

The turnoff to the first beach is marked by a sign for the Punta Uva Lounge (p.477), a great beachside restaurant serving food and drinks (and occasionally hosting all-night parties). Next to the restaurant is the Punta Uva Dive Center, where you can rent snorkel equipment to explore the beautiful coral reef lying just offshore. The Punta Uva Dive shop also offers scuba diving tours and kayak rentals to explore the nearby rivers.

The turnoff to the second beach is marked by a sign for the Arrecife Bar & Restaurant (p.453), which serves cold drinks and tasty Caribbean food. Continuing east, you'll round the tip of Arrecife and continue on to Playa Grande, which stretches east to Manzanillo.

Return of the
GREEN MACAW

As you wander around Punta Uva, be sure to listen for the loud squawks of great green macaws (p.107) in the trees above. These magnificent birds once thrived throughout Costa Rica's Caribbean coast, but their population has fallen 90% over the past 50 years due to illegal capture and habitat loss. The widespread destruction of mountain almond trees, which provide green macaws with the majority of their food and nesting sites, has been particularly devastating. In 2011 ten captive-raised green macaws were released near Punta Uva at a site that contains a small population of mountain almond trees. The release program, which was initiated by the non-profit Ara Project (www.thearaproject.org), marked the first time captive-raised green macaws had ever been successfully reintroduced into the wild. As reintroduction efforts continue, a self-sustaining green macaw population may once again fly free along the Caribbean coast.

Punta Uva

Manzanillo

The tiny village of Manzanillo is located 13 km (8 miles) southeast of the town of Puerto Viejo—literally at the end of the road. Its large, beautiful beach and laid-back vibe are the main draw for most visitors, but Manzanillo is also the main jumping off point for exploring the rugged Manzanillo-Gandoca Refuge (see following page). The village itself, which is home to about 300 people, feels delightfully trapped in time. Originally settled by Afro-Caribbean turtle hunters from Panama in the 18th century, it was cut off from much of the outside world until 1985. In that year a road was constructed between Manzanillo and Puerto Viejo, and the government created the Gandoca-Manzanillo Refuge. Due to strict zoning laws, the refuge limited development and pickled the town in a Caribbean time-warp. Manzanillo's most famous landmark is Maxi's (p.477), a laid-back restaurant that serves traditional Caribbean food. Playa Grande, Manzanillo's famous beach, is a broad crescent of golden sand that stretches over two miles. Lying just offshore are some beautiful coral reefs. If the water is calm, you can rent snorkel gear ($4/hour) and get snorkeling advice at Aquamor, one block west of Maxi's.

Note: On Saturdays and Sundays locals set up a roadblock at the entrance to Manzanillo and ask passing cars for donations. The money goes to a local program that hires schoolchildren to clean up the beach. If you pass through on the weekend, please donate whatever you can.

Gandoca-Manzanillo Refuge

The Gandoca-Manzanillo National Wildlife Refuge, which stretches from Punta Uva to the Panamanian border, is one of the ecological jewels of the Caribbean. Created in 1985, it covers 5,000 hectares (19.3 square miles) of land and 4,400 hectares (17 square miles) of marine territory, providing vital habitat for an incredible range of species.

Over half of the refuge is considered wetland, including the most extensive mangrove site on the Caribbean coast. Red, black and white mangroves are found here, as well as Costa Rica's only population of mangrove oysters, warm water species that attaches itself to the roots of red mangroves. Nearby is the Gandoca Lagoon, which covers nearly 200 hectares and is home to a small population of West Indian manatees. These gentle giants, which grow up to 3.5 meters (11 feet) long and weigh up to 600 kg (1,400 pounds), are endangered and rarely seen. They submerge at the slightest disturbance, holding their breath underwater for up to 20 minutes.

The refuge's forests provide shelter for over 350 bird species, 40% of which are considered rare and 100 of which are North American migrants. Toucans, harpy eagles and green macaws are among the highlights. The refuge is also home to mountain almond trees—an important source of food for green macaws—as well as the last coastal primary forest of giant cativo trees.

The refuge protects 9 km (5.6 miles) of rugged coastline, some of which is ancient coral that was uplifted thousands of years ago. An extensive living coral reef system extends up to 200 meters (650 feet) offshore. It's home to brain coral, elkhorn coral and dozens of tropical fish species. Sea grasses also provide food for sea turtles and manatees.

The waters offshore are home to three dolphin species: bottlenose (left), Atlantic spotted, and the little-known Tucuxi (pronounced "*too koo shee*"). Tucuxi are small dolphins normally found in fresh water rivers and estuaries of the Amazon basin. Until the Tucuxi were identified here in 1997, they were not known to exist this far north.

Of all the amazing animals found in the refuge, perhaps the most impressive is the leatherback turtle—the largest sea turtle on earth and one of the most endangered. Each year between March and July, female leatherbacks arrive at Gandoca Beach to nest and lay their eggs. In the early 1980s, leatherback turtle eggs at Gandoca Beach had a 95% mortality rate due to poaching and predation. Today, thanks to the conservation efforts of groups like ANAI (www.anaicr.org) and WIDECAST (www.latinamericanseaturtles.org), the survival rate of leatherback eggs is over 90%.

If you'd like to explore the wonders of the Gandoca-Manzanillo refuge, both ATEC and Gandoca Tours offer guided tours.

The Best of the Best

For photos, hotel info and guidebook updates
visit www.jameskaiser.com